A PLUME BOOK

JIM CRAMER'S GET RICH CAREFULLY

JAMES J. CRAMER is host of CNBC's *Mad Money w/ Jim Cramer* and cohost of *Squawk on the Street*. He serves on TheStreet, Inc.'s board of directors, is a columnist and contributor for TheStreet's *Real Money* and *Action Alerts PLUS*, and participates in various video segments for TheStreet TV. Cramer is the author of six books, including *Confessions of a Street Addict* and *Jim Cramer's Mad Money*.

Praise for *Jim Cramer's Get Rich Carefully*

"In highly accessible language, Cramer explains how the stock market is influenced by economic data, Fed policy, world events, the actions of hedge funds, and the trend toward sector funds even when the underlying fundamentals of a stock remain stable. Drawing on his long experience, both mistakes and successes, Cramer demystifies the stock market and offers sound investing advice and an insightful overview of the market for cautious investors."   —*Booklist*

"Look to this book for guiding principles rather than specific stock tips. . . . Forget about getting rich quick: The new investment climate, writes *Mad Money* host Cramer, is 'treacherous. . . . [B]izarre stock movements have become the staple, if not the hallmark, of this era.' Cramer, formerly known for his exuberant approach . . . has since taken a visibly more deliberate approach to the matter. This new book reflects his caution. . . . Cramer's long list of dos and don'ts ('Relative valuations don't justify a purchase'; 'Stop falling in love with your stocks') is worth the price of the book."   —*Kirkus Reviews*

"Jim is a whirlwind, a true force of nature. He embodies not only the strongest work ethic extant (something Omega Advisors' Lee Cooperman taught me is at the epicenter of investment success), but in my decades in the investment business I know of no other person that possesses the breadth of knowledge about individual stocks. He is a reservoir of information. . . . And that is why *Jim Cramer's Get Rich Carefully* . . . is a must-read. . . . My advice? Run, don't walk, to read *Jim Cramer's Get Rich Carefully*. Booyah!"

—Doug Kass, TheStreet.com

"Who wouldn't want to 'Get Rich Carefully,' as the title of Jim Cramer's new book promises? The stock market may seem scary, but Cramer says you can make money with research, logic, and prudence. . . . Whether Cramer's advice will make you a boatload of money or not, his rational explanations make stocks seem less intimidating."

—Jessica Gresko, Associated Press

"Careful isn't the word that usually comes to mind when investors think of Jim Cramer . . . [b]ut Cramer says his show has changed, and his newest book reflects this epiphany."   —*USA Today*

ALSO BY JAMES J. CRAMER

Jim Cramer's Getting Back to Even
Jim Cramer's Stay Mad for Life: Get Rich, Stay Rich
(Make Your Kids Even Richer)
Jim Cramer's Mad Money: Watch TV, Get Rich
Jim Cramer's Real Money: Sane Investing in an Insane World
Confessions of a Street Addict
You Got Screwed: Why Wall Street Tanked and How You Can Prosper

Jim Cramer's
GET RICH
Carefully

JAMES J. CRAMER

A PLUME BOOK

PLUME
Published by the Penguin Group
Penguin Group (USA) LLC
375 Hudson Street
New York, New York 10014

USA | Canada | UK | Ireland | Australia
New Zealand | India | South Africa | China
penguin.com
A Penguin Random House Company

First published in the United States of America by Blue Rider Press,
a member of Penguin Group (USA) LLC, 2013
First Plume Printing 2014

P REGISTERED TRADEMARK—MARCA REGISTRADA

ISBN 978-0-399-16818-5 (hc.)
ISBN 978-0-14-218138-6 (pbk.)

Printed in the United States of America
11   13   15   17   19   20   18   16   14   12

Original hardcover design by Tanya Maiboroda

To Lisa Detwiler,
who is everything that's good in this world

Contents

Author's Note

As I put this book to bed, I know we are in for still another year during which Washington will provide no rest for the weary. This book is about getting rich carefully; Washington is writing a serial novel about bankrupting us slowly.

We would have loved to think that after the bitter conclusion of the October 2013 debt ceiling fracas we could at last invest without endless daily intrusions from politicians, many of whom don't know the difference between a stock and a bond. But let's be realistic. Politics has sewn its way into the very fabric of our daily lives, in large part because our nation has spent beyond its means (and yet seems to have so little to show for it). The fabric's going to choke us several times a year now if we aren't mindful of how harmful politicians of both parties have become to our portfolios.

As you will see in this book, I don't think it's for me to opine on what Washington should or shouldn't do about debt ceilings, tax rates or budget appropriations. I don't care if you are a Tea Party member or a tax-and-spend liberal. I care about making you money. I am focused on the savings side of your ledger. Given that Washington's going to be wrangling about matters that directly impact your portfolio for years to come, let me share some tips gleaned from what has worked each time these hideous interchanges have occurred so that you can survive—and possibly even thrive—through the partisan pulverizing that Washington is now guaranteed to do to your savings.

Within the last three years, our stock market has had four separate run-ins with politics that caused you to lose a lot of money: the 2011 federal budget bust, which led to a ratings agency debt downgrade; the 2012 fiscal cliff debacle, with its concomitant tax increases; the spring 2013 failure to avoid the federal sequester; and, finally, the pointless fall 2013 government shutdown and debt ceiling clash. All four battles curtailed business, eroded confidence, and hurt your pocketbook. Even if this litany of pain can't be broken, is there any way to profit from it?

The short answer is yes. Each Washington tussle has the same familiar pattern. All four bitter budget contests were basically scheduled events, meaning that you could tell that they were about to occur because they were provoked by deadlines that were clearly visible to all. In each case, approximately one month before each deadline, you began to hear chatter, typically from political commentators (not businesspeople), that Republicans and Democrats might be at loggerheads over some sort of budget issue or tax resolution that had to be agreed upon or the government would cease to function. Soon after, you got pleas from various money managers, who assured you there was no need to worry about the upcoming turmoil; all you needed to do was "stay the course," because it's just politics and every time we get one of these political dramas, the action may become twisted and tortured but all will work out in the end.

While, ultimately, these "cooler heads" are right that we haven't defaulted yet and most likely won't, their "stay the course" admonition only makes sense if you are willing to experience heavy losses—realized or unrealized—and then hope to recoup those losses once the issues are resolved. That is not now nor has it ever been my style. I say if you can dodge big declines and get back into the market at lower levels, you should do so, at least with some of your money, and not just sit there and take an undeserved beating.

But here's the trick. You must take aggressive action and do some selling the moment you hear these false reassurances and not one second later. You cannot afford to wait. Here's why: In all four of these go-rounds, the stock market lost on average about 8 percent from the moment a potential skirmish began to be talked about—usually one month before the drop-dead deadline that's supposed to trigger a default or a downgrade—to when the war was finally concluded. Given this consistent peak-to-trough decline, you would be nuts *not* to do some selling the instant you hear the words "looming" and "Washington" in the same sentence. You have to overcome the complacency bred by smug money managers who blithely assure you with Shakespearean wisdom that All's Well that Ends Well. That's because when you hear their soothing entreaties, you are at the exquisite moment at which you can still take action to preserve some of your hard-earned dollars before that coming 8 percent plunge.

Then and there, you need to trim whatever stock portion of your portfolio you can trade, be it an IRA, 401k, discretionary, or whatever; it doesn't matter. Try to sell at least 10 percent of your holdings before the alarm bells go off, because that's probably the last moment at which you will get prices that are high enough and worthwhile enough to exit whole. You can take that newfound cash and put it safely on the sidelines, ready-ing it for the inevitable and brutal denouement that all of these phony reassurers didn't see coming during the downgrade debacle, the fiscal cliff, the sequester and the debt ceiling rows. Similarly, if you are about to make your regular contribution to one of those retirement accounts, try to hold off and wait for the ensuing stock decline. Having that money taken "off the table" so as to be ready for the inevitable buy point is akin to saving up for a sale at the mall. You need to have cash at the ready to take advantage of the bargains Washington's about to give you.

Then I want you to be prepared to buy several of the stocks that I recommend here, which I believe will hold up under any politically engen-dered onslaught; they have catalysts that will not be stopped by the shenanigans in the Capitol. You have to pull the trigger at the point of maximum fear, because these are the kinds of stocks that rarely get clocked except in a sell-off that's extraneous to the performance of their under-lying companies.

Now, how will you know when to begin to reinsert your money into the market? Easy: A few weeks after the exquisite sell moment, as the mar-ket has begun to plummet, you are going to hear FROM THE VERY

SAME PEOPLE WHO TOLD YOU NOT TO WORRY that, oops, the divisions in Washington are far more serious than they'd thought, maybe even worse than the last dispute. They will suggest that perhaps it is time to start selling some stocks in preparation for the "coming" decline even though the market's already been rolling over for days now. Sadly, for those who don't understand the rhythm of these events, it will then already be too late to take defensive action. In fact, when the "stay-the-coursers" change their tune and tell you that it is prudent to raise some cash, that's precisely when you must begin to reapply your sidelined money into the best-of-breed names that are described in this book.

As we get closer and closer to each fated deadline, it pays to get more aggressive with that sidelined cash. However, do not wait until the last day to do your buying because history shows that some traders will get wind of a settlement ahead of others. You snooze until that last hour, you lose; the best opportunity will have come and gone.

Now I know that this is an intense way to approach these moments. You can argue that you don't need to avail yourself of these sell-offs, but as you will soon see, if you want to get rich, carefully, it's precisely these kinds of declines that can make a big difference in doing so over the long-term. You are about to read about plenty of other, easier ways to make money, but you now know what's worked before and what I believe can work the next time a divided, dysfunctional government raids your nest egg.

October 2013

Preface to the Paperback Edition

How does something so fascinating, so enjoyable and, yes, most important, so lucrative, keep losing the hearts, minds and wallets of the American people? Every day when I come to work on Wall Street I now ponder the question of how Americans have turned so decidedly against investing in stocks. As I make my way through downtown Manhattan each morning, traversing the canyons that used to teem with eager young associates and stentorian partners excited for the ringing of the opening bell, I now marvel at the neighborhood's symbolic neglect and emptiness. In the thirty years I've toiled in the financial district, I have seen it transformed from the pulsating engine of corporate progress to an ossified antique, a museum of what capitalism used to look like, with the bustling bespoke professionals supplanted by frazzled tour guides, arms extended in the air, bearing different colored umbrellas to be sure their flocks don't stray down some blind alley filled with empty offices that still bear signs of long-ago forgotten or deceased stock broking firms.

Yet at the exact same time Wall Street's star has dimmed both metaphorically and in reality, the profits left for those stalwarts who have managed to hang on have been nothing short of spectacular, among the greatest ever recorded. Interest dwindles even as takeovers and acquisitions, those instant wealth creators, occur with a velocity and magnitude that would have been undreamed of just a few years ago. People avoid the mention of stocks even as we have blown through all sorts of levels of the Dow Jones Average that would have been unthinkable six years ago, when the market had lost half its value and companies were bleeding from their eyeballs. Few even seem to care that we are getting back to those vaunted NASDAQ prices of the turn of this century, except this time the technology stocks that dominate that index represent good values. They aren't about to explode in your faces like the Internet dot bombs did so hideously in 2000 and 2001. In fact, they could be in the midst of a sustained run. Yet, sadly, these growth stocks, both young and old, seem to beckon no one but the most intrepid of investors.

So what's happened? What can explain why fewer and fewer people seem to partake of the tantalizing and realized possibilities of tremendous wealth at our fingertips and right before our eyes? How did the souring continue despite the historic runs so many stocks have enjoyed?

It's not an easily answered question. In truth, many issues weigh on the minds of potential stock investors and they've only grown more weary, not less, as the averages power higher, and the winnings are distributed to fewer and fewer takers. In the old days when we took out big round numbers, Dow 9,000, Dow 10,000, Dow 11,000 and the like, the gains intrigued, enticed, and seduced. Now, sadly *and* shockingly, they seem to repel people and create new levels of trepidation with every breached benchmark. "Oh we missed it all, Cramer" is the sentiment I hear from passersby and see on Twitter @JimCramer.

Before I give you the litany and refutation of unfounded fears that keep so many from snatching the riches stocks create, let me reassure you that the themes, ideas, disciplines and concepts embraced in this book will allow you to triumph over any of the objections that I hear so frequently. If anything, the opportunities since *Get Rich Carefully* first rolled off the presses have gotten only more bountiful, the themes more pronounced, the profits from exploiting them even larger than I had imagined when I was first committing them to paper.

And, of course, I don't share in the increasing hostility toward making money through stocks *after* they have already had some strong gains, provided the fundamentals of the companies underneath them continue to improve. I know better and will show you, empirically, why my methods will allow you to triumph over the critics' castigations that stocks are too expensive and risky and that the entire asset class is tainted and illegitimate.

First, though, let me address the considerable brief against equities and tell you why I think the criticisms fail to measure up under close scrutiny. The most important indictment smearing Wall Street is that it's rigged, and rigged against you, the little guy, in favor of some nameless wealthy people who collude and pull the strings of stocks like they are so many marionettes on a stage of corrupt illusion. We recently heard a prominent and charming author, Michael Lewis, begin his book tour for *Flash Boys* with the rigging siren, a damning critique made pretty much everywhere he visited, often greeted with knowing nods, as if, somehow, after all of the indictments and scams and flash crashes and bank penalties, how could it *not* be rigged.

Let me give you a reality check: there's nothing rigged about Procter & Gamble or 3M; there's nothing phony about Boeing and Intel, nothing corrupt about Google or Starbucks. Yet when we say "the market," we are really talking about a supermarket that contains pieces of paper that are backed up by the real profits and predicted profits of these enterprises and thousands more honest companies just like them.

At times are the prices of their stocks ever so minutely impacted by the machinations of the so-called "big boys" Lewis derides? Yes, they certainly are, and I am sure that each of us has had, at one time or another, a few insignificant pennies taken by them when we took our profits off the table. I don't care for the high-frequency traders, and I cite them as a reason for the lack of faith in this market, throughout many a chapter. But I care more about the psychological impact of the charge that they are rigging the overall markets even more than I dislike their financial avarice and how it can impact your bottom line. I think the jeremiads of one author have once again scared people and frightened them back to the sidelines to where opportunity is nil. That's costly and it is wrong. In the long run, their high-frequency trades won't amount to a hill of beans for you if you pick the right stocks and hold them to ever superior gains.

High-frequency traders do have an unfair millisecond or two edge in trading. I don't think anyone should be allowed to have even that kind of small advantage over anyone else in the financial markets. I have always favored a leveled playing field with equal access to the best prices, something that, because of the prevalence of high-frequency trading, is decidedly not the case right now. The government should change the rules so no one can speedily front run your orders or the orders of the mutual funds you may be investing in. Still, though, remember that the impact on your sliver of a mutual fund that is gaffed by these traders is infinitesimal and certainly no reason to avoid investing in stocks.

Far more important than the pennies they clip are the dollars I want you to make with some of the long-term investments I suggest here. I know from this book and others I have written, as well as from my television shows, *Squawk on the Street* and *Mad Money* on CNBC, and my online blog in thestreet.com, that money can and is made fairly and squarely every single day that the stock market's open. We don't need to fret about making two cents less on a gigantic takeover bid. We can't really care if a nickel is scalped out of the hundreds of dollars that the tremendous themes described within have made us. That's just plain foolishness, brought on by scare tactics of an author to make a profit not by helping you but at your expense because the rigging charge keeps you in the shackles of alternatives like cash and bonds that yield next to nothing. If you think that the New York Stock Exchange is corrupt at its core, you will most likely hide your money in a .5 percent certificate of deposit, if not under the mattress. I think that's nuts. No high-frequency trader is going to keep you from earning a dividend on the average stock in the market that's four times that (and five times if you include the big tax breaks stocks give you). No flash boy shenanigans should keep you from making money over the long term with the terrific investible ideas I suggest and detail here.

The second obstacle keeping people from earning great wealth in the stock market? The impressions left by the judicial system that the big banks have wrecked finance with their greed. When you see billions and billions of dollars being paid into the Justice Department's coffers because of a legacy of financial destruction, you don't want to go near Wall Street and the wares these banks sell.

Now it is true, beyond any reasonable protest, that there weren't just a few rotten apples in the barrels of banking during the past decade; many of the barrels were despoiled beyond belief. But the crooks in the temples of finance were manipulating mortgages and bonds packaged full of mortgages, not the prices of stocks or the companies underneath them. They attacked the fixed income portion of the stock market that I am not much a fan of, in order to fool large pension, hedge and mutual funds into trying to pick up a little extra yield off of baskets of phony, undocumented, loser loans. Even as I think that game's been cleaned up by the prosecutors, lawmakers and regulators, I want you still to have nothing to do with these fancy instruments, especially if they somehow make a reappearance. They were and are always high risk–low reward alternatives to stocks. We want our stakes to be in the Googles and the Celgenes, not pieces of junk still shamelessly being marketed by slick bond salespeople.

Nor am I worried that the remaining banks can bring the whole system down, stocks included, with them if they fail. We have now put enough years between us and the great recession to know that our remaining financial institutions are indeed rock solid, actual models to the rest of the world of what solvency really means. Say what you want about the regulators, particularly former treasury secretary Timothy Geithner, but they forced our banks to raise hundreds of billions of dollars in cash—so much cash that they are no longer a valid reason to stay away from stocks because one bank's problems won't knock down the rest of them anymore. Sure, I wish our prisons were overcrowded with bankers who ripped us all off. That would be sweeter justice than having the current iteration of banking execs writing big checks of shareholders' money to the treasury even as they award themselves obscene raises and bonuses. Yep, those big fines don't come out of the offenders' pockets; they come out of the profits that belong to those who own the company's shares. That's just wrong; but they call it justice.

The third rap against the one aisle of the financial supermarket that can be so rewarding? The charge that stock prices are being manipulated upward by the Federal Reserve. Once the Fed is done trying to boost the economy and stocks through low rates, this thesis goes, it will have to raise rates quickly to combat the inflation its foolish bond-buying program has caused.

Now, let's forget for a moment that we've heard this bogus entreaty for more than 8,000 Dow Jones points. Let's ignore that the Cassandras making this charge, so wrong for so long, are almost never called out for costing you the tremendous opportunity to profit from this magnificent bull market.

The simple fact is that while rates have been trending higher, it's meant very little to the stock market. Moreover, the moves of the Federal Reserve, once so important to a very ailing economy, have actually ceased having much of an impact at all on bonds or stocks. No, the Fed and its new chief, Janet Yellen—more on her a moment—aren't entirely irrelevant. If the Fed were to decide that inflation was raging out of control and it had to take short-term interest rates through the roof, we'd have to re-think some, but not all, of our game plans.

However, the opposite has happened. We have already begun what is turning out to be a smooth and orderly departure from dramatic intervention in the markets by the Fed. All of that hand-wringing was, indeed, pretty much for nothing, not that anyone will apologize for scaring the bejesus out of you. Despite the endless screeds from some often very politically motivated commentators masquerading as honest brokers, it turns out that the policy makers were very good at their jobs.

Finally, the legitimate question of valuation must be addressed. Have we missed the whole run? Isn't it way too late? Yes, it is true that stock prices are higher than when I first outlined how to Get Rich Carefully, some meaningfully higher. But you know what? The profits that back up those stock prices have been even more bountiful than I thought. The dividends that are returned to shareholders have grown at a faster pace than I, a bull, ever imagined. The competition for your dollars, meanwhile, has either gotten way too expensive pretty much overnight, as is the case of real estate, or, in the case of all sorts of bonds, has stayed ridiculously unrewarding with a great deal of risk. In fact, I could argue that stocks are even cheaper versus these other asset classes than when the hardcover edition of *Get Rich Carefully* first came out in 2013.

Stocks, even at these heights, remain the only investable game in town. Given the improving economic backdrop and the much more lucrative earnings streams our companies are pumping out, I could easily argue that stocks remain terrific buys, and when they are placed on sale en masse, for whatever reason, should be purchased with alacrity.

Now that you see why I believe the case against stocks doesn't hold water, let me give you some additional themes that make stocks even more attractive since *Get Rich Carefully* was first published. The year since the book came off the presses has produced ten new, lucrative trends that provide a positive undercurrent and make the arguments for stock investing here even more worthwhile. These are ten briefs *for* the market that are not being factored in correctly by most investors today. They are in their infancy and by next year will be acceptable as gospel and people will be kicking themselves thinking, "Why didn't I realize the game had changed so positively in the favor of the buyers, *not* the sellers?"

First: shareholder activism. It wasn't that long ago that shareholders who didn't like the direction a company might be following simply dumped the stock in disgust. However, in the past decade, many successful hedge fund managers have been able to amass billions upon billions of dollars in capital. These investors with pools of capital much bigger than many companies themselves no longer turn tail when they don't like what's happening. Many dig in their heels and press for change.

The result has been, in just an amazingly short year's time, a revolution in activism. No company, large or small, is immune. Carl Icahn, one of the oldest activists going, took a multibillion-dollar position in Apple, the world's largest company, and through a series of Tweets, no less, helped compel the company to embark on the biggest stock buyback and dividend boost ever. The result? The stock added tens of billions of dollars in value and became, once again, after a prolonged decline, one of the best, most pro-shareholder stocks to own. It's a turnabout put squarely at the feet of activism.

Activism had a hand in the sudden departure of Microsoft CEO Steve Ballmer, even as he was the biggest shareholder in the company. That stunning turnabout occurred in part because the company invited the representative of an activist, Value Act, to the board, who immediately pushed for value-creating changes.

Both results would have been unthinkable a few years back, when huge companies' managements routinely told disgruntled shareholders to take a hike. These ultra-rich activists can buy so much stock now that they can't be ignored—and get seats on the boards of directors where they can make great things happen for you.

The change is even more pronounced among companies, unlike Apple and Microsoft, that are small enough to be taken over or forced to be sold. Consider Allergan. Here's a fantastic drug company that more than doubled in less than a year's time because a wealthy hedge fund activist, Bill Ackman, teamed up with a public company, Valeant, to orchestrate a hostile takeover of the drug giant. Until Ackman's bold move, no hedge fund had ever collaborated with a potential acquirer to take a run at any enterprise. I now believe there are so many hungry hedge fund managers out there that it will quickly become the template, giving you another way to profit from mergers and acquisitions.

Activists have also taken advantage of newfound willingness of boards of directors to entertain ideas for value creation even if current management tries to fight them. Management of Timken, a maker of specialty steels, resisted an attempt by activist Relational Investors to split the company into a steel maker and a proprietary ball bearings and service company. The board of directors hired Goldman Sachs to analyze the alternative proposed by Relational and ended up siding with the activist— resulting in dramatic gains when the company divided into two terrific, separate, publicly traded companies. I think, in the traditional fashion I outline later in these pages, both pieces of Timken, plain old Timken and Timken Steel, will continue to make you money as they grow more focused and receive sponsorship from Wall Street analysts.

Activism's become a major part of the firmament starting in 2014 and, judging by its success, that activist spur to higher prices could continue for years to come.

Second: inversion. The United States has a very punitive, sky-high corporate tax rate that is dramatically more draconian than just about every country out there. However, recently, U.S. companies have been using a loophole in the tax code to change their tax regimes, quickly boosting profits for those who take advantage of it. All an American company has to do is merge with a foreign entity where the resulting company would have more than 20 percent of its shareholders residing overseas. So companies as diverse as Medtronic in the medical device sector and Abbvie, in pharmaceuticals, among so many others, have cheated the U.S. tax man with the remaining profits falling right to shareholders. Both targets and acquirers have jumped on the announcement of each deal.

I know it seems ridiculous that our country's policymakers allow this flimflam that permits billions of dollars in tax avoidance and hurts U.S. job creation all in the name of higher earnings per share. But my talks with administration members, including Treasury Secretary Jack Lew, have led me to believe that there is little likelihood that the loophole will be changed anytime soon, because the Republicans are demanding comprehensive tax reform and are unwilling to work on fixing this one portion of the code by itself. That means much more opportunity for buyers of shares of companies seeking to invert their taxes.

Third major change? The collapse in bond yields in Europe. As recently as two years ago, the principal worry among many investors was a possible collapse of a major Western country, with smaller nations like Greece, Portugal, Ireland and even larger sovereign states like Italy and Spain facing the possibility of default. But an aggressive European Central Bank, trying to save the system and restart hiring, pumped in massive liquidity injections, causing the value of these countries' bonds to soar and yields to fall dramatically. The yields have gotten so low that in many cases they are now *below* the yields of U.S. bonds, even as they are nowhere near as safe as our country's debt.

The result? Europeans are fleeing their markets, both stocks but most particularly bonds, for the United States. Those fund flows have both kept our bond yields down, despite an economic recovery, and have helped buoy our own stocks with fresh capital. When you consider that many of the sovereign bonds of major countries used to yield as much as 7 percent and now give you only a 2.5 percent return, you can understand why we can expect European money managers to continue to flock to the United States for better investment opportunities. Remember Europe's got more than 700 million people with savings that have to be put to work somewhere, and until this last year, very little of it ended up in the United States. Same with funds from China that had been parked in European bonds. Chinese money has been going into our bond markets with a vengeance in 2014, even as the Chinese already hold 2 trillion dollars' worth of our debt. China is our largest lender; its appetite for our bonds seems endless.

In this book, I suggested that U.S. interest rates are most likely going to move up, perhaps not as gradually as we would like, because of the economic recovery. But this European fund flow has so far kept our bonds surprisingly low in yield, making many of the stocks that I describe as bond market equivalents because of their higher yields far more valuable than they would be otherwise.

Fourth major change? How quickly stocks bounce back after a disappointing piece of news. For ages I had a rule about investing: you can't buy a stock soon after an earnings disappointment no matter how low it goes. You need to wait to see the next quarter to be sure there is an all clear. One of the reasons I adopted that rule is because I recognized that even if you thought a company could rapidly recover from and reverse its fortunes, money managers would not be so forgiving and would keep the stock in the penalty box for at least the next three months.

Not anymore. Now we see stocks as varied as United Parcel, Federal Express, Oracle and General Mills report shockingly weak numbers but tell a tale of a more positive future, and the stocks rally right back to where they were after a brief dip, or even go higher than where they were just a few weeks later. This is a remarkable change, an element of forgiveness I have never seen before. It has opened up whole new possibilities out of what once were purgatories.

This change makes for a much more benign stock market. In the old days you took your life in your hands if you bought a sell-off after an earnings miss. Now many of these disappointments must be considered opportunities.

Some of the best money made in 2014 revolves specifically around this newly discounted merchandise as it turns out that the stock was far more damaged than the company itself. In fact, we have taken to buying that first dip for my charitable trust if we believe management has traced out any meaningful, credible way to reverse the current fortunes. It's been working.

Fifth new moneymaking theme? The return of old tech to the fore of market opportunity. For almost a half decade, the market has forsaken the companies that brought you so many amazing products and supported so much of what we think of as technology. The reason? Because they were linked with the personal computer, which many had written off as no longer a growth business.

However, that obituary turned out to be premature. New versions of the personal computer, including ever larger, more functional tablets, and ultra-small "clamshells" began to stem their decline in the past year and are now beginning to grow, albeit slowly but surely, as the world's economy recovers.

This change has seen a remarkable shift in many areas left for dead. Stocks I formerly scorned because they were either personal computer–related or because they used powerful servers that seemed like simply souped-up PCs are now among the hottest equities in the firmament. Given how recent this turn has occurred, I think these stocks have only just begun to make their moves.

Who fits this new pattern? I never like to outthink trends. The two most obvious beneficiaries are Microsoft and Intel. In my meetings with these two companies of which I always maintained close relationships, I am stunned by how quickly the turn has occurred. Some of it is new management. Satya Nadella, the new Microsoft CEO, has been calling for bold change, including layoffs of as many as 18,000 people, and now that Windows has a tailwind pushing it, the company may be able to unlock billions upon billions of dollars in value while at the same time boosting its buyback and its dividend. Microsoft could have many good years ahead of it as the stock has now become very cheap, even without a breakup into Xbox, utility software and cellphone and cloud initiatives.

Same with Intel, the big semiconductor company. I think that Intel, once one of my absolute favorite companies, had lost its way over the years, spending way too much on projects that didn't pan out while at the same time really missing the great growth market out there: the cell phone. Now Intel is being reenergized by new CEO Brian Krzanich, a man who has slashed profitless spending, turned the company back to its inventive roots, and made it, once again, into a semiconductor powerhouse. It, like Microsoft, represents tremendous value with a good yield and earnings estimates that I think are way too low given the company's newfound momentum.

The companies that make parts for personal computers are just now beginning to get better valuations on their earnings. Two disk drive makers, Seagate and Western Digital, while participating somewhat in the bull market, could trade substantially higher as it begins to dawn on more portfolio managers that other devices besides handhelds might be on the increase.

Micron, which had benefitted from a consolidation that I detail in this book, is now seeing not just a tightness in supply of the commodity DRAM chip that it makes; it is also seeing an increase in demand that is causing average selling prices of its wares to lift. That's not happened in years. Same thing goes for its division that makes flash storage.

Perhaps the biggest beneficiary may be Hewlett-Packard, a company that had truly been left for dead after a string of bad acquisitions had been made by a set of truly weak chief executive officers.

Now, under CEO Meg Whitman, Hewlett-Packard has turned around its core personal computer and service business, and it has done so with far fewer people on the payroll. That's allowed her to boost the dividend and increase the buyback of this venerable computer company that has gone from being on the ropes to raking in the profits.

Look for many old tech companies to continue to rebound as personal computer refresh cycles, after years of neglect, kick in all over the world.

Sixth theme? The return of China, or at least Chinese companies, to the investable firmament. After a series of scandals and a Communist Party crackdown of new equity issuance, there's been a noticeable change in the merchandise now emanating from China. We are getting respectable, fast-growing companies that look just like American companies when it comes to the financials, and also have incredible growth characteristics. Stocks like Baidu, VIPshops, JD.com and the newly public Alibaba, all of which I have repeatedly highlighted on *Squawk on the Street* and *Mad Money*, have captured many a growth manager's attention as they should, because these companies are all variations of Amazon but with much better opportunities for profits. Alibaba, in particular, stands out as a potential core holding for those investors seeking long-term growth. Now, I am not yet willing to believe that the Chinese economy is making a comeback. But I think its online retail possibilities, given the Communist Party's newfound predilection to emphasize internal consumption over exporting, present tantalizing opportunities. I also believe that many of the accounting scandals involving new Chinese companies may, at last, be put in the rearview mirror.

Seventh change? The analyst community. For years, ever since the Great Recession, analysts have been given to a level of negativity that while cogent during the dark days, now seems out of step with the reality of better economic times. Hardly a day goes by when we don't catch upgrades of stocks that had been hated for years. For example, the personal computer stocks I just mentioned have all been despised for ages by the research arms of the major brokerages. Now they are being upgraded, and each upgrade takes these stocks much higher. Same with the auto makers and the airlines. I haven't seen anything like the agglomeration of upgrades since right after the Great Crash of 1987, when analysts almost en masse turned negative only to spend the next several years going out positive, and with each upgrade a higher price ensued.

I know the sell-to-hold-to-buy repertoire of analysts shouldn't mean that much, but with the change in tone of the market to a more positive bent, analyst upgrades are boosting stocks like crazy. It isn't unusual to see stocks gap up in price on an upgrade that would have been yawned over for the past half-dozen years. I marvel at this phenomenon almost daily in my "Mad Dash" and "Stop Trading" portions of *Squawk on the Street*. Upgrades matter and they are now coming every day, fast and furiously, as analysts no longer share a collective bunker mind-set.

The eighth new theme? The surprisingly strong pro-growth new Fed chairwoman Janet Yellen. One of the saving graces of this era was the fantastic work Ben Bernanke did as Fed chair to steward the economy toward a comeback after the Great Recession that's been unrivaled by all other Western nations mired in the downturn. It's one of the reasons I dedicated my last book, *Getting Back to Even*, to the former Fed chief. His combination of low interest rates and aggressive money creation triumphed over a federal government so at loggerheads that after an initial, underperforming stimulus package, has been cutting back hiring and job-boosting infrastructure programs ever since. While there were many candidates for the Fed job, the president picked a person most similar to Bernanke in a desire to keep rates as low as possible until a genuine recovery ignites. Yellen's concerned about employment at a time when the recovery's still spotty, knowing that we have had totally inconsistent industrial production, retail and housing reports, albeit certainly stronger than previous years. Aside from one errant comment about the "stretched" valuations of smaller social media and biotechs, she's been as hands-off about stocks as Bernanke. We want the Fed chief not to focus on a few admittedly risky sectors of the stock market and instead be concerned with helping the economy along as Bernanke did, and that's continuing under Yellen. She creates more opportunity to make money in the stock market because her bias is not to slow the economy down through higher rates for fear of inflation, but to stay easy to try to solve longer-term unemployment issues that aren't being addressed by the president or Congress because of partisan rancor. She is proving to be a godsend to the stock market with her thoughtfulness and lack of rash judgments.

Ninth theme: the return to stock picking and the end of a silly season for ETFs. One of the most important changes that has occurred since the initial launch of *Get Rich Carefully* is the recognition by the market of what I call the ETF-ization movement that has finally peaked and is receding. What's ETF-ization? It's a once-prevailing view that stocks are like commodities and can be grouped by sector without worry that one company is truly superior to others.

We are now in a period where we recognize that individual companies and managements are indeed different from each other. Retailers, for example, have had very mixed success dealing with the up and down economy, some blaming the weather for poor results, others even citing a funk in the consumer herself. But some companies, notably Costco and Macy's, two *Get Rich* favorites, have risen above the fray. The same thing has happened in new technology, where the proven winners have just gotten stronger and are leaving the others behind. One of the most important theses of *Get Rich Carefully* is that being careful to identify best of breed and not lumping in the good and the bad through an ETF can lead to much better returns. It's a validation of my homework-derived thesis: the more you know the more you make.

I am not, per se, against index funds if you do not have the time or inclination to research and deploy your hard-earned capital. It's always been my default theory, as I don't want you taking on individual stocks if you don't have the ability to do the homework. I see many people, for example, on Twitter who blindly buy stocks of companies without even knowing what they do. They just like the "action" or the "momentum."

When the action and the momentum cool, they get nervous, and when the stocks swoon, they blow them out. That's become the modern version of buying high and selling low. My bottoms-up approach should lead to the opposite; as stocks of terrific companies go down, you buy more, not less.

The twilight of the homogenized, commoditized baskets of sector ETFs is at last upon us, something that will make it easier for better managements to distance their stocks from the pack. It's a subtle but huge change, and I hope that the ignominious brainwashing of America by greedy professionals eager to get the fees that come from the endless procession of sector ETFs is at last coming to an end.

Final theme, best for last; the renaissance of mergers and acquisitions in the market place. When people ask me how I can still like stocks at these supposedly lofty levels, I always come back and say, "Don't look at me, look at what the companies are doing." We are seeing a remarkable number of deals occurring, in dollar amounts that are so far ahead of any other years that it is astounding to behold.

I used to joke with my CNBC colleague and merger and acquisitions expert David Faber that each week started with Merger Monday, as we would have major deal after major deal be announced after a weekend's worth of work. Now every day seems to be Merger Monday. Plus the consolidation is happening in everything from entertainment and telecom to oil and gas, to auto parts to chemicals to aerospace, defense, materials and, most important, consumer products. We have seen a series of consolidations and bidding wars for companies that make current valuations seem like they are aberrantly low. Amazingly, almost every deal creates a bump in the acquirer, a further verification of my theory that stocks remain too cheap and the opportunities vastly surpass the risks. When the buyer's stock gets rewarded, it inspires ever more deals, which I expect to continue after the longest dry spell of deals in modern memory.

We are seeing these deals in large part because there is a growing sense that while not going back into a recession, we are not going to see the kind of 4–5 percent growth we used to take as a given for both the United States and the world. Thus the only way to really assure your shareholders that they'll see consistent returns is to buy other companies and then take out costs, giving you earnings gains for many years to come. Any improvement that we actually get in any of the worldwide economies, such as Europe, Asia or Latin America, will quickly lead to a boost in sales and enlarged profits because of the streamlining of the labor forces that has occurred during the downturn. The recession gave cover for companies to fire excess workers, which has resulted in some pretty powerful bottom lines wherever a recovery takes hold.

There are simply too many areas where similar corporations compete with each other, including retailers, restaurants, financials, chemicals, metals, oil and gas, health care, medical devices and even social media and e-commerce firms. All of these are rife with deals and ripe with opportunities.

It's not unusual now to wake up to a deal like Merck buying Idenix, a little biotech company, for three times what it was selling for just the day before with the hopes that it might have a formulation that can cure hepatitis C. Idenix is a reminder, by the way, of why I like speculating in small capitalization stocks for a tenth of your portfolio. That keeps you interested in your money and also allows lightning to strike. It is also a verification that Fed chief Yellen's worries about stretched valuations of small biotechs is misplaced. In a world where big pharmaceutical companies are out of ideas and have no attractive, long-term pipelines full of new drugs to speak of, smaller, riskier biotechs are more likely than ever to catch lofty takeover bids giving instant profits to those who speculated wisely.

We see European companies that we thought were dead men walking now suddenly alive and well—and buying U.S. companies, like when a German company recently went after the venerable TRW auto parts maker. Or we get a bidding war for a sleepy Sara Lee spin-off, Hillshire Brands, that, out of nowhere, virtually doubles the price of this left-for-dead sausage maker out of nowhere. I expect many more takeovers in the food and beverage arena as sales decline and companies clamor for growth via acquisitions.

Finally, we have seen the return of the hostile takeover, perhaps the most bountiful of all merger and acquisition activity. Consider the three most prominent attempts, Valeant Pharmaceuticals going after Allergan, Dollar General seeking Family Dollar and Twenty-First Century Fox gunning for Time Warner. Valeant's managed to drive up the price of Allergan by more than a third. Dollar General came in to bust up a deal between Family Dollar and Dollar Tree, something that insured fabulous returns for Family Dollar shareholders. Yes, Fox ultimately walked away from Time Warner, but in the interim you could have made more than 20 percent in just a few days of trading. The excitement and the gains that come from these kinds of deals cannot afford to be missed and many of the sectors where the deals are most likely going to occur are detailed here in later pages.

Now, I am not blind to the risks that are in front of this market. In the past year we have had geopolitical tensions that hadn't been seen since the time of the cold war. The Middle East's Arab spring has turned into a quagmire that threatens to spread to all of the oil-producing countries. The gridlock in Washington pretty much makes it so nothing positive for business can come out of Capitol Hill. There will be no stimulus, no infrastructure spur of any consequence. While in the short term the federal deficit seems tame, in the longer term, as Baby Boomers retire and Social Security and Medicare face demographic threats that are by no means resolved, there'll be a negative impact on the stock market. Meanwhile the nascent hiring boom will most likely be tempered by the implementation of the confusing, jumbled Affordable Care Act.

Nevertheless, all of these problems are, I believe, already well factored in by the level of prices in the market. If any of them is actually resolved positively, you will see an even more powerful, consistent, upward move than even I believe possible.

So fret all you want about missing the big moves. Worry that it is rigged and you can't afford to be more than just a sightseer. Shake in fear about another financial collapse or runaway inflation or an ineffectual Fed or a dysfunctional Washington.

I, on the other hand, prefer for you to get rich using stocks as your wealth builders, as long as you invest wisely and carefully when doing so.

July 2014

Introduction

We've been beat up. We've been struggling to come back. We're finally breaking out to levels that were thought to be unthinkable given how poorly stocks have performed in the past decade and a half. We need to stop getting knocked around and settling for incremental strides. It's time to use the stock market to build wealth again. It's time to get rich, but to do so carefully this go-round, not recklessly and not with blind disregard to this new world of investing. We accept that this market has overpowered most small investors. The big funds too seem to have lost their ability to beat the averages, perhaps permanently, because of their size and because of their collective bunker mentality that has them simply trying to mimic the Standard & Poor's 500. I am confident you can beat the averages if you work with me to triumph over the obfuscating, infuriating and often broken process of trying to profit from short- and long-term stock price movements.

What does it take to Get Rich Carefully? In the past eight years, watching the markets for *Mad Money* and then *Squawk on the Street*, as well as investing in them for my charitable trust, I have had to rethink entirely how you can use stocks to generate the wealth you need to put children through school, buy a house, afford your leisure time and ultimately fund your retirement needs. During my frequent trips to colleges for *Mad Money*, I have seen that a whole new generation has discovered the wonders and dangers of the stock market, but they do not have the tools to profit from its gifts or protect themselves from its pitfalls.

Most of all I have come to realize that the basics continue to elude people, that most people feel left out, that they "never took the course," so to speak, about how the markets really work. Consequently, they feel ignorant and disenfranchised. They know a small number of people are making money again. They yearn to be a part of that select group, but they know that the losses in the past few years have been staggering and that bonds and cash are the only choices for those who don't know how money creation works.

Unfortunately, the thirty-year bull market in bonds—where prices went up and interest rates went down—has now ended. The easy, safe, if not guaranteed money has turned into the risky money that's anything but guaranteed and has been generating humongous losses over short periods of time. That's not what these bondholders expected when they stashed trillions of their hard-earned dollars in these funds. They didn't know they could lose money. But switching that giant hoard to stocks without the tools, without the knowledge base? That's just foolhardy, isn't it?

No, not if you read this book. *Get Rich Carefully* is designed for investors who thought they were being careful playing it safe, storing cash in bond funds and keeping it in low-interest certificates of deposit. It's tailored for those who are befuddled about and distrustful of stocks but seek better returns than they've gotten from somnambulant managers and underperforming mutual funds. It's meant for those who think they can profit from stock price gyrations but don't know how and why stocks really go up or down. They are mystified by the process though eager to learn how to gain wealth from stocks in a prudent but opportunistic way.

What will you find here to help you make the transition from amateur investor to someone who can go toe-to-toe with professionals—although they have hardly distinguished themselves in the past fifteen years—and become the more informed client who produces the best results? How about a novel, fast-paced how-to book that gives you insights into how stocks really work and how you can profit from this market's machinations and mysteries rather than be turned off or freaked out by them?

First I let you in on secrets that you don't know unless you've worked within every part of the process of how the stock market works, a process I've been exposed to throughout my financial career. Then I explain what propels stocks, why they really advance or decline. No matter what I have done and how hard I have tried in my media career, I still run into thousands—yes, thousands—of people who do not understand the anatomy of a one-point gain. How can a stock move up a dollar? Why does a stock shed three points in a heartbeat? How does it actually work? After all the chicanery that's been visited upon this stock market, many people think it's all alchemy. Others think it is just plain crooked. They don't trust the explanations they hear daily about why their stocks moved up or down and why the market rallied or swooned.

They're right to be suspicious and skeptical. After you read *Get Rich Carefully* you'll be wise to what really happened on a given day's trading and, therefore, ready to make money in the next day's session or the next week's, month's or even years' worth of sessions ahead of us. No, I am not able to give you tomorrow's cyber paper today, but I can try to do the next closest thing, showing you how to predict moves with a degree of certainty that will make you more comfortable and better at creating your own wealth.

Next, I show you how to take advantage of the confusion and obfuscation that surrounds the movements of equities to pick the right stocks at the *right* prices. Why not get your portfolio in tip-top shape to profit from what looks to be the chaos of daily trading?

People always ask me what I read, how I get my input, how I have such an edge when it comes to so many stocks and so many sectors. How come it seems to come so easily for me? Believe me, I wish it did. Sure, I have resources that you can't have, but they are way overvalued compared to the information I glean from public information about stocks that is readily available to you on dozens of sites around the web. You just haven't been taught how to parse the releases, how to understand the research and, most important, how you can use conference calls to make sense of things. Yes, these sources can be arcane and difficult to divine, but they are a unique part of the stock market firmament that you must tame so you can try to profit from every earnings report. They are among the most important sources for understanding why individual stocks advance over longer periods of time, sources I am confident you will understand after reading *Get Rich Carefully*. Once you have learned how to do the homework, I bet you will become as good a student of the market as I am, maybe better, because you will focus only on what matters, not on the millions of extraneous details that I have, at last, learned to cull and discard.

Everything I do, almost every stock I pick, emanates from major themes that are playing out underneath the market. What are those themes? I refer to them on television, and I try to flesh them out as carefully as I can. However, I have never done them justice. If you are going to Get Rich Carefully, you are going to have to get rich over time—no shortcuts. So you need longer-term investment ideas, rooted in concepts that can withstand the vicissitudes of a sometimes broken, often confounding market over the next five to ten years. I've got seven of them, seven themes all built to last no matter what the world's economies throw at you. Don't worry, I don't just detail the themes. This book is practical: I give you the best stocks to profit from them, stocks to buy now and hold as the themes unfold over many years' time.

I want you to benefit from some of the insights I have gained, specifically from hosting *Mad Money* and running ActionAlertsPlus.com, the fancy name for my $3 million charitable trust. For example, I have seen chief executive officers take their poorly performing ugly duckling stocks and turn them into extremely profitable swans through acquisitions and breakups. I show you who might be next to create that wealth for shareholders. That means no matter how sick or tortured the market might be at any given moment, there's still a huge amount of money to be made. No one else is talking about this new and amazing money-making process, yet I think it is the most lucrative path to great wealth currently playing out today.

You want proprietary ways to wealth? I have now conducted hundreds of interviews with chief executive officers and spent thousands upon thousands of hours prepping for, sitting with and learning from the best of the best executive talent that America has to offer. Here, for the first time ever, I reveal my Bankable 21, my salute to the twenty-one best leaders who have come on *Mad Money*, and why you should invest with them and ride their coattails to tremendous gains. The list will surprise you, might even amaze you, because most are anything but household names. I want you to pick your favorites of my favorites, invest in their stocks and stay with them through thick and thin. That's what my Bankable 21 CEO list is all about.

As Bob Dylan noted years ago, the times, they are a-changing, and I have had to change with them. For years I have described myself as a fundamentalist, someone who looks strictly at the companies underlying the stocks and tries to discern where, when combined with the news of the day, they are heading. I have shunned technical trading and charting because I thought those methods were lazy and less rigorous than my routine of homework and selection of individual stocks. However, through the regular and wildly popular "Off the Charts" segment of *Mad Money* I have validated the success that can come from interpreting the arcane and seemingly inscrutable stock pictographs that the segment explores. Now, at last, I teach you how to harness the "technical" and divine the charts in a digestible way that makes you better at picking winning stocks and what prices to pay for them. Through my "Charting for Fundamentalists" chapter I hope to augment the timing of your buys and sells and even short sales using better, more precise entry and exit points.

I also want you to glean from my lessons learned after a decade of picking stocks with an open hand through the brutal gauntlet that is ActionAlertsPlus.com. I critique my own moves after examining the contemporaneous bulletins, looking for misjudgments, pitfalls and bogus rationalizations that you must never make if you are going to Get Rich Carefully. I give you the raw, often embarrassing insights and the do's and don'ts these insights spawn. Twenty-twenty hindsight can actually be a brilliant teacher when you learn from my mistakes. Be my student; let me show you how to learn from what I have done right and, perhaps more important, what I have done wrong. Be wary of a creeping lack of diversification, reckless stock picking masked as prudent portfolio management and dozens of other sand traps that you must avoid if you're going to use stocks to get rich.

Finally, you know how important I believe discipline is to managing your own money. When I say Get Rich Carefully, I mean get rich with disciplines that I have pioneered and, hopefully, by now have almost perfected. I say "almost perfected" because I have sometimes let emotions get through the door instead of leaving them outside so I could become a better trader and investor. I give you the coat checks to your anxieties and fears and, yes, greedy tendencies. So sit back and enjoy my keys to "What Matters? What Doesn't? What We Should Care About," "When and How to Sell in the New, More Difficult World of Investing," and how to "Check Your Emotions at the Door" so you know how to discipline yourself. Believe me, after reading those chapters you will be cracking your own whip and will be your own best critic and disciplinarian.

I know, lots of tall, ambitious orders here. And certainly lots of new orders, not anything warmed over or seen in any other investment book, including my own. Because this is a different market. It's a better one than we have had in decades, even though it seems ever more treacherous and unfair. The rallies are happening at a period of tremendous and deserved disenfranchisement for the everyday investor. How in heck are you going to make big money in that case? Personal income levels are stagnant; they have been for years. Bond funds have gone from cautious friends to reckless, wily enemies. Real estate seems played out, gold stymied, commodities kaput. But stocks? Let's go figure them out. Let's go harness them together. Let's go get rich with them, carefully this time, so you don't give it back. Let's go forward and make some hay, because at last the sun is shining, and we have the tools to harvest the money that's within our grasp after years of toiling in the most barren of vineyards.

CHAPTER 1

What Moves a Stock

If we are going to invest successfully in this new, more treacherous environment, we are going to have to recognize that bizarre stock movements have become a staple, if not the hallmark, of this era. Before we even get to the buying and selling of individual stocks in order to create wealth, we have to understand how stocks are impacted by both understandable events and what seem to be random gyrations that baffle and frighten us. We need to fathom these moves because when we become scared and confused investors we become emotional and reckless investors. Ignorance is the opposite of bliss in the stock market.

Let's take the most glaring example of a pernicious quarter-hour event that turned off more people to the stock market than just about anything since the Great Recession: the Flash Crash of May 6, 2010. I happened to be on television when this horrific 1,000-point decline occurred, and I have to tell you that it was one of the most mystifying moments in my career. Virtually nothing of any real import was happening; we were all chatting about riots in Greece at the moment the crash was triggered, explaining why riots aren't a reason to sell off investments. But the market proceeded to decline so precipitously that a giant stock like Procter & Gamble traded at $60 one minute and then at $50 and then sliced right through $40, all within the confines of a commercial break. Fortunately, I was in a position to say there was nothing fundamentally wrong with P&G or a host of other stocks that were also plummeting, but I was at a loss to explain how it could happen.

It was only after the event and the subsequent run right back up that we realized it was just an example of the power of the S&P 500 stock futures running roughshod over all stocks, as the market couldn't absorb a couple of huge sell orders that came into the futures pits in Chicago all at once. The pummeling in the stock futures cascaded over to individual stocks, and the avalanche took down almost everything in its path as stocks broke down, triggering various sell strategies. Buyers were fleeing the market in fear that something larger and more terrible was occurring that no one knew about. When we found out there was nothing fundamentally wrong, nothing that spooked the markets, just a series of overzealous traders selling all at once, it turned out to be a terrific buying opportunity. However, the fact that there was no precipitating event for the 1,000-point decline, no real rhyme or reason for it, only served to scare people even more about the stock market. The whole asset class was tarnished more in fourteen minutes of trading than when banks and brokers crashed in 2008 and high-flying dotbombs went off in 2000. The exit from the building has pretty much continued unbridled since the Flash Crash, aided by several other similar but smaller crashettes, as we call them, including perhaps the most bizarre of all: a total shutdown of the NASDAQ for three hours, the Flash Freeze. Unfortunately, these terrifying mechanistic obstacles have occurred during an incredibly good performance for the stock market. But can anyone blame those who flee? I understand the reasoning. Who would risk their hard-earned dollars on the stocks of even the strongest companies with the biggest dividends, the best earnings track records and most bountiful balance sheets, when their market capitalizations can be cut in half, or even more, during the time it takes to brush your teeth, shower and get dressed in the morning?

It's not just events like the Flash Crash, though, that confound people about this asset class and drive them to either more tangible investments like real estate or less rewarding ones like corporate and treasury bonds. There's the day-to-day interchange between stocks and bonds themselves, where the bond market seems to call the tune regularly over the stock market, even though it seems many companies should be immune to such movements. There's the "macro" tug of events, the impact of important economic influences, like jobless claims or pronouncements by the Federal Reserve or aggregate retail and home sales numbers, and how they can impact many of your stocks that you might believe shouldn't be buffeted by such extraneous issues. Even more disturbing is the role of a Cyprus bank failure, a Spanish employment report, a riot in Brazil or a slowing Chinese industrial production number on your purely domestic holdings, many of which might have nothing whatsoever to do with those overseas events.

And it's not just these big news items that can impact stocks in mysterious ways. These days there is an intense sector pull on stocks that almost at all times overwhelms the individual characteristics of individual companies. People ask me, "What kind of insanity allows good companies and bad companies to trade in lockstep?" How can you be careful and prudent in picking stocks when the worst stocks in a group can pull down the best ones? What an obstacle to the homework that's now become, what a roadblock to serious investing. How can the performance of an individual company not matter if it's put in an index of companies that it's beating the pants off and they all go down at once?

Then there's the impact of the "micro," the individual news coming out of individual companies that you might be investing in. You've navigated the flash crashes, accepted the bizarre role that bonds and big-government data may have on your stocks; you know the Fed's pronouncements can impact stocks in strange ways that you can't figure out and that the bad stocks can take down your good ones. But how can a stock you own not go up on good earnings news? How can it not rally when its quarterly sales are stellar and it raises its dividend and reloads its buyback? What the heck is that all about? That's not the way it used to be. How can you protect yourself from this seeming lunacy, let alone profit from it?

These are all the new mitigating factors that we must now calculate before we can decide whether we should even own stocks, let alone select individual equities for our portfolios. That's why I want to break down, one by one, each of these hard-to-fathom distortions to all stocks before we get into the weeds and learn how to select, buy and own individual stocks for the long haul. We can't possibly be in shape to own stocks until we can live with the roller coaster of volatility caused by all of these mysterious and often profoundly negative events that have taken root since the time my previous book was published.

So let's get started examining the other-worldly forces that can impact your stocks in a way that can often trump the businesses that these pieces of paper are supposed to track. Let me give you the mechanics of how and why stocks can move without anything happening at the underlying companies themselves.

SOMETIMES I JUST have to own the fact that the whole time I've been picking stocks and espousing their virtues, I have skipped over perhaps the most basic part of the stock market's anatomy: the actual pressure put on stocks from buyers and sellers. While every single one of the extraneous forces that I just mentioned plays a role in a stock's movement, it all still comes down to the fact that a stock goes up when there are more buyers than sellers, and a stock goes down when more people want out than want in at any given moment.

As someone who's been analyzing stocks for most of his life, I have often taken for granted this tug-of-war between buyers and sellers. But I know from interactions with so many of you that I had better explain the underlying process of a stock's movement right here, right now, before I suggest which stocks will move and why they will do so. So many times people ask me or tweet me, "Jim, which book of yours can help me, a beginning stock market investor?" While many of my books and articles delve into what can move a stock, none of them has explained why a given stock moves the way it does, something that often eludes not just the beginners but those with years of experience trying, and failing, to pick good stocks. Without that initial understanding, the whole thing feels a bit like alchemy at best, or a rigged contest at worst. Surely, we think, given the prevalence of insider information, lots of stocks go higher because someone has the skinny and we don't. While the now rampant federal prosecutions are needed because plenty of people do know information and trade on that information illegally, that's profoundly not why the vast majority of stocks move up or down in a given session.

What moves stocks, what makes them gain or lose pennies, dimes or dollars, is a process that mystifies many and puts them at a huge disadvantage if they don't know how these jumps and dives actually occur. They get confused, angry even. Why bother to try investing carefully if you have no idea what moves the stocks you own? If you get frustrated because stock movements seem so illogical—a pretty universal complaint these days—then you've come to the right place. I am certain you can improve your financial health if you become attuned to the way stocks really do work.

First, let me tell you a story about how hard it is to even figure out what moves a stock, and why you aren't alone in being confused by it. It's a story about when I was starting out, when I, too, didn't understand what could cause a stock to move up or down a dollar.

Before I got to Goldman Sachs in 1983 as an intern, I was fascinated to learn what was behind a stock's given move, despite nothing new or of import happening at the company the stock was supposed to stand for. Sure, a big earnings surprise could impact a stock's price. But those reports come out only four days a year. How about the 361 other days when nothing material occurs? I know that investor meetings, high-level resignations and appointments, product introductions and changes in analysts' opinions can occur. Nevertheless, those too can be considered to have only an ephemeral impact. When I first walked into Goldman Sachs I considered myself a legitimate student of the stock market, but deep down I was always befuddled when a stock jumped a quarter or a half or a point seemingly based on nothing. (We used fractions back then, not pennies.) Was it stock news I didn't know about but would know if I toiled at an in-the-know place like Goldman Sachs? Was it a cascade of buyers who just couldn't wait for something that I didn't even know about? Did one person know something no one else did, and he left enough tracks that others followed him? Was it insider trading ahead of a good earnings report that a chump like me just didn't know yet? What caused these seemingly random moves that defined the range of that day's trading?

In one of my countless interviews with Goldman Sachs (about a dozen over a year just to get a summer internship), one of the executives said I could ask him anything I wanted about the market. The interviewing process had been tedious if not futile by then, and I figured if I hadn't gotten the job by now I was never going to get it anyway, so I blurted out what was actually on my mind. I believe the same question is on the mind of the vast majority of you reading this or watching my show: What makes a stock move—I mean, really move? What gets it going? What takes it from $9 to $10 in a single session, when nothing's happening, nothing at all, at the enterprise that's being traded?

The market was open for trading, so the exec said, "You really want to know? Okay, watch this: I will make a move happen. Keep your eyes on the symbol SRR." That was the stock symbol for Stride Rite, a shoe company known for its Keds label, which at the time was trading at $9. I was sitting in front of a quote machine called a Quotron, a priceless relic of a different era. Only a limited number of machines had the prices you now see routinely on every PC or cell phone, making you a far more powerful and intelligent trader than I was in the old days, despite the fact that the market has become far more difficult to fathom on a daily basis. The Quotron showed that the SRR stock's last sale was at $9. That was the quote line. Next to that were two numbers, 9 and 9⅛, and two more numbers with an *x* between them: 100 x 100. That meant that someone was willing to buy 100 shares at $9 and someone else was willing to sell 100 shares at $9⅛. Who knows who they were and what they had in mind beyond that, but you could "hit the bid" for 100 shares, selling them at $9, or you could "take the offer" and purchase 100 shares for $9⅛. Markets don't trade like this anymore; now stocks trade in penny increments, and many stocks are so "deep" or filled with so many buyers and sellers that you can sell thousands of shares or even 10,000 shares at the exact same price and not move the stock at all. But the gist of the example remains relevant, as huge buyers can and do overwhelm large sellers every moment in the market. Given that I am trying to show you how I could be so obtuse and almost afraid to learn because it could reveal my ignorance, let's let the example suffice.

I was totally glued to these flashing green numbers, thinking, What's going to happen next? There's no reason for the stock to move. Nothing's new. It's just another random day at the company that makes Top-Siders and Keds Champion Oxfords.

The exec knew he had me on the hook. He said, "Ready?" I nodded. He then picked up the phone and called one of Goldman Sachs' in-house traders. "Eddie, take 50,000 Stride Rite, with a 9.25 top." In English that means Eddie was just ordered to buy 50,000 shares of Stride Rite, with a limit of $9.25 and not a penny more, to "get in," or purchase, all 50,000 shares. The trader could do what he wanted to buy the 50,000 shares, as long as he did not exceed the top of 9¼, or pay more than $9.25. Next thing I know, the green line on the Quotron is going nuts and the stock is jumping straight up to $9.25. Just like that. Yep, in no more than thirty seconds, maybe less, Stride Rite has gone from $9 a share to $9.25. Twenty-five cents gained if you owned Stride Rite because Jim Cramer wanted to see how a stock moves.

Eddie calls back after the green stops flickering at 9¼ and says, loud enough so I can hear it, "You've got 6,500 shares in at slightly more than nine and an eighth," and he's now "working the order," trying to get the rest of the stock, 43,500 shares, purchased at 9¼ or less.

Eddie goes on to explain that he had no choice but to move the stock to $9.25 in order to get that meager amount in. He adds, "Look, there's nothing offered in size right now up anywhere near here," meaning that there are no real sellers offering to part with shares at that moment any-where in sight at the 9¼ level or even above that limit. Eddie then suggests that he might have to take the stock of Stride Rite all the way to $10 per share to get all 50,000 shares in if "your guy" is in a hurry. Hmm, I think to myself, I'm the "guy"! The exec says, "Stay there for a few minutes," code for Eddie to bid up to $9.25 "out loud," meaning "Show my bid on the green screen to see if that will draw out sellers." Suddenly, I see on the screen "9.25 9.375, 1000 x 100," with Goldman's trader trying to execute my order, bidding for 1,000 shares and some nameless soul offering just 100 shares an eighth above where we are willing to pay. It stays that way for about a full minute with nothing happening at all. The last sale is $9.25 and there's nothing doing. Bored, point proven, the exec tells Eddie to "walk away," to hold up the order for now, "and let's see if someone shows up as a seller." A few minutes go by and no one surfaces as a seller, so the exec gets Eddie on the horn again and cancels the remaining buy ticket.

The exec turns to me and says, "You want to see that stock move up a dollar, you take the top off," meaning if he doesn't limit his buy order of 50,000 to $9.25 he will have to pay perhaps as much as $10, in Eddie's judgment, to bring out enough sellers to get the job done and complete the order. There, right in front of me, was my anatomy of a one-point gain. The $1 move up in Stride Rite would occur not because of a terrific earnings report, not because of a takeover, not because of an analyst upgrade and not because of a new model Ked, but because this Goldman exec placed a very large order relative to the market capitalization of the entire company, at that time $500 million, and demanded that it be filled quickly with no limit.

When you've wondered why a stock went up on no news, you might have heard reasons like "more demand than supply" or "more buyers than sellers." You probably wanted to shoot the person who gave you that kind of glib answer. You wanted to know what the buyer knew, what insight he had that you didn't, what the "real" reason was. You thought the response was totally lacking in candor. I too always hated that kind of "explanation"— until I saw Stride Rite jump from $9 to $9.25 in less time than it takes to run from one end of a football field to another and back again. And I know it could have gone to $10 if that exec simply pressed the issue to demonstrate how a stock can rally a dollar on nothing, indeed nothing at all.

I could only imagine what the good people sitting in Stride Rite's headquarters, then in Cambridge, Massachusetts, would be thinking if SRR suddenly rose to $10. Takeover? Some news that even the CEO didn't know about? The absurdity of it all was palpable, but in the end, there was simply more demand than supply and a larger buyer was overwhelming all sellers at that moment. The supercilious answer was the correct one. And the scales were lifted from my eyes. I had been part of a vast conspiracy to move Stride Rite higher—at least that's how it would have appeared to the outside world if we had continued to press it—and all that had really happened was a larger order had been placed than the volume of the Stride Rite market could handle at that minute. I am sure that had we reversed course and tried to dump 50,000 shares all at once, we could have just as easily smashed through the $9 level and taken the stock to the $8s if we were in a hurry. And yet all that would have happened at Stride Rite that day was a bunch of shoes would have been made and still another bunch would have been sold. Just like any other day.

Of course, not all stocks are like Stride Rite was, a thin or lightly traded stock with a relatively small market capitalization. But you get the picture.

Stocks move when supply overwhelms demand over a very short period of time. That's what propels or pushes down stocks when nothing's happening. That was the real answer to my question.

This exercise isn't an idle one but one that could have serious consequences for you if you don't enter your order right, with a limit and not "at the market." Let's go back to the original purchase order. Think of the options the buyer had. Instead of putting a limit on his buy, he could have said, "Buy me 50,000 shares at the market." Given that 6,500 shares took the stock to $9.25, it is entirely possible that a market order, meaning "Buy everything in sight until you got to 50,000," might take it to $10 or even beyond, because a market order without proper guidance is just an order to pay whatever you can, even if it moves a stock. Now, most of you won't be buying stocks in that quantity. However, it is entirely possible that in the time between when that market order is placed and when it is fully executed, you might be putting in an order to buy 100 shares of Stride Rite at the market—no limit. You have no idea what's happening with the stock. But I bet you thought you could buy it around the price you saw it trading at, $9 a share. Next thing you know, because of someone's aggressive market order, you just paid $10 for a stock you thought you could purchase for no more than $9.25 at worst. You've just made a horrible trade. You have a miserable basis, and you feel totally betrayed by the process. Then, of course, now that the buyer is done, next thing you know, SRR's back at $9 as sellers at last see nothing's going on at the company and decide to take advantage of the temporary rise and get out at better prices than they deserve. That's why, beyond solving the mystery of why a stock can jump on no news, you need to protect yourself from this insanity by using limit orders. That's also why I always admonish you to stick by a price and not deviate: precisely because you now know what—or who—can move a stock.

Of course, if there actually is some news, some positive surprise to earnings, we accept this hazard. We're in there buying with everyone else on the news, and we accept the consequences. It's just that, as I said earlier, that kind of instantaneous earnings reappraisal happens only four times a year. The rest of the time it's pretty much as I have just traced out. That's why the wise customer puts the top, or limit, on the order.

Let me tell you the much larger takeaway of this story in the new world we find ourselves in now. The whole Stride Rite exercise is actually a mini-version of what happened that day in the Flash Crash, except the orders that day caused the whole stock market to plummet, not increase. For reasons I am about to show you, the stock futures are very powerful, and with a surprisingly small amount of money relative to the actual size of the stock market, a seller can overwhelm all buyers very quickly, especially in a skittish market where some extraneous event might be occurring that you don't know about that's now linked electronically to our market at the speed of light.

Just as there were no sellers lined up in time to meet my 50,000-share Stride Rite buy order until I took the stock up to $10, there weren't enough buyers lined up that fateful afternoon to match the selling that stemmed from stock index futures selling. If the orders had been smaller—there were multiple sellers at that level, not just one "guy"—and the sellers were willing to take their time rather than burst in with market orders that had to be executed immediately, the disaster would not have occurred. But the sellers at that moment had much more stock "to go" than the buyers had to buy, all the way down in price, so that stocks could get cut in half in a few minutes. That's, again, why I say, *Please, people, use limit orders!* Can you imagine if you went in to sell 200 shares of Procter & Gamble when it was at $60, using a market order, and you ended up getting a report that you sold it at $40? Yet that's exactly what happened to thousands of people on that Flash Crash day. That's why a limit order is prudent and a market order is reckless, and always will be until the government figures out how to stop trading in the whole market when these events occur. And it sure isn't doing that now.

The Distortion of Common Stocks by Index Futures

The whole thing seemed ridiculous to me. I was sitting in my Corporate Finance class at Harvard Law School in 1982, reading the *Wall Street Journal* as always, just trying not to disturb the zombies around me with my page-turning. I liked to hide in the back during class; that way it was much less likely that I would be called on, because I either hadn't read the material or didn't understand it. Plus, who could concentrate on the stock tables and take notes on a meaningless class at the same time? Better to have your priorities straight in order to get your money's worth for the $25,000 a year you'll owe in student loans at the completion of the exercise.

Anyway, there was an article in the paper that day about some stock index that was going to start on the Kansas City Board of Trade, an exchange I thought just traded those agricultural products you didn't care about unless you were in the food business—you know, grains, winter wheat, whatever. Yet there it was. Some wise guy was putting together not a basket of grains or pork bellies but a basket of stocks, specifically a basket of the stocks in the Value Line Index, which represented the same stocks as the Value Line Investment Survey, at one time the bible of all stock research for the home gamer and the professional alike. Those were the quaint days, when individual stocks were studied and owned, not the quant, or quantitative, world of today, when whole groups of stocks are charted and traded via machines that are supposed to tell you the optimum purchase price and let you exercise the trade within the blink of an eye.

This newfangled package of stocks was meant to trade as a futures contract, meaning you would bet on the future direction of all the stocks combined in the index, except, unlike a grain index, at the future's conclusion you wouldn't have to deliver the stocks themselves. The prices would settle in cash, and you would be able to take your gains from where you first made your bet. And it *was* a bet, not an investment, because you weren't actually buying the individual stocks in the package. Just like a future, you could sell short the basket too, if you thought it was going to go down.

So if you thought the collective value of all the stocks in the Value Line Index was going higher, you bought a future that gave you the right to the gains at a specific point in time. If you thought they were going lower, you could short the index and then buy it back and pocket the difference, if indeed it went lower, as you hoped and wagered. Of course, if you bought, thinking the index was going higher, and it went down, you had a loss of the portion of the money equal to the decline, just as you would with an individual stock.

After I read about this new index futures market, I asked one of my securities professors, "How can this be legal?" Stocks, I said, don't trade in lockstep. There's nothing in a group of stocks that is comparable to winter wheat, which is uniform and not meant to have any differentiating statistics or characteristics. Stocks trade on their own mettle. They have so little in common there could be no point in homogenizing them in an index. The repercussions could be huge. Stocks might cease being representative of the enterprises behind them and take on the characteristics of an entire market, even as that market had little to do with the profits or sales of the individual companies. I said it was absurd and I couldn't believe the Securities and Exchange Commission would allow such an irresponsible grouping of stocks to trade together.

I questioned whether this Kansas City Board of Trade idea would pass muster given how it might play havoc with how we value individual stocks. Surely the SEC would see the detriment and distortion a Value Line Index could cause down the road if it caught on. My professor, clearly oblivious to who the heck I was, as he would never have seen my face behind the front page of the *Journal* I read each day in class, informed me that there was nothing insane at all about this basket of stocks. This new index would be a risk tool for portfolio managers, just as the farmers needed risk tools for their crops. If someone owned a portfolio of stocks and wanted protection from events and feared the downside, he could sell a Value Line future against his portfolio, hedging that risk, just like a farmer or a grain buyer who might fear a drought or a frost. In fact, a stock future could work even better for a portfolio manager than it might for a winter wheat farmer. If the portfolio manager truly feared some sort of catastrophic event, he wouldn't have to blow out each individual stock, incurring all sorts of imperfections, commissions and time pressures. Instead, with one order, he could put a hedge on that would insure against the downside during a very specific period and then have that hedge taken off when the event concluded or was safely behind him.

If someone wanted to accumulate exposure to stocks, meaning he just wanted to bet that all stocks were going to go higher, my professor explained, he didn't have to do all of the work on the individual stocks or tediously buy each one; he could just buy a future and get all the exposure to the stock market he needed in one immediate, seamless transaction. No hedging in this example, just an outright instant accumulation. The professor reminded me that many portfolio managers simply viewed stocks as part of a broader allocation of stocks, bonds, real estate and gold, and that this future simply gave the portfolio manager the chunk of stocks he needed to get the proper exposure to this one portion of the investment supermarket. It was a beautiful expedient, in his opinion.

I bridled. How could it not matter what the companies in the index do? What about all of the work people put in to discover or purchase an individual stock? What about the research process, the process of finding the best stocks, not just stocks themselves as one unit? Why would anyone want to own the bad stocks with the good? Who would want to check his stock-picking abilities at the door? The haughty professor lectured that perhaps I didn't understand what was about to happen to stocks, that portfolio managers were moving away from the futility of individual stock picking and into a "can't beat them, join them" strategy. They were just trying to equal a benchmark or try to slightly exceed it, rather than trump it. They simply wanted to put, say, 40 percent of their entire portfolio in stocks and, say, 50 percent in bonds, because they preferred bonds over stocks in general, and not specific stocks. That way they couldn't fall too far behind the stock market with their allocation and would be "truer" to that allocation than they would be otherwise. The stock future *was* the future, and he saw it coming.

But wouldn't the index influence the action of the stocks in the index itself? I persisted. The professor, who knew exactly what the SEC was doing (he was a corporate finance professor tied in to Washington), told me that the SEC was unconcerned because the government believed—and to a degree still does, by the way—that stocks themselves were much bigger than the index and the index was a tail that could never wag the whole dog. The idea that an index could ever control a stock's particular movement was antithetical to the purpose of the hedge or the accumulation. No single portfolio manager or even a group of portfolio managers would ever be big enough to influence an index to the point that it would impact the stocks in the index themselves.

The certainty of that statement annoyed me, but I didn't make the rules. I realized that at one point in life I would have to live by them, as I already had my heart set not on practicing law but being a real-life stock-picking portfolio manager.

Thus, with one obscure index on one obscure exchange, the index future was born.

Two months later the much, much larger Chicago Mercantile Exchange began trading futures on the Standard & Poor's 500, a sainted group of stocks, considered the best representation of the stock market since 1923, when it was first created. (Older, more desultory investors still seize on the Dow Jones Industrial Average as the benchmark, and I start each *Mad Money* show with how it fared that day, but portfolio managers compare their performance to the much more broad index that is the S&P 500, the benchmark that one must beat regularly to be considered a successful, or outperforming, manager.)

Pension funds, huge portfolio managers and mutual funds almost immediately took to the S&P 500 index futures as a cheap, low-commission way to get exposure to the market and yet not have to deliver stocks, as they would wheat or pork bellies, because the settlement, what happens when the future comes due, like the Value Line future, was in cash. One of these big institutions could put, say, $20 million to work in some S&P futures contracts that allowed it to get a gain six months out. If the S&P 500 rallied 10 percent in that period, the account stood to make $2 million at the time of settlement.

Not only were futures convenient, but the managers didn't have to put up the entire amount that they sought to buy or sell. In fact, they could borrow money and put up only a fraction of that $20 million in real money. Of course, the logic extends to large numbers: $20 million could get you $200 million in exposure in seconds. The rules for futures are very different from those for stocks. With futures you can use leverage and put up much less cash than with stocks and get much more bang for the buck—still another advantage for those who want to use these commodity-like instruments. Simple as that.

Too simple.

Almost overnight these contracts became a sensation as the big funds fell in love with them. They got to be so popular, at the same time that funds were growing ever larger as money flowed into the stock market, that within a few years the impossible had come true: they began to have a more powerful impact on stocks than anyone had dreamed, including the people who run the companies in the indices. I always felt they were too powerful, and I railed against them in the 1980s in the few press outlets available to me. I suggested that they would one day cause a stock market crash because the futures could easily overwhelm the actual stock market, as the little amount of capital needed to control a stock future could turn millions of futures dollars into billions of stock dollars.

Sure enough, by 1987 they were so sought after that a bunch of financial consultants decided that they could use the futures to hedge out all risk to stocks, no matter the size of the fund. They created a product called "portfolio insurance," and they peddled it to big institutions that owned a lot of stock. The consultants said that for a fee they could protect any fund from the downside because, as the market went down, the consultants could dynamically hedge out any losses using these S&P 500 futures.

The product initially worked terrifically well as the market drove ever higher through most of that year. Then, when the stock market started to crumble in August 1987, culminating in the crash of '87, portfolio insurance began to fail. It directly contributed to that record-smashing one-day 508-point decline as the consultants threw the equivalent of acetylene on that raging fire of selling by trying to short the futures ahead of the plummeting stocks. The Chicago-based futures had overwhelmed the New York–based stocks. The stock that came in for sale because of the S&P 500 futures sellers arrived too fast and in too large amounts, so that buyers couldn't be found. As a result, the stock market lost almost a quarter of its value in a day. The dynamic hedges, the insurance, failed to protect the portfolios properly, so the clients lost huge amounts and the consultants went under.

After that fateful day, it dawned on many market participants that the S&P 500 futures were now bigger than the stocks, and big sellers of futures can knock down stocks with impunity, even if they didn't deserve to be knocked down.

A Treasury Department investigation of the crash identified the interaction between the futures and the stocks themselves as a proximate cause of the precipitous decline simply because the leveraged selling of futures could impact stocks faster than buyers could be found to offset them. Just think back to that Stride Rite example to understand how speed can overwhelm volume; multiply that speed by ten, the approximate ratio of futures selling to stock buying on that fateful session. Rules were put in place after the crash to slow the futures-to-stock linkage on big price declines, but the whole portfolio-basket approach was already ingrained, and, being just a few years old, it was never even called into question as a possibly manipulative and pernicious entity.

Stocks eventually climbed back up after the crash, when it became clear that the whole episode was caused by a problem with the mechanics of stocks versus futures, and not with the underlying economy and its impact on stocks. The futures had simply caused the stocks to go haywire, but the economy never skipped a beat. Never again, though, did any of us have any illusions about how futures had changed the stock market. From then on, for many of the biggest funds, stocks might as well have been soybeans or corn or wheat. For many managers, it never again mattered what companies did. They decided to just trade the whole index as an asset class, regardless of the individual stocks that made it up.

From the birth of that now obscure Value Line Index until the present day, we know that perhaps the biggest influence on a stock beyond its sector and its own business is whether it's in the S&P 500 index. And at times of real crisis, the S&P futures are a far more powerful influence than the fundamentals of any individual company. If the futures roar higher or plummet, your stocks will rise or fall if they are in the index. They react as if there is one giant buyer or seller of everything, from the tiny Stride Rites to the Exxons and Apples. The futures are so powerful in their influence over individual stocks that a stock you own might get a real beatdown as part of an S&P futures sell-off, even on the day of a good earnings report or positive analyst chatter. It's just the way it is. I got used to it, even though I hate it, just as I hated the Flash Crash, which was very similar to the Great Crash of '87 in its speed and almost in its size.

You too have to get used to this reality, and you have to recognize that, as in the individual stock example I gave you, nothing a company does can stop the tide. The movement in the stock price simply has de-coupled from the underlying stock because of this financial innovation. The genie jumped out of the bottle three decades ago, and we have not been able to stuff it back in, no matter what the companies in the index try to do about it, including aggressive buybacks and even bountiful dividends.

Sector ETFs Overpower Individual Stocks

Traditionally, a stock's sector plays a tremendous role in performance. Sector gravity has been considered responsible for close to 50 percent of a stock's move. These days, however, during very big stretches in time, and certainly on any given session, it can be as much as 75 to 80 percent of the move in short-term bursts. So sectors are worth exploring and fleshing out when we talk about what causes your stocks to move intraday on no news. Sector groupings, like broader index funds, are still one more obstacle that mocks the notion that homework and knowledge of individual stocks can play an important role in the money-making process. You must learn to respect the power of sector exchange-traded funds (ETFs), because you must understand how they can impede, mystify and distort what should be a totally rational process. Yet, like stock futures, the ETF-led sector propulsion gets in the way of the fundamentals on a very regular basis.

Why does the sector pull matter so much? Because stocks are hostage to them, even if individual companies don't deserve to be. That's because of the immense popularity that sector indices and the ETFs that mimic them have gained among huge institutional money managers. To put it bluntly, they would rather play with big, liquid ETFs than mess with trying to get in and out of individual stocks. These baskets, designed by firms to, once again, give big-portfolio managers large and quick exposure to a group of stocks instead of one stock, fulfill the same role the S&P 500 futures play for the entire market. You like the banks? There's an ETF that mimics the banks. You hate the gold miners? There's an ETF that you can use to short them at the drop of a hat. You can even own or go long on an ETF that represents gold and short the miners that pull the precious metal out of the ground to come up with a perfect hedge, as the miners have performed poorly even when gold is stellar, and when gold cools the miners totally tank.

The federal government has blessed these individual ETFs, and in many cases has even allowed particular ETFs to be traded in a leveraged fashion. In other words, you can get two or three times the buying or shorting power over a sector with a leveraged ETF. Once again, the government, oblivious to the impact of the tail that can wag the dog, has approved these machine-gun instruments in a field formerly dominated by the individual rifle-toting stocks. In a matter of minutes all members of these ETFs can be blown to bits or elevated to outrageously high prices with small amounts of selling or purchasing power. In the past few years this financial engineering has become gospel, and those who don't take into account the individual stock fallout from these ETFs are doomed to make a lot less money than those who do. They defy prudent investing.

How do they impact stocks on a day-to-day basis? Let's take the oil service group, one of the sectors most keenly dominated—I would go so far as to say it has been wrecked—by ETF trading. Over the past thirty years, we have seen tremendous differentiation and a superiority-inferiority dichotomy emerge among the players in this industry. For example, Schlumberger, the largest oil service company, has been considered vastly better run than the other well-known players, particularly Baker Hughes and Halliburton. Schlumberger is more global in reach and is less levered to the fickle nature of North American drilling. It is more lucrative than most of the other players and is the open envy of the industry. While there are brief periods when Halliburton and Baker Hughes execute well, the consistency of the company the Street calls SLOB for its SLB symbol is a marvel to behold. Even when its longtime CEO, and a personal favorite of mine, Andrew Gould, stepped down in 2011, the performance of the company didn't skip a beat.

Same with the actual drilling concerns. Most of the time Transocean, Ensco and Weatherford trade in lockstep on a day-to-day basis, but their true colors do surface at certain times, typically during earnings reports, when the fundamentals exert themselves in a most definite and material fashion. Ensco is the best of these three because of its technologically superior and younger rigs. Transocean is second best, but it became deeply scarred by the Macondo fiasco, as it was contracted to do the actual Gulf drilling for BP. Weatherford is third best, dogged by unfathomable accounting issues and a confused and out-of-touch management. Yet for most of the year, none of these seemingly germane characteristics matters at all because of sector domination over individual securities. They might as well be the Transocean-Ensco-Weatherford Company.

It is obvious and logical that when the West Texas and Brent oil futures, the principal pricing structures of crude oil, rally, all of these stocks should and will trade higher, as they all stand to make more money when oil is moving higher than when it is going down. What's mystifying for most of you, though, is that even though the gradations of management and performance are severe, they are not differentiated when the underlying oil futures do their tugging.

While there has always been a similar relationship to the group's oil gearing, the nature of the sector pull has gotten increasingly pronounced in the past few years—pronounced, frankly, to the point of absurdity, with the stocks of the worst companies often increasing in price almost exactly as much as the stocks of the best. That's because of the underlying pull of the extremely popular OIH, the Market Vectors Oil Services Sector index, which includes all of these stocks. Consider the OIH to be the sun that all of these stocks revolve around, both good and bad, with equal speed. Yes, the gravitational pull is that overwhelming. When big institutions want quick exposure to the stock market, they buy the S&P 500 index. When they want instant exposure to the oil service industry, they don't bother with the individual stocks; they just come flying in to purchase the OIH, or call options on the ETF for more leverage. That has become the de facto way for big institutions, particularly the hedge funds, who don't want to bother to differentiate—or are too lazy to differentiate—the individual members of the index, to play the group. It's just much easier to buy the basket of stocks than to select which ones you want in the endless chit of oil-related stock movements. Heaven forbid you decided to play—and it *is* playing, believe me—the wrong stock, say, a Weatherford, and you miss the oil sector move you are trying to catch when Weatherford is hit with another restatement because of its obviously inferior internal controls. So big institutions are willing to buy the known best with the hideously bad, and somehow they consider this homogenized purchase actual investing.

This is where you can find the fun and the profit, because, remember, I am at all times trying to meld the market's overall mechanical imperfections with opportunities for you to profit from individual stocks. We hear endlessly from academicians and proselytizers of index funds, and myriad proponents of ETFs in particular, that you can't possibly stock-pick and make money. They think it is too hard for us, that we are kidding ourselves and should just throw in the towel on managing our own portfolio. But these "sages" are either out of touch because they are not boots-on-the-ground students of this market, or they are self-serving because they are conflicted. They will profit only if they convince you of your own inability to take care of your money and your utter inadequacy when it comes to spotting the differences between companies. Remember, ETF proponents incorrectly regard stocks as pretty much the same, regardless of the fundamentals, something that has been proven to be false, empirically, time and time again, and anecdotally by the thousands of viewers of *Mad Money* who regularly tell me otherwise. Nevertheless, once the S&P futures commoditized stocks, it was an easy leap for individual sector ETFs, like the OIH, to commandeer and commoditize whole sectors on a short-term basis.

Of course, this index-to-ETF nexus isn't an accurate picture of the long-term fortunes of the individual companies. I know dozens of people who work in the oil patch and interview them frequently on *Mad Money*, and the in-the-know execs scoff at this commodity-based view of the stocks. They know it is patently incorrect. We know that these service companies are competitive, and they win business from each other based on the merits. I deal with the index participants themselves, and they, not the short-term performance of the ETF, influence my opinions. Their input plus my homework gives me the ability to make informed judgments about which companies will be most successful longer term at profiting in different environments.

Now, here's the real irony: the academics and the ETF purveyors have been able to brainwash enough participants, and the hedge and mutual funds have fallen so in love with the ETFs, that they have created their own reality-distortion fields, to appropriate a terrific term normally associated with the late Steve Jobs. In other words, the academic-ETF–money management complex has successfully been able to homogenize short term what can't be homogenized long term: the differences between the best-of-breed, the so-so, and the worst-of-breed participants. But you *can* differentiate. So when the linkage with oil sends the ETFs and their components in the attendant direction, you can sell the bad ones, often at considerably higher prices than you deserve, when oil goes higher, and you can buy the best of breed at lower prices than you should normally be able to obtain when the oil futures plummet. In fact, you can do this trade until the cows come home, or get a better basis for your investment if you choose to go longer term. The same scenario goes for any of the powerful ETFs and their leveraged brethren, especially in housing, banking, retail, real estate investment trusts, semiconductors and restaurants. Yep, the movements of these stocks are now largely dictated by the ETFs that lord over them. But the short-term frustrations of stocks divorced from their fundamentals can lead to healthy long-term opportunistic marriages between you and the best ones in each industry.

This against-the-grain stock picking has never been as bountiful as it is now, and the lack of short-term correlation between the companies' performances and their stocks is something you must not only accept but profit from if you are going to get the best basis, and ultimately the best performance, from an individual stock in the ETF basket.

So let's be granular and more practical. Let's say you are stuck in Baker Hughes because you mistakenly thought it was inexpensive enough relative to its peers, or perhaps because you incorrectly disagreed with some downgrade, or you didn't see an earnings shortfall coming. Believe me, Baker Hughes will give you a shortfall quite regularly. You shouldn't just blow it out. You should use ETF-engendered artificial, ephemeral strength to sell it. The opposite side holds true too. If you think oil can rally after a downturn, then I can almost guarantee that Schlumberger is mispriced in your favor because the ETF has been mercifully whipping it down along with the second- and third-tier players.

What an amazing opportunity to take advantage of fabulous imperfections created daily by the overpowering ETFs!

This same strategy works in virtually every major sector these days.

You can buy the best-of-breed bank stocks at ridiculous discounts to the worst of breed because of the XLF, the banking ETF. That's how I was able to snare the top-notch U.S. Bancorp at about the same valuation as the worst of the worst players at the moment for my ActionAlertsPlus.com portfolio. It is also how I was able to get an excellent exit price for the underperforming SunTrust for the charitable trust.

Retailers, technology stocks, you name it, are all subject to the ETF sector shackles. If you think, for example, that the holiday shopping season will be a good one, you just need to wait until the ETFs have their pernicious lockstep impacts on the better-managed companies like Costco and Home Depot and the inferior Kohl's and J. C. Penney.

Use this incredible instant distortion of the reality of the stocks of individual companies to your advantage when managing your own money and get the best entry and exit points imaginable for individual stocks. Oh, and yes, thank you, academicians, theorists and ETF creators. You have sufficiently impacted stocks in such ludicrously effective ways that we can all profit from exaggerated sector distortions to give us bountiful outperformance that we could never obtain otherwise.

You will need to keep in mind this new trick of the trade when I show you how to compare the fundamentals of individual stocks in individual industries so you know what can be sold and what needs to be bought at the artificially inflated and deflated prices that now predominate because ETFs have become, along with S&P Index funds, the chief determinant of stock price action.

The Power of Bonds and the Fed on Stocks

We've covered the impact of supply and demand on stock movement, the power of the S&P to play a role in a stock's performance and the incredible sway of sectors to move as a stock in lockstep with its cohort, whether that's right or not, which we now know it isn't.

Before we get to what you think probably causes the lion's share of the movement, the now rendered quaint impact of the company's fundamentals on the stock, at least on a short-term basis, let's consider a few more extraneous factors influencing stocks. These have grown far more important in the past few years than at any other time in history and will only gain in importance going forward.

Let's start with the bond market. I know the mere mention of the word "bond" drives you up a wall. Bonds are incredibly boring even to me, and I am a financial junkie. I don't even want to hazard a guess about what you might be thinking about them. But when it comes to the stock market, they can have a really powerful, often unseen impact. Bonds act like bullies toward stocks; they are always behind the scenes, throwing their considerable weight around—the bond market is much larger than the stock market in actual dollar size—distorting prices all over the place in a pretty significant way. These days, if you don't know about the impact of this colossal "fixed income" asset class, as it is called, on your common stocks, then you are now investing imprudently and taking far more risk than you realize. Let's fix that now. You are not reading "Get Rich Recklessly."

Remember to always think about your common stocks within the broader context of all the investments there are to choose from. Imagine that stocks are just another form of goods, some sort of merchandise that gets sold in an aisle in the vast financial supermarket. The bond market section of that supermarket dwarfs the stock market section, where aisle after aisle is filled with treasury bonds, corporate bonds, mortgage bonds, convertible bonds, municipal bonds and all sorts of other esoteric instruments. The commonality in the bond section? They offer a "fixed income" return—paying you a regular interest stream—backed up by the issuing entity, whether that is an individual corporation, a municipality or the federal government. The last is, by far, the largest issuer, which stands to reason given the size of our nation's deficit.

The competition for your dollars is steep. Stocks, we know, offer lots of upside, but they offer lots of downside too, making them riskier investments than bonds, but ones that carry bigger rewards. Bonds can also be volatile. They can gyrate up and down in price, especially of late, as the Federal Reserve tries to extricate itself from buying bonds on a regular basis to depress interest rates to increase business, especially home building, and decrease unemployment. But bonds do have a guaranteed element that stocks don't have that is tremendously appealing to any investor. When you buy a stock it may not offer much income, if any at all, after inflation, and you can't return it to the supermarket for the full price once you've checked out at the register. But bonds give you a fixed income stream and a money-back guarantee on top of it.

If that confuses you, think about it like this: if you have a mortgage, you are in the same situation as a bond issuer. You borrow money, you pay interest on that money and then you pay back the initial principal when you are finished with your loan. However, if you don't pay back the loan, the bank can and will—as we know from crises past—take possession of your home. When you consider that guarantee, wouldn't you rather be on the other side of your mortgage? That's how bondholders feel. They love the surety and protection bonds give them because they get a regular income stream over the life of the bond, and then they get their money back, guaranteed.

Corporate bond holders, for example, can take over the issuing enterprise if they are stiffed, because bonds are often backed up by the assets of that enterprise. When corporations file for bankruptcy, corporate bond holders seize the assets and sell them to make themselves whole. Investors who purchase mortgage bonds—bonds backed up by the principal and income stream of a basket of mortgages—can seize and sell the houses that make up the basket if the bond defaults. The lion's share of the foreclosed homes caused by the Great Recession are houses that were seized and sold by mortgage bond holders. Even municipal bond owners can at least try to seize the assets of the municipality if it has any worth seizing, as the municipal bond holders in Detroit are discovering.

The only bondholders who can't seize the enterprise are owners of U.S. government debt. The federal government, rather than allow itself to be taken over by its lenders, gives bondholders what's known as a "full faith and credit guarantee" that they will get their money back. Yes, countries can default. It's been known to happen. The mere whisper of a potential default by the U.S. government on its trillions of dollars in debt can cause huge turmoil in all assets, even in stocks, as we found during the U.S. debt crisis in 2011, when stocks declined almost 20 percent, in part because of fears that the U.S. government debt would be downgraded by the agencies that rate debt: Standard & Poor's and Moody's. Ultimately the S&P did take U.S. government bonds down a notch because of the runaway deficit, but actions taken to try to control government spending salved the agencies, and worries about the integrity of the debt and its issuer died down. We saw this pressure again in the government shutdown and debt ceiling fracas in 2013, when the government again almost defaulted. That's why, although it sounds glib, we regard treasuries as "risk-free" assets. The federal government's promise to pay is considered inviolate among debt holders, and even in the darkest of moments of the financial crisis, that promise has not been in question by most treasury debt holders.

AT VARIOUS TIMES bonds can give you a higher yield than stocks, and historically they have. However, because of the hideous rise in unemployment that the Great Recession engendered, the Federal Reserve, as just mentioned, has tried to keep bond rates lower than normal by buying huge amounts of bonds in order to jump-start the economy. Makes sense. The Fed's trying to influence the whole financial system with its interest-depressing bond buying, so you can get a low-interest mortgage or refinance your mortgage at a lower rate, or a corporation can borrow for less or can issue bonds with lower coupons—the income stream—to expand or pay down the higher-cost debt. The Fed has wanted everyone to take advantage of its largesse. And, to some degree, that has worked, as housing prices have rebounded and jobs are more plentiful than they've been since the Great Recession started. It has also led to a rise in stock prices from a multitude of directions. Companies, for example, have been able to borrow money cheaply to go into the stock market and buy back their own shares, driving up stock prices. They've borrowed low-cost money to pay out higher dividends. They've paid less in interest charges, which leaves bigger profits for shareholders. It has been a very virtuous circle that has had an immensely positive impact on stocks, which is why we have often had to hang on every word from the Fed, fearful that it might be bringing this halcyon period to a close.

Let's go back to the financial asset supermarket so I can show you the impact treasury bonds have on the entire bond and stock food chain. All fixed-income assets are priced "off of" treasuries, meaning that any other bond issuer is going to have to pay more in interest than the Treasury because its bonds can't be backed up by the full faith and credit of the government after the wrangling of 2013, although the better the balance sheet, the lower the interest rate the company might have to pay to bond-holders. You may scoff at our government, but bondholders know that explicit guarantee is still the safest guarantee, worth more than any other promise to pay by any other entity. Because of the risk-free nature of federal government debt, the yield on government bonds is going to be lower than any other issuer's debt at any period in time: six months, one year, ten years, thirty years, it doesn't matter. So if the Fed keeps rates down on treasuries, every issuer gets to issue debt at lower rates than it might otherwise.

It would be terrific if all of this bond market interaction could be kept within the fixed-income section of the supermarket, but it's too big and too powerful to be contained. We recognize that stocks have flourished ever since the Great Recession because the Fed has kept all interest rates artificially lower by buying hundreds of billions of dollars of U.S. government debt. That has made bonds less competitive with stocks, particularly stocks that offer yields that are higher and therefore more attractive than you can get from fixed-income alternatives. But as the economy gets better, the Federal Reserve can let the interest rates return to more natural, higher levels. That's where the competition sets in. As interest rates on debt go higher, supermarket shoppers seeking income are more attracted to the bond section and less interested in the stock aisle. Why take the risk that a company might cut its dividend when times get hard again? Why not just go buy a less risky bond with a guaranteed income stream? Not only that, but stocks have had a big run. The collective yields on stocks have come down as stocks have rallied because the yield is simply an arithmetic equation: the size of the dividend divided by the price of the common stock. A $20 stock that yields 5 percent because the company pays out a $1 dividend yields only 2.5 percent if the stock goes to $40.

Sure, that's terrific if you owned the stock while it ran up and you got the dividend. But imagine you are a new shopper. You walk into the financial supermarket, peer down the stock aisle and see a piece of merchandise that has doubled recently and pays only a 2.5 percent yield. Then you walk down to the fixed-income section and see bonds backed up by the full faith and credit of the United States that now yield more than that stock. You're likely to be tempted to buy the bond rather than the stock because the bond is less risky. Other shoppers want to cash out of that stock entirely and put the proceeds in bonds.

The pressure from bonds as competition for stocks has heated up so much that now bonds are far more important than at any time in recent history. The higher the interest rates on bonds, the more pressure you will see on stocks, particularly stocks that had become "fixed-income equivalents," meaning that they were being used by savers instead of bonds to get a good income. For example, many investors seeking decent yields rotated into the stocks of consistent utilities, like Con Edison, American Electric Power, or Southern Company. For a time they were able to get double the interest rate they could on treasuries. The switch made economic sense even though utilities, as safe as they are, certainly aren't risk-free. However, with bonds now yielding similar to utility stocks after the increase in interest rates, these stocks simply aren't as attractive, especially given their price increases, so they, too, get sold down when interest rates tick higher. This switch from once higher-yielding stocks into now higher-yielding bonds takes place every day, and it puts pressure on the market regularly. The competitive threat from bonds is now fearsome and is a huge influence on stocks pretty much on a daily basis. As long as you recognize this, you can use it to your advantage because (1) you now know what might be behind the selling of a lot of the higher-yielding companies you own, and (2) you too might want to take profits on those stocks because they simply aren't as attractive as before, given their run-up and the better, less risky returns that bonds offer. Of course, as always, I urge you to consider each stock on a case-by-case basis. The themes and methods I will trace out in this book can transcend this impact and allow you to profit from it, but not if you don't understand why it is happening and how it has led to a dramatic and rapid change in how stocks are being viewed and bought and sold.

None of this bond and stock interplay that the Fed has stirred up is new; it's just more salient because rates are coming off all-time lows. That whole supermarket section has come alive with competitive activity, and it's pretty darned distracting and compelling to all investors.

However, as part of being a more prudent investor than in the old days, we now also have to consider the traditional influence of the Fed on the economy in general because we've enjoyed such a prolonged period during which the Fed has been friendly to stocks. That's not going to last as long as the economy keeps percolating and the Fed starts worrying about the need to curb inflation. Remember, the Fed has two mandates. We've been living with the first mandate: getting the economy moving when it is slow, so more jobs and wealth are created. Now, though, the second mandate, the cooling of an economy that's gotten too hot because of low rates, is coming into play, and careful investors must adjust accordingly. I always say, "Never fight the Fed." If the Fed is keeping rates low to get the economy moving, there are tons of opportunity in stocks. But when the Fed is exercising its second mandate, raising rates to fight inflation, the options narrow accordingly. We've got to recognize that new and negative reality if we are going to be prudent about our investment choices.

We've already discussed the supermarket impact of the interest rate rise. We understand the instant attraction of bonds that comes from the sudden jump in rates after years of declines. We recognize the competitive threat they now offer, especially when we consider the reduced yield stocks give you because of the terrific rally we've had from the stock market's bottom in 2009.

But as the second mandate of the Fed, the need to slow down the economy to prevent inflation, comes into play, we have to be concerned about the impact higher rates have on the companies themselves, not just the yields on their stock prices relative to the yields on fixed-income alternatives. The Fed's moves have always had a real impact on the pace of economic growth, which then affects the sales and profits of the companies we invest in. The Fed has been trying to keep interest rates low and steady to quicken that pace, but when it moves to cool the economy and prevent inflation from raging, that's a different story. When the Fed raises rates, money managers who control trillions of dollars in assets tend to flee from stocks en masse, particularly those of economically sensitive enterprises, because they know that earnings estimates might have to come down as a consequence of the Fed's actions. Most companies simply can't make as much money in a rising interest rate environment. Many have to borrow money to do business on a regular basis, and when the cost of that money goes up, it has a real impact. A retailer may have to pay more to finance its inventory. Customers may have to pay more for credit to buy goods. There is a repercussion to higher rates that causes analysts who follow stocks to automatically want to cut earnings estimates. There is also a mitigating factor, however. If the economy is recovering, some companies may be making more money and the increase in rates won't matter as much. Why cut earnings estimates because of interest costs if sales are so much better because of a stronger economy? Can't a housing company that is hurt by higher interest rates sell more homes because the economy is better and more people have jobs and will look to buy houses? It's a real tug-of-war across many industries as analysts set out to determine which companies might be doing so much better from a stronger economy that higher rates don't matter.

Still, though, the overall implication of higher rates is not a positive for the stock market; it's a negative, regardless of the improvement in earnings companies might experience from a stronger economy. So with every rate increase, you get selling in stocks and, more important, stock futures. Given the lockstep nature of the S&P futures and stocks that I described earlier, you get that uniform impact on all stocks when institutions move quickly through the futures to reduce their exposure to equities. As usual, I don't want to just describe these actions. You will get plenty of that from others. I want to tell you how you can prudently profit from this bond market pressure on all stocks. For example, when stock index futures plummet because of worries about the impact of higher rates on corporate profits taking down all stocks, that could be a terrific opportunity to buy the stocks of companies that aren't all that sensitive to rate increases. You want to be looking to buy the stocks of companies that aren't hurt all that much by the slowing of economic activity the Fed is bringing about, meaning that they are not as cyclical or beholden to the economic cycle that the Federal Reserve is trying to slow down. That's the time to pick up growth stocks like Celgene, Regeneron, Amazon and Netflix, whose earnings streams are not dependent upon the economy continuing to prosper. It might be the time to trim the stocks of companies that need rates to stay low and economic activity to increase in order to beat the estimates Wall Street is expecting, stocks like Alcoa or Freeport-McMoRan

Copper. Most important, these interest rate–induced sell-offs are precisely the time to fall back on the stocks that benefit from the major themes I am going to tell you about in a coming chapter, themes that are much bigger and can transcend the entire interest rate discussion. Still, though, the careful investor must feel comfortable with the role of the Fed because the Fed may not be as friendly as it was. And just as we don't fight the Fed when it is trying to help us make money and get the economy moving, we don't want to be oblivious to the Fed when it is no longer as friendly to our attempts to build great wealth by buying the best stocks in this new environment.

Let me give you a simple example of how this interplay can impact your stocks, so you can profit from the turmoil it produces. Let's use the stock of Bristol-Myers Squibb, because everybody knows the company as a high-quality maker of pharmaceuticals that isn't beholden to the economic cycle at all. Its growth is considered secular, not cyclical, meaning that its prospects are influenced by long-term trends like the aging of the population or the increasing ability of the middle class worldwide to obtain life-saving drugs. Neither of these secular trends is impacted by the Fed and its attempt to control the pace of U.S. economic activity. Yet the stock of Bristol-Myers will get tossed down like all others in the S&P 500 when institutions sell S&P futures because they fear the impact of higher rates on economic growth. Yep, even though Bristol-Myers can thrive in this environment, its stock gets pummeled initially, like all others, as if its earnings were going to be depressed by the Fed's actions. So you might want to bid for that stock below the last sale price when this interplay is triggered so you can buy it more cheaply than you would otherwise expect, if you believe interest rates will stabilize or peak in the near future. It's the natural way to profit from the unseen forces I have traced out.

Now, though, as with everything else in the past few years, things are not as easy as they used to be. We have to recognize that the supermarket impact I talked about earlier also comes into play with a higher-yielding stock like Bristol-Myers or any of the older pharmaceutical companies. The careful investor simply *must* take into account this complex competitive yield issue, because many investors in the past half-dozen years have sought the relative safety *and* higher yield of the stock of Bristol-Myers as an alternative to low-yielding bonds, not just because of its terrific earnings prospects. That means if interest rates keep rising, you have to recognize there could be extra selling pressure on a stock like Bristol-Myers not just because all stocks are coming down but because investors in higher-yielding stocks might be dumping them to take profits and go back into less risky bonds. These "fixed-income alternatives" don't hold up all that well when rates go up because those investors who used them as alternatives to bonds aren't all that interested in the characteristics and fundamentals of the individual companies that paid the dividends. In fact, some investors might not even care about how the company that is Bristol-Myers is doing. They may not know, for example, that Bristol-Myers could be on the verge of a breakthrough cancer drug. They may not know that Bristol might be about to report an upside surprise. They may not even care if it is about to increase its dividend, something that bonds can't do. They just want to own something that gives them good income with safety, and they think that bonds, not stocks, give them a better opportunity now that interest rates have increased. To put it another way, while Bristol-Myers is a really good, safe company with a growing earnings stream that is secular in nature and not cyclical and beholden to economic growth that the Fed can squelch, its dividend is backed up only by its income stream, not the full faith and credit of the federal government. These fleeing investors care more about the yield and its guarantee than they do about the possible increase in Bristol's price that they might leave on the table. They seek capital preservation, not capital appreciation, and so they sell Bristol and buy treasuries or other bonds with more attractive, safer yields. It's just one more reason why, in this new, more treacherous environment, you have to disabuse yourself of the notion that what a company does and how it does should determine whether its stock goes up or down in value. I know, it's all rather counterintuitive, but it is vital for the prudent investor to understand if she has any hope of using stocks to create bountiful wealth. The tug-of-war between a company's dividends and earnings prospects versus the band market's pull of interest income and safety may be a paramount concern for years to come.

HOW, YOU MIGHT ASK, can you figure out when a run on the stock aisle into the fixed-income section of the supermarket might occur? How do you stay on top of this process so you can profit from it? I could say, "Just keep an eye on the stock market at all times." But I have a better way. I monitor the action by following the TLT, the iShares 20+ Year Treasury Bond ETF. This security goes down when interest rates go up, and vice versa. When the TLT goes down, you can expect the stock index futures to go down soon after, as stock index futures react to every minute move of this security. To put it in the new vernacular of the stock market, if you want to know what will happen to BMY over the extremely short term, just watch what happens with the TLT, because it's more in charge of Bristol-Myers stock right now than anything that happens inside that giant pharmaceutical concern.

I believe understanding bonds' gravitational pull on your stocks is integral to being an effective investor. Get used to it. You will see it as a theme for many years to come, as interest rates likely saw historic lows during the past few years and we won't be visiting them again, perhaps in our lifetime. The TLT will tell the tale. To give you some perspective on its newfound importance, I now have it at the top of my screen, right next to the S&P 500, above the Dow Jones Average.

The Over-influence of the Macro

If we are going to be thorough in our discussion of the new unseen and extraneous influences on stocks, we have to address the impact of the rest of the world's economies on our stocks, particularly China and Europe. As someone who is acutely aware of how the United States has diminished as a global economic power, I recognized that ROW, the rest of the world, could become an important influence on our stocks. But even I have been taken aback by the incredible linkage between the problems in Europe and the performance of the stocks of our own companies, particularly the banks but also the industrials. Some of the linkage was empirically true.

Many of our industrial companies barreled into the Continent after the European economies banded together under one currency, the euro, in part to diversify away from what they thought would be the permanently sluggish U.S. economy. They seemed to get the latter right, but the former has been nothing short of disastrous. The extent of the pull, though, brought even entirely domestic industrial companies to their heels, again because of the power of ETFs centered on American manufacturers.

The banking linkage mystified many but wasn't totally unfounded. Our money-center banks had pronounced exposure to borrowers in Europe as well as to the European banks and even the sovereign nation bonds, as our financial institutions put their own capital to work there to pick up better yields than they could with U.S. treasuries. The pain of the linkage is lighter now because of European stabilization and an American retreat from European banking, but the inevitable flare-ups will still impact the stocks of this cohort.

Because of the ETF gravitational pull that I outlined earlier, we saw the bizarre homogenized stock performance from the untouched and uninvolved domestic and regional banks right along with the deeply impacted money-center players like Citigroup, JPMorgan, Goldman Sachs and Bank of America. I expect this falsely commoditized linkage to be with us for many years, so instead of shrugging your shoulders about the tie-in, accept it, account for it and profit from it by buying the stocks of domestic banks, notably the terrific Wells Fargo, on signs of European trouble that knocks down the XLF, the key financial sector ETF. Wells Fargo has nothing to do with Europe. Doesn't matter, short-term: it's in an ETF dominated by international banks and, therefore, it trades just like them. Longer term, however, it does matter a great deal and you can profit from the ETF-imposed discount.

The final countervailing force to the direct fundamentals of companies? The impact of China on the global economy. The vast migration of 400 million Chinese from a rural to an urban environment is a trend that will be with us for many decades, if not longer. And as you will see later, it is one of the great themes for us to profit from via individual U.S.-based stocks and foreign ETFs that track the stocks in markets where otherwise we could not trade. That migration stands behind much of this largely positive influence on markets, even as, on any slowdown in China, there can be an obverse effect. There are three strands of impact. The first is on the materials and industrial sectors. Any acceleration or deceleration of growth will directly impact the oils, like Chevron and Conoco; the coppers, like Freeport-McMoRan; the coals and iron ores, such as Peabody and Cliffs Natural; and even the rails, particularly CSX and Norfolk Southern because of their dependence on shipping coal to ports that send coal to China.

The larger industrials are directly impacted because China affords them the greatest growth. I now regard General Electric, Caterpillar, Cummins, United Technologies and Joy Global as more China plays than American concerns.

Second are the consumption chits in the Chinese game, including Yum!, Nike, Coach, Starbucks, General Motors and, increasingly, McDonald's, Ford, VF Corporation, and PVH. These companies need Chinese growth to accelerate to report better-than-expected quarters. We also know that technology can be impacted by China; think of all the back and forth about Apple's sales growth and the billion-person smartphone market.

Finally, there are the negative impacts from China. The Chinese can put a damper on aluminum when they choose to dump it—oops, I mean export it—and they have decimated the steel industry with their willy-nilly sales, as they try to put many people to work in the industry. Be careful of dumping targets like Nucor, US Steel, AK Steel and Reliance Steel & Aluminum. Timken, because it actually has a sizable steel business in China, remains the sole exception.

The Fundamentals and How They Really Impact Stocks

We've now covered all of the unseen but incredibly important forces that can move stocks: basic supply and demand, index fund futures, ETF-led sector pull, the bond market, and economies of foreign countries. All of these newfound influences have coalesced just in the past few years to make investing more treacherous than it has ever been. But if you master these inputs, they can help make you more money than you have ever dreamed, particularly because so many people are baffled or confused by them or are entirely oblivious to them. Now, and only now, can we focus on what the vast majority of investors still believe is the be-all and end-all of stocks: the fundamentals, or how the business is really doing. The fundamentals do seem almost antiquated when stacked up against all of the extraneous impacts and inputs I have just detailed. Nevertheless, they can still determine some of the fate of shorter-term stock movements, and they remain the most powerful forces when it comes to creating longer-term values, even as they seem to have been rendered irrelevant on a day-to-day basis, except during periods when they report earnings or release material information that can actually impact the worth of the enterprise.

WHEN I STARTED investing I cared only about the fundamentals. And for the longest time that really was about all you should have focused on, beyond some traditional sector analysis. Think about it: we didn't have index funds or sector ETFs; our companies hadn't grown as global as they are now; the government hasn't been this interventionist since FDR and the New Deal; and interest rates didn't affect stocks as instantaneously as they do now. But what a company does and where it fits into the vast economic scheme of things still matters tremendously, even after all of these other influences are gamed. And that means we need to be as shrewd as ever about how to examine fundamental inputs.

The first and most important fundamental influence? The company's growth rate. While a company's past—how much revenue and earnings it has booked historically—can be very important, it's not the most significant factor when we are determining how much to pay for an individual stock at any given moment. What matters is how fast a company's sales and earnings are growing, especially in the context of what is expected of the company. The expectations are set by the analyst community, which is why we have to pay so much attention to the consensus of those expectations. Fortunately, you can find these analysts' aggregate expectations for sales and earnings at a whole host of websites, including CNBC.com, Yahoo! Finance and TheStreet. While I have stated my case that the invisible forces outlined above now tend to dominate the day-to-day pricing of stocks, the ability of an individual company to generate earnings and sales in excess of those expectations remains the biggest factor in trying to figure out if the stock is going to go up or down over both the near and longer term.

At all times we are trying to figure out how fast a company can grow, compared to both all other stocks and the stocks in its sector. We need to know how to assess how a company performs in times of not just domestic but worldwide economic acceleration and deceleration.

Earlier I detailed the notion of cyclical versus secular growth, the growth that is hostage to economic forces and the growth that is dependent upon longer-term themes that don't revolve around the increase or contraction of the gross domestic product. We are always on the lookout for companies that can better both their sector's growth and the economy's growth as a whole. If we can profit from secular-growth companies, that's terrific, but we may have to pay a too-high-to-sleep-at-night price for it. In other words, the price-to-earnings multiple, what we will pay for that stream of future earnings, is higher or more expensive than what we might be willing to pay for a stock with a far more variable, economically dependent earnings stream. That's nothing new. But since the Great Recession, there has been a big change in the price tag of stocks with this kind of consistent growth, because worldwide economic activity has slowed and is now so sporadic that it can't be counted on to produce excessive earnings gains from cyclical stocks. The world has become a much more difficult place for companies to grow earnings consistently. So many economies are now experiencing sluggish, intermittent growth that we treasure any company that can maintain any constant level of growth. Who's got that? Many companies, but the ones I regard as classic growth stocks include Kimberly-Clark, Procter & Gamble, Johnson & Johnson, General Mills, Coca-Cola, PepsiCo, Hershey, Kellogg and Clorox. These stocks are trading at historically high levels because they can deliver consistent, albeit slow, earnings growth in a tepid economy.

On the other hand, if your company's fortunes are linked to the slings and arrows of global or domestic growth, then you have a classic cyclical on your hands, and you need to anticipate any reacceleration or deceleration or both, something that's become exceedingly difficult to monitor. That's why if you own Caterpillar, Ford, General Motors, General Electric or Cummins, the engine company, to name some examples, you have to be on top of world events, particularly in China, pretty much every day.

Some stocks, like 3M, Honeywell and Emerson, are what we call growth cyclicals, hybrids that have the characteristics of both kinds of stocks. They hold up at times of mild acceleration and stability.

Of course, some companies are levered to individual cycles. Deere, Monsanto and Potash are all about the farm cycle, chiefly whether or not the farmers are flush. Boeing and Precision Castparts and to some degree United Technologies hug the aerospace building cycles and track worldwide aircraft demand.

Others have their own secular-growth themes, such as the renaissance of oil and gas, the desire to look and feel well, and the aging population. Those themes are myriad and pervasive, and I spend the next chapters describing the best ones to profit from over the long term and which stocks best fit the long-term winning theses.

But all stocks, whether they be cyclicals, growths or hybrids, get graded the same way by analysts: Are the underlying fundamentals of the enterprise better or worse than expected, as expressed by the consensus of the analysts' estimates? Consider this whole investment process as an Olympic diving match. The analysts are the judges, and they grade on many different inputs. The ones we care about are sales expectations, or the top line, and the earnings expectations, or the bottom line. Many people are fixated just on the top line, the revenues, as a way to judge whether a company is growing faster than the global economy or its own cohort.

I agree that the top line is a very important input. A company's stock will be walloped if it "misses" on the revenues. However, I think the bottom line is more important, and here's why: the earnings—what a company has left after it takes out the costs of all of those goods sold, expenses, taxes and depreciation—certainly need to please the analysts, but on top of that, bigger earnings can lead to bigger dividends, which are such a huge part of a stock's upside over time and can be traced to about 40 percent of a stock's long-term performance, dating back to the 1920s. Profits matter even in this new, crazy world, because profits can put dividend checks in your hand and help propel stocks higher over time due to those ever-increasing dividends. Thank heavens something remains true to the old days!

As part of our judgment process, we have to compare the numbers in the earnings and sales reports to the expectations set by Wall Street analysts. Perhaps more important, though, we care about the company's outlook for the future, and how that jibes with the expectations. This outlook is typically given cursorily in the company's quarterly earnings release, but is much more in-depth on the conference call, at the end of management's discussion of the earnings and right before the question-and-answer session. That outlook is the single most important consideration when you are trying to decide whether to buy or sell a stock at the time it reports. That's why I always laugh—with scorn, mind you—when I see people trading stocks after hours without listening to the conference call. If the largest determinant of the future price move comes usually about ten minutes into the call, what the heck are these bozos trading off of? It's shameless and stupid, and I sure hope I don't catch you doing it.

What are we listening for in that outlook? We want to hear forecasts, particularly for the rate of change of sales and earnings growth. But the portion of the forecasting I care the most about is the direction given on future gross margins, because that can be a true indicator of what the business can earn in the future. The gross margin guidance is what will be used to try to figure out next quarter's earnings estimates. That will set the benchmark that has to be beaten next time. When you hear "Such and such company beat the estimates," I say, "That's nice." It can help a stock and won't hurt it, for certain. But when you hear "Such and such a company beat estimates and raised guidance," then I know the stock is going higher. That's because a raising of the guidance by the company in that one little moment on the conference call before the Q&A means that analysts have to change their views to be more positive about the stock, which means more upgrades, more price target increases and more promotion. Those are the fundaments of immediate increases in stock prices. That's the only earnings "surprise" you should really care about, not the "better than expectations" stuff that you are normally told should matter.

"Beat estimates" can matter. "Beat and raise," shorthand for "beat the estimates and raised guidance for future quarters," is what matters most. That's the crucial phrase you need to hear to bet with a stock instead of against it. That's when you know you have a winner, even if the unseen forces are playing havoc with the stock that day. If you keep a file of the "beat and raise" stocks and you buy them on down days, you are going to be investing carefully and making a boatload of money despite the noise that seems to weigh on stocks on a daily basis.

Summary

So what have we learned here? First, we have to accept that stock gyrations often don't have much to do with the day-to-day success or failure of the individual companies they are meant to track.

What can be more important in this new world?

1. The impact of supply and demand is critical. Is there stock for sale near the current price? Do buyers have to pay up to get their stock in? Do they have to sell the stock down to get their order done? The supply-demand imbalance can control minute-to-minute pricing more than pretty much anything else that's going on, as our Stride Rite example showed.

2. Stocks now trade like commodities because index futures have overwhelmed the stocks that are in them, in part because the buyers and sellers of futures are putting an immense amount of money to work in rapid fashion. Stocks can't withstand that power and are helpless in the face of it, as we saw in the Great Crash of 1987 and the Flash Crash a few years ago.

3. ETFs have created a homogenized environment among different stocks in the same sector that is often more powerful than the fundamentals of the individual companies. You can't judge a company by its own cover; you have to judge it by the sector's cover.

4. Bonds and the Fed matter far more than ever because we have now seen the bottom in interest rates and they are climbing, impacting

stocks in lockstep, particularly the stocks of higher-yielding equities that had been used as bond market equivalents.

5. International influences must be grafted onto your thinking about stocks pretty much on a daily basis because of the electronic linkage of all markets and because the U.S. market is no longer as dominant as it once was.

6. Only after you understand all of these other forces does it pay to consider how the fundamentals will impact the prices of stocks, and the fundamental input we most care about is whether a company is raising its guidance for future sales and earnings. If we find companies that do raise guidance, we need to cherish them, given how little growth there is in the world and how hard it is to find consistent earnings power in this day and age.

If you want to invest carefully, and not just think you are investing carefully, consider this checklist before you buy or sell another stock.

CHAPTER 2

Getting a View of the World from the Source

We put an amazing amount of trust in the data the government releases, way too much if you ask me. We put our faith in all sorts of figures about industrial production, purchasing managers' reports and durable goods—not just here but abroad as well. We get these spoon-fed statistics and we accept them without skepticism. We take them as gospel.

That's fine if we are in a current-events class and there is no money on the line. It's not so fine, though, if we are investing hard-earned dollars trying to get rich in the stock market. I find the officially disseminated reports more often wrong than right and not worth relying on when I am analyzing the future direction of stocks. They let you predict nothing, or at least nothing that gives you a worthwhile investable thesis.

Nevertheless, I am a great believer in having an economic worldview, a vision of where I think the world is going, before I invest in stocks. You need this larger context because this market is too given to "shocks" that shouldn't be all that shocking yet cause immediate selling panics. Without a broader sense of what's happening in the world and at home, you may be too gun-shy to take advantage of the bargains those panics create. Or you yourself might panic, and panic is never a strategy for building wealth; it's a reaction that destroys it.

I learned a long time ago that successful investing entails having a view of more than just a company's prospects. If you seek to own an international company, you need to know how the world is growing—both the developed and the emerging markets. If you want to buy the stock of a domestic company, you have to have a sense of our own economy. Then you need to know how the sector the company fits in is performing. If you do not have a vision of what's happening in the world, the nation and the sector when you invest in the stock market, then the odds of successful individual stock picking drop dramatically. I know you have a bias toward picking winning stocks or you wouldn't be reading this book or watching my show. So I need you to understand how I form my top-down view— how I arrive at what I think is even worth looking at or avoiding—before I make my stock choices. I believe if I show you how I do it, giving you the tools and metrics I use, you will become a better personal portfolio manager or a better client, as I have no desire to take you away from a trusted adviser who does a good job for you, but I do want you to be informed enough to make judgments about that person's work.

So who and what do I trust to help me build this overarching view? I trust statements from the companies themselves when they report their earnings and conduct their conference calls. I trust the visions and the opportunities and the worries that managements utter about the world, their sector and their own businesses. I treasure and put faith in the color that the best executives give you in their reports to the public. That's because the companies, like you and I, have a lot on the line, certainly more than any government agency or industry group that releases data or offers a view of what's about to occur. You can bet that when a solid executive is investing his company's money, he has done a thorough, boots-on-the-ground study of the world and the portion of it that is the company's bailiwick. That analysis, even if it is gleaned from insights given routinely on calls typically devoted to the company's particular prospects, is worth a fortune to those trying to determine what to do with their investments. It's worth a heck of a lot more than any Commerce Department or purchasing manager statistic or certainly any blather from the chairman of the president's Council of Economic Advisers, as I know all too well. As part of my job, I have had to interview these chairmen many times, and I know they speak only the party line. In contrast, there's nothing political and nothing polemical about a CEO's take on the world; it's all business. In fact, I am surprised we take seriously most of the data or statements turned out by the government, given that politics has suffused every aspect and every disseminator of information that so many people count on. Your money is way too important to take action on anything the government might put out, with the sole exception of the Labor Department payroll numbers, and even there we've heard criticism from respected businesspeople like former General Electric CEO Jack Welch that they, too, can be fudged to suit political needs. Though, unlike almost all other times Jack has spoken, I can't agree with his tweets on this one.

The only problem with getting the worldview from the companies is that it's an awful lot of work to assemble. You have to pull it all together yourself. It doesn't come out in some release delivered to the media. There's no spoon-feeding. It's not given in a campaign speech by the president, an obfuscating bit of testimony from the Fed chief, a garbled transmission from the Chinese or a multi-tongue missive from the European Central Bank, despite the media's endless attempts to proclaim that such information should truly influence proper stock picking.

I can't say I have done all of the work for you about which corporate calls matter most, although I do pepper my shows and my writing with this kind of information. But I can give you my "must-reads," the conference calls that I devour for their information about the world. That way you can develop a view yourself and not have to waste time reading hundreds of calls looking vainly for the information you need to draw the proper conclusions. Remember, really good, actionable information isn't static; it's fluid and needs to be updated regularly by using the information gleaned from these calls.

Why do I need what's known as "top-down" analysis, or "macro" insight, when I am trying to discern the "micro," the data that help me pick the best individual stocks to invest in? Because business doesn't occur in a vacuum. I need to know what's likely to happen in the world to be able to drill down on the best stocks that fit the conundrum of good stock investing for long-term wealth. Consider the stock market landscape as a gigantic malfunctioning jigsaw puzzle, for which you are given hundreds of pieces, most of which don't even fit. You have to discard the incorrect pieces before you can even try to assemble the correct ones. Having a broader, macroeconomic thesis helps you eliminate pieces that would otherwise send you into culs-de-sac and dead ends as opposed to fruitful roads to big profits.

You need to understand the tenor of the economic times if you are going to discern the growth rates both in this country and in the world that often control company performance and which kinds of stocks do best at given moments in various business cycles. If I know the pace of economies around the world, I can make more informed decisions about the types of companies I should be looking out for at that moment.

This kind of thinking is so important to professionals that we divide the universe of stocks into those companies whose fortunes depend on economic growth and those whose future earnings are independent of these macro forces. Companies that need economic growth to perform well are called "cyclicals," like the industrials I mentioned in the previous chapter. Companies that can produce positive earnings regardless of the vicissitudes of the economy are called "growth" stocks, such as the equities of the aforementioned consumer packaged goods companies. These two terms are general rubrics, some would say overly general ones, so we will have to break them down further so you know which ones are truly right for the moment.

A prudent stock picker's job has two stages: First we need to form our outlook on growth, and I will tell you in a moment how I go about that process. Then we need to pick stocks to fit that outlook. In general, if we think economic growth is strong or improving, we bias our stock picking toward cyclicals, the companies that are geared to the economy and generate high returns accordingly. If we expect slowing, tepid or intermittent economic activity, we should be seeking growth stocks, the stocks of companies that should still perform up to expectations or even slightly better than that without an economic tailwind.

There are different types of cyclicals and growth stocks for different environments. Consider for a moment that the entire stock market is like a giant restaurant. You've got a whole menu of stocks to choose from to suit investors' tastes for different growth rates. Portfolio managers "rotate" in and out of groups depending upon those growth rates. I know it sounds like a giant game of volleyball, where rotations dictate which stocks are in the first row and which ones are in the back. But all that's really happening is that investors are rotating into stocks that fit a changing economic climate, while they flee from stocks that are no longer, at least historically, able to go higher in that new climate.

Let's say my homework tells me that worldwide growth is going full speed ahead, perhaps as high as a 3 to 4 percent clip or even more. In that environment I might be tempted to buy the cyclicals, stocks like Caterpillar and Cummins, the heavy equipment makers, or Timken and Alcoa, the steel and aluminum companies, that thrive when we have boom times. Those leading industrial companies get lots of new orders when the economy is going full tilt, as big customers need more capital equipment to expand their businesses. These manufacturers could surprise "to the upside," meaning they could generate earnings far in excess of what Wall Street might expect, because they have the wind at their back as their customers feel confident to buy more and more of their wares. That kind of bountiful return attracts money managers who are constantly seeking the stocks of companies that can "blow away" the estimates. Managers shun consistent growth stocks in that environment because it's the magnitude of the surprise that is important to them at that stage in the cycle. The big-time money managers with trillions of dollars at their disposal are always willing to trade the sleep-at-night returns of consistent growers for the upside surprise value of the more robust earnings streams of the cyclicals when times are getting better or are already humming.

If the world's economies aren't growing at full bore but seem to be accelerating at a healthy pace, managers like to choose a different cohort from the stock menu. In that mixed to good environment, say 2 going to 3 percent growth, the classic "deep" cyclicals are prone to missing earnings estimates. So managers rotate into what are known as "growth-cyclicals." These are well-run companies like 3M, Honeywell and Eaton that perform better than many other companies when things are improving, but they also have some divisions that offer moderate earnings power, that hold them back from the spectacular growth that the pure cyclicals have when economies are roaring. We call the Honeywells and the 3Ms "chicken" cyclicals, because most managers are too chicken to step up to the true heavy industry cyclicals when growth is improving but still a tad uncertain. These timid managers fear the shortfalls that the pure industrials often deliver. They hate the big one-day declines that are so common when a cyclical that has had a big run "misses" the estimate, or fails to deliver on what the analysts were expecting from the company. Instead these managers hide in these more mellow companies, with smoother earnings patterns and therefore less risk, albeit also less reward.

Now, let's say the economy is growing only slightly, at 2 percent, and shows little sign of accelerating or decelerating. Managers then feast on a type of growth stock called a "discretionary." The kinds of companies in this cohort depend on the discretionary spending of the consumer to generate good earnings, and the consumer, at that 2 percent pace, still spends fairly consistently. Managers in that slow but not contracting economic climate are on the hunt for investments like Starbucks, Panera Bread or Chipotle and perhaps Disney or Macy's, all of which should do well when the consumer is willing to spend to eat out or travel or shop at places that aren't too costly but are certainly more expensive than other destinations. Those companies can meet or top Wall Street estimates in a slower growth environment, while the classic cyclicals and the chicken cyclicals might fail to do so.

When we know that growth is decelerating or meager, the big money managers who control the prices of stocks with their buying will ignore the cyclicals, the chicken cyclicals and the discretionaries and go for the "staples" portion of the menu, companies that should make good money even in a subpar economy, such as drug and food companies like Pfizer and Merck or PepsiCo and General Mills. Or they may choose Walmart or the close-out retailer TJX, or even the dollar stores like Dollar General and Dollar Tree. People still take medicine, eat and drink, and shop, although admittedly in a more downscale fashion, in even the hardest of times.

Some managers with a greater risk tolerance, when faced with decelerating economic activity, like to buy companies that have "secular" growth, meaning companies that have long-term tailwinds behind them. That's because these companies can take advantage of certain big-picture themes that transcend the business cycle's gravitational pull, including some very powerful concepts like combating obesity, finding new sources of energy or corralling the web to dominate social media. Or they may be biotech companies with novel formulations that fight disease. Obviously, none of these kinds of companies needs much of an economic push to deliver their numbers and beat the estimates that are so important to the investing process.

If there is no growth at all or the economy has hit a wall and many sectors fall out of favor, managers will augment or replace their staple stocks with stocks that are *purely* defensive, stocks like utilities, oil and gas master limited partnerships and higher-yielding real estate investment trusts that offer just enough growth to, hopefully, raise dividends each year, while performing in line with what analysts are expecting. We can't expect these stocks to appreciate all that much given their minimal earnings trajectory, but they should do better than most other stocks because there is so little risk to their business faltering, therefore causing them to miss estimates. These are capital preservation, not capital appreciation, equities, with safety of principal being a primary concern.

Normally, at that point in a slack portion of a business cycle, I would also be recommending that you put a portion of your wealth in fixed-income instruments, particularly as you get older and can't handle the risk of a loss of principal. That was my strategy in all the other books I have written. But in the years since the Great Recession, economic growth has been so halting that the Federal Reserve has attempted to keep interest rates especially low to jump-start the economy. While the success of those efforts is debatable, what isn't open for debate is the impact the Fed has had on savers. You simply can't get much of a return from treasury bonds—the bonds the government issues to pay for its ridiculous spending habits—because the Fed has been in the market pretty much every day buying treasuries to influence pricing in a negative way for savers. The rate has remained at such low levels—although not the incredible depths of late 2012 and early 2013—that you earn almost nothing on these bonds after we take into account the historic rate of inflation. Any investment that doesn't leave you with a real return after inflation is inherently a threat to wealth building, and I don't take those threats lightly. So we seek to find a higher return than treasuries can offer without taking on too much risk of principal loss.

You might ask, "Well, why not buy other bonds that give you higher interest rates than treasuries?" That's a totally legitimate question. There are many different kinds and qualities of bonds out there. However, as detailed earlier, all bonds are priced off of, or are governed by, the interest rate on treasuries. The Fed's efforts to try to maintain low rates through its bond buying has brought down the interest rates for all bonds in what's known as the "credit" market. That pressure on bonds has rendered many of them poor investments, either because the rates of the higher-quality bonds are too low to beat inflation or the risks from lower-quality bonds, the ones more likely to default if times turn tough, are too extreme compared to their meager rewards. For example, Apple, the company with the best balance sheet in the world, was able to borrow money at a rate of 2.4 percent for a ten-year bond. That's ludicrously low, and I would never recommend that piece of paper. Other companies with more checkered balance sheets might offer bonds that yield 4 to 5 percent but may not be worth the risk given the limited upside of fixed-income securities.

The Fed's strategy has caused investors to go to nontraditional places to get higher interest rates, including stocks themselves, or at least the ones that pay higher yields. As mentioned earlier, we call these kinds of stocks "bond market equivalents" because they have a mix of some of the characteristics of the safety and yield that bonds give you with a possible upside that bonds can never offer. The bond market equivalent stocks have solid balance sheets—meaning they don't have a lot of debt and have no problem paying their bills—and they consistently return capital to shareholders with higher dividends than the average equity. Often these bond market equivalent stocks can be much better investments than bonds because they can raise their dividend distributions, while the coupon, or the interest rate payment you get from owning bonds, is fixed at the time of its issuance. However, as we saw in the spring and summer of 2013, when interest rates did rise, especially suddenly, despite the Fed's best efforts to keep them low, these bond market equivalent stocks can stumble, and stumble badly, even if their yields are in excess of the interest rates that most bonds are offering. The decline in the price of a bond market equivalent stock can often wipe out whatever the return might be from the dividend. Plus, unlike bonds, which give you your money back when they come due, stocks don't offer similar guarantees. There's a caveat emptor quality that many who adopt this strategy seem to forget about. Here's my rule of thumb: If you are trying to preserve capital over time, as opposed to have your capital appreciate, and you want to "hide out" in stocks, make sure that your stock selection gives you a yield that is at least 50 percent higher at a minimum than the average rate of the traditional alternative to stocks, the ten-year treasury. That way the yield should give you some protection against a sudden rise in rates by arresting the fall of the stock, as other investors will seek out that even higher yield that you get as the stock declines in value.

NOW THAT YOU know the menu, how do you figure out what to pick and what to avoid? What do we want to accomplish? First, we have to accept that in these uncertain times, when we need to be so prudent in how we pick stocks, we must always be nimble. While we certainly want a diversified portfolio, we must be careful not to skew too much toward heavy industrials when times are weak or the staples and the pure safety stocks when boom times are upon us. The economy fluctuates, and we must adjust with it or else we will find ourselves endlessly dodging shortfalls and downgrades or earning a subpar return with stocks that offer only sedate returns when the economy starts humming and we could be winning big with a more industrial set of stocks.

We must never forget that the fundament of good stock picking revolves around finding companies that can do better and grow faster than we think, given the state of the economy. When I say "we think" I am actually talking, as I described previously, about what Wall Street thinks will happen, as expressed by what's known as the "consensus estimates" of what the analyst collective believes a company might rack up in sales and earnings. We may not trust analysts to correctly predict what individual companies will earn; in fact, I have almost given up on that possibility because their analysis is so hit-or-miss. But I do use their aggregate work to benchmark what a company is expected to make in the environment I believe we face, in order to be able to predict disappointment and therefore sell-offs versus approval and stock advances. You tend to get analyst downgrades if companies fail to beat estimates, and upgrades if they succeed, and those actions drive shorter- *and* longer-term performance of the stocks you own.

Analysts score companies by how much and how fast they are growing their revenues and how much they are earning on those sales. They estimate how a company will do in both the coming quarter *and* the coming year given their expectations of worldwide and U.S. growth, depending upon the percentage of international or domestic growth a company may generate. They arrive at these estimates individually, and then these projections are pooled to form the consensus that a company must beat, a process I detailed earlier.

Here's a real-life example. Analysts project both quarterly and yearly sales and earnings. So let's say the consensus holds that a growth cyclical like IBM will sell $25 billion in products and services this quarter and earn $5 a share on those sales, and for the year it can sell $100 billion in product and services and earn $20 a share on those revenues. Now let's say IBM reports and it beats both the quarterly sales, known as the top line, and earnings estimates, the bottom line, and then raises sales and earnings projections for a given year.

If IBM hurdles all of these top and bottom benchmarks and does so in fine fashion, meaning a few pennies more for earnings for the quarter and a few percentage points for revenues—no mean feat—then the analysts will collectively raise IBM's estimates for both the next quarter and the year to come. That's what I call the holy grail of investing, and barring a broad market sell-off, you are more than likely going to be rewarded with a stock that goes higher both short- and long-term. That's what defines a good investment. That's what I am on the hunt for all of the time both for my charitable trust, as our bulletins from ActionAlertsPlus.com tell you, and for the recommendations I make on *Mad Money* and *Squawk on the Street.*

At the same time, it is worth pointing out that anything short of that, a miss on either top or bottom line, will more than likely produce a sell-off. A miss on both will almost always produce a decline, sometimes of great magnitude, as was the case with IBM in 2013. That said, if the world's growth is about to accelerate (the macro) or if the areas that are disappointing for IBM are about to get better (the micro) or if management makes positive changes to its business (perhaps a restructuring), the stock can then rebound from that sell-off if the company can make a convincing case to analysts, who are always willing to trust IBM, that its prospects are about to improve.

The future of the macro environment—what might happen to the world's growth—can play a huge role in a company's prospective sales and earnings. But once you have determined how the world's economies or the economy of the United States may grow if you are analyzing a multinational or a domestic company's performance, there's much more to do before you get to the prospects of an individual company. You are only partly along the way to reaching a successful conclusion about the stock. Next, you have to determine the growth rate of the sector that a company may labor in, factoring in that menu of cyclical, growth-cyclical, discretionary, staple and no-growth stocks. You need to know if the sector, at that moment, is growing faster and performing better than the world as a whole is faring. The stocks of companies in any sector that can exceed the world's growth are equities worth concentrating on. Remember that the company's sector determines a great deal of its stock performance. It's only after you have estimated the world's growth, and the sector's growth within the world's prospects, that it is worth figuring out how a given company is performing in that sector and what management is doing to exceed the average performance of the companies in that sector.

If you can approximate all three—the macro or world economic growth, the sector growth, and the micro achievements, including sales and earnings by the companies themselves—then you are going to be successful at growing your wealth carefully through superb stock picking.

I KNOW, I KNOW, it all sounds impossible. Believe me, when I break it down, when I show you how to best determine all three inputs, it will be less daunting. I do it every day, day in and day out, to the point where it is second nature to me. It is so ingrained in me that I can use the three-step process—macro analysis, sector analysis and company analysis—to offer buy and sell recommendations rapidly in the *Mad Money* lightning round and I want you to be as familiar with this checklist as I am. You now realize, though, why trying to get rich quickly can be a dangerous game, given the homework that's entailed to get all three scenarios right. But gaining solid wealth carefully, over time, is an attainable goal.

The Only Conference Calls You Will Ever Need

I glean the best data about the worldwide and domestic economies not from official sources but from piecing together the mosaic of conference calls that companies present when they have material news to report. If you can't catch them in real time, they are available, in audio or transcript, on the websites of the companies you are researching. I urge you to get comfortable doing this kind of homework if you want to invest prudently. In fact, you are being reckless if you don't. Which conference calls of which companies can help you the most when you want to hone your worldview to pick stocks?

The first and most important call I turn to of the hundreds of companies I follow is the quarterly earnings call from Caterpillar. Here's a company that sells heavy equipment that is used everywhere. They make engines for trucks. They make construction equipment used to build roads and commercial real estate. They make mining equipment used for the excavation and transport of all sorts of commodities. They sell worldwide, and their key markets are the markets I care the most about when I think about world growth: America, Brazil, Western and Central Europe, and, most important, China. This Peoria, Illinois–based company has the pulse of the entire developed and emerging market planet.

There's a real irony about Caterpillar's conference calls. The company itself has made a series of missteps, including some big shortfalls in 2013, owing to some poor execution by management. Nonetheless, it is a superb evaluator of what's happening in each of the countries it sells in and it does give you the most thorough description of each economy it serves. Despite these glaring recent company miscues, I still trust Caterpillar's long-term vision because when you are selling heavy equipment, you must try to make accurate forecasts and important judgments about inventories, judgments that directly impact earnings per share. You can't send too much product to one dealer or one network of dealers or one country because you will then have to discount the product if it can't be sold. When a company discounts its product, that means it fails to make enough on each sale; then its margins fall, and the sales and earnings numbers are therefore bound to disappoint.

Normally, when a company isn't able to make enough on each sale, you can question its execution or even its product. But not with Caterpillar. It works as a perfect "tell" of all the world's economies because it makes the world's best product, as acknowledged globally. If Caterpillar doesn't get the sale, there very well may not be a sale to be had. So I accept that there's a slowing, not just excuse-making, if business is off in a given country. I use the lengthy CAT press release and ensuing conference call to figure out where we are in the cyclical-growth continuum more than I use just about any other input. That's why this one's a must to listen to.

There are many other important reasons why the Caterpillar conference call is my gospel, my go-to call on which many of my decisions are based. First, Caterpillar's tractors are our single most important gauge of the Chinese economy. Many people do not trust the statistics the Chinese Communists release. They fear that the numbers are too rosy and too fudged. But Caterpillar is scrupulously honest in its depiction of the Chinese economy, and given that Caterpillar sells gigantic machines for hundreds of millions of dollars, I consider its Chinese revenue numbers the most reliable gauge we have of that opaque but key driver of the world's economy. We so often hear, for example, that the Chinese are trying to stimulate their economy, typically through gigantic infrastructure projects and road, bridge, tunnel and commercial real estate. You don't know if this is bluster or the truth unless CAT tells you that its orders are going higher. In another time, China typically would like to export its way out of a slowdown, but because it relies on a sluggish, depressed Europe for 25 percent of its exports, that part of the Chinese economy has slowed, although Europe's awakening of late has certainly helped a bit. Still, when CAT says things haven't picked up, you know the stimulus isn't working. It's not all been rosy for Caterpillar in China. In a notable misstep, Caterpillar bought a Chinese mining-equipment company in 2012 and later had to write down the purchase because of fraud at the unit. Also, Caterpillar called the bottom in the Chinese economy two quarters too early in 2013.

Nevertheless, I listen to get a contemporaneous, boots-on-the-ground view of the Chinese economy, and CAT, even with its flaws, is the most authoritative voice out there.

The only other indicator I find remotely as important as CAT's window into China is the electricity data that Joy Global, CAT's biggest mining equipment competitor, releases on its call. Joy has a very large coal-mining equipment business in China, and that business coincides with electricity use. Given that China's principal method of energy generation is coal—China opens a new coal-fired plant every ten days—Joy has access to the electricity consumption number and can meet demand with more equipment. It may not be as predictive as we might like, as the number is coincident with usage, not forward-looking. But given how little we really know about the Chinese economy, I will take it.

The second reason to pay attention to Caterpillar's conference call? If we want to know what direction the world is moving in, we have to pay attention to commodities. Some look at the prices of the commodities, and only the prices of the commodities, and then make a judgment about world economic growth. That's a decent method, and I too have used it. But I want to know what the big miners are thinking, because they make budgets with real money on the line and are forced to deal constantly with growth as they see it for their raw wares and adjust constantly to the changing global fortunes. For that, again, I need to know CAT's order book as it is the best indicator of what the most important companies that mine copper, iron and aluminum think about the longer-term view of things. That's far more valuable to me than a snapshot of the price of a commodity at a given time. If CAT is seeing outsized, above-average orders from companies that mine copper, that's a good clue that the world's economy may be expanding. Caterpillar has the best read on the key commodity, steel, not just because its machines are used by coal companies that supply coking coal to steel companies but also because it uses so much steel itself to make its equipment. I prefer CAT's view on steel demand far more than any of the steel companies themselves; they can see only their own order book, while CAT sees the entire panoply of the industry. I regard steel demand as a terrific tell on where the worldwide economy is headed.

Third, you can't build huge new communities or giant office buildings or massive pipelines or mining projects without using Caterpillar equipment. These kinds of projects are preludes to hiring. Large commercial and big infrastructure projects require a demonstrable amount of hiring, numbers so huge that they can move the needle. That's another piece of the economic puzzle that CAT can help you solve.

Fourth, lots of people like to use the transport indices as good predictors of the future of world commerce. I like to do one better: I look at truck orders, the number of trucks that the big shippers order to move product from one part of a country to another. Caterpillar's extensive truck engine business gives you fabulous insight into both the Chinese and the American economies, with a fantastic breakdown of what's selling. By the way, these truck engines play a major role in the shale oil drilling in Canada. I have been able to monitor the growth of the largest oil fields in the world by reading the CAT tea leaves on large-scale trucks.

Fifth, because Caterpillar's business is global, it has to have views on the world's major currencies; it can't be caught selling in a currency that might rapidly depreciate against the dollar. When many were doubting the viability of the euro, I trusted CAT when it didn't question the currency's staying power. Good call by the manufacturers in Peoria.

Sixth, I like Caterpillar because it has a colossal finance arm. CAT's machines are so expensive that almost every company must buy them on credit. Very few customers have that kind of cash on hand. CAT therefore also has a call on what interest rates will look like going forward, and, given how long I have followed the company's call, I can tell you that I find their information more accurate than most when it comes to worldwide interest-rate forecasting. Caterpillar, if you paid attention, gave you an early warning into the depth of the downturn before the Great Recession hit because the company made it clear that it was getting harder to obtain the letters of credit from banks it needed for customers to make big purchases. I was also able to track down Caterpillar's corporate bonds when they announced this troubling bit of news, and they were selling off very hard. That's a major red flag that only those who follow CAT would know about. Yep, CAT's own finances give you a terrific insight into the credit markets.

Caterpillar's *the* primer, the source for your global outlook. If I had only one document to form my view of the domestic economy, the Chinese economy and the global economy, I wouldn't use a government number or an economic forecast from any research house. I would just listen to the Caterpillar conference call and read the presentation and make up my mind from those two well-thought-out inputs.

SOME COMPANIES, due to the breadth of their product lines, can give you a fantastic read on how the world is doing, particularly when it is presented to you by a man of the world like Klaus Kleinfeld, the CEO of Alcoa. I first met Klaus years ago, when he first came on *Mad Money*, and I recognized immediately that he is every bit a global economist as well as a master of the aluminum trade.

That's why his conference calls are quarterly epiphanies. First, Klaus breaks down aluminum use by product line. Its most important use is in aerospace, because aluminum is durable and light. Plus, Alcoa has a gigantic business in fasteners, and each large commercial jet can have as many as 2 million fasteners in it. The aircraft cycle employs millions of people and is one of the world's chief growth engines. The major players are all viciously competitive, so I can't count on any of them to have the view I need, as one of the aircraft manufacturers might say things are slowing in the whole sector, but that might just be an alibi for sales lost to a competitor. That's why I turn to Alcoa, which gives me the long-term growth rate it expects for aerospace—as it does for all of the industries it sells to— based on its own order book, which includes contracts from all the aerospace concerns. Alcoa is so tied in to the aerospace industry that you would have nailed Boeing in the $60s a year ago when you heard Kleinfeld talk about Boeing's orders. It was a prescient moment; while most people were preoccupied with near-term Dreamliner issues, Alcoa was simply trying to meet multiple-year demand from an important customer.

Again, because of one of the unique properties of aluminum, its extremely light weight, Alcoa has been taking share from other metals in the factories of all automobile makers worldwide. The importance of autos to the growth of economies is crucial, and Alcoa's forecast of car builds is priceless. Plus, we know from "light-weighting," the process by which heavier materials are replaced by aluminum, that if Alcoa's orders fall off, it isn't because aluminum is losing share; it's because business in autos has slowed. The same goes for heavy trucks, an important part of the industrial economy. While I like Caterpillar's forecasts for trucks, I think Alcoa, because Kleinfeld is so meticulous and because CAT could always be losing share to other companies like Cummins or Navistar, always does it one better.

Aluminum's other principal use is in commercial construction. While many economists signaled that construction would come roaring back after the Great Recession, Kleinfeld told you otherwise because he simply wasn't seeing large orders for aluminum used in commercial real estate projects. I wait with bated breath to hear whether he is, at last, able to increase his forecast—and when he does say that commercial construction's picked up, that will be the clarion call to buy a host of companies that participate in building projects.

We don't think we should put too much weight on the consumption of beverages, but I like Alcoa's forecast, if only to temper my enthusiasm for two companies I like very much: PepsiCo and the Coca-Cola Company. Slow growth in Alcoa's business for years has kept me from being too excited about the growth prospects for the carbonated soft drink business of either. Fortunately, PepsiCo has an excellent snack business in Frito-Lay, but Alcoa's read on aluminum beverage cans has been crucial in keeping me from plunging into Coca-Cola's underperforming stock.

I have had a strong call on the increasing use of natural gas over other forms of electricity, and I have Alcoa's conference call to thank for that, as Kleinfeld issues a quarterly projection on the pace of increased switching from coal-fired plants that don't need a lot of aluminum to natural gas plants with turbines that are voracious aluminum users. Kleinfeld's against-the-grain forecast of a slowdown in orders in 2013 took a lot of people by surprise; many were predicting that natural gas turbines would really begin to be built in earnest to replace coal. But Kleinfeld pointed out that it wasn't coal to nat gas that was slowing; it was the need for less electric power altogether because of renewable energy, better conservation and a decrease in manufacturing. That's the kind of jumping-off point that could send you buying First Solar, or put a further nail in the coffin of coal, just when you thought that maybe, just maybe, the EPA was going easy on that dirtiest of fuels and that's why turbine orders weren't that strong. I love that kind of derivative thinking. It's a fabulous edge that you can glean from the call that those who don't listen just won't have.

Finally, Alcoa makes the commodity of aluminum itself, and aluminum, like copper, can be a great thermometer of world growth. When there is a surfeit of aluminum you have to sell those big cyclical stocks I wrote about earlier. Believe me, if Alcoa's aluminum order book is bare, there's no way an economic boom can be on the horizon. There are way too many ties to all sorts of construction for that to happen, so temper your enthusiasm for faster economic activity.

IF YOU WANT to gauge global growth further, four other companies—General Electric, Honeywell, 3M and United Technologies—can give you calls on pretty much everything that matters; they fill in or verify pieces of the puzzle that Alcoa and Caterpillar haven't given you. The global nature of all four of these businesses is unsurpassed, and while their CEOs do not spend nearly as much time giving you a view of the world's economies, they can offer incredibly valuable insight.

I use General Electric, first and foremost, to gauge energy spending, as it has been at the heart of creating and saving energy for years, particularly with both nuclear and natural gas power. GE has a big window into health care spending as well as aerospace and aviation. I have found out everything from how governments are allocating limited resources to how fast our energy bill may be growing globally by listening to General Electric. China is a major focus for GE, so you always want to pay attention to any sign of an increase or retreat in orders. A slowdown in European orders for the big equipment that GE manufactures for health care systems gave you a heads up that the European governments were so broke they were even cutting back on health care reimbursements. Given the purchases GE has made in the energy field, I now regard the growth or shrinkage of their energy order book as a good gauge of capital spending by the major worldwide oil companies.

Honeywell, by virtue of its dominance in all aircraft, not just the majors, allows you a terrific edge in trying to figure out the growth of an industry that has been leading in its job creation. I use its climate-control business as a gauge of office construction spending, and its best-in-class turbocharger business as a tell for automobile builds, particularly because Honeywell offers a superbly accurate five-year plan for these businesses. Remember, I am trying to use these calls to create my own worldview, both short and long term, and Honeywell clues you in on both. Dave Cote, the CEO, takes pains to forecast well in advance, in part because he likes to plant "seeds" for future businesses, and I always want to know where he's gardening.

I pay attention to 3M because it sells a lot of global glass, including a gigantic business in Southeast Asia, which is almost impossible to get a read on without 3M. Why does it matter? Because so often I am stuck trying to figure out how the PC makers and television companies are doing, and only CEO Inge Thulin seems confident enough to give a forecast out more than three minutes about those economically sensitive goods. 3M has also got the best call on the rest of Asia, where it does a ton of business, so I get a good picture of how Korea and Taiwan might be performing.

Finally, United Technologies is the world's largest elevator and air-conditioning company, and these are at the core of world commercial real estate activity. Once again, I have to stress that most viewers and readers simply do not understand the importance of commercial real estate as a predictor of world growth. It is the largest user of labor and materials, and who would know more about that than a company that develops the actual interior infrastructure of so many buildings? After United Tech bought landing-gear maker Goodrich, giving them an even bigger piece of the aerospace industry, I have come to rely more and more on the aircraft forecast laid out by United Tech. It's impeccable.

Sector Reads

The transport companies can also give us a great read on both global and domestic growth pictures. We are blessed to have not just one but two incredibly thoughtful shipping companies, Federal Express and United Parcel, both of which have gone global in a key way. Federal Express gives a renowned conference call because Fred Smith, its chairman, founder, president and CEO, is an economist by trade, and he offers an amazing summary about whether the world is accelerating or decelerating by looking at package shipment counts. But not just any kind of package shipment counts. When things are humming, companies spend more on overnight delivery. When things are leaner, they pay only for regular delivery. Both FedEx and United Parcel Service give you geographic breakdowns and strengths and weaknesses that have been terrific gauges of where the world is growing. United Parcel has also given you the best read on the domestic holiday season, with helpful compares against previous years. These numbers tend to elude the economists and the brick-and-mortar bean counters because UPS ships tons of Internet-ordered packaging, including Amazon's, which typically isn't being monitored any other way. I often scoff at those who predict early on how the holiday season is going to be. UPS tells you what it is by looking at package count. What are those other guys looking at? Their thumbs?

When it comes to overall domestic strength, look no further than the rails; they ship huge quantities of cargo that allow you to make excellent predictions of growth. Just consider the freight that Union Pacific hauls: autos, housing-related products (everything from lumber to appliances), coal, oil, fracking sand, agricultural products, chemicals, and intermodal—the hauling of trucks from one place to another.

From Union Pacific's traffic numbers you can get a handle on the oil and gas boom in this country, as the railroad ships a huge amount of crude from the wellheads to the refineries as well as carloads of sand used for hydraulic fracturing, or "fracking," of new oil and gas wells. You can tell from their chemical business how that building-block industry to so many products is doing. The company has been a fabulous forecaster of new commercial construction that can take advantage of the oil and gas revolution in this country. You get a terrific handle on auto sales, because Union Pacific also brings in the autos being made in Mexico, a number that is supposed to double in the next couple of years. I can't wait to get my hands on either the Union Pacific call or the slides that go with it, because the company is an authority on the big industries that drive this country. They gave you an early read on the housing slowdown with a decline in lumber traffic. They gave you a heads up that the natural gas industry was cutting back on drilling when fracking-sand shipments cooled. Sometimes I can't believe how specific chief executive officer Jack Koraleski and his team can be. I also have to commend Norfolk Southern and CSX for their insight and statistics, although I find those two too geared toward coal to be as important a barometer as Union Pacific, and they don't do enough traffic with California, which means a not-so-hot read in China compared to UNP. You almost always get a few successful trades off this call, and, more important, your worldview, how fast you think the country is growing, should be influenced by this well-run company.

Then there are the specific sector calls that must be listened to, the ones that tell you the state of that sector so you can figure out whether the sector is worth participating in at all, before you get into which ones might be the best in that sector. Good stock picking requires you to know what kind of neighborhood you are in. If the neighborhood is bad or on the decline, you don't need to consider any stocks in that sector. If it's at rock bottom or improving, it might very well be fertile ground you might want to examine.

Given the long duration of aircraft orders, something Alcoa goes over in great detail every quarter, I am drawn to Boeing's sector analysis for more information. Boeing is one of those companies that spends far more time on its own business than on the sector, but you can tell what inning we are in on the next aircraft cycle—they tend to last seven years—by reading through the call. Boeing's management gives you a twenty-year outlook, the longest of any company I follow. I think they spend months and months debating this outlook, so the final exposition that Jim McNerney's company puts out is authoritative and incredibly reassuring. And you need reassurance if you aren't going to be shook out by some Dreamliner news flash. I also like Boeing's take on the defense budget. Perhaps because, unlike most defense companies, they have other businesses, they aren't fearful of saying that things are bad or getting awful; it isn't the chief determinant of their earnings. Still, their exposition of where the orders are coming from gives you an idea of the sustainability of this business and allows you to assess the scores of companies that supply this crucial industry.

Consumer spending can be fickle. There are so many factors involving execution, weather risk, new stores and cannibalization that I like to use a neutral barometer, one that allows for excellent comparisons: the Walt Disney Company. Given that Disney measures everything from theme parks to movie gate, cruise ships, and advertising rates for ABC and ESPN, when you are finished with the Disney call you know more about the state of the U.S. consumer than you are going to get from any economist, Commerce Department official or industry survey. The information and the predictions are impeccable, in part because CEO Bob Iger likes to give you a thoughtful view of how much the consumer is spending on travel, merchandise, theme parks, cruises and the movies. If you can't make a judgment about consumer spending after listening to a Disney call, then it simply isn't going to come to you.

We are in the midst of a long-term housing boom, and I use two companies to monitor how far we are into it and how far we can still go, given the quick increase in mortgage rates we experienced in 2013: Toll Brothers and Home Depot. I fell in love with the Toll Brothers call because they were early in predicting that housing was overheating—they were doing their best to try to restrict buyers to take only one home at a time. Yes, when things overheated, any joker could get credit to buy any new home and then hope to flip it as soon as possible. If you listened to a Toll call in that period you would have known that the industry was at a precipice. For the longest time Toll would actually grade areas to tell you how they were doing, but they pretty much gave it up when every single area started flunking as housing started to crash. And when many thought housing was bottoming, Bob Toll famously predicted on *Mad Money* that while some think that there might be light at the end of the tunnel, it is more likely to be the light from an oncoming train.

These days the Toll call gives you a good read on demand by talking about the number of communities it is selling in and how many units are being sold. The backlog number is hugely important, as are the gross price mix, the gross margins and the cost of land. Plus, the Toll Brothers cancelation rate shows how hard or easy it is for potential buyers to get credit. This number is especially important when it comes to Toll because their houses are high-priced, and that means many of them don't conform to federal agency standards for guaranteeing. So an increase in loans for Toll houses shows the banks are getting less stingy about big purchases. However, I do want to make one thing very clear: home builders haven't seen rate increases in ages, and they tend to think that increases don't really hurt sales. That's just untrue. So, take their pooh-poohing of the importance of rising mortgage rates with a grain if not a box of Morton's salt.

Home Depot, in many ways, may give you the most thorough exposition of what's happening with the consumer and spending on her biggest purchase: her home. More than 63 percent of the people in this country have homes, so spending on them may be the best way to figure out where the consumer is putting her extra dollars. Home Depot gives you which regions are strongest and which aisles are doing best. They actually lay out sales data on pretty much every commodity sold and tell you whether it is above or below the average comparable-store rate. We should pay them for the right to be on this call. You can gauge demand for everything from appliances to paints, kitchens and baths, to flooring, giving you a chance to score on stocks like Whirlpool, Lumber Liquidators, Weyerhaeuser, Stanley Black & Decker, Sherwin-Williams, Masco, and Fortune Brands, all of which I have recommended for ages because I listen to the Home Depot call. They also let you know how much of an individual's dollar is going into her house versus other spending priorities. I get a ton of important tidbits from HD's calls, including, recently, an amazing piece of data on the correlation between spending on homes by those who are underwater on their mortgages and spending by those who are currently whole. Someone who has negative equity in a home is likely to spend only about $1,000 a year on it. But someone who has a good loan-to-value ratio spends three times that. Many people are still underwater on their mortgages, but that's changing rapidly, so I can only conclude that we have a multiyear path to the housing and home spending story, with intermittent breathers as rates go up and customers get skittish before returning to the house hunt after years and years of pent-up demand and a real dearth of new supply.

It's tough to gauge how any of the really big retailers are doing, as they are pretty unwilling to tell you much these days, and many have given up monthly updates that were the norm just a few years ago. Plus, I think perhaps for competitive reasons, their calls tend to be skeletal and lacking in any conclusion-forming data. That's why I turn to their suppliers, notably, VF Corporation, with its North Face, Wrangler and Lee jeans brands, and PVH, with its Tommy Hilfiger, Calvin Klein and Phillips–Van Heusen labels, to make the best estimates about how their end markets—the stores themselves—are doing. These are two of the most forthcoming players in the industry, and they offer a level of transparency I wish their customers would emulate, particularly Target and Walmart, which tell you way too little to be helpful in making any determination about this key industry. Oh, and remember, when their sales get tepid, reach for some TJX Companies or Ross Stores. They are the winners in a slowdown because they buy the merchandise that didn't move in a particular season. When VF and PVH do poorly, that means there's way too much inventory in the system, ideal for Ross and TJX, the closeout kings.

Most people seem to be mystified about how well technology is doing at any given time. I don't know why. You want to know how it is going? Just ask Avnet, which gives you an intense and thorough breakdown of what hardware and software is selling by giving you an insight each quarter into how its more than 100,000 customers are doing. I call Avnet the world's largest tech supermarket chain; its gigantic distribution network will tell you whether there is more ordering than there are supplies available. I cannot tell you how many times I have gotten the jump on everyone else just by parsing Avnet's conference call and then following up each quarter by having the CEO, Rick Hamada, come on *Mad Money* for a further drilldown. Given that they sell virtually all components needed for technology, nobody has a read on the industry like they do—not Apple, not Microsoft, not Hewlett-Packard, not IBM, not Google, and not Intel. Pay close attention to what they say about flash memory, drives and commodity semis. This company moves stocks like Western Digital Corporation, Seagate Technology, SanDisk, and Micron Technology each time it opens its mouth.

There are hundreds of banks out there. I go through about three dozen bank conference calls every quarter, and most tell a compelling story about their own successes and positioning. You can skip almost all of them, though, if you want to know how banking, credit and finance are doing in this country. Just read the JPMorgan quarterly conference call.

CEO Jamie Dimon doesn't get that solid reputation—and I don't think it is lastingly tarnished by the mistakes made in London trading or the mortgage market—just from doing better and having that fortress balance sheet. It's because he has tremendous knowledge of every aspect of banking: commercial lending, corporate bond issuance, commercial and consumer mortgages, credit cards, private banking, and money management, among others and he explains how banks in general are doing in each area. Then he follows up with how JPMorgan is doing in each of those segments. You simply need to pit any bank you are thinking of buying against what JPMorgan is saying about how it is doing in the important sectors before you should pull the trigger. JPM is the benchmark against which all are measured. Jamie's quarterly state of credit is bested only by his must-read annual letter to shareholders. I know that Warren Buffett's letters are treasured for their wisdom about so many topics, but at this stage of things, I prefer Jamie's, if only because Warren is always bullish, no matter what the circumstance. That's not the case with Jamie; while he always speaks positively about the nation's prospects, he isn't always bullish on some business lines. So stay close and parse all of his words.

When it comes to autos, you can count on the Ford Motor Company to give you the best read. Alan Mulally, the man who kept Ford from having to take a federal bailout, is always forthcoming about how his company is doing around the globe, region by region. If people would simply listen to his conference calls and read his presentation that comes with each quarter, they would know that as important as the United States is to auto sales, Ford is also a very European company and was the first American company to tell you that Europe was done going down in 2013. That was a home-run call from the guy from Detroit, although the company was late in seeing the emerging European recession coming.

Consumer packaged goods data are very subjective: Who's taking share? Who's winning the hearts and minds of the global consumer? But if you want a "just the facts, ma'am" rundown of how this key global industry is doing, pull up a series of Procter & Gamble conference calls as well as its annual report, which, despite management turmoil, remains a must-read if you want to know how much a consumer is willing to spend on razors, hair care, laundry detergent and so many other products in both developed and emerging markets. Sometimes I can't believe that P&G is willing to divulge as much as it does. If it gives me a competitive advantage in figuring out the stocks, who knows what it does for Colgate, Unilever and Clorox.

We've got a great growth story in oil and gas going in this country, but oil and gas is a global industry, and in order to get a read on the state of the exploration and production of petroleum and petroleum-based products, you need to listen to Schlumberger, the greatest oil service company in the world. I have learned so much from their conference calls and their explanations that I invited former CEO Andrew Gould on just to thank him not only for making his shareholders so much money but for sharing his insights about this incredibly important industry. I don't know if I could divine much at all about the future of the oil and gas industry if I didn't have Schlumberger to help me find the way. If your eyes glaze over when industry people seem to talk in code about all sorts of issues and products and proposals in the oil patch, take those arcane terms and plug them into the Schlumberger glossary. It's incredible how many times the online Schlumberger dictionary has bailed me out when I am interviewing oil and gas execs. I always keep the site open on my computer when one of the execs from that cohort appears on *Mad Money*.

I've saved the best and the worst for last. If you own the stock of Deere, you know the pain of listening to its conference calls. There's always something going wrong at Deere, and it's always what is highlighted the most, much to every shareholders' chagrin. Recently I was on *Squawk on the Street* and Deere's stock was flying before the market opened, trading up almost three points. I told people to sell it right then, before the conference call, because Deere would screw it up or be downbeat. They were even worse than usual on that call, and the stock plummeted from where it was in premarket trading to several points *below* where it had traded the day before—a five-buck swing in just a few minutes' time.

However, if you are simply trying to figure out the state of the world's agricultural businesses from a gargantuan industry with many important players and therefore stocks, Deere's conference call is superb. Deere tells you what to look for, everything from how much will be spent on equipment to the lean or fat years that are ahead for the farmers around the world. I use the Deere call to help me evaluate everything from the state of renewable fuels—ethanol—to the prices of grains, and ultimately the costs to the supermarkets, restaurants and you, the food consumer. They also give you a terrific geographical read of the agricultural world. Although I think the stock of competitor AGCO is much better to own than Deere's, if you want data and insight, Deere is a better source.

I AM NOT SAYING that this list is complete. I am saying that if you listen to these calls, you will be able to craft an informed view of both the world's growth and the growth of every important industry out there that might matter to good trading and careful investing. But if you want a worldview based on what actual businesspeople are saying before you decide to buy or sell any stocks, these calls will make your decisions a heck of a lot smarter than those who haven't heard them, thereby increasing your odds that you will pick the right stocks and avoid the wrong ones. In a world where trust is hard to come by and the road to getting rich is filled with land mines, these conference calls give you a leg up and provide the mine detector you need not to get blown out of the water.

How to Grade High-Growth Stocks

Only after arriving at a worldview based on the judgments of actual businesses, and then analyzing the sectors that fit that worldview, am I actually in good enough shape to make effective stock choices. While the process to get to where we are now seems difficult, remember: It isn't like you have to read hundreds of conference calls. You now know what to listen to, and you can tune out a lot of the noise that passes for intelligent information that is of no value whatsoever to picking stocks.

Once you have examined the relevant conference calls, you can pretty much figure out which sectors are in the sweet spot for investing at that moment. I have shown you how we grade cyclical stocks against a particular kind of economic backdrop. If they can outperform other kinds of stocks and top the sales and earnings estimates with alacrity when the economy is doing well, they can go higher. We are familiar too with how traditional growth stocks work. If they beat the estimates in a slower-growing economy, they too can go higher. Defensives are also easy to gauge; if their earnings hold up in a no-growth environment and they have nice-size dividends relative to bonds, then they are worth owning. But there's one group of stocks that will defy these traditional benchmarks and are bound to confuse you if we don't stop to figure out how to grade them. These are the super-growth stocks that need to be a part of your portfolio if you are going to beat the averages in what may be a permanently slower-growth economy. These miraculous stocks require a different set of metrics from all others because they all seem overvalued versus cyclical, regular growth and defensive stocks, yet they are precisely what you need in your portfolio when so many are befuddled that any stock can advance when weak hiring and sluggish business conditions prevail. Before we get any further in choosing any stocks, we have to spend some time learning about these unique kinds of equities; they are integral to trumping this particular market at this particular time. They will mystify you and shake you out if I don't explain how they are graded.

When I make my highest-growth stock selections, ones that often fit the themes I will be giving you in the next chapter, I like to go through an exercise that illuminates the strengths and weaknesses of these kinds of companies. I think I have it down to a system, and I want to share my methods with you so you can use the same methods to measure uber-growth stocks. It's my ten-point test that I use every day to isolate my favorite stocks for my favorite themes. I will demonstrate my system by using three super-growth stocks—Google, Amazon and Starbucks—because they are synonymous with the kinds of high-powered equities I am talking about. These are all superbly managed companies, all best of breed. These aren't test flunkers. Consider them icons to pit your own high-growth stocks against in my ten-point quiz. Grade your stocks on a scale of 1 to 10—10 being the best—and then add them up to see which wins. In a diversified ten-stock portfolio you must limit how many of these supergrowth stocks you can own because they do tend to trade together as if they are in their own cohort, even though they might originate from different sectors. Just go for the one or two that trump the others.

First Test: Is there potential for multiyear growth that we can put a value on, a clear growth path that provides long-term visibility with multiple revenue streams?

Wall Street prizes growth among all other characteristics when it comes to what can withstand a selling onslaught. So we need to be sure that we are dealing with companies that have that growth staying power and are not exhibiting flash-in-the-pan performance. On *Mad Money* I often say that growth is the magic elixir. That's because there is a tremendous amount of money dedicated to finding growth, particularly in the out years, so that's what we are searching for. It's also why I am listing this criterion first, because it's the most important.

Let's start with Amazon, perhaps the quintessential growth stock of the era. The global retail opportunity here is enormous, and Amazon is the best-positioned company to continue to gain market share. A scan of the available research from most of the websites out there shows that revenues could increase ten times over the long term. Today U.S. commerce is growing in the mid-teens, and international is slightly faster. The trends here are Amazon's friends: smartphones, tablets and digital goods, while worldwide Internet connectivity will fuel growth. Plus, the company has exactly what we want in a non-bricks-and-mortar retailer: (1) the widest selection of product worldwide; (2) the lowest aggregate prices and fast delivery, often for free with Amazon Prime, perhaps headed to same-day service once the extensive warehouse system is built out; (3) strong and unique customer relationships, particularly with Prime members; and (4) high repeat purchase activity and strong portability of the model to international and mobile users. In the past decade Amazon has moved from a single-function book retailer to a global e-commerce powerhouse, which is key to long-term growth. Additionally, the company's newer business units in digital, Amazon web services (where they fulfill the orders of other retailers trying to master e-commerce) and hardware represent optionality in an expanding revenue pie. All of these initiatives add up to superior multiyear growth that is precisely what we are looking for. If you were scoring on a 1–10 scale, with 10 being the best on growth, then Amazon is the quintessential 10.

How about Google? Here's the dominant player in the key and growing category of search. With more than 66 percent share of queries in the United States and 75 percent of search advertising budgets, it is still the most obvious and effective form of advertising on the web. Google is the acknowledged king of growth on the Internet. These trends are global—Google's biggest market is in Europe—and search is still in secular-growth mode worldwide.

Google's open-source Android operating system is now on 52 percent of U.S. smartphones and is headed toward similar adoption globally, even as it has yet to be monetized effectively; that will come later. Same with its YouTube monetization, which should be a multiyear growth stream as Google attempts to expand this product into a multichannel form of broadcasting. I have no doubt of its success in this endeavor.

However, the greatest growth market in the world right now is China. That's where you have to be if you want to be able to add millions, not thousands or even hundreds of thousands, but millions of new viewers and readers. Google, for political reasons involving free speech, is not able to tap into the world's fastest-growing Internet market.

Let's go beyond tech into consumer growth with Starbucks. Does SBUX have the potential for multiyear growth we can put a value on because it gives analysts the path they need to develop models that can be beaten on both top and bottom line?

We know that Starbucks has a portfolio of assets that include 19,000 stores serving 70 million customers each week. It has the most effective social media initiatives of any company I follow; these include 40 million Facebook followers, 5 million Twitter followers, more than double just a few months ago, and a potential for more than 10 million loyalty cards at the current pace, ensuring a loyal customer base. While some fear saturation, at least in the United States, CEO Howard Schultz has made it very clear that there's room for thousands more stores here, particularly since the acquisition of Teavana, the tea accessory chain. Given the recent acceleration in U.S. same-store sales, it's tough to argue with the founder, chairman, CEO and president of the company. I see almost no sales cannibalization in any region in the country.

The real growth, however, unlike Google's, is in China, where Starbucks intends to triple the number of stores from 500 in 2011 to 1500 in 2015. There are similar plans to double the number of Starbucks in most of East Asia and to penetrate India, Russia and Latin America aggressively. I have never heard Howard more upbeat than he's been lately; he sees same-store sales continuing to accelerate in the United States—remember, that's the key metric for retail—gaining in China and even turning in Europe, which had been a problem for the chain. Starbucks also has new products, including single-serve K-Cups, new pastries and juices that can ignite retail sales, so there's a lot of room for this company to run. That said, no matter what Howard might argue, at a certain point Starbucks will exhaust its U.S. growth. We're just nowhere near that level yet.

All three of these companies score well on this criterion, but I believe Amazon has got the widest path ahead of it. Starbucks could be limited at a certain point by how many coffee stores *and* tea stores it might be able to erect in mature markets. Google has a ton of irons in the fire, but without China it's not going to be able to justify endless growth.

My takeaway: Edge to Amazon, even as it is extremely highly valued on earnings, simply because it still has lots of domestic categories to exploit and hasn't scratched the surface in international. Starbucks has plenty of room to grow, especially now that it is embracing consumer packaged goods and opening aggressively in China. Google? Not clear. It has to be able to figure out how to monetize its growth better, and it might be capped by the lack of Chinese exposure. Amazon is a 10, Starbucks an 8, Google a 7.

Second Test: Is the total addressable market big enough for the companies to sustain their growth?

Amazon's easy. This company is the Walmart of the Internet, and much growth remains because of the size of the market and its dominance. Amazon has seventy warehouses and is adding scores more to be able to handle their merchandise and the merchandise of others that use their web service for fulfillment. It's expanding into every single kind of good that it sells. Since 100 million people shop each week at Walmart, and Amazon offers lower prices than Walmart on most items, I think the market is more than big enough. Plus, there are still plenty of brick-and-mortar stores that can be "Amazoned," meaning that they perform the showroom function for this amazing retailer. That means Amazon has a total addressable market (TAM) that may be bigger than any other company in the world. That's why this company has defied the skeptics for many years and, I think, will continue to do so going forward.

Google has several different markets that it sells into that are all growing like weeds. It has search, which is a $45 billion market with double-digit growth potential for years to come. Its paid search model could easily grow at a mid-teens compounded annual growth rate. If you take a much wider view of the TAM, especially with Google's efforts with YouTube and DoubleClick, its ad server business, plus its tools to place ads on a programmatic basis, meaning an auction-based system that places ads automatically in the best sites to deliver worthwhile impressions, you could argue that Google might be able to take a gigantic portion of the $600 billion global advertising market. Google's share of plain old display revenue can grow from its current $6 billion base to twice that as it builds out YouTube.

Most important, Android, its remarkable operating system, has shown an ability to beat Apple in any head-to-head competition because Samsung, which runs the Android system, is priced through Apple's iPhone at all global telecommunications providers. There is no short-term plan to monetize Android, but it is only a matter of time, and that means the TAM can be much bigger than we currently think.

Google is even moving aggressively into selling personal computers, with its inexpensive Chrome device, which recognizes that most of the features and functions of a regular PC simply aren't used. Eighty million personal computers are bought every year; no one has even factored in yet how big Chrome can be.

Starbucks plays in two markets. It's in the ready-to-drink beverage market, which is valued at $60 billion in the United States alone and is far bigger than that worldwide. Starbucks would tell you it still has so much room to grow that it's impossible to put a number on it. And it has a growing consumer packaged goods market with K-Cups; it could ship 500 million K-Cups a year, as well as brand-new proprietary yogurt and juice offerings. Don't rule out Starbucks taking yards and yards of space in your supermarket with these products in the not-too-distant future. Around the world, coffee is a $50 billion at-home market, and I would contend that SBUX has barely scratched the service of that business. There are 130 million coffee drinkers in American alone, so the total addressable market is truly far larger than we need to fret much about when we measure how much Starbucks can sell. Be on the lookout for the build-out of Teavana, the tea and accoutrements store Starbucks bought in 2012. Before Starbucks purchased Teavana it was more of a tea accessory emporium; Starbucks wants to turn the stores into tea bars like the coffee bars it is known for. The total addressable tea market, according to Howard Schultz, is $40 billion, so I don't expect growth to run out any time soon.

My takeaway: Amazon has just started scratching the surface of retail and can take a huge amount of share from brick-and-mortar retailers around the globe. Google's addressable markets are large, and it too can take away a huge number of dollars from television, print, radio and all other sorts of ad forms. Starbucks is tougher. Sure, the coffee and tea markets are gigantic, but at some point they will be saturated by SBUX and its competitors. Still, I can see the TAM being big enough to last for many years before SBUX exhausts it, because of its new inroads in consumer packaged goods and tea. I say 10 each for Amazon and Google, 8 for Starbucks.

Third Test: Does the company have the ability to stay competitive?

To some degree the companies I have picked to highlight these tests are the best of the best, but that doesn't mean they can't be felled by a competitor. Ask yourself about the transformation of the post-Jobs Apple. While initially the stock moved higher without Jobs, it was quite evident nine months later that the string had been played out, and not only had Apple become less competitive but Google had become more aggressive. So this test requires some real vision and a reversion to orthodoxy.

Amazon has developed tremendous loyalty in e-commerce. Prime membership and fulfillment are driving purchase frequency and locking in customers. The Kindle is always in danger of being passed by a better mousetrap, but the fact that the Nook from Barnes & Noble, arguably a superior product, has struggled so mightily is a testament to the staying power of Amazon. So is the lack of a decline in sales when states enact sales taxes on its products. Amazon's mobile offering is consistently one of the most popular apps on both iOS and Android.

Only eBay has been able to successfully challenge Amazon's web services fulfillment business. However, it is much more of an adjunct to its own normal auction business, and eBay has its hands full trying to harness the explosive growth of its PayPal franchise. I guess you could say that eBay is a distinctly second-fiddle competitor.

Google is dominant in search and has consistently been able to pull away from competitors Bing and Yahoo! in its capabilities. Google is so strong here that the only thing I worry about, the only entity that could stop them, is the Justice Department's Antitrust Division. Don't laugh. Some say Microsoft under CEO Steve Ballmer never recovered from its bout with Justice, and it was still talked about when he retired not that long ago. However, there are two factors that you must worry about if you own Google: (1) a resurgent, well-capitalized Yahoo! under Marissa Mayer, and (2) the potential for Facebook to cut in to their search business with clever graphical search, a supersmart search that is more targeted and could become more trusted than Google because it's not perceived to be "bought" by advertisers.

Starbucks has many rivals, including, domestically, Dunkin' Donuts, a very good company and an excellent stock, which offers a cheaper alternative to Starbucks. But brand loyalty, fabulous social media, excellent affinity programs and stores that are considered to be a "third place"— Howard's term—between home and office have allowed Starbucks to distance itself from the competition. I feared that Green Mountain Coffee Roasters could cut down the growth of in-home coffee, but a recent alliance with Green Mountain ended that. At one point I also fretted that Teavana would start serving tea at its stores, blunting the Tazo initiative by Starbucks, but the merger eliminated any worries on that score.

All three of these companies are innovators, which allows them to stay one step ahead of the posse. Often companies flunk this question because they have failed to keep innovating or have let others pass them by, such as Procter & Gamble when a newly invigorated Colgate took share from them in virtually every global market. Remember, though, no company stays on top forever. I am old enough to remember when IBM vanquished Burroughs, Univac, NCR, Control Data and Honeywell, the old BUNCH, all of which were making big iron—as we called mainframes—back in the 1960s and 1970s. I never thought a company could become so dominant in my lifetime. Now IBM is a shadow of its former self, defeated by Intel, Microsoft and the triumph of personal computers that are now more powerful than mainframes and sell at a fraction of the cost.

My takeaway: Amazon has already destroyed the competition. I'm not worried about its ability to stay competitive. Google? Tougher call. It has been dominant so far, but smart competitors are making inroads into the very core of its business. Starbucks will always have competition; that's the nature of the coffee beast. But the more it can enhance the experience, the more it can stay competitive. Still, once again, edge to Amazon with a 10, Google with 8 and Starbucks with 7.

Fourth Test: Is there a possibility for the company to return capital over time, through either dividends or well-timed buybacks? Or does the company have such a well-defined growth plan that it can just continue to pile the money into the business to get consistent or accelerated revenue growth?

This is a two-pronged test because we never want to eliminate companies from our portfolios simply because they aren't paying good dividends or buying back stock—the former I treasure, and the latter can be good if done in a more than desultory way. In fact, if a company is not generating dividends, it can be a good sign that its total addressable market is so huge that the company needs every penny to exploit the situation. I also consider this question a referendum on what management is willing to do for its shareholders. I will spend a great deal of time in this book describing some of the ways a company can bring out value besides increasing a buyback or a dividend. Perhaps it can split itself up, which has been a magnificent way to unlock value. It can be willing to sell out to the highest bidder. Or it can take its cash or its high-priced stock and purchase another company to grow. All are terrific ways to bring out shareholder value.

Clearly Amazon and Google can pass the first test and do so with flying colors. They have oodles of capital. For Amazon's stock to keep going higher, it needs to continue its investment in warehouses and technology to block all other comers and solidify its position as the Walmart of global commerce. In fact, I wonder whether the stock wouldn't fall, perhaps dramatically, if it suddenly issued a dividend; that would be a sign that growth has peaked and that the company is now more mature than we thought.

Google has a ridiculous amount of growth in front of it, with initiatives that require it to spend as much money as possible to continue to get consistent if not accelerated revenue growth. Again, Google would disappoint if it suddenly became more "shareholder-friendly" by returning capital. In fact, it is innovation, like Chrome, like the extension of YouTube, like the Maps initiative that draws investors to the stock in the first place. However, Google spends a lot of money on projects that don't seem to be oriented toward making a profit or seem uneconomical, or even foolish. It also shelled out $12.5 billion for Motorola Mobility, a maker of smartphones that has a large stable of patents. It's an acquisition that has not paid off much yet and may turn out to be an expensive mistake.

Starbucks is different. It is a mature growth stock that throws off a huge amount of cash, more than it can use to grow its store base. That's why its quarterly dividend has been growing at a pace far greater than just about every large cap growth company out there. Its outsized dividend payments have not kept it from expanding rapidly in China, nor has it stopped the company from remodeling or expanding its offerings. The cash flow is strong enough to support both without worry.

My takeaway: Here there's a clear winner, Starbucks. The company is deploying its cash wisely. It's returning plenty of capital to shareholders without crimping growth whatsoever. Google is very problematic. It seems to spend a lot of money on things that might not pay off, which could hurt its valuation over time. Amazon gets a pass. It is in a rare league of its own. We don't want it to slow down; we want it to spend, spend, spend. And that's exactly what it is doing.

Starbucks 10, Amazon 9, Google 7.

Fifth Test: Can the company expand internationally?

The international markets may be weaker at times than the domestic markets, but if analysts are going to take a longer-term view and offer multi-year growth forecasts, then a plan of expansion overseas, where there's unexploited turf, is a must.

Amazon already controls one-fifth of U.S. e-commerce, but that's still not enough to sate the growth hound mutual funds. To put it in perspective, U.S. retail sales were $4.16 trillion in 2011, meaning Amazon's $36 billion in U.S. gross merchandise value (GMV) is less than 1 percent of that sum. If one assumes that U.S. retail sales increase by 3 percent annually over the next ten years, and if Amazon were to capture 5 percent of U.S. retail sales, then its implied GMV would be $280 billion.

But the global opportunity for Amazon is even more attractive, as Internet user adoption rates—e-commerce penetration of total retail and Amazon's presence in international markets—pale in comparison to the more established U.S. market. Amazon already has captured 13.5 percent of international e-commerce, but it controls less than 1 percent of world retail sales. So, as I see it, the opportunity is simply humongous.

Google currently generates more than half of its revenue overseas— and this is without China. The opportunity for share gains in the $600 billion world ad market makes Google one of the most attractive global plays, and core international search markets continue to grow at a rapid pace. But not having access to China makes its international efforts very problematic.

Starbucks has laid out ambitious targets for China by 2015, with a target of 1500 stores—triple the 500 stores that existed in 2011. After speaking recently with CEO Schultz, I am convinced this is easily achievable. If Starbucks follows the trajectory of Yum!, whose Kentucky Fried Chicken business is the largest chain in China, it could triple again, from 1,500 units to 4,500 units, in seven years. Much of the growth in China will come from expansion into some of the smaller cities with tremendous growth that have very few Starbucks and very long lines of people waiting to get coffee. The European expansion has been stalled by the slow growth of Europe. But I believe that India will be the next big phase of international growth, hence the importance of the Teavana acquisition in December 2012.

My takeaway: Amazon is triumphant simply because it has just begun to tap international, and there's no reason to think it can't pull off what it is has done here when it goes abroad. Google already gets about half of its business from international. I worry that without China it might not have the growth from overseas that the others have. Starbucks is already in most countries, which is a negative, but there's still plenty of room within those countries to build out more stores. Edge, again, to Amazon.

Amazon 10, Starbucks 6, Google 8.

Sixth Test: Can the balance sheet support strong growth?

We used to see many companies' growth plans become constrained by their balance sheets. Then the Federal Reserve lowered interest rates to the point that the vast majority of companies with high-cost debt were able to refinance, just as you have been able to refinance your mortgage.

Still, though, that doesn't mean we should forget about a firm's finances. Many economies around the world are on unsteady ground. Many companies hope to be able to maintain a growth path; they have spent a great deal to do so, and the credit markets won't always be as available and as friendly as they are now. So the balance sheet is always an issue.

This trio of companies passes with flying colors. Amazon has more than $7 billion in cash and $3 billion in debt, plenty of cash to continue to expand. Google has more than $50 billion in cash on hand and has a staggering amount of free cash flow, more than $13 billion of it, so even though it is spending aggressively it has no problem funding its expansion plans. Starbucks maintains a much smaller cash position, usually about $1.5 billion, as it likes to return cash to the shareholders that it doesn't reinvest in the business. That is certainly still an acceptable level.

My takeaway: All three stand up well against this criterion, as there is no dearth of investors willing to give capital to high-growth companies that want to expand rapidly. The more rapid, the more capital! No clear winner this time: 10s all around.

Seventh Test: Is the stock expensive on the out years?

Up until this question I haven't stressed the notion of the company's actual earnings. Remember: All companies must be put through the brutal quarterly earnings gauntlet, when not only must each company's reports beat the consensus on top and bottom lines, but the company must then raise forecasts for both to ever higher levels. When it comes to traditional industrial, technological or financial stocks, the near term means a great deal.

But when you are examining classic long-term growth stocks, you have to look at the out years, typically the potential for the next five years of earnings growth. This "out years" concept is extremely difficult for even the most seasoned managers to understand because they regard out-year logic as lacking in rigor. If you can't figure out what the next quarter is going to be, who knows what the quarters will look like five years from now? These skeptics think that you are simply giving a growth company a free pass. For example, billions have been lost betting against Amazon because its near-term earnings cannot support its current valuation. It always "looks" expensive on its multiyear estimates, but then, when it ends up beating those estimates handily, you see that it wasn't as expensive as you thought, although it was hardly cheap.

Always know that if Amazon wanted to slow its growth, it could easily trade at half of that elevated price-to-earnings (PE) multiple. But when it comes to growth stocks, remember, we want the fastest growth possible, and we don't want to miss the opportunity simply because it is too costly near term. Plus, when a company like Amazon has the wherewithal and the balance sheet and the, yes, love of supergrowth aficionados, then another competitor won't try to challenge it, allowing it to be the undisputed champion. It's difficult to map out a five-year growth path if there is a ton of competition. But Amazon has already crushed the competition and won the arms race, so the game is AMZN's to lose. As unpalatable as Amazon's PE might be for wizened investors, it can be justified by thinking about how much it will earn many years from now, when its entire worldwide network is built out—although the risk is palpable, given possible execution problems and a sky-high multiple.

Google's valuation is more reasonable than Amazon's here, but gets notably cheaper in the out years. It's been selling at about twenty times forward near-term earnings, pretty great for a company that's been growing at about 18 percent. But if you try to discern how it will be doing versus estimates out a few years, it is in the out years that the stock seems especially cheap, selling for single-digit multiples. That means it actually sells at a discount to the average stock as expressed by the price-to-earnings multiple on the S&P 500, and yet it is far from being just an average stock. Now you see why so many people believe that the stock is so undervalued. They are willing to look out a few years and make a judgment, especially because, like Amazon, most of the competition has been vanquished. Plus, with new products it is always possible that we could see an acceleration in growth that could lead to even greater surprises in the future, something I do not anticipate happening for the other two companies.

Starbucks currently trades for about twenty-three times forward earnings, but it has about a 20 percent sustained earnings growth path. Forward projections on these out-year numbers put the stock at a lower price-to-earnings multiple, of course, but under no estimate do I think this one is cheap compared to Google.

My takeaway: Amazon better keep growing as it is now and take advantage of international, because it's way too expensive on a pure earnings estimate basis. Google, on the other hand, is surprisingly cheap on those out-in-the-future estimates, and Starbucks is pretty much in between. That's a big edge to Google, giving it a 10, Starbucks a 7, and Amazon a 5.

Eighth Test: Does the company have the right management?

There is no doubt that Jeff Bezos is the right man for the Amazon job. Many companies came public during the so-called dotcom explosion, but only a handful are still alive, and none has thrived like Amazon because

Bezos knew that he had to both scale the business and maintain first-mover status. My only fear with this stock is that I have no idea who else there is besides Bezos. It seems frighteningly like a one-man-band outfit. But what a band!

When Larry Page, the cofounder, took over as Google's CEO in April 2011 from old hand Eric Schmidt, there were visible changes made at the top of the organization as he reorganized the company around individual product areas, which helped streamline decisions and make individual product heads more accountable. He also empowered executives in some of the newer emerging revenue streams to grow their business lines faster, including Android and mobile, display/YouTube, Chrome and commerce, plus the enterprise businesses that had been neglected. Getting a job at Google is the single most difficult hire on earth, courtesy of Page's outstanding leadership.

Starbucks' Howard Schultz is the definition of bankability. First, he has taken a small regional coffee company that went public more than 20 years ago with approximately 150 stores, 3,000 employees and $100 million in revenue and transformed it into a company with over 17,000 stories in 57 countries serving over 60 million customers a week, employing 200,000 people, with net sales of $15 billion and $8 billion in gross profit.

Schultz retired from the day-to-day running of the company in 2000, and the chain fell down dramatically. When he returned in January 2008 he inherited a bedraggled and, yes, dirty coffee shop company, with same-store sales growth of just 1 percent in the United States. He's taken that all the way back to 7 percent, and he's closed scores of underperforming stores while expanding in the right places both domestically and overseas. We do not want to imagine what Starbucks would be without him, but this time I believe he is grooming a deep succession bench. Still, let's just hope he stays around to fulfill the decade's worth of growth that lies ahead of the company.

My bottom line: The current leadership at all three is superb. My concern here, because we are thinking long term, is succession. I believe that Schultz has learned from his mistakes the last go-round and is building a remarkable team. Google has got tremendous young bench strength. Frankly, though, I have no idea who is really running the show at Amazon besides Bezos. That's worrisome. I would give the slight edge to Google over Starbucks in this category. Amazon is a black box. Google gets a 10, Starbucks a 9 and Amazon an 8, purely over worries about what happens next.

Ninth Test: Does the company need macro growth to meet the numbers?

This is not a trick question. There will be many companies out there that do need world growth to do well and can't excel until world growth accelerates. That's why I spent so much time filling you in on who I listen to in order to gauge long-term growth. If you think the growth is sluggish, though, you know that there are many companies that are difficult to own unless they are willing to try to unlock shareholder value because they are too likely to miss Wall Street estimates and be punished when they do.

Amazon and Google are secular growers, meaning they don't need strength in either the U.S. or the world economy to hit or beat the numbers. Plus, they are taking share, so even if the world slows they can still augment their earnings. There are many secular trends in their favor, including the inexorable speed improvements by the telecommunications providers, the finer resolution that new equipment is giving all devices and the rapid adoption of mobile, which, for Google in particular, represents a major breakout in round-the-clock user ability, even as Google has yet to harness it successfully. I am not sweating that issue; Google will figure it out, just as Facebook did not that long ago. However, Google does have some cyclical advertising issues. Advertisers will cut back in times of economic hardship.

Starbucks is a tougher call. In a time of economic weakness, when many of its competitors' growth rates were stunted, Starbucks still delivered consistently good numbers. Plus, there has been a tremendous insensitivity to price for even the highest of the high-end lattes Starbucks offers. Starbucks' loyalty program, perhaps the most sophisticated one of its kind, does reduce the cost of a cup of coffee. I am also mindful that Starbucks has indeed created a "third place," as Schultz calls it, a home away from home where the ambience makes the more expensive coffee worth it. That experience will only be enhanced by three new additions to the Starbucks experience: homemade baked goods, fresh juices, and computer charging stations. That said, we did see a slowdown in European sales when the Continent experienced an extreme downturn, but even then Schultz adjusted once he realized the depth of the issue and managed to stem the declines in an impressive way. So Starbucks, while not immune to shrinking world growth, has been viewed skeptically by many big investors, something that Schultz has told me will be a wrong call as long as Starbucks offers the combination of value and choice to its millions of minions.

Still, though, since we are scoring these companies on a 1–10 basis, I think Amazon is a shopper's solution to harder times. Google may be susceptible to the wiles of customers not wanting to pay up for search and ads. Starbucks, we know, had problems in Europe during the downturn. The nod goes to Amazon. My scores are Amazon 10, Google 9, Starbucks 7.

Tenth Test: Can the company maintain or grow its margins?

Ahh, the hardest for last. This, the tenth test, has laid low many a company that you might want to buy, whether it be a tech, a bank, an industrial, an oil, a retailer or even a pharmaceutical company. Both Amazon and Google have been making substantial investments in growth initiatives, which have pressured margins over the near and medium term. But investors are giving both companies the benefit of the doubt, as these are strategic investments that are poised to grow the businesses long term. These investments have been key in sustaining continued penetration in developed and developing markets.

Despite some recent margin expansion in the latest quarter, Amazon is still at decade-low operating margins, and it needs to spend colossal amounts to maintain a global retail footprint. Its warehouse-build-out costs alone dwarf what most companies are willing to spend for any project. Margins are a bit of an afterthought for Amazon because it can show whatever margins it wants if it wants to sacrifice growth. Contrast this with, say, a packaged goods company, which is lucky to grow at 3 percent organically. The only way a packaged goods company can keep generating good earnings per share growth besides buying back stock to shrink the denominator that's used to divide into profit growth is to keep improving its margins. That's not the Amazon way, and we don't want it to be that way. Amazon isn't going to cut corners and fire its way to a higher stock price, it's going to grow there organically.

Google's margins have been declining from its high in 2009 because of heavy spending for new initiatives. I believe that if they don't stabilize, people will begin to question whether Google is spending too much, which at times has been a recurring theme. But as long as it keeps rolling out new products, the margin issue will not be a deciding point on a go–no go buying decision.

Starbucks has an entirely different set of margin issues. First, there is the raw cost of coffee. After spiking for multiple years it has now leveled and is even trending down, though I am still paying $5.07 for my triple venti cappuccino with skim, wet. It has tremendous labor costs; however, its throughput efficiency, augmented by mobile payment and advance ordering technology, has allowed for earnings leverage, as the same labor costs are amortized over many more clients per hour. When I recently attended the Starbucks analyst day, I gleaned that the expansion into China will raise overall gross margins as each store there makes more money per sale than stores in the United States. That's extremely important because the reverse leverage in Europe—from maintaining the labor force but fighting to grow sales—cannot be allowed to bring down margins, or the stock will suffer.

My takeaway: While the margins can't be as good as Google's or as unimportant as Amazon's, the price you pay for Starbucks' earnings is low enough that you can handle some gross margin degradation, even though that's typically unacceptable for most retailers and consumer goods companies. But then again, most retailers and consumer companies aren't Starbucks and they aren't led by Howard Schultz. Here I favor Google because, while it has been under some margin pressure, it still has a very low cost of goods sold; it's mostly done by computer or self-generated content, or by paying customers. Amazon, by nature, can't have good gross margins and will always struggle to maintain them. Starbucks has done a remarkable job at maintaining or improving gross margins. But I question whether that can be sustainable, because, at its core, Starbucks must reward people well to get the best associates, and coffee is a very fickle commodity.

Let's give Google a 10, Starbucks an 8 and Amazon a 7.

Who Triumphs over the Ten-Part Gauntlet?

So, when you add them all up, what do you see? They are pretty closely clustered, but I have Amazon as the winner with an 89 versus an 87 for Google and an 82 for Starbucks. Obviously if the stock prices were to shift, and shift dramatically, you might see a change in the ordering. There would certainly be a radical revision if any of them stumbled in their execution, which is why you must always do homework before you buy any stock, including these. For example, if the stock of Starbucks gets hit hard with no change in the fundamentals just described, it just might be too cheap to ignore versus the other stocks. But Amazon surfaces as the supergrowth vehicle to buy, with the biggest potential return and the lowest possible risk. Funny, because it trades at such a high absolute dollar amount it seems so risky, scary even, but I trust my test to elucidate and illuminate the reality of the situation.

SOMETIMES THIS RIGOROUS GAUNTLET can show you, in an unemotional way, how a company has fallen from Wall Street's grace and therefore needs to be cut back or eliminated from your portfolio.

Let's be brutal. Let's deal with the elephant in the room: Apple. The decline in Apple's stock price has mystified and befuddled both those who made so much money in the stock for so many years and those who love its products. How can a company with the greatest brand, the best devices, the most beautiful balance sheet, a sizable dividend, and the largest stock buyback perform so poorly in the time since it hit its high of $702 in the late summer of 2012, slightly less than a year after Steve Jobs's death? I think once you see how Apple fares in the ten-part test you will never ponder that question again.

First, does Apple have the potential for multiyear growth? The answer is yes, as the company's iPod, iMac, iPad and iPhone are all industry leaders. Apple sold 31 million iPhones in a recent quarter, up more than 10 percent from the previous year, and it is still a growing franchise, one that could accelerate with its latest, very well-received iPhone 5c and 5s. The company is executing well on the other business lines too, although growth is slowing for personal computers and iPods. Its tablets are taking an increasing share from the personal computer space, but growth is slowing and competition is increasing. However, without new, dazzling and unheard-of products this company does *not* have the potential for multiyear growth as defined by year-over-year comparisons. Given that Apple's only real growth comes from the cell phone, I would put the stock a notch down from the weakest of the trio just tested; call it a 6.

Second, how big is Apple's total addressable market? When we think of Apple's TAM, we are thinking about the sales capabilities of all the devices it is currently manufacturing. We know that the personal computer market is gigantic, but there is a degree of saturation that calls into question how much growth there really can be. iPods are essentially a no-growth business. Tablets have the ability to take sales from personal computers, but cannibalization isn't the kind of growth money managers are looking for. Finally, there are cell phones, particularly the kind of smartphones Apple sells. Right now there are about 5 billion mobile devices in use, but there are 7 billion people in the world, which makes for a 71 percent mobile penetration rate. About 30 percent of cell phones are smartphones, so 70 percent of the world's people can be considered potential customers. Plus, we are headed toward a multi-device world, where a person can be expected to have a cell phone, a tablet and a personal computer. Apple therefore has a lot of runway. I can see giving it a 10, like Amazon and Google.

But how about question 3: Does it have the ability to stay competitive? Under Jobs that was never an issue. No one could keep up with the explosion of fabulous products from Apple, products that could always command a premium price. Why not? Apple's products were vastly superior to those of its competition. Now, though, Apple's products, while still loved and respected by many, have lost their considerable advantage over Samsung, particularly when powered by Google's Android operating system. The issue isn't so much the superiority of Samsung as it is the inability to differentiate between the two, except when it comes to price, as Samsung's product costs much less than Apple's similar device. Think about this question in relation to question 2, the total addressable market. It is true that 70 percent of the world may not have smartphones, but a huge portion of that 70 percent is made up of poorer people who, most likely, will not pay up for Apple's brands. Give Apple just a 5 on this competitive scale.

The fourth category, the return of capital, is a solid 10 for Apple: it has the best balance sheet in the world. The company has an impressive buyback, and it has both initiated and then boosted its quarterly dividend to $3.05 as of the end of 2013. Nevertheless, as bountiful as that dividend might be, it didn't come into play as a floor for the stock until the mid-$300s. Not only that, but in the past couple of years the buyback has barely shrunk the shares outstanding, so it can't be counted on as a reason to buy the stock, unlike those buybacks I favor that take a huge chunk of stock out of the market. If it were truly reducing the number of shares, and if the dividend were to be boosted to a level commensurate with its cash generation, than Apple would be a 10. As it is, though, I can give it only an 8 because the buyback's not doing the job I like to see and the dividend was set too low to begin with.

Fifth, can it expand internationally? The company used to have a terrific record of international expansion, but it has hit a bit of a wall of late because its phones are often too expensive for most of the world's emerging markets. Apple's pricing scheme isn't an issue in the developed world because telecommunications carriers subsidize the consumer, choosing to eat some of the cost to keep its customers happy. But that's not the way many of the carriers do business in the emerging markets. There the consumer bears almost 100 percent of the cost. In those markets the poorer customers are buying low-priced handsets from a variety of providers. The wealthier customers, not as attuned to Apple's greatness and often enamored of Android, will not pay up for the iPhone, especially in China, the world's largest untapped cell phone market. This lack of an inexpensive device is a huge impediment to international growth, so Apple can be given only a 5 in this category.

Sixth, can the balance sheet support growth? Like question 4, Apple can do a lot of things with its overflowing cash hoard. Unfortunately it is not being used to support growth. The way to leverage that cash is to buy something that is growing. I have often suggested that Apple should use its cash to build an ecosystem that would dominate the living room and take share from the cable companies. For example, let's say that Apple had bought a content provider like CBS and then married that with a satellite provider like DIRECTV or a phone company like Sprint or T-Mobile if DIRECTV satellite technology can't scale. Then, to top it all off, it could have purchased the much-beloved Netflix, with its 40 million domestic and 10 million international subscribers, and its clear path for international expansion. That combination would have given all of the cable companies a run for their money. Or let's say Apple had decided to pony up $20 billion for Twitter. It could then have had a credible social strategy. Or it could have bought Yelp and have a platform for a new social and mobile initiative. It did none of these. It just sat there with the cash or returned capital via the dividend. While these acquisitions would have been expensive— and would now be very costly—Apple could have given the aggressive money managers the growth they want, not the dividends they don't need or care for. Apple needed to put that cash to work creatively. My conclusion: The balance sheet can't support growth because management doesn't care to buy that growth. Give Apple a 5 on this score. It would get a much higher grade if it used that money to buy more growth and less stock.

Seventh, is Apple expensive on the out years? No, it is ridiculously cheap. Too cheap, which is actually a bad sign. When you see a price-to-earnings multiple as low as the one Apple sports, that can mean only one thing: The earnings estimates for the out years are *too* high and are going to come down. That's right, Apple looks cheap, but if the estimates are going to be slashed, then it is very expensive because growth managers will not suffer through down years. Apple gets a 5 on this brutal part of the exam, as I fear that once the 5c and 5s sales run their course, Apple could have some leaner times ahead, even with a new, improved iPad on the horizon.

How about question 8: Does it have the right management? This is a loaded question. Who can follow in the footsteps of perhaps the greatest CEO of all time? Even as Apple has since produced some superior products, management may not have the kind of vision necessary to keep

Apple well above the fray. Give the team a 6. Why not lower? Because the trains run on time; the company does have clockwork precision in each iteration, with just a small number of mishaps.

Question 9—Does Apple need macro growth to meet numbers? This is a tough one to answer. In the United States the answer seems to be no, as sales held up extraordinarily during the Great Recession. Overseas is a different matter. Because of that high price point and low carrier subsidies, Apple's products are out of reach for much of the unserved and under-served market, given the world's lack of income growth and the percentage of the population in poverty. Poorer people are not going to upgrade devices to Apple's higher price point. Again, another 6.

Finally, question 10: Can the company maintain or grow margins? If you listen to an Apple conference call, you will hear question after question about declining gross margins. The analyst community is deathly afraid that Apple will have to cut prices to stay competitive with Samsung, and that would leave its margins in tatters. At the same time, I think Apple's management believes that its devices are so much better than Samsung's that the company can still command premium pricing. Without new devices that dazzle, however, margins will be under pressure for a long time. Again, Apple's stuck with a 6 rating. Why not lower? Because Apple still has a phenomenal brand name, and that has not been tarnished by the people currently running the company. The real issue here, however, is that Samsung now has a brand name too.

You add them all up and you get a 62, much lower than the number for Amazon, Google or Starbucks and definitely subpar when it comes to the possibility of Apple fulfilling the growth stock role for your portfolio. In fact, Apple's become much more of a value stock, and an attractive one at that, but not what you want if you are looking for a hyper growth stock. It's easy to lament, as we know when Jobs was alive this company might have been able to score a perfect 100. But, alas, he isn't, and it should not be a surprise that the company is not the same without him.

THIS STRINGENT TEN-PART TEST isn't just good for analyzing individual stocks in a vacuum. You can pit two stocks together to see which fares better, particularly when one stock "seems" a lot cheaper than the other. When I look back at comparisons I have made, for example, between

Pfizer, a slow-growing pharmaceutical company with a very low price-to-earnings multiple, and Celgene, a fast-growing biopharma with a much higher price-to-earnings ratio, it was obvious that Celgene was the cheaper of the two on a long-term basis, and it rallied accordingly. A few years ago I pitted Panera Bread with Chipotle and reached the conclusion that Panera was far cheaper with much less risk but more reward, particularly if anything goes wrong, and sure enough it did—for Chipotle, whose stock dropped 100 points in a day, although it did manage to recover, ultimately, from those losses. Sometimes the stock smackdown shows, however, that stocks are basically six or a half-dozen, as it did when I put MasterCard and new Dow Jones entrant Visa against each other. It was a total split decision.

These kinds of comparisons can lead to fewer mistakes and more confidence in the inevitable downturns, and I often use them when people email me or tweet me @JimCramer and want to know how their stock stacks up against others. I know the metrics and the quizzes. After that, it's pretty easy to figure out the answer.

I know that answering these ten questions before you pull the trigger on a stock is laborious, but as I point out, this book is not an exercise in getting rich quick, it is about getting rich over time, and when I say you have to do the homework before you buy a stock, and you have to continue to do it even after you have bought it, you now know which questions you have to ask when you do that homework. There are no shortcuts to great wealth. I sure didn't take any. You shouldn't either.

The Hidden Metrics

In every case when I am judging a sector, I find myself trying to assess how a company is doing versus others in its group on what we would consider an apples-to-apples basis. After many years as a generalist scrambling to figure out what the analysts really care about, I have put together this cheat sheet so you can quickly determine how your stock stacks up on the issue that matters for its industry. In each case, in light of that hidden metric, I will give you the best of breed in the sector it dominates.

AEROSPACE: Order backlog is all that matters for aerospace concerns. That's why each bulk purchase by a particular airline company means so much. Each adds to backlog, which then gives visibility to the earnings in the out years. The average new plane cycle—for the 787 Dreamliner, for example—lasts about seven years; the most lucrative years are the end of plane life, as the costs to make each plane at that point have dropped dramatically, sending margins through the roof. Right now you can't get a Dreamliner until 2019, which, of course, makes Boeing the best of breed in the group.

AGRICULTURE: Everything in the agricultural stock complex is based on the futures contracts for the individual crops. As long as they stay robust, farm equipment, fertilizer and seed stocks will all trade higher. The Department of Agriculture's crop reports impact the futures but have been unreliable because of changing weather patterns. So be careful using them as a predictor. Deere may give you the best predictions of the price of these commodities, but AGCO is now the undisputed best-of-breed stock.

AIRLINES: Airlines are judged by multiple inputs: fares, fees, seat miles and fuel costs. (Factor in age of planes, as the older ones burn too much fuel, the principal variable cost for airlines.) The industry lacks a best of breed right now, given that the Justice Department blocked the US Airways–AMR deal, which would have given us the best-of-breed player, but I do like the way Delta seems to be running things of late.

APPAREL: There are two key variables here: raw costs, which tend to be the same for every apparel company, and inventories, which control margins. If the stores won't take the apparel, it has to be discounted and usually sold to the Ross Stores and TJXs of the world. VF Corp. and PVH are both best of breed, with Ralph Lauren coming in third because it has been less consistent in its earnings reports.

ASSET MANAGERS: Assets under management determine the direction of these stocks. It's a simple metric, but when assets are coming out, look out below. The winner, hands down, is BlackRock, run by Larry Fink.

AUTOS: We measure autos on their percentage of the seasonally adjusted annual rate of cars sold. While U.S. sales matter, almost all auto companies are now global, so we care about units sold in both Europe and China, the former currently overshadowing the domestic market and the latter soon to eclipse the domestic market in terms of importance. Here Ford is the best-of-breed auto company and Magna is the best-of-breed auto parts concern.

BANKS: You would think that banks should trade on the number of accounts they have or their ratio of bad loans to current loans, but banks are measured almost entirely on their net interest margins, how much they can make off their deposits. Banks usually try to play it safe, investing this money as conservatively as possible, which often means that they are making very little money off your money. The way they can augment their net interest margin is by lending more, as they can make much more on loans than investing your deposits in safe bonds. These fixed income instruments do not currently give banks much of a return but they are superior to what banks pay depositors. However, lending has risk, and after the devastating times these banks have been through and the regulatory scrutiny they are now receiving, they have been reluctant to take on much risk, which compresses their net interest margins. JPMorgan is the best international bank, and Wells Fargo is the domestic champ.

BROKERS: Employee compensation determines how we build models that show profitability in the brokerage industry. Other data do matter, including number of trading days with profits and the amount of capital versus debt. But if you had only one metric, you would want to know how much the firm is sharing with its employees versus you, the shareholders. Goldman Sachs takes the honors here.

CASINOS: We care about "the handle," which is the total amount bet, and the "drop," the total amount exchanged for chips, including loans and the interest they generate. While all the major casinos are based in Las Vegas, Nevada, increasingly we care more about the guest count in Macau, where the Chinese are allowed to gamble legally, then we do about U.S. gambling numbers. Right now Wynn's got the edge over a very close-second Las Vegas Sands, as both have fabulous Macau operations.

CHEMICALS: Raw costs and volume growth are the metrics needed to compare chemical companies. Given that natural gas is the principal feedstock, the price and direction of that feedstock, coupled with posted price increases and decreases, determine the price of the stocks themselves. PPG is hands down best of breed.

COAL: Here's a business entirely based on inventories. If a company is stuck with a lot of inventory, its stock is headed down. I use the train company figures to assess the coal companies, as I trust the train companies to give you the straight dope. Peabody is the best, but only because the others are so horrible.

CONSUMER PACKAGED GOODS: These companies generate huge cash flows and buy up gobs of stock, so the actual earnings per share is no indication of how the business is really doing. What matters are margins and organic growth. Are the sales actually growing, particularly from new products, and is the company making as much money off those products as it should? Right now Colgate is the champ.

CRUISES: The metric here is an equation, called net yield. You take the ticket price, minus the cost of getting there, plus onboard spend, minus commissions paid to travel agents. This never fails to order the group. You measure the net yield against the overall bookings number. Obviously if a cruise ship is cutting ticket prices, you couldn't tell from the raw bookings number, so you must use net yield. The newly public Norwegian Cruise Line is the best of breed in part because of glaring operating problems at Carnival.

DEFENSE: We measure all defense companies based on their backlogs, *not* the announced projects out of Washington. If you followed backlogs, you would have known not to sell or short the defense contractors after the federal sequester, as they kept on increasing when the perception was that they would decrease. I think Lockheed Martin earns the crown in this sector.

DIAGNOSTICS AND DEVICES: These companies trade on approvals from the FDA plus hospital adoption. If approval is rapid and adoption strong, I usually expect a takeover within the next few years, as the companies in this space are serial acquirers. I prefer Becton Dickinson in this category, but Bard is also terrific.

DRINKS: The carbonated-soda companies all trade on sales volumes, and each company has a projection set by analysts that must be beaten in aggregate for the stocks to advance. Liquor trades on depletion, which means the sell-through from the warehouse to the retailer/restaurant. Nothing else really matters. PepsiCo does it for me, especially if there is further unlocking of value.

DRUGS: Here's an industry that is based on the pipeline: How many drugs might soon be up for approval and whether governments and insurance companies will reimburse users and for how much. Drug companies receive patent protection, which is normally twenty years, but the patent is applied for before the clinical trials begin. The time between patent and approval tolls against the protection, and that can mean that the actual protection may last somewhere between seven and ten years. I prefer to recommend the stocks of companies that make orphan drugs—drugs targeted for a smaller population that the federal government gives special incentives for and the insurers often pay hundreds of thousands of dollars a year for—because otherwise the costs of maintaining the patients without the drug could vastly exceed the cost of the drugs themselves. Johnson & Johnson steals the big pharma show under its new leader, Alex Gorsky, and Celgene is best of breed in the biopharma sector.

ENGINEERING AND CONSTRUCTION: The E&C group trades entirely on backlog. If it grows at a respectable pace, the analysts will raise numbers. If it drops, analysts will slash numbers aggressively and downgrade with abandon, which makes it a very tough, volatile group to own. Those engineering and construction stocks more geared to commercial real estate and the contractors and equipment they use live by the American Institute of Architects' monthly Architecture Billings Index, which is a terrific leading indicator, although it does not help determine which stock to buy. I like Fluor because, while it has a substantial energy business, it develops enough purely commercial property projects that it won't be hostage to power plant construction, which dominates the books of most of the competitors.

FOOD STOCKS: While all food companies have to purchase the raw commodities that go into their products, the price of the foodstuff itself matters little to the bottom line. What matters far more is the cost of the package, including the plastic and the cardboard, as well as the shipping to the store for sale. New products add to the bottom line and also preserve and augment shelf space, so I am intensely focused on the amount and number of new successful launches. However, if the company has to coupon, pay additional slotting fees to get good placement in supermarkets, and advertise heavily, then I am less likely to buy that stock, especially in an era when the store brand has been making such serious incursions in all supermarkets. After a long period of dormancy, Hershey has come on as best of breed here, reining in costs and taking aisle share, all in a very well-executed fashion.

FOOTWEAR: So often people react to the immediate sales and earnings numbers of footwear companies like Nike. That's not what matters. Those numbers are already past. You need to wait to examine the "futures" orders, which measure worldwide growth and estimates of product orders. Their acceleration and deceleration determine the direction of the stock, *not* the recent earnings or sales. Nike's a fabulous senior growth company with an amazing business in China and a growing one in Europe. But, believe it or not, Under Armour is now the gold standard in the group because of its superior growth pattern and large overseas opportunities that the hard-charging chairman, president, founder and CEO, Kevin Plank, is just beginning to exploit. If you have a lower tolerance for risk, go with Nike. If you want oxygenated growth, pick up UA.

GOLD: You would think that what matters the most with gold stocks is how much gold is selling for. But the metrics everyone is focused on are finding and developing costs. As gold gets tougher and tougher to prospect for and retrieve from the ground, we care about the cost it takes to find and get that gold to a smelter. The environmental costs of siting mines is enormous. The extraction costs have gone through the roof because of the now desolate and/or dangerous locations of the mines. The stocks have been a terrible way to play the price of gold because these costs have multiplied at a time when gold has stopped going higher. Randgold Resources is the best of a real bad bunch.

HMOS: The one metric you need to know about these wild traders is the medical loss ratio: the ratio of total losses incurred divided by the total premiums paid. The lower, the better. Tough call, but I think Humana has become the most consistent player in the sector.

HOSPITALS: These days, the only thing you need to know about hospitals is the reimbursement rates from the federal government. Given that they are pretty much the same, they trade in lockstep, so there's little stock differentiation. Just have to go with HCA despite the company's balance sheet and sluggish numbers.

HOTELS: We may care about which hotels we stay at, but when it comes to selecting stocks, all that matters is revenue per available room, also known on the Street as RevPAR, which is calculated by multiplying the hotel's average daily room rate by its occupancy rate. That's the perfect apples-to-apples comparison. Wyndham has done the most to bring out value. Starwood is the best operator.

HOUSING: Housing companies are graded on their backlog numbers, sales and how much they make per home. If a company can't close as many deals as expected, or if a lot of its deals are canceled, the stock will likely be downgraded *even if* it has legitimate reasons for the shortfall. Toll is the finest, but I like to play housing in ancillary ways, typically through the tremendous housing-related retailers like Lowe's and Home Depot.

INSURANCE: This industry trades on two components: the combined ratio and the quality of assets the company owns. The former is the only one that used to matter; it's a ratio of the losses and expenses incurred through claims to the amount of premiums taken in. If an insurer pays out more in claims than it takes in, the stock will get whacked. Of late the investment side of the ledger has meant a great deal too. The companies that took on the least amount of risk when they invested your premiums, notably Travelers, received the highest price-to-earnings ratios. Travelers deserves it; CEO Jay Fishman's shop is best of breed.

INTERNET: Traffic acquisition cost (TAC) has been the key metric we use to determine which company is doing best in the Internet world. TAC consists of payments made by Internet search firms to affiliates and other online companies to acquire traffic. It's a measure of whether or not a site is organically hot. We also care about the advertising cost per thousand viewers, or how much advertisers are willing to pay Internet sites for ads. Google's the benchmark here.

MEDIA: Advertising dollars and subscription dollars both matter now that many media entities charge for access to the web. Before the sub model changed, we cared about circulation, but that has diminished in importance now that sub fees have made up an increasing amount of revenues. I like what Gannett has done to augment both streams. Time Warner has done a fabulous job too. The Publicis-Omnicom combination will produce the best-of-breed player in advertising.

MINERALS: The cost of mineral extraction and the cost of getting the minerals to the market both matter. The location of the minerals to the big market, China, will determine the end prices, so if the cost to extract goes up while demand from China goes down, the stocks will crumble.

Vale, the Brazilian iron-ore company with many other fingers in other mineral pies, has done the most to improve itself and is now the strongest company in an industry with a history of overexpansion that has almost felled all of the entries at one time or another.

OILS: It is nuts to focus on oil earnings. They are impossible to understand. But oil replacement? That's the ticket. A growth oil is one that can find and replace reserves faster than they are being used. We also care about finding costs for domestic oil companies because if OPEC were to crater the price, many of these companies would instantly be on the ropes. Ask anyone: EOG is the clear best of breed in the group. ExxonMobil has been terribly inefficient at replacing its reserves, which is why the stock rarely seems to do much of anything and has way underperformed most other stocks in this, one of my favorite sectors.

OIL SERVICE: Monitor these through the Baker Hughes rig count. While these are international companies, they all mistakenly trade on how much drilling is going on in the United States. The rig count, released once a week, gives you the story, even though it shouldn't be the key metric. Sometimes you just have to let things go and say, "Even though this number shouldn't count that much, it does," and move on. Fortunately, one company, Schlumberger, rises above all others and is the must-own in the group.

PAPER: Paper stocks tend to trade in lockstep off the always fluctuating price of containerboard. But lately there has been enough consolidation in the business that we are able to distinguish among them by looking at raw cost inputs. International Paper, for example, has gone from a high-cost to low-cost producer through consolidation and cost cutting, so it goes up the most every time there is a containerboard price hike. International Paper is phenomenally run and is by far the best of breed.

PIPELINES: You pick a pipeline stock on whether it can raise its distributions. To forecast those, you have to look at their pipeline expansion plans. The more projects, the higher the distribution down the road. I also look at two metrics: the fee metric and the variability-to-price metric. I like pipelines with fixed charges; they are like toll roads. But some pipelines take price product risk. Those can yield more at times but are far more risky. When in doubt, just go with the fee-based carriers that have many projects in the works that will allow them to increase distributions.

Kinder Morgan Energy Partners is regarded as the Tiffany play, even though it does have some commodity risk, albeit small compared to most of its pipeline competition.

RAILS: We measure rails by contract roll-offs and repricings of new contracts. When contracts end and new contracts are entered in this business, they are almost always agreed upon at a much higher price than before. That's because there's not a lot of competition within the railroad business specifically or from other transport carriers in general. The more roll-offs, the higher the earnings. We also care about coal loadings and oil loadings. Coal can be shipped only by train, and the use of coal has diminished rapidly in this country. Oil can't make it up, but it has been the biggest factor in offsetting declining coal. Watch new track growth for oil as another important metric. If pipelines are going to be blocked because of environmental concerns, oil companies will shift to rail to bring their product to refineries. Union Pacific has been the most aggressive about building out train lines to the newly discovered oil shales, much faster than the others. Michael Ward has done terrific things with CSX, but it's too coal-dependent, which is why I think Union Pacific is the standard to measure all others against.

RESTAURANTS AND RETAIL STORES: We live or die by same-store sales numbers because overall sales tell us nothing. All you need to do is add stores to bring overall sales up, but when we compare how the same store did the year before with the current year, we get a much more accurate view of the health of the enterprise. I also care about inventory levels, but those are pretty much expressed within that same store sales number. Some like to use a sales-per-square-foot metric, but to me that's a nonstarter—it always leads you to Apple, which isn't much of a retailer at all.

For restaurants, we care about food raw costs because when they spike, the restaurants have to raise prices, and many can't do that without losing customers. Similarly, if a chain can "take price," or raise menu prices and not lose customers, then you could have a home run when food costs come down. Most restaurants aren't sensitive to specific costs, except for Buffalo Wild Wings, which requires you to monitor the price of wings to compute earnings. We also care about throughput numbers at quick-serve restaurants. Given that the labor costs are static, the more people that can be run through the restaurant at key hours, the more money the restaurant can make. So those that are most efficient in a measured way will see their stocks go higher. Two Seattle-based companies, Starbucks and Costco, stand out as best of breed in each category.

REAL ESTATE INVESTMENT TRUSTS: Lots of people try to use fancy ways to measure real estate investment trusts (REITs). All I care about is the occupancy rate and whether rental rates are going higher. If the vacancy rates are low and the rents are going higher, then I know the stock's a good REIT to buy—barring a huge spike in interest rates—because it means that the distribution will increase. That's why I recommend REITs. Don Wood, the CEO of Federal Realty, has turned FTR, a shopping center REIT with a tremendous history of boosting its dividend, into the best of breed of the traditional real estate players.

SHIPPERS: We monitor the Baltic Dry Freight Index, which measures the price of shipping dry goods by sea for the bulk carriers. We care about the Suezmax day rates (large oil tankers) to monitor how oil tankers are doing. Any spike in either leads to an immediate increase in the stocks of the ships that carry those cargoes. For packaging delivery companies, like Federal Express and United Parcel, we care about volume growth, both domestic and international, and we care about yields, as expressed by revenue per package. I also like to monitor overnight shipping versus regular, as a judge of economic strength, but that tends to be the same for all carriers. Both companies are best of breed; hard to distinguish between two of the best-run companies in the United States, although UPS has the superior dividend policy.

SOFTWARE: It's very difficult to compare apples to apples in the software business, but I like to look at the unearned revenues as a guide to future earnings. Advanced payments—or unearned revenues—are recorded as a liability until services are rendered, so they aren't obvious but they are disclosed. These are usually sizable because they represent licensing fees and annual maintenance charges that must be prorated. They give you the best indicator of what's to come. Salesforce.com takes the crown here.

TECH: It may sound quaint at this point, but we can still measure the health of a tech concern, like a semiconductor or a disk drive company, by its book-to-bill ratio, whether it is receiving more orders than it can ship. If it is, then it is possible that the average selling price can go higher, which would expand margins and increase earnings that would allow companies to beat and raise estimates. I follow the construction of new factories that would add to capacity and therefore trigger an oversupply of product. I also monitor yields, meaning how much product companies like Intel have to throw out because of imperfections before the assembly line starts to hum. You always have to be careful of new assembly lines because of poor yields; sometimes the manufacturers have to throw out about half the product at the start of a new run. Each quarter it gets better, but the bad yields have a huge impact on gross margins, which are critical to the bottom line. Tough one, but I still have to go with Google, as it is the best run and most creative in the sector.

TELECOMMUNICATIONS: You need to focus on churn when you think telco. These companies are always locked into dogfights, and the only real way to tell who is winning and who is losing, meaning losing customers, is to look at the magnitude of customer base churn. You were able to nail the bottom in Sprint when churn turned more positive, meaning that Sprint was able to start gaining customers and no longer losing them. You could bet on Verizon over AT&T because of low churn. Issues like spectrum and network quality matter, but that's exactly what churn takes into account and why it is so important. Verizon is the best run and shows no sign of losing its best-of-breed title any time soon, even as it just spent $130 billion to buy the rest of the Verizon Wireless stake that it didn't own from Vodafone, in a highly accretive deal.

UTILITIES: The overwhelming reason why you would choose one utility over another is a higher yield. Until the yield gets too high: that's a red flag that it's not sustainable, as holders of Exelon, the giant Chicago utilities company, found out the hard way not that long ago when the company slashed its payout by 41 percent. Utilities are regulated by states, and the states usually try to give the utility shareholders a break and allow for regular increases in dividends. But some utilities have opted to be merchants of power, and when electricity goes down in price their regulated businesses can't save them from profit shortfalls. I like to invest in plain old utilities that aren't trying to shoot the lights out with growth. Utilities that have consistently increased payouts because they have had nice slow rises in earnings are the safest bets to make, but remember, utilities are benchmarked against treasuries and they will all go up or down depending upon whether the interest rates on treasury bonds are rising or falling. That's far more important to the price action than anything fundamental to the companies themselves. Management of AEP has done the most to bring out value, but I think Dominion has the finest assets, the most shareholder-friendly management, the greatest growth story, and is the best-positioned player in the group.

Summary: Getting a View from the Source

1. First things first: Build a worldview of the macro forces at work around the globe so you can access the growth rates that determine so much of what ultimately makes a stock go higher.

2. Decide if you want a cyclical stock that needs worldwide growth, to "beat the numbers" or a growth-cyclical that needs less, or a discretionary play that's good for a slow growth environment or staples if there is little to no growth at all. Utilities, real estate investment trusts, and master limited partnerships can also work with no growth, but be careful of fixed-income equivalents. They might not be equivalent at all in a rising-rate environment and might mean more risk than you can handle.

3. Measure your company's growth rate against both the rate of growth in its own sector and the rate of world growth, if it is an international company, or domestic growth, if it is a company that sells only into the U.S. market. You need to make all of those comparisons if you want to identify less risky stocks that can give you a bigger reward in a difficult environment.

4. Get your top-down growth views from managements of companies on their conference calls. Caterpillar and Alcoa are best, but there are many others you must listen to if you are going to be informed about the global growth picture.

5. Run every stock through my ten-point test of growth metrics to see if it can match the gold standards of Google, Amazon and Starbucks.
   • Is there potential for multiyear growth?

- Is the total addressable market big enough to sustain growth?
- Can the company stay competitive against all comers?
- Will the company return capital to shareholders through dividends and buybacks, or are the growth opportunities too great and such capital returns would be a poor use of money?
- Can the company expand internationally?
- Can the balance sheet support strong growth?
- Is the stock expensive on the out years?
- Does the company have the right management to handle the growth?
- Does the company need macro growth to meet the numbers?
- Can the company maintain or grow its margins?

6. Understand which hidden metrics really matter in each sector, as they won't necessarily be the earnings per share. Know the best of breed of each sector if you want to invest in it and don't you dare trade down; it's just too risky.

CHAPTER 3

Seven Major Themes Built to Last

What's the key to successful long-term investing, to making money even in the most malevolent and confusing markets? You need to be able to identify the big-picture themes, megatrends that are ripe for the era we are in. And then you need to find the best-of-breed ways to play those themes. The right thesis can be a gold mine as long as you know how to get digging with the right stocks. These themes are what I call "secular-growth wealth creators." They aren't defensive; they don't have stunted growth but pay big dividends; nor are they cyclical, in need of a tailwind of economic growth to excel. They tend to be free of the everyday vicissitudes, ones that can hurt stocks, like Washington intrusion or a slowdown in Europe or China, and they are well positioned for upside in pretty much any environment. We always look for big-picture investment ideas that give you something to fall back on when the market gets hammered and that should participate when the market is strong—themes and names that transcend near-term disruptions. Doesn't mean that they won't go down; they do. Does mean that they bounce back harder and faster than most other stocks.

Remember, identifying these themes and the stocks encompassed by them isn't a license to buy and hold. Just because there's a powerful long-term thesis behind a company, that doesn't necessarily mean its stock is worth owning. You absolutely must do the homework, as I always empha-size. A theme is not an excuse for taking endless avoidable losses either. Wall Street is capricious, with different groups of stocks or sectors con-stantly gaining or losing favor. For example, when the economy is growing at a healthy clip, safe, consistent stable growers like the foods and the drugs will tend to get hammered or drift lower, no matter how good the underlying company, because money managers can always be counted on to play the rotation game I outlined previously and buy less safe, faster-growing cyclical stocks that happen to be in style at that particular mo-ment. But, believe me, that moment never lasts very long, so you need to think longer term about your selections.

So what's the use of banking on a nebulous theme if it won't make you money all the time? Simple. By familiarizing yourself with the best-of-breed plays on unstoppable trends, you'll know when their stocks become cheap as they go down and aren't just road kill that correctly roll over and are going to be consigned to the stock dumpster. When these best-of-breed stocks in the most long-lasting themes get hit, you know you'll get them at a bargain. In fact, they may be part of themes so strong that the only time you will be able to buy them at a discount is when the entire stock market throws a sale. Consider the best-of-breed players in the most compelling themes I am about to outline as being on a perpetual shopping list that must be activated when the entire stock market takes a tumble and pan-icked sellers conspire unwittingly with the stock futures and the ETFs to send down the whole market.

There is no such thing as a stock that you can own forever, one that works in any market, that's eternally in favor in the Wall Street fashion show, and is perpetually working its way higher. The investing game just doesn't work that way. But there are themes that you can count on no matter what, ne'er-to-fail themes with tremendous staying power, which you can always fall back on as a source of terrific, multiyear investment opportunities.

I'm betting these themes hold up not just for one or two but perhaps as long as five years as they play out in pretty much any environment. Careful investing requires you to have the wind behind your back because so many mistakes can be made unless you have the bigger picture in mind.

With that, let me give you the key themes I believe are built to last that you can return to, again and again, when others are drowning in the rough waters that surround you. Then I will give you the best-of-breed players in each of the seven built-to-last themes.

The first is new tech, the companies that have embraced the holy trinity of mobile, social and cloud and will be profiting from investments made now for years to come. Second, the beneficiaries of the desire of all Americans to look good and be healthy as they live longer than most ever thought possible a few dozen years ago. Third, the newfound virtue of value, as consumers demand bargains wherever they can find them and want goods that are known to last. Fourth, companies that buy other companies to take advantage of scale and synergy to dominate whole industries. Fifth is what I call "stealth tech," companies that innovate where you didn't think there was innovation in order to stay ahead of their competitors. Sixth, the new pharmaceutical companies, the biotechs that are replacing the old behemoths that crowded our parents' portfolios. And seventh, the renaissance in oil and gas that's happening in our country because of new techniques in finding and extracting crude oil from the ground.

1. Embrace the New Holy Trinity of Tech—Social, Mobile and the Cloud

Can anyone invest carefully in technology stocks? Do any of these stocks, which used to be the primary source of wealth creation in the stock market, belong in a prudent portfolio anymore? Aren't they just too risky? Well, yes and no. In the past few years, the vast majority of tech has become too risky to own. That's because so many companies in this group are beholden to the growth of personal computers, and that growth has all but disappeared. Personal computers are now in secular decline, meaning that each year we can presume that fewer and fewer will be used and that they will get cheaper and cheaper in value. That means the tech sector is filled with dinosaurs, unable to come to grips with the changing universe.

But not all of tech is part of the Paleozoic era. In fact, there's a cohort within this sector that's thriving, and it's just in its infancy. It's untethered tech that takes advantage of the Internet chiefly using mobile devices and uses the cloud, not expensive in-house servers, to store easily retrievable data. A successful tech company in this new world has to embrace at least two parts of the holy trinity of social, mobile and cloud. Tech stocks that don't harness at least one of these horses are destined to fail or fall behind to where they can't catch up, modern-day equivalents of the mainframe-based Goliaths, like Control Data or Burroughs, that were reduced to nothingness by IBM, with only Honeywell reinventing itself as a diversified industrial and the rest merging and stumbling into oblivion or holding on by the skin of their teeth.

That titanic struggle for relevance infects many a household tech name, everything from Microsoft and Intel to Hewlett-Packard and Dell and all of the companies that sell parts into their devices. How ironic that these companies, especially Intel, would be left behind when Intel's former chief executive officer Andy Grove detailed, in one of my favorite business books, *Only the Paranoid Survive*, how disruptive technologies, "10x changers," he called them, can wreck not just one-time technology innovators but any dominant, incumbent enterprise. "What such a transition does to a business is profound," Grove wrote, "and how the business manages this transition determines its future." These personal computer companies, with so much at stake in their core businesses, refused to abandon them and failed, spectacularly, at least so far, in managing that transition to be part of the cloud, mobile and social revolution.

The 10x game-changer that is the new tech trinity also felled the one-time colossuses Nokia and BlackBerry, both of which failed to recognize the need for smart mobile devices with touch-screen technology and open architectures, until it was too late and they too fell by the wayside, dragging many of their suppliers with them, although Nokia has been able to reinvent itself as a telecommunications infrastructure enterprise with the help of a gigantic payment to the company from Microsoft.

Even Apple, the inventor of the smartphone and the creator of the wildly successful tablet, has, to some degree, fallen behind because it failed to foresee the power of social media and exploit the cloud to its fullest. I have no doubt that had Apple bought Twitter, for example, and engaged deeply in social media, or had it purchased Netflix before that stock quadrupled, Apple's stock would be much higher. And if it had decided to dominate the living room with a cloud-based television network, the stock would be twice as high as it is today.

But enough of those who have stumbled against the holy trinity. Who has embraced it, and how will they continue to profit from it? Here are the five best-of-breed social, mobile and cloud plays that could reign for years and years. They not only saw the future but had no legacy to keep them from falling behind.

Google

Google, as I detailed earlier when I used it to show how to rate a super-growth stock, is the sultan of search, with more than 66 percent of queries in the United States and 75 percent of search advertising budgets. Its paid search business is still growing at more than a 20 percent annual clip worldwide and is incredibly lucrative precisely because the firm is so dominant. Of course, we're seeing a big migration in online advertising away from desktop-oriented ads and toward mobile, and Google excels at mobile. Here in America, more than half of smartphones run on Google's Android operating system. Unlike so many other web-based companies that were caught flat-footed by the speed of the switch to mobile, Google saw it coming. They'd been giving away Android for years, precisely so that they'd be ready for this moment. They make up the cost on the back end with queries and video, as they do own YouTube and all of its lucrative channels, but it won't be long before they monetize the front end too.

Google's AdMob business sells mobile display ads; in 2012 they captured 51.7 percent of the market, and they're still the number one player. Plus, the business is growing quickly because of its programmatic ad service that allows advertisers to skip the middleman and let Google place ads as advantageously as possible using proprietary algorithms.

Advertising is a $660 billion global market, and less than 10 percent of that is online. I think that percentage gets much bigger going forward, especially given the advertisers' desire to reach the younger demographic, particularly the millennials. That means a lot more money for Google, and that's just in the core business. Don't forget, Google is a truly global company that gets 54 percent of its sales from outside the United States, and the international side is growing rapidly. Can you imagine what would happen if they ever worked a deal with China, where Google has refused to compromise with the authorities? Unfortunately, I don't think that will happen, and it is the biggest drawback to the company's growth.

Google's balance sheet is a thing of beauty, with more than $50 billion in cash and marketable securities and a very small amount of debt. I'm also a believer in the management. It's cheap on the out-years' earnings and it's relentlessly focused on social, mobile and cloud innovation. Who doesn't want to own a stock that beat both Starbucks and Amazon in the growth stock bake-off?

Facebook

There's no question that the much-anticipated initial public offering of Facebook was a debacle. After coming public at $38/share on May 17, 2012, the stock started a hideous slide downward, bottoming at $18 a few months later on concerns that it couldn't monetize its 1.1 billion customers, who were quickly migrating from desktop to mobile. But all of that criticism dissipated when, in July 2013, Facebook reported a quarter showing accelerating revenue growth precisely because of its stunning newfound success in selling mobile ads. Now the company has gone from being scorned and belittled to being the belle of the growth stock ball. It's become a must-own for all who seek the highest of growth rates for both sales and earnings, even if it means buying the stock at a price-to-earnings ratio well in excess of Google's PE and nearing Amazon's stratospheric valuation.

After a couple of quarters when Facebook did seem genuinely baffled by the speed with which mobile had taken over as the primary way users identified with it, mobile has now gone from almost zero in sales to 49 percent of revenues a year later. In fact, Facebook now generates more mobile revenue per quarter than its entire advertising business did at the beginning of 2010, when it already had nearly half a billion users. Even though Facebook is showing its users more advertisements through sly embedded news stories, user engagement has actually never been higher. Skeptics had been worried that users would flee if they were subjected to too many ads, but in reality, as CEO wunderkind Mark Zuckerberg pledged on several of his conference calls when he said he would never allow ads to intrude on the user experience, the opposite has happened and users actually seem to like them.

After all, though, where the heck are users supposed to go? There's only one Facebook. Google is trying to compete with its Google Plus initiative, but the whole point of a social network is that lots of people need to be on it, and that's why Facebook is going to remain unrivaled in this business for years to come, a generation at the very least. So much for "Facebook fatigue" or arguments that it was losing its audience to the 140-character world that is Twitter.

The company's average revenue per user is increasing across the globe, and total monthly active users are increasing at a strong pace. So, not only does the company still have many more people using the site, but it's also able to make more money out of each set of eyeballs.

But what really impresses me about Facebook is the fact that the company is investing in its future. The company is hiring, and it plans to spend $1.4 billion on capital expenditures this year in order to expand the business. My friends' kids who are at the top of their college and business school classes seem to be clamoring to work at Facebook even more than they want to work at Google and much more than they want to work at Apple, but they expect to be rejected because of the degree of difficulty in landing a job there. This is an honest-to-goodness accelerating secular-growth story, one of the few out there, and I believe it could remain that way for many years to come.

Salesforce.com

Salesforce.com is the dominant software as a service company taking advantage of the cloud to revolutionize customer acquisition and relations management throughout the globe. Salesforce.com helps clients build deep relationships with their customers in a world where mobile and social media have transformed the digital landscape. Most important, this is *the* social media company for the enterprises, the large-scale corporations trying to increase sales for whatever business they might be in. This company and its visionary CEO, Marc Benioff, understand the current tech environment perhaps better than anyone else out there. So it's no wonder that Salesforce.com has given my viewers a phenomenal 800 percent gain since Benioff came on *Mad Money* in November 2008, right when everyone was convinced it would be the end of the Western financial world, and he told us that his business would be just fine. Benioff recognizes that this moment is a once-in-a-lifetime opportunity for him to acquire as many companies as he can to dominate in customer relations management—hence the symbol CRM. So, while many people criticized him for making too many expensive deals and moving too quickly, Salesforce.com was the quickest company to reach $4 billion in revenues, and I think $5 billion is right around the corner. I really like his most recent acquisition, the $2.5 billion ExactTarget deal, because it gives Salesforce a hammerlock on email marketing, which it has lacked in its considerable arsenal. The stock's not for the squeamish, and the bears are relentless in their dismissal of the company's success, in part because it is so richly valued even after it reports upside surprise after upside surprise—like the one in the summer of 2013, which moved the stock up about 20 percent in a single session. But I think Salesforce and Benioff have what it takes for CRM to be the dominant force in social, mobile and cloud marketing for years to come. If you doubt me, go to both Benioff's masterful conference calls and the company's website, where you can see countless well-known companies explain how Salesforce.com boosted their sales dramatically through the use of social and mobile marketing.

LinkedIn

LinkedIn has proven to be among the most successful offerings in the social media IPO cohort that blazed through the stock market in 2011–12. The leading professional network has over 250 million members globally, with a disruptive business model to address the recruiting market in a social fashion.

Revenue generation is diversified across three segments: Talent Solutions at 55 percent of sales, which provides recruitment solutions to enterprises; Marketing Solutions at 25 percent of sales, which helps brand development of enterprises targeting professionals; and Premium Subscriptions at 20 percent of sales, which helps individuals and small businesses access LinkedIn's network for recruitment and sales needs.

LinkedIn has focused in particular on emphasizing mobile technology, and it has a long runway of initiatives in the pipe. As the founder of TheStreet, a survivor of a bygone era, I am deeply in favor of Internet companies that can have both an advertising and a subscription model in case the advertising cycle turns even more vicious than it is now. That's why LinkedIn has been so successful; it is not overly reliant on frugal advertisers who know they can blanket social media without having to spend too much money to acquire customers. Plus, LinkedIn has become a loved brand, with many of us clamoring to be part of its Key Influencers program of writers who offer tips for work and life. I am looking for its international initiatives to provide the bulk of new revenue growth in the coming years, as this company and its dynamic CEO Jeff Weiner seem to have this growing category all to themselves, a virtual monopoly in a whole new industry that the company pioneered and in which it will be peerless for a long time.

Amazon

Amazon is already an online retail powerhouse, the Walmart of the web, with the widest selection of products, the lowest prices and the fastest, cheapest delivery. Amazon is a beloved company that has cultivated fabulous relationships with its customers, and most important, it's still taking market share all over the world. Amazon is like a bulldozer, putting brick-and-mortar retailers out of business first in books and then in consumer electronics, and perhaps soon in food retailing and apparel. Now the company has moved beyond retail with a huge cloud business, selling its own hardware, like the Kindle, in order to dominate online publishing. It's become a true online marketplace, where people and businesses can go to sell as well as buy things on the Internet, and Amazon's web services division takes care of all the shipping and handling. It's no wonder that some analysts believe Amazon's revenues can ultimately increase tenfold over the long term. That's the kind of growth trajectory that can get people salivating, as I showed you when I ranked Amazon so high using my ten-part high-growth stock test. Remember, Amazon has built this amazing network of warehouses and offers to handle the back office of so many companies that need an online strategy that it is now the dominant servicer of all Internet retail commerce.

Now, even though Amazon controls nearly 20 percent of all e-commerce in the United States and around 13.5 percent of international e-commerce, I think it still has tremendous capacity to take share. Why? Because this isn't just about e-commerce. When you look at total retail sales, online and off-line, Amazon accounts for less than 1 percent both in the United States and overseas. I have to believe that number is going to go much higher, as it's so much more convenient to buy things from Amazon, especially when you're doing any kind of comparison shopping.

Amazon has fabulous management, led by its tremendous visionary founder and CEO, the quiet, nonself-promotional Jeff Bezos. The balance sheet is terrific, with over $7 billion in cash versus just $3 billion in long-term liabilities, giving the company all the capital it needs to grow for years and years. Amazon has been ramping growth, and its third-party fulfillment business is especially profitable. Given that Amazon's growth path overseas is in its early stages, and given its ability to take share from brick-and-mortar companies worldwide, you can see how growth stock managers don't mind overpaying now for what could be gigantic earnings in the out years. In the end, as I detailed earlier, you are paying a premium for growth, but in a tech universe with very little growth to speak of, Amazon has become a cult stock for mutual fund managers. They can always justify buying more Amazon whenever new money comes in over the transom because the growth story here is more powerful than for any other company in the universe of stocks these managers follow. Oh, and of course, every portfolio manager shops there.

I KNOW THIS LIST is incomplete. Right now I have my eye on Yelp, which has embraced social, mobile and cloud to become the modern-day Yellow Pages, where customers pay to be listed under their services but users steer others to their favorites, harnessing that social touch that's so genuine. I also can see how HomeAway and Zillow can use social, mobile and cloud to help rent and sell real estate with meritocratic and empirical ease. Even a fallen star like Groupon, which uses on-the-go coupons, can regroup and exploit portions of the trinity, despite its sordid stock history. But these companies have a long way to go before they can stride among the fabulous five that are so profitable in the new world of tech, which looks nothing like the landscape of just a half-dozen years ago.

Summary: The Holy Trinity of Tech: Social, Mobile and the Cloud

Forget about old-fashioned technology. It's usually too tethered to personal computers. You need to hitch yourself to the new tech stars, those dominant companies that have social, mobile and cloud application. You need Google for search, Facebook for social media, Salesforce.com for customer relations software, LinkedIn for a professional services network and Amazon for all things retail. Only those techs will let you Get Rich Carefully. If you can buy only one, I'd pick up Salesforce.com; it has the best of social, mobile and cloud under one roof in the category and is reinventing the way companies sell just about anything to their customers.

2. Companies That Keep Us Healthy

Sometimes a fabulous investing theme is so immense it will cut a swath across a whole series of sectors. Eating more healthfully to live longer is one of those themes, and companies that keep us healthy will also make us wealthy. It's not obvious to the everyday investor where to find these stocks because we tend to take our cues from Wall Street analysts who follow certain groups of stocks by silo, and there is no "healthful eating" sector. There should be, though, because these kinds of stocks encompass the fastest-growing portion of several groups that analysts follow, whether they are in the supermarkets, restaurants or consumer packaged goods segments of the markets.

Stocks of companies that appeal to the desire of everyone, from aging baby boomers to teenagers, to look and feel healthier by watching their weight, monitoring their diet for the "right" foods and, perhaps most important, steering clear of the wrong ones, have been among the best-performing equities in this market for several years now. This theme is gaining steam, though, and we've got some terrific stocks with tremendous resiliency to invest in to exploit it. The companies that can prove they have the ethos and understand the needs of the skeptical, health-seeking consumer will have multiple years of success ahead of them, mostly at the expense of the companies that either haven't figured it out or don't have the DNA to do so because they are so rooted in the old ways of unhealthful eating.

Perhaps because at one time or another I've had to feed vegetarian and vegan daughters, I've been wise for ages to the companies that purvey natural and organic foods. It used to be difficult to find restaurants to take the girls to or food to bring home. Not anymore. Organic food is now a $63 billion industry worldwide, and it's growing at a 9.5 percent clip here in the United States. That's incredible, considering that food plays tend to be slow and steady growers, not ultra-fast ones. But the real source of strength here has less to do with the numbers and more to do with the culture of the consumer and the inability of most businesspeople to adjust to the change.

The fact is, nearly 36 percent of American adults over the age of twenty are now obese. We're in a desperate fight against fat, and everybody knows it, especially the younger generation. That's one big reason why people increasingly care more and more about what they put into their bodies. And these days, eating healthfully isn't just about looking at the calorie count on the back of the packaging or eating fewer servings or going all Atkins and cutting out carbohydrates. It's not just about the ingredients in your food, although obviously all of these things matter. For the truly food-conscious today—and they have become a large cohort—it's about the provenance of the ingredients, the way the fruits and veggies and grains were grown, the way the cows and chickens and pigs were raised. Is your meat shot full of hormones and unnecessary antibiotics? Were your coffee beans picked by Juan Valdez personally and paid for using the best fair-trade practices available? And so on.

Of course, that's a lot to keep track of, and for the rising tide of people who really care about this stuff, it's very difficult to just go to a regular supermarket and put every single product you're thinking of buying under the microscope. Doing that for your entire diet would be a full-time job. Which brings me to the first group of stocks that dovetail the theme: organic, health-conscious grocers where we're going to buy our ingredients. Many people marvel that a place like Whole Foods, the country's premier natural and organic supermarket chain, can get away with charging such high prices for its food—hence the old saw "Give a man a fish, he eats for a day; teach a man to shop for fish at Whole Foods, he'll be broke within the year." But for the dedicated organic and natural food crowd, and even people who are just looking for good-tasting food that's also good for you, Whole Foods has something incredibly valuable: their trust. You go to Whole Foods and you know that everything in there has the company's good housekeeping seal of approval. And believe me, these guys make it very difficult to get food in their stores unless it meets their exacting standards. Besides the organic crowd, you also have a cohort of wealthier people who are willing to pay up for food that's simply a cut above what you can find in a typical grocery store in terms of quality. Given the *Tale of Two Cities* nature of our economy lately, where those at the top of the income spectrum are doing just fine, the kind of consumer who shops at a place like Whole Foods is far from strapped.

At $20 billion in market capitalization, Whole Foods is the biggest and best-run purveyor of natural and organic food, with 350 stores in the United States, Canada and the United Kingdom. The company regularly puts up the highest-growth comparable-store sales numbers of any large supermarket chain, and it has the ability to expand to a thousand locations, nearly triple the current store count. In other words, the growth story is still in its early innings. The company plans to add thirty-three to thirty-eight new stores in 2014, which would be 8 to 9 percent store-count growth, and I anticipate that expansion to accelerate to as many as fifty new locations per year after that. So the growth is still almost as far as the eye can see. Meanwhile, Whole Foods' older stores, ones that have been open for more than eleven years, they're still performing quite well, with 5.8 percent same-store sales growth in the latest quarter, unusually high numbers for any retail chain in this environment.

Right now Whole Foods is selling for thirty times 2014's earnings, with a long-term growth rate of nearly 19 percent—not too pricey—and it's only trading at twenty-seven times earnings when you back out the $6 of net cash per share on the balance sheet, money that could be used for buybacks, dividend boosts or growth-enhancing acquisitions. Look, always remember that the best-of-breed stock in a space never comes cheap, and Whole Foods is no different.

I have spent a lot of time with the Whole Foods team, especially co-CEO Walter Robb, and I can tell you that this company is constantly incubating ideas to bring out value for shareholders, from rolling out private-label goods that customers seem to like more than much of the branded product out there, enabling the company to charge more for its store brand than just about any other retailer, to developing smaller stores to fit into smaller areas in ever smaller towns or to open near college campuses, where the demand is off the charts. It's developing new concepts, like the gigantic store built next to the Gowanus Canal in Brooklyn, with a massive greenhouse on its roof to grow fresh vegetables instead of having them shipped from far away. It's going to underserved urban areas, like inner-city Detroit, which has few supermarkets as it is. And for those who think that the company may already be cannibalizing itself with too many stores, consider that the Brooklyn store is the only Whole Foods in that borough of 2 million people across the East River, or that Boston, where Whole Foods just added a half-dozen Johnnie's Foodmaster stores all at once to an area already supposed to be saturated with seven stores, has among the best comparable stores within the chain. Whole Foods has had tremendous success developing regional offerings, everything from fresh Whole Foods beers to spas within stores. Perhaps most important, in an era when loyalty programs using social and mobile methods have been accelerating sales at outfits like Starbucks and Panera, Whole Foods will soon be rolling out an affinity program that's meant to put all others to shame in its ability to entice loyalty in what's becoming a crowded contingent in the supermarket universe.

What about the competitors? Wall Street knows a good thing when it sees it, and the investment banks have been pumping out new stocks to meet the demand of investors who seek the best natural and organic supermarkets, finding the "next" Whole Foods, if you will. There's The

Fresh Market, a rapidly growing competitor, with 130 locations, mostly in the Southeast, which, like Whole Foods, believes it can triple its number of stores. TFM trades at twenty-eight times earnings with a 20 percent long-term growth rate, but I'm somewhat concerned about the company's regional to national potential. It's going to be tough for The Fresh Market to break into the Northeast, where the private Trader Joe's and Whole Foods have such a strong hold. There's reason to worry. In a recent conference call, Fresh Market admitted that numbers coming from its newer stores have been subpar, something that's never happened to Whole Foods when it had rolled out new iterations.

How about the recent IPOs in the organic grocery space? These have all been on fire, but I find them suspect. Natural Grocers by Vitamin Cottage (NGVC) came public in 2012 and almost immediately doubled in market cap, and the sixty-eight-store chain is expanding rapidly. But it's too expensive for me, trading at fifty-eight times next year's earnings estimates, almost twice what Whole Foods sells for. You can't pay up for not-tried-and-not-true versus the best of breed.

Then there's a store chain that New Yorkers know well, Fairway, which came public in April 2013 and roared up 75 percent almost immediately. Again, while a popular favorite among the extreme loyalists who shop there, the chain is in its infancy and yet sells at an exorbitant ninety-one times next year's numbers. And even though I initially misjudged the power of Fairway's name and its luster—something that's pretty silly when you think about it, as the gigantic billboard above its beautiful Harlem store had a picture of me and my *Mad Money* logo for a huge part of 2013—I am not going to countenance paying ninety-one times earnings for anything, not even a biotech.

Then we have the most recent IPO in the group, Sprouts Farmers Market, which came public in 2013 and immediately jumped 122 percent on its first day of trading. While many say that Sprouts is the first real challenge to the natural and organic emphasis of Whole Foods from this group, I am urging you to wait and see. The pressure of growth coming from Wall Street to grow willy-nilly is often too great for young managements to bear for this already expensive-on-earnings growth stock. I found it telling that most of the big Wall Street firms were neutral or suggested you sell this stock when they rolled out coverage shortly after it came public. They must be worried too.

What matters to me is that you own the best of breed. Remember, we are trying to game an uncertain market that can send stocks down, and down hard, for no obvious reason. You don't want to be buying Fresh Market or Fairway when that happens. You want to buy the stock of the proven operator with the best balance sheet and some of the best management in any industry. You want to buy Whole Foods.

How about the companies that actually make natural and organic foods? I like this theme because consumers in America, especially younger consumers, are increasingly conscious about what they eat, not just in terms of whether or not it's fattening but where it comes from and whether the ingredients were raised naturally, without all sorts of chemical junk added to them.

There are currently three organic and natural food stocks. Hain Celestial is the largest player in the space, with a host of brands you might recognize: Celestial Seasonings, Earth's Best, Terra, Garden of Eatin' and Greek Gods Yogurt, among many others. Then there's Annie's, a smaller player that just came public in 2012, which is focused on selling healthful meals, snacks, dressings and condiments. Last but not least, there's WhiteWave Foods, the organic and natural player spun off from milk titan Dean Foods last October. WhiteWave sells organic dairy products, as well as soy- and almond-based dairy alternatives—think Silk brand soy milk.

How do we decide among these three healthful-eating names? First of all, we need to consider their growth prospects. Let's start with White-Wave. Here's a stock that has done little since its spin-off because of supply chain issues that have held back its growth. It has basically been trading sideways. But I can see Wall Street warming up to WhiteWave, because it has some terrific growth drivers and because portfolio managers want more than just one entry in this fast-growing category. The company's premium dairy business, Horizon Organic Milk, is growing in the mid-single digits. However, the area where WhiteWave really excels is plant-based beverages, basically soy and almond milk. Soy milk has been around for a while, but almond milk is the hot new thing, which is why this category has solid double-digit growth. Plant-based offerings are much cheaper to produce than whole milk, but WhiteWave can charge pretty much the same price, a tremendous advantage that's still not "in" the price of the stock. The company also has a strong dairy and nondairy creamer biz, although it has to compete with Nestlé, which currently dominates this category.

Then there's Hain, run by the irrepressible Irwin Simon. This company is controversial because it's expanding like wildfire, including into Europe, and it has been aggressively taking aisle space with everything from organic cleaning and personal care offerings to juices, teas, snacks, soups and baby foods. Hain already has a killer position in Whole Foods, with a ton of aisle space, but these guys really know what they're doing, they are the unparalleled experts, and I think there's more room for the company to expand. Short-sellers had been gunning for Hain for several years now, saying that it has no real growth and has masked that weakness with expensive acquisition after acquisition, in categories of dubious value. I think that's nonsense, and the earnings Hain put up in 2013 prove that. Not only has Hain now delivered growth at twice the pace of most food companies, but its European bets are paying off with stronger growth even than in the United States. No wonder the stock rallied ten points on one of its best quarters ever, which put to rest the short case, perhaps once and for all.

How about Annie's? Here's the company with the fastest growth in the cohort, but because Annie's is also the smallest of these three players, you need to remember that it's growing off a pretty tiny base. Annie's is coming out with new categories, like microwavable mac-and-cheese cups, as well as more frozen foods, all exciting stuff. But they just don't have the product breadth of a Hain Celestial, and that does concern me.

However, when I interviewed the CEO, John Foraker, on the floor of the New York Stock Exchange not that long ago, I could see where this brand, so popular with young mothers, has the possibility of accelerating revenue growth. That's because its healthful snacks are viewed as the alternative to so many packaged goods offerings from Campbell Soup's Pepperidge Farm division as well as Kraft and Frito-Lay. Its frozen foods entries are also gaining in popularity. Annie's is one to watch. I just wish it weren't so expensive compared to the much more entrenched Whole Foods. Nevertheless, I would recommend its purchase when there's any broad market weakness; I think this company could ultimately supplant the competition from the old-line behemoths Kraft and Campbell's, as younger shoppers simply don't trust the DNA of those older, somewhat fossilized companies. Plus, Annie's has a halo that can't be tarnished because it is viewed as the healthful alternative to the Goldfish and macaroni-and-cheese that parents used to serve up, before we started worrying about preservatives and excess amounts of sugar and salt.

While all three of these companies have runways for tremendous growth, I think the best of breed here is Hain, in part because it has been at it for so long and in part because CEO Simon has the pulse of this sector and, most particularly, the stores that he sells into. WhiteWave is the cheapest of the group relative to its growth rate, and Annie's has the fastest growth of the three. But I want tried-and-true, and that means Hain's the best choice for your portfolio. I could easily see it go up another 50 percent within the next couple of years, given Simon's shrewd acquisition story and his recent line expansions into juices that are grabbing aisle space in all sorts of conventional stores desperate to show organic and natural food credibility. And I would never rule out the possibility that if Hain stumbles, even for a quarter or two, a General Mills, a Nestlé, a Kraft or a Kellogg will come in and buy the whole company, because this part of the supermarket is starting to take a great deal of share from the old-line packaged goods companies. That's a threat to their very existence that only an outright buy of Hain might be able to cure.

The healthful and organic theme has been a huge spur to certain portions of the restaurant industry too. Chipotle and Panera are two chains that have become the "more healthful" quick-service restaurants. They have a huge hold on the millennial demographic, especially when compared to the complex exemplified by McDonald's and its peers, Burger King and Wendy's.

The superbly managed Chipotle has ridden a wave of skepticism to outright anger about the way food is made and sold in this country, and its Food with Integrity program and the tremendous loyalty it inspires has given Chipotle a growth path that is the marvel of the industry. In the world of quality quicker serve, Chipotle is about as amazing as they come.

I marvel at the commitment to infuse all of its management with the ethos of organic eating. I am blown away by management's careful and considered expansion, choosing employees from the best stores to manage new stores. Sometimes I think that those who go to Chipotle are part of a club—or even a cult—of people who are mad as hell at the processed-food chain and aren't going to take it anymore. These customers seem to be motivated more by the quality of the food than the fact that it's Mexican, and that means the company can charge more for its food than it would otherwise, hence the higher gross margins than most restaurants are able to obtain. Frankly, from my point of view as an interviewer, it is a delight to work with Chipotle because I think the team who runs it has a better understanding of the need to eat healthfully in order to live longer than any other management team save Whole Foods. That allows them to stay on point despite the difficulties of procuring food and finding employees that can measure up without having to charge a price that's beyond the average consumer. Of late Chipotle has been a tad inconsistent given its extremely high price-to-earnings multiple; that's why it could fall 100 points after a shortfall of some magnitude. But I chalk that up to the difficulties of expanding in a way that pleases Steve Ells and Montgomery Moran, the co-CEOs. They take their time. They do it right.

The big concern I have is that the management is so doctrinaire in its policing of the food chain that this nation will not have enough farmers equally as committed to their ethos to be able to produce the ingredients up to the standards of their Food with Integrity culture. But so far they have been able to pull it off with just a little bit of same-store lumpiness.

Of course, maybe that's why I like to go to Chipotle so much and trust the company's food implicitly, which is a lot more than I can say for most other quick-serve outlets. Chipotle is one of just a handful of companies, including Amazon, Google and Facebook, that younger investors like to buy simply because they like the experience. That's something worth considering every time the stock is hit, as that young stock-buying cohort will be with us for many years to come.

That said, Chipotle has become more of a trading vehicle than I prefer, which means it's a buy when it has come down a great deal. And it does need to be traded around after most big advances, ringing the register and taking some stock off the table in order to buy it back lower, a strategy you have to accept after the company's stock dropped 100 points in a day on a missed quarter.

That could change, however, as Chipotle begins to expand overseas, where I believe its greatest growth could be had. People in other countries have an even greater commitment to eating natural and organic food but lack quick-serve restaurants committed to the same culture. I believe Chipotle's best years lie ahead of it because of that international growth path. Plus, Chipotle is readying a second concept, ShopHouse Southeast Asian Kitchen, which may be able to augment the Mexican-based chain's growth. If it's as successful as the similar Noodles & Company, a chain of over 360 stores that recently came public, run by the Chipotle émigré Kevin Reddy, then you could see accelerated growth from CMG, which could smooth the occasional rough patches that have caused such volatility in its stocks.

The only rival to Chipotle's commitment to food that's thought to be better for you is the Panera Bread company, run by Ron Shaich, the chairman, CEO and founder, whom I salute elsewhere in this book as one of the Bankable 21 CEOs. Panera is a terrific story, and I believe can remain one for some time, given the dearth of urban Paneras in what is basically a regional-going-national chain. I would not have put Shaich in my personal pantheon if I didn't think that his company has the consistent growth needed for its stock to continue to power higher. Panera has a constantly changing menu of reasonably priced fresh foods, many of them low-calorie, and it has inspired an incredibly loyal following in the millions. But the restaurant chain is not necessarily dedicated to the concept of organic food as much as it is simply a really good place to eat fresh food, so it may not be fair to lump PNRA into this powerful long-term secular-growth theme. A recent earnings stumble has me concerned here, although I think that Shaich has the management skills to right the ship quickly, especially given strong customer loyalty, as the My Panera loyalty program has more than 15 million customers enrolled.

I also am keeping an eye on the aforementioned Noodles & Company, which has a totally new concept, a faster-food restaurant that produces individually made, natural-ingredient foods served by a waitstaff that is not supposed to be tipped. I have met management and tried the food; both are superb. But the stock trades at north of 100 times earnings;

that's just too speculative to be included in a theme that's meant to be put into place when the market goes awry for reasons extraneous to this sector. I just fear that there could be a stumble in this fresh-faced offering and that it will come back to haunt us. More years as successful as 2013, however, might make me less reluctant to recommend the stock in the future. It's most definitely one to watch, though, and I am excited for its long-term prospects.

Finally, I would recommend taking a hard look at GNC Holdings, which is rapidly becoming the dominant player in vitamins and supplements in this country. The retail vitamin business has become a crowded segment, but GNC, through its intense loyalty program, which includes an upfront payment for a card that 6 million people have been willing to buy, has been able to pull away from the competition. It's clearly best of breed in the supplements space. The company has been an innovator, with multiple new private-label product lines refreshed regularly, and its online business has been exceedingly robust, growing at about 35 percent a year, negating worries that it is losing share to Amazon. It has had consistent high-single-digit comparable-store sales, with more than 6,000 stores in the United States and 1,800 outside the country. I like GNC's growth path; it doesn't have all that much execution risk, and its price-to-earnings multiple is lower than one would expect, given how it has been eviscerating the competition.

This health theme will, I believe, make you wealthy over many years to come. As the millennials age, you can count on the total addressable market to continue to expand. The theme is so disruptive that all packaged goods providers, supermarkets and restaurants that don't embrace the ethos could become like the dinosaurs of tech, made obsolete by something that's simply not good enough for the discerning consumers of the future.

Summary: Healthful Eating, Wealthy Portfolio

The desire to live longer by eating organic and natural foods is a theme that's still in its infancy. You have a variety of ways to invest in this theme. Whole Foods now stands for a good housekeeping seal of approval for its entire line of natural and organic foods. Hain, WhiteWave and Annie's represent the best bets in natural and organic foods. Chipotle and Panera are both about eating out in a more healthful, more natural way. And GNC Holdings is the growth retailer when it comes to nutritional supplements. If you can own only one, it's worth buying Whole Foods.

3. The New Frugality

While the Great Recession may be behind us, it has spawned a whole new generation of penny-pinchers that, though not as severe as those with a Great Depression mind-set, are certainly not going to revert to their previous free-spending ways. Bargain hunting has gone from being the province of the lower and middle class to being the mainstay for many, including the wealthy, who are committed to finding value in every purchase. Frugality has become an ethos extending across all forms of consumer spending, from where to shop to where to vacation and where to get goods and services.

This theme has multiple prisms. One of the strongest is the desire to buy hard goods, goods that last, versus more ephemeral purchases. That change cuts to less extravagant spending on apparel and more on goods for the home, particularly now that home prices are rising. Of course, the obvious themes here are Home Depot and Lowe's, both of which are doing exceedingly well. Their aisles are stocked with the best merchandise at prices far lower than the local hardware store. As Frank Blake, the amazing CEO of Home Depot, has said on his recent conference calls, homeowners who have mortgages that were underwater and are now above the surface are willing to spend far more on their homes than those who haven't yet been able to get out from under. That's produced an acceleration in sales for both Home Depot and a newly aggressive Lowe's, which, in 2013, at last closed the quality and earnings gap between the two. I like them both.

Of course, Amazon is part of this cohort, as its price-comparison work for all goods, but especially hard goods, has given value a transparency unheard of before the Internet and has led to the downfall of many a retailer who couldn't deliver value.

But I think the foremost retailer for value is TJX Companies, run superbly by the totally nonself-promotional Carol Meyrowitz. TJX, which includes T.J.Maxx, HomeGoods and Marshalls, has delivered the most consistent set of numbers of any retailer I follow. These days, though, because of the woes of retailers who are perceived as not offering bargains to consumers, TJX has really begun to shine. Inventory is the bane of all retail, and traditional retailers who carry a great deal of apparel have now been caught for several quarters with too much of each seasonal offering. That means they have to dump clothes at fire-sale prices, and it is TJX that has the cash to take that merchandise off their hands. I believe TJX will exploit this edge for many years to come, as there appears to be a wholesale shift away from expensive apparel until it gets marked down, and TJX is the ultimate markdown store. Plus, Meyrowitz has brought this same concept to Europe, where TJX stores have shown amazing numbers, once again because the European economies have been quite weak for some time. Don't overlook the incredibly powerful HomeGoods store as a place where homeowners with houses that are rising in value will shop for housewares.

There are other off-price retailers that are beneficiaries of this value trend and the need for larger chains to lay off merchandise, but I think another obvious and consistent way to play this shopping theme is with Tanger Factory Outlets, a secular grower within the real estate investment trust sector that has tapped into the desire of upscale retailers to own the bargain-basement customers who would not normally be inclined to shop at a strip mall. Steve Tanger, a frequent visitor on *Mad Money*, has chosen locations near expensive vacation areas, perfect for the inevitable rainy days. "In tough times people need a bargain," Steve often says, "but in good times they want a bargain." He's captured the theme well. Tanger malls include entries such as Off 5th, the Saks Fifth Avenue outlet, and Nordstrom Rack, as well as retailers we don't normally expect to find in outlets, including Pottery Barn, Armani, Barneys, Ralph Lauren and Eddie Bauer. Tanger has been able to raise rental rates consistently because of a dearth of new mall construction, courtesy of the long-running credit difficulties that all contractors face. That shortage of new space has allowed the company to bump its distribution every year in a fashion that only a handful of REITs have been able to deliver.

Where else is the consumer finding value he loves? Private label is a great example, and the best at it is Perrigo, the premier manufacturer of so many of the store brands that we've all become accustomed to seeing at a Walgreens, Rite Aid or CVS as well as many supermarket chains. Perrigo's strengths are many. First, it has been first to market with many drugs that go off patent and go generic. Second, it has become the best way for big chains to boost their gross margins; drugstores can charge the public almost the same price they would offer for the wares of the likes of Colgate, Procter & Gamble and Johnson & Johnson, but they pay Perrigo far less for the privilege of supplying these store-branded products. Third, the recent recall fiascos of all sorts of over-the-counter drugs made by Johnson & Johnson shifted consumers to the store-label brands in many aisles of the drugstore. Consumers rarely return to the branded breeds because the quality is almost entirely the same. Before the Great Recession these products had a stigma that made customers feel poorer. Now they just feel wiser. I expect Perrigo's recent acquisition of the Ireland-based Élan to produce accelerated earnings growth, as Perrigo is able to reduce its tax bill by two-thirds because of the cheaper tax rates Ireland offers. I don't believe those gains are currently reflected correctly in the earnings estimates that analysts are using, and that could create a nice spur to the stock in the years ahead.

Consumers are far more aware of costs in pretty much every corner of their life, and that extends to car repair. That's led to some fabulous price appreciation in AutoZone, the best-of-breed do-it-yourself car servicing company. AutoZone is the country's leading auto parts retailer, and its business, always consistent, has accelerated markedly ever since the Great Recession. It's got more than 5,000 stores in the United States and Puerto Rico, as well as about 150 hub stores for commercial customers. The company has posted consistent, turbocharged growth, with perhaps the most aggressive buyback of any major company, allowing it to shrink the float by 50 percent in six years' time. Plus, AutoZone is benefiting from all the dealerships that have been closed, courtesy of the Great Recession and the restructurings of GM and Chrysler. Importantly, AutoZone has focused its do-it-yourself businesses in blue-collar areas and offers service bays in more white-collar areas to capture their do-it-for-me business—an area where it is focusing on growth.

Almost all restaurant chains have noticed a marked slowdown since the Great Recession, as consumers have been far more willing to forgo trips to these eateries to make meals at home. McCormick, the Baltimore-based spice king, had seen sales humming along in a fairly slow and steady clip until a recent acceleration directly related to this all-encompassing bargain theme. McCormick has huge market share in almost every supermarket in the United States, not to mention a big presence in Europe and a growing one in the emerging markets in the Middle East and Africa. If you're looking to buy spices, herbs, marinades, seasonings or mixes, you're probably buying McCormick's brands because they practically own these categories. And if you buy private label, you're buying McCormick too, as the company controls roughly 50 percent of the domestic market for private-label spices and seasonings. CEO Alan Wilson has managed to beat back plenty of competition with that dual branded–off-brand model. McCormick's institutional business, mostly to restaurants, has been slow since the Great Recession, but that's been more than made up by stay-at-home cooks.

Consumers now seek out value in vacations as they never have before. It all starts with the use of Priceline, the online bargain-hunter site for airlines and hotels. This company has put up fantastic numbers while it expands from domestic to international, and harder times across the globe have led to increased sales as it has pulled away from all of its competition. Wall Street analysts, perhaps because they are often rich and, yes, snobs, have continually misunderstood and underestimated this terrific company, which has become the de facto way to travel for tens of millions of people around the globe.

But just as important is finding a bargain in the vacation itself, which more and more often means a trip to an amusement park. Disney has been a big beneficiary of this trend, but with all of its other entertainment arms, it's not much of a pure play. The two best selections to fit this portion of the value theme? Cedar Fair, with the easy-to-remember symbol FUN, and Six Flags, known by its SIX symbol. Six Flags is the largest regional theme park operator on earth, with nineteen theme parks, water parks and zoological parks across North America. And Cedar Fair is not far behind, with eleven amusement parks, seven water parks, and five hotels.

These two companies pay out very high distributions, far more than most publicly traded companies, because they throw off a huge amount of cash. They routinely raise those dividends each time they open new rides. Given the difficulties of opening competitive parks because of insurance, zoning and permitting concerns, there's not a lot of competition coming in to this space any time soon. And the only other publicly traded player in this industry, SeaWorld, is a high-cost operator that failed to deliver on earnings forecast in the first quarter of public trading. That's an "avoid at all costs" situation.

Both Cedar Fair and Six Flags, whose representatives are frequent guests on *Mad Money*, have terrific, conservative managements that have been able to harness technology to improve customer service and build up brand loyalty, while at the same time keeping their balance sheets relatively free of debt. It's remarkable how amusement parks, which experienced a remarkable resurgence during the downturn, have not lost their appeal as the economy rebounds, a classic example of the new American mind-set. In fact, both companies have accelerating revenue growth precisely because they offer such bargains to American consumers.

Finally, and best for last: Costco, the ultimate in new value. Anyone who watches *Mad Money* knows that Costco is my favorite place to shop, and when I go usually someone nabs me wheeling my two carts around for a Twitter pic. I do love shopping bulk, and like everyone else I love the bargains that Costco gives me. And yes, it is true that I do not like to eat the night before a trip to Costco because those free samples are just too fabulous to pass up.

Costco is immensely profitable because of its unique club model. More than 70 million members have a loyalty card to Costco and are responsible for about 75 percent of the earnings before income taxes. It has incredible shopper loyalty; it recently put through its first price increase in many years, and almost no customers balked. How can Costco offer such low prices? The dues help offset the costs, and Costco's private-label brand is much loved even versus the branded products. But most important, it's the employee retention. Costco prides itself on keeping its employees happy, offering the best benefits of any major company not just in retail but in all businesses. Not needing to constantly train new employees has kept down training costs, which can be as high as 30 percent of the cost of labor at other stores. That's a legacy of former CEO Jim Sinegal, who has stressed to me over and over again the need to give employees health care and, more important, dignity, which competitors regard with a degree of insignificance that marginalizes them on a daily basis. Craig Jelinek, the terrific new president and CEO of Costco, is steeped in that tradition, and the best retailer just seems to get better and better.

When I took the *Mad Money* team to the opening of a new Costco in Harlem, Jim showed me how some high-end merchandise is priced so low that he sees employees of traditionally priced stores buy up whole offerings to mark up and sell at their own emporiums.

Jim constantly refreshed his stores with new, low-priced goods to inspire what he calls a "treasure hunt" feel; that tradition has been kept alive by the excellent managers who have succeeded him at this great and growing chain.

One more sterling set of value plays: the dollar stores, led by Dollar General. This cohort has shown remarkable growth and is taking share for the likes of Walmart and Target with ultra-low prices augmented by private-label offerings. All of the dollar stores have benefited from two inexorable trends: (1) 46 million people currently on food stamps, up from about 30 million just six years ago, an average growth of 13 percent per year, and (2) a much better-looking set of stores than in the old days, when no chain was known for its ambience—or cleanliness, for that matter. These stores are the ultimate trade-downs, but that said, they can be truly terrific places to shop because, these days, their offerings are so much less expensive than the traditional mass discounters and drugstores. They've also expanded into tobacco, and sales are much stronger than even the stores anticipated, as Dollar General called out on its recent, much-better-than-expected quarter. My personal favorite? Dollar Tree—not the stock, but the stores. I have a terrific one I go to that's bright and airy and truly inexpensive, especially if you have a sweet tooth. But Dollar General remains the cheapest and has the best growth path ahead of it, as it is just now expanding into California, which includes one-fifth of the nation's entire population.

Summary: The Need and Love for Value

The consumer learned a tremendous lesson after the Great Recession: You don't need to spend as much money as you used to, so rein it in and get more bang for your buck. That means shopping at an off-price retailer like TJX or a club like Costco. It means buying knock-off products made by Perrigo that are every bit as good as the branded issues. If you can go to an outlet, it's worth it, and Tanger Factory Outlets has the best real estate. Fixing your own car means going to AutoZone, and fixing your own meal means buying McCormick spices. Vacations are now staycations, great for the high-yielding Cedar Fair and Six Flags. Priceline has become the de facto travel site for transport and lodging. And dollar stores now take business from even the best mass discount stores, because their prices are so low and their selection much better than in the old days—perfect for penny-pinching customers, including the 46 million people on food stamps. If you can own only one of these, I would go with TJX; the off-price apparel store chain has demonstrated the best ability to get the cheapest and best merchandise, mark it up to a level that's attractive to the broadest array of customers, and give shareholders the best of returns, although Costco shines as by far the best place to get both hard- and soft-good items at incredibly low prices.

4. Shareholder Bounty from Anticompetitive Mergers

Most secular-growth themes that work tend to surf natural waves, big sea changes that a handful of companies have been able to capitalize on. But there's an exception, a big exception, that's proven to be strong and lasting and must be dissected here. In a growth-starved world, where revenues are increasingly hard to come by, some bold companies have taken it upon themselves to create value simply by buying up the competition. It's ironic that we are in a time of relatively few mergers, given the remarkable success we have seen in the stocks of so many of the acquirers. Not only that, but the acquirers tend to enjoy multiyear moves in their own stocks, highly unusual behavior pre–Great Recession mergers.

There are two types of mergers that have created tremendous value for shareholders: acquisitions that produce oligopolies and mergers that have allowed companies to become dominant in their categories. Both have been stupendous wealth creators.

Shareholders in the airlines and rental car companies have been the biggest beneficiaries of the former trend. When I first came out for the airline stocks on *Mad Money* in late 2012 it was almost as if you could hear a collective sound of shock. That's because I haven't recommended the stock of an airline since 1985, when I was at Goldman Sachs and put my father into American Airlines. It promptly lost more than half of its value. I swore to myself after that debacle that the group simply wasn't worth it because of its cutthroat nature and its inability to control costs.

But sometimes you have to approach even the most hideous of industries with fresh eyes when you are confronted with game-changing events. That's what has happened to the airlines in the past few years, when the Antitrust Division of a liberal Justice Department decided to look the other way at a host of mergers that essentially quashed competition and have led to consistent profits for the first time in the history of the airline industry. That's right, an industry that seemed addicted to bankruptcy has, at last, broken through into the investable category, because, for the first time ever, there is oligopolistic pricing that, while terrible for the hapless consumer, has been fabulous for the airline companies and their stocks.

But let's go back in time for a moment to set the scene. Since 2005 we have seen a host of airlines either disappear—there have been more than a dozen bankruptcies—or get swallowed up by larger players. In 2008 Delta was allowed to buy Northwest Airlines. In 2010 the government blessed United's merger with Continental. These combinations have led to a situation in which five large carriers now not only get 80 percent of the passenger revenues by volume, but they now also barely compete against one another anywhere, which makes this situation the virtual definition of an oligopoly. If the Antitrust Division at the last minute hadn't blocked a deal that would have seen US Airways purchase AMR, the old American Airlines, out of bankruptcy, you would have seen a four-player oligopoly that would have led to a thousand additional routes having no competition, and thus sharply higher ticket prices.

Just as important, the airline industry itself has changed. There used to be very few barriers to entry, as planes were relatively inexpensive and fuel was relatively cheap, as little as 62 cents a gallon at the turn of the century, and fuel represented only about 20 percent of the entire cost of operations. Now, though, with the much higher cost of fuel, north of $3 on average, this huge variable cost represents between 40 and 50 percent of operating expenses. That means only those with the most fuel-efficient, newer planes can operate profitably, which has radically cut down on competition. Because Boeing and Airbus, the two principal companies in the industry, can't make them fast enough, there are long queues to buy new planes. So don't expect to see upstarts upsetting the bountiful pricing now in effect on so many routes in the country. At the same time, the legacy airlines have radically rearranged their labor forces, including trimming their employee head count from 450,000 to 300,000.

Although there's been no shortage of critics of these mergers, including the American Antitrust Institute and the Business Travel Coalition, both of which point out that huge hub airports were designed for multiple competing airlines rather than single-airline dominance, the industry has finally gotten its way. The lack of competition has allowed airlines to raise prices even for the more competitive routes, sometimes as much as 30 percent in recent years on some very popular destination routes. They've been able to tack on a host of fees and at the same time add more seats to planes, while serving little to no food beyond snacks. These days there's barely an amenity you don't have to pay for.

My favorites? A merged US Airways–AMR would have been my top pick. But Delta is in excellent shape, with only one unionized work group, the pilots, with whom they have a cordial relationship to date. United Continental works too. It is still seeing synergies from the big merger, and the company's international and corporate focus makes it a good bet in an environment where the economy has a modicum of growth.

What could go wrong with this thesis? The Justice Department might seek to reopen previous decisions to bless other mergers after it woke up to block the US Airways–AMR deal. Or a new well-capitalized carrier could come in to challenge the multiple duopoly route structures. However, the only potential challenger I see is Spirit Airlines, with the brilliant symbol

SAVE. But its CEO, Ben Baldanza, a frequent guest on *Mad Money*, has repeatedly assured me that the last thing he wants to do is compete with these new behemoths. Instead he concentrates on going where the big carriers will no longer go, which, by the way, is a considerable part of the nation, because any route that can't generate a solid return for the incumbent players has been or is in the process of being dropped. Spirit offers the lowest fares and the lowest service, some would say the worst service, which Baldanza assures me means little, because in the end those who choose his airline accept the devil's bargain-basement offering and simply want to get from here to there. So don't look for Spirit to bust up the competition any time soon. But charging for printing out tickets, as well as for baggage and even for boarding the plane, seems a little over the top for most value-seeking travelers. It's been working, though, and the stock has been a real winner.

The second brand-new oligopoly has again changed the landscape and taken a group of stocks from total purgatory to the pantheon of profitable enterprises: the rental car business. This once cutthroat industry, with dogfights among a half-dozen players at every turn, has now become so egregiously anticompetitive in the past few years that I am amazed the Obama Justice Department looked the other way on this one. Don't let all the rental car desks at the airline terminals confuse you: there are only three big rental car companies left standing: Hertz, Avis and the privately held Enterprise. Once you step up to the counter, you will know why these stocks are worth buying on any weakness, because if you choose additional features beyond the posted day rate, you will be revolted by the price tag. Buying the stocks of these outrageously expensive purveyors may be the best and, now that the competition is sparse, the only revenge.

A decade ago there were nine major rental car companies, all competing against each other and keeping rental rates low. Then Enterprise bought Alamo and National in 2007 to become the top dog in the group. Avis bought Budget in 2002 and then, in late 2012, acquired Zipcar, the newly minted car-sharing service, in what looks to be a successful bid to win over the tech-savvy millennial generation. Then, at the end of 2012, Hertz was able to buy Dollar Thrifty.

By 2013 Hertz, Avis and Enterprise controlled a whopping 87 percent of the rental car market by revenue. How good was this Dollar Thrifty deal for Hertz and the industry? Here's an easy way to tell. Hertz had been pursuing Dollar Thrifty for two years before the closing of the deal. It initially offered to buy Dollar Thrifty for $1.2 billion. Avis then countered with a higher offer, and then Hertz preempted the bidding with a $2.3 billion offer, fully $1.1 billion more than the original entry. Yet when the news hit, the stock of Hertz, rather than going down on that much higher purchase price, actually soared 11 percent. The stock of Avis also jumped 4 percent as it dawned on the market that oligopolistic pricing had come at last to a once competitive industry.

Ever since this last deal, price increases, augmented by the one-time surge in demand stemming from Hurricane Sandy, have become a regular occurrence. Once again, the customer gets hurt, but the stockholders have received a huge windfall, one that I suspect will last for years. A surprising slowdown in airport rental car travel in the summer of 2013 produced a rare shortfall for Hertz. Given the lack of real competition, it was just another good opportunity to buy this slaphappy oligopolist.

I also like the power that individual mergers give the acquirers, something that the prices of the combined entities would certainly confirm. You don't need an oligopoly to emerge to make a merger worthwhile for shareholders. In fact, just the prospect of greater market share gains while costs are taken out have benefited a host of forward-looking players that have otherwise been challenged to find revenue. Again, you know when you have stumbled on one of these winners when the stock of the acquirer jumps, first, after the initial reports of the deal, and then, a second time, after the completion of the transaction as analysts, in lockstep, bump their earnings estimates higher because of the synergies and the newfound dominance of the combined companies.

Consider the case of Gannett, the communications company that purchased the venerable Belo Corporation, once the pride of Dallas, in June 2013 for $1.5 billion in cash. Gannett agreed to pay a 28 percent premium for its fellow newspaper-and-television company, initially thought to be an extremely high price for what had seemed to be a declining entity. Sure, Belo rallied, as would be expected. But the real shocker came from the stock of Gannett; it jumped 34 percent on the day the deal was announced.

Why did the stock of the acquirer jump so high? Before this deal Gannett was mainly a newspaper company with more than half of its business coming from publishing, and though Gannett is a terrific operator, the owner of *USA Today*, which has been revitalized in remarkable fashion by Larry Kramer, president and publisher of one of my favorite morning reads, newspapers have been in a secular decline. But by buying Belo, Gannett transformed the very nature of the company, moving the business away from print and toward television broadcasting. Gannett went from being 51 percent print and 35 percent broadcasting before the deal to 38 percent print and 52 percent broadcasting after the deal. Instead of a newspaper publishing company with a TV kicker, the combined entity will be a TV company with a publishing kicker. Therefore Gannett, by moving more deeply into a business that still has growth, is able to obtain a higher price-to-earnings multiple.

The combination creates one of the largest broadcast groups in America, with stations that reach nearly a third of the country. The company owns forty-three stations, mostly network affiliates, and twenty-one of those are located within America's twenty-five largest media markets. Plus, the synergies will be immense for years to come. I suspect the new Gannett will be the growth publishing company that mutual funds crave, given the higher barriers to entry, lack of competition to local television and multiple years of cost takeouts.

Or consider the amazing 35 percent run-up in the stock of generic drugmaker Actavis, during and after the announcement that it had purchased Warner Chilcott, a rival company, for $8.5 billion in 2013. The reason? Actavis was a strong generic player, but it lacked entries into gastroenterology and dermatology. Warner Chilcott solved that problem and, at the same time, gave Actavis a powerful women's health drug portfolio and a branded birth control franchise. The deal also handed Actavis a ready path to much higher profitability, given that Warner Chilcott is based in Ireland, where corporate taxes are incredibly low. Yep, Actavis is taking advantage of the same tax break that caused Perrigo to buy Élan in 2013. This deal should boost the earnings of Actavis by as much as 30 to 35 percent in 2014 alone—a brilliant transaction. No wonder the run!

The best kinds of acquisitions, though, are the ones that take old-line companies not thought to have tremendous growth and turn them into serial earnings growers that keep giving you raised numbers for years and years to come. My favorites are the acquisitions by PVH, VF Corp. and the Walt Disney Company, all of which have stocks worth buying. All three executives behind these acquisitive companies—Manny Chirico, Eric Wiseman and Bob Iger, respectively—are saluted in my Bankable 21 chapter. But it's worth taking a moment to point out how well these companies have been able to acquire brands that build out their businesses.

There was nothing wrong with Phillips–Van Heusen when Manny Chirico took the reins in 2006; it had a host of venerable brands, including Van Heusen shirts, Bass footwear, Izod and Arrow as well as some Calvin Klein brands that it had chosen not to license out to other companies. The fact is that the company now known as PVH had been around since 1881, so it has been doing something right and has long held huge apparel share, as much as 25 percent of the department store shirt market and even greater dominance in ties.

But Manny has never been satisfied with anything less than creating a growth apparel company with heft and scale, something so necessary if his company was going to have pricing power over the behemoths in the retail industry. That's why, in 2010, he shelled out approximately $3 billion to buy Tommy Hilfiger, a brand thought to be played out in the United States but which has been a powerhouse for years in Europe, particularly the wealthier portions of the Continent, where it is considered a premium brand. Manny reinvigorated the U.S. portion of the business and built out Hilfiger in the stronger areas of Europe, allowing it, and therefore PVH, to far exceed expectations for several years. Then, just when Wall Street feared that all the gains that could be had from the Hilfiger acquisition had been played out, Manny struck again in 2012, buying the horribly mismanaged Warnaco, a company that had international licensing rights to Calvin Klein products, a signature brand for PVH. The $2.9 billion deal united all of the Calvin Klein brands under one roof and has given PVH another clear growth path, this time in Asia, where Calvin Klein brands are revered as top of the line. This acquisition, which hit a speed bump in the first quarter of the combined company, as Manny learned of the much sloppier execution by Warnaco than he had realized, has now begun to produce remarkable synergies. I think that not only will the Calvin products that had been licensed to Warnaco be upgraded, but the deal will allow PVH to expand Hilfiger into Asia, where it currently has no real presence. This deal will be a win for years to come.

VF Corp. used to be a jeans and bra company. But in the past few years management has gotten aggressive, acquiring fallow brands, breathing new life into them and then blowing them out across the globe. Eric Wiseman, the CEO, calls these brands "coalitions," and he's got coalitions that touch every aspect of apparel. You may know VF as North Face, which is indeed its signature brand, known the world over for the highest quality sportswear. It's hard to believe, in retrospect, that VF paid only $135 million for that billion-dollar brand. But VF Corp.'s been a serial acquirer of brands, including Nautica for $586 million in 2003 and the 2007 acquisition of 7 for All Mankind for $775 million.

Then in 2011 VF made perhaps its gutsiest acquisition to date: the $2 billion purchase of Timberland, the shoe company. Almost immediately Wiseman was able to revitalize the brand and expand it more aggressively overseas while cutting costs. The gains could last for several more years, during which I fully expect VF to make another acquisition or two to keep its growth going and to continue to play hardball with its retailing customers, all of whom seem to want far more than just one of its coalitions in their stores.

No company has been more adept at adding to its stable of brands, though, than the Walt Disney Company under Bob Iger. With the 2006 acquisition of Pixar for $7.4 billion, the $4 billion buy of Marvel in 2009 and the Lucasfilm purchase for $4 billion in 2012, Iger has created a virtual hit machine. The *Toy Story* creator coupled with the *Avengers* franchise and the legendary *Star Wars* series have given Disney the ability to actually time its hits for quarters and years to come, allowing for a very smooth earnings path. Iger is so smart. While he's developing the new hits, he's busy paying down the costs of the acquisitions and keeping the firm's balance sheet in unquestioned shape while expanding an already immense buyback to be one of the most vigorous on the New York Stock Exchange. I have often joked with Bob that he has almost as many billion-dollar brands as Procter & Gamble. But given the hard times P&G has had of late and the amazing success of multiple hits emanating from Pixar and Marvel, not to mention a slate of *Star Wars* movies as far as the eye can see, I think Iger's Disney will one day surpass P&G for the brand crown. Don't forget, these houses of characters can be amortized over many different venues, including merchandise and theme park rides.

The best thing about these acquisitions? Their movies are almost guaranteed to be successful because the characters already have a loyal following from past endeavors, which makes the possibility of a big miss, the bane of an entertainment firm, much less likely—as long as Disney sticks with the tried and true and doesn't deviate from the plan, as it did momentarily and egregiously with one of the biggest bombs of the era, *John Carter*.

David Wenner, the CEO of B&G Foods, may not be known to you, but with a series of terrific niche, left-for-dead brands like Old London, New York Style, Mrs. Dash, Shed Guard and Pirate (known for Pirate's Booty), he's been able to cobble together a nifty consumer packaged foods company with a very stable earnings stream as well as offering a hefty dividend. Wenner's a terrific manager; every acquisition he has made has always been accretive within the next year, and he's never allowed any of them to dent his pristine balance sheet. The combinations have allowed him to consistently boost the company's payout, which was already among the highest in the packaged food industry. I am looking, by the way, for the newly public Pinnacle Foods to make similar kinds of acquisitions; its purchase of Wish-Bone salad dressings in the summer of 2013 led immediately to an almost 10 percent jump in the stock's price, with a promise of more deals ahead to continue propelling the stock higher for several years to come. Pinnacle and B&G Foods, with their terrific and disciplined acquisition strategies and high dividend payout ratios, are the perfect stocks for those people who are looking for solid, albeit staid, growth with solid income.

We've seen some tremendous value creation in the basic industry segment too. My favorite? When Eaton, an electronics conglomerate, purchased Cooper Industries, its number one competitor, for $11.8 billion at the end of 2012. Cooper, like Eaton, makes a variety of electrical equipment products, including power transmission, distribution, lighting and wiring components. This deal allowed Eaton to lessen its cyclicality and increase its exposure to the U.S. residential and commercial housing markets. The rap against Eaton for years was that it was hostage to the much more cyclical trucking industry, but by acquiring Cooper, Eaton changed its stripes and now has a secular-growth tailwind because of the need for companies and homeowners to use the combined entity's products to increase energy efficiency in construction and remodeling. Cooper's business carried higher margins, allowing Eaton to raise its forecast for the out years immediately upon the completion of the deal. And there are the synergies that come from selling twice the product into what amounts to a very similar customer base.

Those may be the most visibly successful acquisitions we've had in recent years. I do believe, given that each acquisition has been bountiful for the stock of the acquirer, that we are at the beginning of a renaissance of deal making. It hasn't happened yet. In fact, there has been far more money made in breakups and initial public offerings than in M&As. But how much longer can companies wait on the sidelines as more successful companies acquire targets in their spaces and then watch their stocks zoom in return? In the meantime, every company mentioned here should give you enough multiyear returns to help you get rich without taking on too much risk given the now tried-and-true formula for these very winning companies.

Summary: Acquiring Your Way to Shareholders' Hearts

In what seems like a permanently low-growth environment, some companies take matters into their own hands by consolidating their industries. With the airline and rental car industries now de facto oligopolies, I like Delta, United Continental and Hertz. Gannett in newspapers and television, Actavis in generic drugs, PVH and VF Corp. in apparel, B&G Foods in consumer packaged goods, and Eaton in electronics have all bought competitors, streamlined their combined companies and outperformed almost all others in their industries because they know growth has become so hard to come by. If I could own only one, I would go for Eaton because it's doing so well with low global economic activity. When worldwide growth returns, it will perform spectacularly.

5. Stealth Tech: The Power of Innovation

These days Wall Street takes a pretty dim view of technology stocks. While I am often at odds with the Wall Street consensus, you won't find me disagreeing much on this one. After years of innovation, including the evolution of computing power from giant mainframes to extremely powerful small-scale devices, such as the personal computer, the laptop and ultimately the smartphone and the tablet, we've come to realize that, at least for now, we may be at the end of the line for the traditional growth of this cohort. I have isolated the portion of tech that can still be considered a major theme: the holy trinity of social, mobile and cloud. While the cloud has produced a renaissance of sorts in how we can do everyday things such as buy music, rent movies and make purchases online, traditional tech stocks don't necessarily generate great wealth for shareholders anymore, except those lucky enough to own shares in companies that sell out to bigger companies. These days what I see from traditional technology companies away from social and mobile value creation isn't all that innovative, especially when I contrast it with what other companies, non-tech companies, are doing to innovate. And isn't innovation what tech is supposed to be about?

That's why I think it's time to recognize that we are looking for tech in all the wrong places. We want to find it in servers or cell phones or tablets. We keep expecting, for example, that Apple will blow our socks off with some new gizmo. I just don't see that happening. The real innovation is happening elsewhere, specifically in what I call "stealth tech" companies, where new products are being invented to serve needs that old tech, retro tech, doesn't hold a candle to. That's why I need you to start looking for tech in all the right places, even if their births seem to be occurring in the most prosaic of incubators. It's time to redefine what it means to be a tech stock and start thinking outside the tech box weighting that's actually weighing down the indices.

Why bother to make this distinction between old-fashioned tech and stealth tech? It's simple. The market's inability to recognize the innovation in the humdrum—the apparel companies, the restaurant chains, the consumer packaged goods—creates an unfounded discount that you can exploit for your own profit. The companies I am about to regale you with remind me more of the great tech stocks of old because they use proprietary technology to invent new markets and then dominate those markets, giving these innovators faster growth, better gross margins, higher price-to-earnings ratios and therefore, ultimately, higher stock prices. In some cases, notably oil and gas enterprises and big pharmaceutical companies, the innovation is so palpable that they've caused revolutions in energy and medicine. I'll cover those in more depth later. Right now I want you to understand the innovations that are going on right in front of you: in your closet, in your kitchen and in your bathroom.

In the same way we used to look to Dell, Hewlett-Packard and Compaq for innovation, I now look to consumer packaged goods companies like Colgate, Unilever and Clorox. You may think of these companies as some of the most mundane, copycatted companies around, creatures of "all new" advertising and unchallenged hype that lacks any scientific rigor. You'd be wrong. That's because these companies are now in constant dogfights for share, and the only way they can distinguish themselves in a world where advertising claims often ring hollow is to innovate.

Consider Colgate. Many people have been mystified about how Colgate continually sells at a premium to the rest of the consumer packaged goods stocks. What makes Colgate so special? How did it pull away from the others? The answer is that Colgate is a true innovator in an area where we all think that "new and improved" is just advertising hype. Colgate is actually creating solutions that are better than the other guy's, using science and technology as difference makers. What Colgate delivers actually *is* new and *is* an improvement, a substantive improvement, over previous household product iterations.

That's why, despite intense competition from established companies in the consumer packaged goods space as well as offerings from the lower-priced private-label concerns, Colgate is still gaining share in many markets worldwide. Colgate's innovations have also allowed it to raise prices on many of its newer products, something that's quite unusual in a world where downward price pressure seems to be exerted on anything that's thought to be at all commodity-like.

As is often the case with terrific consumer packaged goods companies, Colgate's inventiveness starts with the customer. The company has been the best at gathering insights from what customers want from its products, everything from soap to toothbrushes, toothpaste and dog food. It then develops new concepts within each of its categories to suit those consumers, keeping in mind all sorts of local concerns that most global companies aren't sensitive to, and then rapidly brings those concepts to life as new products. Colgate develops these new products in nine Consumer Innovation Centers, centers that are scattered all over the globe so that they can target new products for specific regions.

Just a few examples of its recent successes might shed light on this phenomenon. For example, Colgate's been winning the endless toothpaste share war, chiefly against a confused Procter & Gamble, with its new Optic White toothpaste, which uses the same ingredients found in whitening strips to give people whiter teeth in just one week. It also recently launched a new toothbrush, the Colgate 360 Surround Sonic Power, which is packed with technology. It's powered by a battery and comes with bristles meant to surround teeth for a gentle yet powerful clean. Sorry to sound like an ad, but the darned thing really does deliver what dentists have been looking for. The brush also has a feature that allows the user to scrub his tongue and the inside of his cheek. It's kind of like the Swiss army knife of toothbrushes, and it's been met with great enthusiasm. They've got a new Palmolive dishwashing liquid that cleans not only dishes but also the dirtiest instrument in the house, the sponge, washing away any lingering odor-causing residue.

In the dog-eat-dog pet food market—sorry, couldn't resist, but it does have the added advantage of being true—the company launched Science Diet Healthy Advantage, a wellness food that's exclusively available from veterinarians, and its distribution is now well ahead of schedule because the company's done such a good job of convincing vets and pet owners that they have a superior product. We're used to medical doctors recommending medicines, but this product's success with the veterinary profession ensures its breakthrough status versus store-bought food. A perusal of the aisles at PetSmart shows the value of the brand name, as Science Diet commands a premium price on all of its goods. Colgate uses the doctor endorsement strategy for skin care products too, developing technologically advanced bath and shower gels approved by dermatologists as break-throughs in skin recovering moisture naturally.

These breakthroughs have brought Colgate the most success of any consumer packaged goods company in the fast-growing emerging markets. Colgate just introduced its Luminous teeth-whitening system across Latin America. The company is now producing a Speed Stick deodorant that's tailored, successfully, for both men and women, which it recently launched in Mexico and is now being rolled out in other parts of South America. Plus, Colgate's research has produced an antibacterial bar soap, Protex, that consumers believe to be superior to other brands in the category, and it too has been gaining share in Latin America over the past few years. These innovations explain how Colgate has been able to generate an astounding 69 percent toothpaste share in Brazil and an amazing 80 percent share in Mexico, two of the fastest-growing markets.

Colgate's "regionalizing" tooth-brushing in Asia too, where the tapered bristle category is growing very rapidly. There they've introduced the Slim Soft toothbrush with tapered bristles designed to clean between the teeth and the gum line.

Interviewing chief executive officers from many different industries as part of my work for *Mad Money* has taught me to look at innovation in all sorts of places in the packaged goods segment, from foods to drugs to grooming and cleaning. Take the prosaic-sounding International Flavors & Fragrances. The company has long been known as the taste and smell behind many of the big consumer packaged goods offerings. What I didn't know until I interviewed Doug Tough, the chairman and CEO, was that IFF is actually a science company, with labs worldwide trying to come up with compounds that meet customers' needs in an ever-expanding developed world. IFF benefits from the needs of food and beverage companies to distinguish themselves and take share. I like to think of the company as an innovative global arms dealer providing weapons that keep companies competitive. IFF develops proprietary scents to help personal care and home care companies differentiate their deodorants and fabric softeners. You can't tell unless you look at IFF's annual report, but this company is the key behind-the-scenes player helping to fuel growth for consumer product giants like Procter & Gamble, Unilever and Coca-

Cola. The company is the innovator behind many of the celebrity-branded fragrances and counts Estée Lauder as one of its largest and most important customers.

Perhaps most important in an age when food and beverage companies must fear government intervention because of the epidemic of obesity and the role these companies play in abetting it, IFF has been inventing flavors that allow these companies to reduce potentially harmful content without altering their attractive taste. For example, IFF sodium modulation technology seeks to reduce the amount of salt in consumer products and IFF is making food sweeter without layering on additional sugar, which is a proximate cause to obesity that could lead to diabetes. As IFF says in its annual and on its conference calls, "Innovation equals differentiation."

Maybe the most fertile ground for nontraditional technology companies today can be found in the apparel category. For most of the previous century, clothing companies didn't even bother to differentiate themselves using science. Occasionally you would get innovations like nylon or Dacron by DuPont, but these were hardly scientific differentiators because DuPont shared its technology with all its customers. These days, though, the apparel segment has become a hotbed of innovation, moving the needle for companies, particularly upstarts that are challenging entrenched competitors.

The most aggressive innovator in the sector? Under Armour, the Baltimore-based purveyor of the much-loved sportswear that came out of nowhere to challenge Nike with technological breakthroughs in fabric. From its start in 1996, Under Armour has distinguished itself by inventing an entirely new category of sportswear: a moisture-wicking compression-fit apparel made from advanced synthetic materials that keeps your body at a healthy and comfortable temperature and dries out faster than clothes made by others in its category. Under Armour is to compression apparel what Coke is to cola or Kleenex is to tissues: a brand name all to itself.

Kevin Plank, the chairman, president, CEO and founder, has built his company on what he calls "relentless innovation." Plank doesn't just toss out platitudes about innovation. He actually devotes a huge amount of time on his conference calls to explaining the scientific breakthroughs, behavior that is highly unusual for a consumer goods company; most just go right into the numbers. Plank knows the numbers for his company stem directly from innovation, and he wants you to understand that. Otherwise you would simply believe that the stock has to be overvalued and you would want to sell, not buy, on the quarterly report.

For example, in 2011 Under Armour introduced "charged cotton" as an alternative for customers turned off by the synthetic fibers that are so often used in sports apparel. Charged cotton dries five times faster than normal cotton and has the durability you would typically associate with polyester fabric. Plank said on his recent conference call that he sees charged cotton as "a path to nearly quadrupling our addressable market," since the market for cotton activewear is much larger than the market for synthetics. The company has had tremendous success in the past few years with its "cold black" technology, which reflects the heat of the sun to make athletes feel cooler. This differentiated technology has been cited by Dick's, the nation's biggest sporting goods store chain, as a main reason for that store's year-over-year success in apparel in an otherwise very difficult time for all other apparel vendors.

The company recently rolled out another innovative product, "Storm," a line of water-resistant hoodies; water literally rolls right off. It just introduced a shirt that tracks the body's natural motion and biometric signals. Now the company is introducing an ultra-lightweight running shoe that uses UA-developed technology to keep feet dry and allow them to flex as they would naturally. That's the kind of differentiation that gives the $8 billion Under Armour a fighting chance in the sports shoe business, which has been dominated by Nike, the $65 billion behemoth. I was skeptical when UA decided to go head-to-head with Nike in footwear, but the inroads are impressive and, I think, lasting. After sitting down with Plank recently, listening to him trace out his vision for extending his company's reach internationally, where Under Armour presently sells only 6 percent of its wares, I am convinced that in a few short years Under Armour will be giving the fabulously competitive Nike a run for its money around the globe.

Lately, UA has been getting into the multibillion-dollar business of fitness monitoring with its Armour39, which measures athletic activity and gives users a "WILLpower" score, likely similar to Nike+ FuelBand. This technology was recently showcased at the NFL combine, where college stars compete to show their strengths, and it's been adopted by premier football players like Carolina Panthers quarterback Cam Newton and elite Atlanta Falcons wide receiver Julio Jones.

Without this kind of innovation I don't think Under Armour could take on an entrenched player like Nike or be featured prominently both in sporting goods stores and department stores that would most likely prefer featuring their own private-label apparel. With this innovation, Under Armour can extract premium prices for its goods, which then allows the company to spend more than it would otherwise to continue to innovate. Technological superiority in apparel is how the stock of Kevin Plank's company can sell at fifty times earnings versus Nike's twenty times earnings. It's a tangible differentiator that's just now being recognized by growth stock investors who simply never expected that there could be anything so different about sweatpants, hoodies or sneakers that it could move the needle for a company itself. Sometimes innovation really does come from perspiration: Plank told me that he had to invent something new to wear to the gym because when he worked out in plain old cotton apparel he became "the world's sweatiest man."

Perhaps the most ironic example of the importance of innovation comes from, of all things, Domino's, the pizza chain, which has used customer relations management technology to separate itself from the pack and compete more effectively against mom-and-pop vendors who don't have the financial wherewithal to offer similar products. At a time when personal computer makers, software companies, semiconductor companies and disk drive companies seem to be stuck in the 1990s when it comes to new breakthroughs, outfits like Domino's, under Patrick Doyle, another one of my Bankable 21 CEOs, recognized that the age-old ordering process for pizza could be reinvented by using new mobile, social and cloud applications. In just a couple of years' time Domino's has switched from an error-prone verbal phone-based system to a foolproof desktop or cell phone system where the onus is on the customer, not the store, to get it right. The new system, which can be reached right from a customer's

Facebook page, allows for any kind of pizza topping change, adjusts for any specials, and gives consumers a chance to pay by credit card, so no cash is needed when the deliveryman reaches your door. It also allows you to monitor the progress of the pizza to be sure that things are going smoothly. It has taken much of the guesswork out of the process and has led to a level of adoption that has already generated billions of orders and has accelerated same-store sales dramatically at the expense of local pizza parlors, which cannot even begin to counter Domino's technological edge. That's why Domino's stock, a phenomenal performer since this innovation began, can continue to pull away from the pack and deliver better-than-anticipated earnings for years to come.

Finally, it's worth exploring "stealth technology" in industrial space. Of course, no company these days can afford not to innovate. Cummins, the engine company, has made remarkable advances in clean engine technology, enabling a dramatic decline in diesel emissions. Westport Innovations has developed technology that allows natural gas to power truck engines in a way that could revolutionize the trucking industry and allow for domestic energy independence, given our nation's bountiful shale gas deposits. 3M has always been an innovation powerhouse, with new products in health care, glass, and adhesives adding to earnings per share every single year. Honeywell has developed additives that have enabled more efficient refining of heavy oil and has created turbochargers that allow cars to use less gasoline per mile. Boeing has pioneered materials that are much lighter and stronger than older, heavier alternatives and allow planes to burn less fuel. There's been consistent innovation everywhere. But what I care about and what you need to focus on is when an industrial company actually changes it stripes via technology, going from a low price-to-earnings cyclical to a higher price-to-earnings proprietary growth company. The finest example? DuPont.

Here's an old-line chemical company that's being reinvented before our eyes by its CEO, Ellen Kullman, who has been shedding low-technology businesses that have long been the bedrock of DuPont, like paints and coatings, and instead is turning the company into a hotbed of innovation centered around agriculture, health, safety and the food chain. With the $6.3 billion acquisition in 2011 of Danisco, a company that develops more healthful food ingredients, Kullman has been able to shift her product portfolio into science that's geared toward noncyclical businesses and away from low-value-added auto and housing materials. Danisco dovetails perfectly with DuPont's agricultural seed business, allowing Du-Pont to produce the materials that farmers want worldwide and that consumer packaged goods companies need to feed the world. Plus, many of her agricultural innovations are allowing for new renewable fuels to be created from plants that don't necessarily disrupt the food chain, causing unintended cost consequences, as corn-based ethanol has done for the average American food shopper. And Kullman also announced sale of the more commodity dependent performance chemicals unit. The old Du-Pont was hostage to the gross domestic product growth of the United States. The new DuPont is leveraged to the need to feed the earth's relentlessly growing population and the secular trend of a growing middle class that wants food rich in protein.

At the end of October, Kullman announced on *Mad Money* that Du-Pont will spin off the company's performance chemical division, which includes its commodity titanium dioxide unit, creating even more value for existing shareholders.

Summary: The Dawn of Stealth Technology

In a world where most technology companies aren't worthy of the tech rubric, you have to find innovation where you can. Fortunately, companies like Colgate, International Flavors & Fragrances, Domino's and Du-Pont are willing to pick up the mantle of innovation, albeit in a way that's not yet visible to most investors. Companies that invest in stealth technology have been able to take on entrenched competitors, triumph over less technically inclined opponents or reinvent themselves into more highly valued, less cyclical companies. The irony of a shirt company innovating more than a personal computer company shouldn't be lost on you. Neither should the profits the stealth tech plays can generate for your portfolio. If you can buy just one of these, I would make it Under Armour, as its growth prospects are probably the least limited of all the stealth techs out there.

6. New Pharma: The Four Horsemen of Biotech

When I first broke into the business of picking stocks in the late 1970s, the health care sector, specifically the pharmaceutical business, was a bit of a backwater. The concept of the blockbuster, the drug that could rack up a billion dollars in sales, was very elusive, and frankly, it was difficult to distinguish the differences among them.

But beginning in the 1980s, the major pharmaceutical companies delivered some breathtaking breakthroughs in cardio care with anticholesterol drugs, in cancer treatment with more sophisticated forms of chemotherapy, and in mental health, first with antidepressants like Prozac and then with antipsychotics like Abilify. These drugs made immense profits for a handful of what we now regard as staple companies for all portfolios: Merck, Pfizer, Bristol-Myers, Eli Lilly and the like.

These days the big old pharmaceuticals still have plenty going for them. They have established franchises and throw off huge amounts of cash. They pay consistently high dividends and are often viewed as bond yield equivalents, although that value is losing appeal given the rise in interest rates. They almost all have terrific balance sheets. However, they are no longer the hotbeds of new wonder drugs, nor can any one blockbuster still move the needle for them. Meanwhile, their breakthrough drugs of the past century are slowly but surely going off patent. This has dramatically slowed their growth rates, as once a drug goes off patent it can easily lose 90 percent of its value overnight. These patent-cliff troubles are now the stuff of daily chatter whenever we talk about why these companies can no longer maintain high price-to-earnings ratios. These stocks seem very cheap, but because they have not been able to innovate aggressively they deserve to stay cheap, unless they split themselves up to bring out value.

In their place have come a new class of drug companies, the biotechs, which are now providing the kind of growth that we used to expect from Merck, Pfizer, GlaxoSmithKline and Eli Lilly. In a time when growth is hard to come by, particularly growth that has nothing to do with the business cycle or the wealth or poverty of various governments, the success of these biotech companies stands out as a lasting theme for many years to come.

As part of my duties as host of *Mad Money* I try to put on as many biotech companies as I can. I am always looking for the next company that might be able to deliver a blockbuster drug that renders the current market capitalization of the company way too small versus the opportunity ahead. However, four companies have jumped to the fore of this group, and they have become the logical heirs to the household-name pharmaceutical companies that have so often been integral to a diversified portfolio. They are necessarily more speculative than the big drug companies because they tend not to offer dividends and they don't necessarily have a wide breadth of product to lean on. However, they have real growth, growth that isn't about to be impinged upon by patent expirations or competitive me-too threats that now plague the older-generation companies.

So, let me introduce you to the revolution in drugs and the players that are leading that revolution: Celgene, Gilead, Biogen Idec and Regeneron.

Celgene

Few companies are as underestimated as the $63 billion Celgene, located in Summit, New Jersey, about a mile down the road from where I live. Despite its fabulous CEO, Bob Hugin, and its sterling track record, the company doesn't get the respect it deserves considering the huge number of offerings it has and the many years' worth of approvals I expect the company will be getting both here and abroad.

Right now Celgene is basically a three-legged stool of innovative drugs, three legs that each could turn out to have multiple billions of dollars of revenue in the next few years. The first and most lucrative is the company's multiple myeloma franchise, a series of drugs that combat an especially nasty type of blood cancer. Celgene's main drug here is Revlimid, a reformulated version of the old thalidomide that caused birth defects in the early 1960s but has had remarkable effect against blood cancer. The drug's on track to do well over $4 billion worldwide in 2014 and has the potential to do $6 billion in sales at peak, just for treating multiple myeloma. At the moment, Revlimid has FDA approval only as a second-line treatment for patients who don't respond to first-line therapies. Even so, Revlimid has about 40 percent of the frontline market here in the United States, as doctors like it so much that they prescribe it off-label.

The big opportunity for Revlimid is in Europe, where Celgene is attempting to get first-line approval for the drug against multiple myeloma. When Celgene had to withdraw its application in 2013 in order to be able to do more testing on the drug, the stock plummeted, but Hugin came on *Mad Money* to suggest that you haven't heard the last from Revlimid in Europe and that other drugs in Celgene's pipeline could be kicking in while you wait for an expected European approval. Meanwhile, the company is also studying Revlimid as a treatment for non-Hodgkin's lymphoma, chronic lymphocytic leukemia and other forms of leukemia. Any one of these could be a huge opportunity for Celgene—it's like they have a whole pipeline here in a single drug that had, incredibly, been given up for dead after the horrendous birth defects it caused. Celgene has developed another multiple myeloma drug called Pomalyst, which is used for patients who aren't responsive to Revlimid. While this indication could be worth as much as $1 billion dollars, other uses for Pomalyst are most intriguing, including systemic sclerosis—a potentially lethal autoimmune disease—as well as a bone marrow disorder called myelofibrosis and even, perhaps, sickle-cell anemia.

The second leg? That's Abraxane, Celgene's potential billion-dollar breast cancer drug that has a host of other applications. Recently, the FDA approved Abraxane for non–small cell lung cancer, and Celgene is seeking approval for its use against pancreatic cancer and metastatic melanoma, the potentially lethal form of skin cancer. With these two new indications, Celgene sees Abraxane sales going to $1.5 billion by 2015. The pancreatic cancer indication alone could ultimately be worth $2 billion in peak sales.

The third leg of Celgene's mighty stool is Apremilast, an immunology and inflammation drug candidate that I believe could be a huge blockbuster for currently incurable arthritis, although it's being tested for psoriatic arthritis, another colossal indication. The drug could ultimately generate $3 billion in peak sales.

Despite having bankable management and a terrific stable of prospects, as well as one of the best pipelines in the industry, the stock is remarkably cheap given that it could earn as much as $13 to $15 a share by

2017. Even at the low end of the range, we're talking about a stock that's trading at just 8.6 times its earnings in the out years, a price-to-earnings multiple that's lower than the old-line pharmaceuticals with prospects that are nowhere near as robust as Celgene's slate of new and prospective drug approvals. That makes the stock ridiculously undervalued, even as it appreciated more than just about every other stock in the S&P 500 in 2013.

Gilead

I was first drawn to Gilead for its breakthrough AIDS drug, which, when used with a cocktail of medicines, has been shown to arrest the disease, something that seemed impossible just a few short years ago.

But Gilead didn't enter the major leagues until it spent $11 billion to purchase Pharmasset at a whopping 89 percent premium for the little Princeton-based company with just a handful of employees and no track record whatsoever. I remember being on air for *Squawk on the Street* when this deal broke and saying to my colleague David Faber, "Wait a second, has Gilead lost its mind, throwing that much away on a company with no track record at all?" But Pharmasset is working on the first real breakthrough drug for hepatitis C, a disease that, if undetected, can be fatal, as it can cause liver cancer and liver failure. Hep C is a huge worldwide problem, afflicting more than 170 million people with extremely painful and sometimes only spurious treatment for the illness. Even if the disease is discovered early, the survival rate is only about 50 percent with current care. Pharmasset's initiative requires only a pill, and almost no side effects have been detected to date.

Aside from the promise of the hep C drug and the anti-AIDS franchise, which could bring in $4 billion in peak sales several years from now, Gilead has a healthy pipeline, including more HIV drugs, cardiovascular drugs and some potentially lucrative cancer treatments, including drugs for leukemia and myelofibrosis that aren't even considered in the earnings estimates for the future.

Make no mistake about it, though, this hep C drug could be as big as the anticholesterol drugs were for Merck and Pfizer, perhaps even bigger.

With each hep C milestone crossed, I expect Gilead to go higher. It is one of my top picks to buy on any global macro event that causes our market to tumble. No wonder this is the first biotech to approach a valuation close to the older generation of drug companies, with an astounding $100 billion market capitalization.

Biogen Idec

Biogen has been around seemingly forever. I remember when I visited its offices while a student at Harvard in the 1980s, puzzling about whether this company could break out of the pack of obscurity one day to be a major pharmaceutical.

But it has since developed a breakout franchise treating multiple sclerosis, a horrible, chronic disease that attacks the body's central nervous system, interrupting nerve impulses between the brain and the rest of the body and causing fatigue; numbness; difficulty with balance, walking and coordination; bladder and bowel dysfunction; even paralysis and loss of vision. The disease afflicts some 350,000 people in the United States and perhaps 2 million worldwide.

There is no cure for MS, and that's absolutely terrible for people who suffer from this awful illness, but it's the kind of illness that pharmaceutical companies love to tackle because the most lucrative form of pharmaceutical is a long-range maintenance drug. Multiple sclerosis is a chronic condition that comes and goes, and the goal of every MS drug out there is simply to prevent relapses, keeping the disease at bay. It's one of the biggest indications out there, said to be worth nearly $18 billion just a few years from now.

Biogen's biggest MS bet had been Avonex, which has more than $3 billion in sales. Other companies, however, have been nipping at Biogen's heels, which is why it is imperative that its newly approved MS drug, Tecfidera, takes off, as it might be able to produce $1 billion in sales without cannibalizing Avonex too severely. Early sales indications are extremely positive for this new compound. Biogen has still one more multiple sclerosis drug that's already on the market, Tysabri, but it has had severe side effects, including death, in a small number of patients. Still, even with this handicap, Tysabri has managed to rack up 10 percent market share in a very short period of time. The company believes it can obtain $2.3 billion in sales by 2015, but I think the peak number could be more like $3 billion because it's been able to effectively isolate those who might be susceptible to the worst of the side effects, fatal brain infections. I know Biogen is hopeful about this label change, because earlier in 2013 it bought the 50 percent of the rights to the drug from Élan pharmaceuticals that it did not own for $3.25 billion and some contingency payments down the road.

What else? Biogen also gets 20 percent of the sales of Rituxan, a Roche drug for non-Hodgkin's lymphoma and rheumatoid arthritis. That stake brings in more than $1 billion in sales for the Weston, Massachusetts, company. And Biogen has the potential for a hemophilia-related blockbuster that could do $3 billion in sales by the second half of the decade.

Still, MS holds the key to Biogen's earnings for the foreseeable future, and I think the future looks very bright.

Regeneron

When we started *Mad Money* back in 2005, executives were reluctant to appear on the show. Was it an entertainment show? Was it just the musings of an ex–hedge fund madman? Or was it a work in progress that led to the teaching and educational show that it is now? One executive, Dr. Len Schleifer, stepped up to the plate early on to talk about the long-range prospects for his company, Regeneron, a biotech company that had been kicking around for seventeen years but had yet to develop any drug that could move the needle. At the time, Regeneron was trading at less than $5 a share. It was a pure speculation.

Since then, though, the stock of Regeneron has been unstoppable because of a cornucopia of new approvals, including one of the most remarkable drugs in history, Eylea, an age-related macular degeneration medicine that requires half as many eye injections as the previous standard of care. Ever since Eylea was approved in November 2011, Regeneron has far exceeded all earnings estimates on a routine basis, and the drug is well on its way to super-blockbuster status. The company is also studying this drug for a host of other conditions. Eylea is in phase 3 trials for diabetic macular edema as well as branch retinal vein occlusion, and it's in phase 2 trials for central retinal vein occlusion. Altogether, when you include each of these indications, Eylea could potentially do peak sales of $4 billion, as it is advancing at a pace of roughly 50 percent a year in usage.

Regeneron also has a bowel cancer drug on the market called Zaltrap, which helps destroy tumors by starving them of their blood supply. They're partnered up with Sanofi on this one, and while I do not expect the drug to be a blockbuster, it is possible that it could produce several hundred million dollars in sales in a few years' time. Regeneron has a third drug on the market, Arcalyst, for a number of rare, inherited autoinflammatory conditions, but this one isn't expected to amount to more than a $50 million drug.

Beyond these drugs, though, Regeneron is a research and development machine. The company has an incredible antibody discovery platform that drives its new drug pipeline, and this platform is so good that Sanofi recently inked an agreement to provide $160 million in annual funding for Regeneron's preclinical work. Sanofi pays for basically all the clinical development costs, and in exchange the French giant gets to select the antibodies it wants to develop with Regeneron. Meanwhile, Regeneron gets to keep 50 percent of the profits in the United States and anywhere from 35 to 45 percent internationally. Sanofi also bought 16 percent of Regeneron and has the ability to buy up to 30 percent.

As exciting as those drugs and relationships are, it's the pipeline that has me most excited about this new biotech star. The company has a hypercholesterolemia product that's entering phase 3 development, which could potentially do $3 billion in peak sales as an alternative to the current generation of statins that reduce cholesterol. If the drug works as an alternative for those of us who are allergic to statins, it could easily bring in more than $1 billion. The company has a novel anti-arthritis compound that could also be worth more than $1 billion. Plus, it has a drug with an anti-asthma indication that might be able to do $500 million a few years from now. As Len recently reminded me, "When it rains, it pours."

Summary: The Four Horsemen of New Pharma

Celgene, Gilead, Biogen Idec and Regeneron may be the most consistent growth stocks in the entire market. They have become the ultimate go-to names when stocks are gripped by virtually any panic or are overwhelmed by hedge funds heading for the exits or political machinations that threaten nascent economic growth. They are stocks that you should always keep at the top of your screen, right next to the S&P and Dow Jones indices. I would pick Celgene if I could own only one of the Four Horsemen of biotech.

7. Gushing Profits from America's Oil and Gas Revolution

We keep hearing of the energy renaissance in America, the one that has brought us back to where we are producing oil at the same pace as we did twenty years ago. This oil and gas exploration revolution has allowed us to dramatically reduce our need for imported oil. In fact, it is so bountiful that the United States is actually exporting 2 million barrels of refined gasoline every day; we have too much of the stuff and can't ship it cheaply to the domestic markets that need it, the Northeast and the West, so it's sent overseas. We've found enough oil and gas on this continent that the dreams of continental energy independence—not domestic, but continental—are no longer a pipe dream. In fact, I fully expect it to be the case by 2018. And if we harness our bountiful natural gas—some would say our glut of natural gas—as a surface fuel, replacing dirty diesel with cleaner liquefied natural gas, we could be domestically energy-independent by the end of the decade. That would be terrific in terms of cleaner skies, our national balance of payments and domestic security. It is highly doubtful that an Arab-led OPEC would have any teeth if we were to turn the tables by using natural gas to run trucks. But this book is about Getting Rich Carefully, not about getting energy-independent. We would love the revolution to happen, but my job is to help you make money from the transformation.

First, I want to make some things clear. Many money managers go on air and talk about investing in industries that are taking advantage of the cheaper price of energy to make things in this country. I wish that were the case. In fact, other than Dow Chemical and Nucor, the steel maker, nobody's doing much of anything to take advantage of the abundance except some of the pipeline companies and several enterprises dedicated to shipping natural gas overseas. It's a pathetically overhyped story. I only wish it were true.

What is true is that some of the oil and gas companies and their service brethren are making vast fortunes as they harvest the enormous energy resources we have both onshore and offshore. Those fortunes have come in large part because of American technology, specifically the technology that allows us to use hydraulic fracturing to bust up oil formations that had been left for dead or were thought to be too expensive to extract from before drilling and mapping became more technologically driven. Fracking, as it is known now, has led to the viable tapping of vast shales that we always knew were there but that were simply uneconomical to drill before the world price went sky-high and the new technology brought drilling costs way low.

Who will benefit the most from exploring and producing from these reserves? I've spent a lot of time analyzing this question on *Mad Money*, taking my show to the oil-filled Bakken shale in North Dakota and then to the natural gas–dominated Utica shale in Ohio. The Utica and its sister shale, Marcellus, in Pennsylvania, have been terrific for the companies that exploit it, and I do think that natural gas companies are in for long-term gains. I even have a couple I could suggest you buy; they can make big money thanks to their ultra-low exploration and production costs.

But the big profits are being made in oil. That's because we have too much natural gas in this country and it is very difficult to export. The landlocked nature of the fuel keeps the price low, much lower than it would be if we could ship it overseas. But oil is a worldwide commodity with a price set in London, and it is a price that is substantially above the current cost of extraction from most of the big shale discoveries in this country.

My trip to the Bakken shale in 2011, touring the acreage held by one of the winners, Continental Resources, was a real eye-opener. As I flew over the vast fields, seeing the drilling and pipe-laying and railroad for miles and miles, I understood why Harold Hamm, the chairman, CEO and founder of Continental, says that the Bakken shale is the largest find since Alaska's Prudhoe Bay in the 1960s. Hamm has made fortunes for himself and his shareholders, so I know that you want some Bakken exposure for certain. You only need to see the wonders of American technology applied to fields like the Bakken to understand how prolific these old fields can still be. I stood in the cabin watching a young fellow play with two joysticks that sent drill bits in two different directions, perpendicular to the original drill column, to capture all the oil that's underground for a two-mile radius, courtesy of the genius of horizontal drilling.

As good as the stock of Continental Resources might be, though, there's another shale that rivals the Bakken's bounty: the Eagle Ford in Texas. You want to win with a company that has chits in both, and that would be EOG Resources, run by the shrewd old oil hand Mark Papa at the company once known as Enron Oil & Gas. Don't worry, it left the Enron fold long before that company was blown to smithereens by greed and corruption. The Eagle Ford shale underlies an area 50 miles wide and 400 miles long, spanning 23 counties in South Texas. While other oil companies, including Marathon, Pioneer Natural Resources, Carrizo Oil & Gas, and BHP Billiton, have substantial holdings—BHP paid through the nose for its acreage, buying Petrohawk Energy not that long ago for $12.1 billion—it's EOG that dominates the play. We tend to think that technology and biotechnology companies have high growth rates, but EOG is growing its oil production at more than 33 percent, a rate of growth well in excess of almost all tech and many of the larger biotechs I follow.

EOG isn't the only independent oil company worth owning, though. Anadarko Petroleum, headed by Al Walker, chairman, president and CEO, and Noble Energy, run by the brilliant chairman and CEO Chuck Davidson, own tremendous U.S. prospects. Anadarko also has some magnificent acreage in the Gulf of Mexico and off the coast of Africa, which it recently began monetizing by selling a small stake in its acreage to India's Oil and Natural Gas Corp. for $2.64 billion. Noble, which is in many of the big domestic plays, has a stake in perhaps the largest natural gas field in the world, the Leviathan, off the coast of Israel. Normally, a natural gas field can't be too much of a needle mover in this country, but in the Russian-dependent, high-priced European market, it's gaseous gold, and I believe the stake is considerably undervalued because of geopolitical concerns. Noble also dominates the Niobrara shale near Denver, which is just now beginning to produce a huge number of new barrels of oil a day. Make no mistake about it, Davidson is one of the most shareholder-friendly managers in the oil world, and he will be able to monetize these holdings, including the Niobrara shale in Colorado, dramatically increasing the price of Noble Energy's stock over time.

All of the oil companies mentioned so far are high-growth vehicles with little dividend protection. If you want slower growth and more dividend protection, even as rising rates have nullified some of the protection higher dividends give you, it may pay to consider ConocoPhillips, which owns Burlington Resources, one of the largest natural gas holders in the country, or Chevron, with vast operations around the world and some of the best acreage in the Gulf of Mexico. Both are conservative, low-risk plays in the American oil and gas revolution. But the most exciting integrated oil, from the point of view of unlocking value, is easily Occidental Petroleum, one of the largest companies in the world and, most important, with vast holdings in California, the last great fracking frontier. I think if OXY decided to split into three parts—a refining and marketing arm, which would include its huge chemical segment; international oil; and its domestic exploration and production operations—you could see the stock trade easily to $150, which is why it is a core holding for my charitable trust. I don't think this is pie in the sky, as Occidental was, for years, the stand-out performer of the major oil companies. Though it has fallen behind of late, it remains the independent with the biggest upside because of its 1.2 million acres in California's Monterey shale, the last big unexploited shale play in the country. For those of you who fear that California governor Jerry Brown would fight the exploration, Occidental has assured analysts repeatedly that the state will not intervene to block the drilling.

Now, I am not against the idea of betting on natural gas rising in the near future; I just fear that the best stocks in that portion of the patch have had big runs. My favorite, on a pullback, is Cabot Oil & Gas, with 200,000 prolific acres in Pennsylvania's Susquehanna County, a part of the Marcellus shale that is uniquely configured to be able to export nat gas to the energy-starved Northeast, particularly New England, where pipe is being laid to open up that market to our natural gas and shutting the door on imported heating oil. Cabot not only has the best acreage, but it is growing production at a 50 percent clip, while its production costs are declining by 15 percent. That's allowing Cabot to generate 35 percent earnings growth, making the stock inexpensive at twenty-seven times earnings. We simply don't find that kind of growth much anywhere in America, and you can bet that an acquisitive overseas company would love to get its hands on Cabot and its bountiful assets.

How about finding the oil and getting it out of the ground? In the old days prospectors used divining rods or simply spudded holes, thinking that there might be oil down there somewhere. That's no longer the way it's played. Now companies hire sophisticated oil technology service companies to be sure their maps are right and to get the most out of each hole. The best? Core Labs, a company that's been on *Mad Money* more than just about any other since the show began. I have been recommending this stock for years because the company has the highest return on invested capital. It makes its money three ways: (1) reservoir description, where it analyzes core samples and tells oil companies how much economic value lies beneath to save the company millions of dollars on dry holes and poor prospects; (2) production enhancement, which allows an oil company to get the maximum out of each hole; and (3) reservoir management, which combines the first and second skills so oil companies can exploit new and older fields to maximum profitability. I consider Core Labs a terrific, high-growth, stealth tech play on the long-term need to prospect and drill for oil and gas.

If you want the cheapest play on the technology behind fracking, that mantle belongs to Halliburton, which has been a fracking pioneer. I ought to know. When environmentalists were engaging an endless war against fracking, replete with movies showing the hazards of fracking fluid, the president of Halliburton's Western Hemisphere operation had me down a beaker of HAL's revolutionary fracking fluid on live TV. It tasted kind of like a McFlurry, and I was none the worse for wear—at least not that I know of. HAL's been the biggest technological driver for fracking, but I hesitate to be too aggressive about recommending the stock because fracking, of late, has become a very competitive market. However, Halliburton is also the biggest innovator when it comes to the process of drilling and is very shareholder-friendly, recently completing a gigantic $3.3 billion above-the-market Dutch tender auction for its own shares.

The largest player and the one I consider the best-of-breed oil service? That's Schlumberger, which has invented some of the best technology to become the first company major oil enterprises bring in to be sure that the exploration process is done cheaply, efficiently and without peer. Schlumberger is a technology marvel that serves as project manager for the biggest initiatives that both national companies and the largest publicly traded companies undertake.

I also like some ancillary plays, like Chart Industries, which makes the liquefied natural gas containers that are used to turn natural gas into a surface fuel. Chart's business is booming; its most successful market is China, where the government has made natural gas a priority because it pollutes less than regular gasoline. But Chart has had a huge move, so it has become more speculative. The same goes for Cheniere Energy, which is going to be the first company to export U.S. natural gas now that the glut has made it economical to do so. Cheniere Energy has gone up almost fourfold since I first recommended it a few years ago; it has to pull back to the low $20s before I would feel comfortable telling you to buy it.

WHAT'S THE BEST WAY for a conservative investor to play the energy revolution? I like the pipeline master limited partnerships, specifically the ones that operate like toll roads, where they have very little exposure to the actual prices of the commodities they transport and charge a fee that's based on volume: the more oil and gas they move, the more money they make. Right now we're in a world where pipe is in incredibly high demand. It is the most efficient way to transport oil, natural gas, and nat gas liquids from where they are produced to where they're needed, which is often very far away from the new discoveries that are transforming the business. It's also by far the safest, as some of the recent rail tragedies have shown us. Right now we simply don't have enough pipeline capacity in this country to shift all the oil and gas to where it needs to go.

So there's huge demand nationwide for more pipelines, which means toll-road-like earnings for years to come for those companies skilled at transporting all of these fuels to refineries and chemical plants around the country. The additional pipes, along with the current pipelines, which generate huge fees, give these master limited partnerships the growth they need to raise their distributions consistently over time. Hence their out-sized yields, which, unfortunately, are not meant for retirement accounts because of an arcane tax law, but can be a terrific way to save in discretionary accounts.

Among the giant pipeline operators, my most valued player is Kinder Morgan Energy Partners, the largest pipeline operator in the country, with a bountiful yield and truly fabulous management in the form of CEO Rich Kinder, a dollar-a-year man who has never sold a share of stock in his company. KMP acts as a giant toll taker for more than 73,000 miles of pipe and roughly 180 terminals.

Kinder Morgan has made some brilliant acquisitions recently that have allowed the company to get more exposure to the domestic natural gas business. Back in October 2011, KMP announced it was acquiring El Paso, another pipeline play, which gave them $10 billion worth of interstate nat gas assets. So far the El Paso acquisition has gone extremely well, with the cost savings from the deal exceeding the initial projections. That's why I feel so good about Kinder Morgan's 2013 acquisition of Copano, another oil and gas partnership that I had been recommending. The Copano deal gives Kinder Morgan Energy Partners much more exposure to natural gas gathering and processing activities in the major shale plays in Oklahoma and Texas, including the robust Eagle Ford prospect. I expect KMP to participate in more than $10 billion worth of expansion plans in the next few years, which could fuel repeated increases in distributions over time.

At various times I have recommended other master limited partners, including Enterprise Products Partnerships, at one time the largest in the group, but it has run so much that I hesitate to endorse it. I feel the same way about two other high-quality pipeline companies, TransCanada and Enbridge, which have advanced to levels where I no longer find their yields that attractive but would be excellent buys on pullbacks. I have also recommended MarkWest Energy Partners, a northeastern pipeline that has done a series of attractive equity offerings in order to build out pipe to New England.

But, just as with every other sector, you should always try to go with the best of breed, and no company can touch the master limited partnership that Rich Kinder has put together over many years of acquisitions and build-outs in an endless quest to blanket the country with the pipe, and at times the rail, it needs to bring the oil and gas to the right markets at the right times.

There are so many terrific oil and gas companies in the country, as well as the suppliers to them. You should consider EOG, Core Labs, Occidental, Schlumberger and Kinder Morgan Energy Partners as possibilities for your portfolio. If you can buy only one, I would go for EOG, which has just about the best growth of not just oil and gas companies but of almost all publicly traded companies that I follow.

Summary: Seven Major Themes Built to Last

Major themes built to last can be the ultimate antidote to the daily hazards that have driven so many people out of this asset class. If you listen to the pundits, they invariably return to the idea that all stock trading is short term in nature, and we have to accept a new world ruled benignly by central banks and maliciously by high-frequency traders and hedge funds that flit in and out of stocks, chasing whatever fad captures their fancy. I think these misperceptions erode confidence and make it seem impossible to get rich with any sort of prudent philosophy. That's why I emphasize long-term themes. These seven themes are built to last for years and years to come:

1. New technology that embraces social-, mobile- and cloud-based initiatives will dominate a sector that's been decimated by the commoditization of so many yesteryear enterprises. Companies like Google,

Salesforce.com, Facebook, LinkedIn and Amazon will be the dominant plays because they recognize the need to continue to pioneer in this new world of progress and innovation.

2. If you can find companies that stand for wellness and health when it comes to the food chain, companies like Whole Foods, Hain Celestial, Panera and Chipotle, you will be able to surf a wave that can generate tremendous profits over time.

3. The post–Great Recession consumer wants value wherever it can be found, whether in retail with TJX or vacations with Priceline and Cedar Fair or knock-off goods with Perrigo. You find companies that can save people money, that respond to the new frugality, and you will be able to beat other investors who simply can't spot this trend. Costco's the best long-term way of playing this theme.

4. Companies can better themselves by merging either with competitors or with other companies that entrench them in their industries. Acquirers in the new world like Eaton, Gannett and B&G Foods are bold enough to transcend the meager growth that other companies just accept and therefore deliver subpar returns.

5. The best money-making technology may no longer be found within the confines of that cohort once known for it. It's more lucrative to look for stealth technology in food, apparel and consumer packaged goods companies like DuPont, Under Armour, Colgate and International Flavors & Fragrances.

6. Biotech has replaced traditional big pharma for growth and consistent profits. Celgene, Biogen Idec, Gilead and Regeneron have produced and will continue to produce superior returns for investors for many years to come.

7. The revolution in oil and gas in this country has produced tremendous profits for the companies that have exploited it to date, including the likes of EOG, Pioneer Natural, Schlumberger, Anadarko, Noble Energy, Core Labs and Kinder Morgan Energy Partners. I believe these shale success stories are in their infancy and will produce bountiful returns for many years to come.

CHAPTER 4

Breaking Up Is Easy to Do

Sometimes the parts are, indeed, worth more than the whole. More and more chief executive officers are reaching that heretical conclusion these days as they recognize that corporate divorce may be the only way to bring out the real value of their cobbled-together entities. In previous times, investors would be no more likely to profit from predicting corporate breakups than from prophesying Hollywood divorces. But spotting corporations that are on the rocks, on the verge of splitting, can be very lucrative. Sticking with the pieces—the newly minted companies—can be even more rewarding.

First, chief executives are almost always loath to separate their companies into different pieces because, invariably, they were involved in the building of the enterprise. You don't dismantle what you've built. That's just admitting that you did it wrong to begin with. Second, chief executives like empires. They like the striding of a global colossus, and they don't want to give up any authority. But they also recognize that Wall Street increasingly doesn't know what to do with their companies. When I started out at Goldman Sachs we had a research department with a fantastic conglomerate analyst. So did everyone else. We thought of these companies as terrific hedged bets. If the economy is getting stronger, one portion of the enterprise could have its earnings accelerate. If there's weakness, another division in a totally different industry might save the day.

Over time, though, Wall Street stopped carrying analysts who just scrutinized these combinations. They were too varied, too hard to understand and way too difficult to analyze or categorize. They lost their sponsorship because there are no cross-disciplined research departments. We may not think all that much of the analyst community, in part because it does seem to be gripped by terrible groupthink—group-nonthink would be more like it. But when you have an analyst putting her name to a stock, standing behind it, offering information about it and taking the company to meet managers of large pools of capital, that stock will invariably outperform a stock without that sponsorship. It will get a premium multiple to a stock with lack of sponsorship. And when we get a flash crash, or a thunderous wave of market or ETF selling, these analysts can provide the reassurance some need to be able to buy more stock instead of cutting and running.

But how can an alcoholic beverage analyst sponsor a company that also has an office supply and home furniture division, as was the case with the old Fortune Brands before its fabulous breakup? Who can get behind the stock of an electronics company with a health care division? Why buy a cereal company that has a private-label food business buried within it for no logical reason save legacy?

Remember, sector analysts are like medical specialists who report to general practitioners; their specialty keeps them from making a judgment on a company because they do not know how to analyze its divisions away from their ken or their expertise. So a drug company that may have a fast-growing medical device division buried within a slower-growing pharmaceutical division gets ignored for a purer play in the group. An exploration and production company with a refining and marketing division might be overlooked for a dedicated oil company that divorces itself from its refining and marketing division. A food conglomerate with a fast-growing international division gets a valuation discount because it's attached to a slower-growing domestic division. But when separated into two companies, the same entity will be worth more, maybe much more, as shares in the fast-growing international business get snapped up by growth managers, and the stock of the slower-growing domestic business attracts new kinds of owners by offering a hefty dividend.

When a company separates into two or even multiple companies, the results over time, as I will show you, can be staggeringly positive. Managers increasingly understand that such de-merging is the way they can deal with ETF discounts and S&P futures selling pressure. It's how they can combat the ennui, if not the antipathy, the stock market now generates for the average investor. A manager who breaks up his company is a manager who is saying, "Look at me, look at these terrific bite-size, easily understood companies. Don't you want one of these for your portfolio?" These breakups can transcend many of the roadblocks the market now seems to place in front of the everyday investor as she searches for ideas that can augment her paycheck. They can relieve the pressure on so many stocks engendered by the always opaque actions of the Federal Reserve. Will the Fed taper its bond buying? Will it stay accommodative? Who cares? We're breaking up into a couple of companies that are going to be worth a lot more regardless of what the Federal Reserve does! The bounty from corporate divorcing, with its instant wealth creation, can transcend the endless parade of depressing economic stories.

When you spot these breakup candidates before they occur, you could be embarking on a journey that ends with a fourfold win. The first victory comes when the market speculates that a breakup is a possibility and the stock is buoyed by behind-the-scenes chatter. The second bump occurs with the announcement of the actual breakup. The third increase comes as the soon-to-be-split-up stock creeps toward the dissolution. The fourth boost happens when they actually separate into different, publicly traded stocks. You get new sponsorship from excited analysts always looking for something new to write about, and you simultaneously get the blossoming of the new entities that occurs because they each had been held back by the unwieldy, unfocused management structure. Every stage of the metamorphosis can be extremely lucrative, provided you have the patience to go along for the *entire* ride.

Maybe because of the voracious way we tackle *Mad Money* every night, coupled with my desire to find stocks that would be worth much more than they are selling for if the people at the top showed some imagination, we've been able to isolate many of these potential breakups before they happen. Still, the trend is in its infancy. There are many more breakups to come. So let me show you, empirically, why the process isn't alchemy and how it can substantively increase values. We'll examine some typical breakups and the stages of wealth creation they produce.

Breaking Up: Why We Care— American Standard, Tyco, Altria

American Standard, one of the most unwieldy conglomerates ever created, may be the granddaddy of the breakup process. This venerable company specialized in three disparate businesses: heating, ventilation and air-conditioning systems; bathroom fixtures such as toilets and faucets; and vehicle control systems: three totally different and wholly unrelated businesses. That's why, in February 2007, Fred Poses, a visionary CEO and all-time wealth creator, decided to break up American Standard into three separate units: Poses sold the kitchen and bath division to Bain Capital, a private equity firm; spun off the vehicle control business as the now publicly traded WABCO; and changed the name of the remaining company to Trane, a superbly run heating, ventilating and air-conditioning company. Trane was subsequently sold to Ingersoll Rand, itself an industrial conglomerate that, ironically, is itself just beginning to break up. The erstwhile American Standard had little appeal to anyone. It traded at a deep discount to other industrials because it couldn't be siloed by Wall Street analysts. No would-be acquirer could be tempted because it was such an odd duck with zero synergy.

Before anyone speculated that American Standard would be broken up, the company's enterprise value—the market capitalization plus the debt on the balance sheet, minus any cash—equaled $11 billion. The core kitchen and bath business immediately fetched $1.7 billion, while Trane was sold for $10.1 billion. The value of these two divisions alone, with a simple pen stroke, exceeded the enterprise net worth of its predecessor company. WABCO, a superb electronics, suspension and transmission company, came for free. It now has an enterprise value of $5.2 billion and, I believe, is worth far more than it is selling for. All told, the American

Standard corporate divorce unlocked a hidden value of more than 50 percent almost instantly, a sobering story of how much of a discount there was to the true worth of this ill-thought-out conglomerate.

The second anchor breakup? Tyco, the once huge conglomerate put together by Dennis Kozlowski, who was subsequently convicted of fraudulent accounting when he was putting together this health care, electronics and security conglomerate.

At the beginning of 2006, rumors began to percolate that Tyco was going to split itself into three separate companies, a move Kozlowski's replacement, Edward Breen, then executed in just eighteen months. Tyco spun off its health care business, chiefly a medical device company, into a new entity known as Covidien, and its electronics business as TE Connectivity—two venerated companies that actually stood above most others in their respective categories. Then, in September 2011, the remaining portions of Tyco broke into ADT, a home security business, and a flow-control company that was then purchased by Pentair, a conglomerate dedicated to the safe flow of water, for $4.9 billion. Tyco kept its fast-growing fire control and security business as part of the stub company. Before the rumblings of a breakup, Tyco's enterprise value stood at $65 billion. The entities, once separated, created more than a 30 percent increase in value from the initial speculation to the completed breakup. The pieces continue to produce value, as Covidien recently spun off its drug division into Mallinckrodt, which immediately generated even more value for shareholders who stuck with the company. TE Connectivity, even after its doubling since the breakup, is incredibly inexpensive, even though it is the best-of-breed connector company, one that makes all of those ubiquitous cables that attach devices everywhere.

The best example of the joys of divorce? The amazingly brave decision by the old chief executives at Philip Morris to break the company into a food business, Kraft, and a domestic tobacco company, Altria, and international tobacco concern, Philip Morris International. The old Philip Morris was an unwieldy worldwide food, beer and tobacco enterprise, led by flagship brand Marlboro, that never seemed to be able to shake off the conglomerate discount. The company, always considered among the most shareholder-friendly concerns, hit upon a multistage plan to unlock buried value upon buried value, and it became the acknowledged blueprint for others to follow because of the incredible value creation that a divided company could engender.

In January 2007 management first spun off its Kraft food division, the iconic consumer packaged goods concern that included cookies, cheeses, salad dressings and, of course, Oscar Mayer meats. Then, after a terrific burst of value from that split-off, Philip Morris management cleaved the tobacco company into a fast-growing international conglomerate, Philip Morris International, with a below-average dividend, and Altria, a slower-growing domestic business with a huge dividend relative to all other companies in the S&P 500. Looking back, I can't believe how prescient the people who ran Philip Morris were. Analysts from two different spectrums sought to champion each part because some managers craved a pure play on developing and largely unregulated tobacco markets and others feasted on a company that gave shareholders a higher-than-average stream of income. And everyone liked Kraft.

Not long after, in 2011, the team at Kraft, recognizing the virtue of a fast-growing international play and a slower-growing, higher-yielding company, split into the domestic Kraft and the international Mondelēz, a silly-sounding moniker but one with a ton of promise. The Kraft piece, funded by the traditional, slow-growing Kraft products Velveeta, Miracle Whip and Jell-O, immediately instituted an above-average dividend. The Mondelēz portion offered a lower dividend but much faster earnings per share growth, with emerging markets craving snack brands such as Oreo, Chips Ahoy, Halls, Trident, Cadbury chocolates and Ritz crackers.

In January 2007, before the speculation of the original breakups, the predecessor company had an enterprise value of $175 billion. Today Philip Morris International, with an enterprise value of $165 billion, is, alone, worth nearly that much, while Mondelēz and Kraft together are valued at more than $110 billion and Altria is valued at another $85 billion. Add it all up, and the component parts of the old conglomerate have more than doubled in value—before dividends—from the days before the first spin-off was announced in early 2007, while the S&P 500 advanced just 14 percent during that time period. Philip Morris is the prototype for all of the splits that have been created since then and all that are now currently on the drawing board, including many I suggest in the rest of this chapter.

The Pieces Exceed the Whole

Before we embark on spotting the next breakups, let's not sell short the companies that have already broken up. Remember, there are four stages to this money-making process: (1) the run-up in anticipation of the split; (2) the announcement of the event itself; (3) the slow creep to the day of split; and (4) the blossoming of the pieces. Each stage is rewarding, and it's not too late to consider buying some of the best of the breakups, including the splits in the oil field. Let's take three of the most recent splits: the de-merging of ConocoPhillips, the oil and gas company, into Conoco, the exploration and production entity, and Phillips 66, formerly the refining and marketing division of the predecessor Conoco; the breakup of Abbott Labs into the new Abbott Labs, a fast-growing diagnostic, cardiovascular and nutrition company, and AbbVie, a high-yielding drug enterprise; and the split-off of Zoetis, an animal health concern, from the drug behemoth Pfizer. At each of the four stages you received a bump in price as the marketplace recognized the desire to have two different divisions, a faster-growing spin-off and a slower-growing dividend payer. All six companies are still enjoying a boost from all the new attention and the better-than-expected numbers that continue to be pumped out by the more focused managements. I think they still have further to go.

Similarly, every deal in the food and beverage business has given you a terrific return on both pieces as the evolution occurred. The breakup of a sleepy Sara Lee produced two pieces, a meat company, Hillshire Brands, and a European coffee company that almost immediately received a take-over bid that brought out an immense amount of hidden value versus what the two divisions gave you under one roof. Not long after that a mundane Ralcorp divided into a cereal company and a fast-growing private-label enterprise. The latter company, which kept the parent's name, soon after received a $5 billion bid from ConAgra, a food conglomerate that would have had no use for the entire Ralcorp but needed a private-label arm to flesh out its full line of brands sold into supermarkets.

The separation of the traditional milk purveyor Dean Foods into the slow-growing namesake milk company and WhiteWave Foods, a premium producer of organic milks and dairy alternatives, has produced market-beating gains for those who held both. I am convinced they will continue to do so, as I suggested earlier.

The breakup of the conglomerate that was Fortune Brands into Beam, the liquor company that produces Jim Beam, among other brands, and Fortune Brands Home & Security, a home-building supplier, has rivaled both those splits with gigantic wins for both pieces. Again, I still like both, the former because the spirits market is incredibly strong, something to be expected in a sluggish economy, and the latter because it is a premier play on home building and remodeling. The breakup of Fortune Brands, which was at one time a spin-off of the now vanished American Brands conglomerate, is emblematic of a neither-fish-nor-fowl company that lacked coverage because neither a housing materials analyst nor a liquor analyst could dissect the company's worth. Separately they each wholeheartedly endorsed the pieces.

Finally, I believe the separation of Timken, a fabulous proprietary steel company, into a best-of-breed steel manufacturer and a fast-growing specialty steel company geared to the aerospace and auto businesses, could generate gains for years to come. Here's a breakup, spurred on by a shareholder activist, that was initially fought by management but then, with the help of a very independent board, came around to seeing the wisdom of separating the two entities.

With these successes in mind, let me give you ten potential breakups that make sense to me and I am sure will make sense to the new breed of activists reading this text. In no case am I recommending any stock that would not work as a stand-alone entity, so if management doesn't attempt to bring out value in one fell swoop, you could still be expected to profit from the single unit.

Likely Breakup Candidates

As we have seen from the stellar results generated by the Abbott Labs split-up and the Pfizer-Zoetis split-off, the parts of a colossal old-line drug and health care provider are often worth far more than their whole. It typically takes an aggressive management to recognize that there are several gold mines buried within the current silver mine of valuation, but I think we can expect that if these stocks continue to trade at discounts to their former valuations, we just may be in the early innings of this sector's unlocking of riches. With an eye to never recommending a stock on a breakup basis if its fundamentals aren't first intact if nothing happens— always the mantra for all my suppositional picks—who could be next for a lucrative divorce for investors in this area? I have three that could rival the wealth generated by the managements of Pfizer and Abbott: Baxter International, Johnson & Johnson and Merck.

1. Baxter

One of the most perennially undervalued companies in health care is Baxter International, which I often refer to on *Mad Money* as the redheaded stepchild of its cohort. Baxter is a classic example of a company whose underlying businesses simply don't belong under the same roof. On the one hand, Baxter has a humdrum medical device and instruments division that makes everything from prefilled syringes to intravenous delivery systems, IV nutrition products, infusion pumps, vaccines, anesthetics and kidney dialysis systems. On the other hand, Baxter also has a fast-growing biosciences division that develops and sells treatments, based on recombinant and plasma-based proteins, for hemophilia and other bleeding disorders, along with immune deficiencies, burns and shock.

Using the Abbott Labs template, Baxter could easily split into the slow-growing medical products business with an above-average dividend, and a fast-growing biotech company. Currently, the stock is getting lost in the shuffle, trading at a discount to its peers because of its confused structure. The two pure plays would be much easier to value and would appeal to different sets of managers, who would pay more for each separate unit than they would for one jumbled stock that's difficult to understand.

Baxter has already shown an inclination to take action. In July 2012 the company officially restructured itself into two segments, the biosciences division and the medical products division, making it much easier to organize and implement a potential breakup, something Wall Street analysts applauded but also acknowledged did not go far enough to cure the inherent discount of this Deerfield, Illinois, health care conglomerate.

How much would Baxter be worth on a breakup? The biosciences division—the drug side of the business—is expected to earn $2.94 billion in 2014. The highfliers in this space trade at twenty-one times earnings, so let's be conservative and say Baxter's bioscience business could trade at nineteen times earnings; that gives you a $55.86 stock. The medical products division, meanwhile, should earn $1.84 billion, and it has a 15 percent growth rate; say it trades at seventeen times earnings on its own, you get a $31.28 stock. Add them together, and the sum of Baxter's parts could be worth $87 a share, a substantial premium to where it has traded for ages. And, again, that's simply the value Baxter could create with the stroke of a pen by announcing a breakup; it doesn't factor in all the improvements that could be made by splitting up the company and letting each business focus on what it does best.

Portfolio managers seeking growth would love to get their hands on Baxter's bioscience division, which racked up $6.2 billion in sales in 2012. The company has a terrific pipeline with many shots on goal, including a hemophilia B treatment that has been designated an orphan drug and could be extremely lucrative for the company for the rest of this decade. Meanwhile, on the medical products side, Baxter acquired a company called Gambro that gives them more exposure to kidney dialysis machines and should provide a nice boost to the segment's growth when the deal kicks in during 2014.

In the meantime, you are being paid to wait with a bountiful $1.96 dividend and a stock that might do fine until management figures out just how badly Baxter needs to be more than one company.

2. Johnson & Johnson

When I first started at Goldman Sachs in the 1980s and was asked what stock I would put away for my kids, invariably I would say Johnson & Johnson. It was an easy call. In September 1982, Johnson & Johnson had just executed the biggest recall in the history of the United States. A never-apprehended homicidal maniac had fatally poisoned seven people in the Chicago area who had taken Extra Strength Tylenol, JNJ's biggest product, responsible for 17 percent of the company's income. Almost immediately JNJ recalled 31 million bottles of the drug and offered to replace any purchased containers for free. The recall cost the company $100 million, a huge sum in those days, but it bought the company a level of loyalty that has never been challenged. That recall, plus the company's renowned triple-A balance sheet, was enough for me to recommend the stock to everyone in my client base as a core holding. It paid off huge: $1,000 invested in Johnson & Johnson in 1982 turned into $22,000 twenty years later.

But in recent years the company everyone on the Street calls JNJ has squandered that fabulous image with a series of recalls and mishaps, including faulty hip replacements produced by its DePuy division and poorly manufactured children's health care products, the latter made at JNJ's McNeil Laboratories, ironically the same division that produced the tampered Tylenol. The recalls, twenty-five in number, cost the company $1 billion in sales and hastened to close the disastrous ten-year reign of William Weldon, an oddly revered wealth destroyer and one of the most prominent members of the *Mad Money* Wall of Shame until his departure in 2012. Weldon did more than just preside over the ruinous recalls. He also ruled during a period when Johnson & Johnson grew its top line at just 2.5 percent, with 4 percent growth in pharmaceuticals and 4.6 percent growth in medical devices, minus 3 percent growth in consumer products because of the horrendous recalls. When you compare those numbers to JNJ's peers, which delivered 10 percent increases in pharmaceutical sales, 5 percent increases in consumer products, and 6 to 6.5 percent increases in medical devices, you can understand why Weldon merited his ignominious spot on the Wall of Shame.

Fortunately, the board of directors wasted no time finding the best successor imaginable, Alex Gorsky, a former army captain and top executive who had managed to keep the JNJ device business in decent shape under Weldon's heavy hand. We don't know yet how Gorsky intends to reshape JNJ, although there's certainly no gun to his head because the stock's been roaring like a rocket ever since Weldon's era concluded and Gorsky's began. And it is possible that JNJ could stay as it is, which, given what I have seen so far from Gorsky, might be good enough, particularly when you consider Johnson & Johnson's bountiful and oft-raised dividend.

But from what I have seen, "good enough" is not good enough for Gorsky. What I hope he will realize is that a far better way to bring out instant but lasting value would be to divide JNJ three ways: pharmaceuticals, consumer products and medical devices. Right now there is a clear lack of synergy among these businesses. Each has different customers, different buyers, different manufacturing processes, different distributors, different product developers, different regulatory processes and even different investment needs and management philosophies.

And, of course, in classic fashion, no one on the "sell side," meaning the Wall Street research firms, knows who should cover JNJ. Should it be a consumer products analyst because of the over-the-counter products it makes, including fabulous household names like Band-Aid, Neutrogena, Johnson's Baby Powder and Listerine? Why not? Those products look a lot like what Colgate or Procter & Gamble have to offer. Should it be covered by pharmaceutical analysts, given that its new drugs have been the chief driver of earnings in the past couple of years? Or should the honors go to medical device analysts, as is pretty much the case right now, even as only 40 percent of sales come from the device business?

While JNJ's stock may have been mired in a Weldon-inspired lost decade, each of these three divisions is a standout leader as a stand-alone entity. Its pharmaceutical division has one of the best oncological pipelines, including a very promising prostate cancer drug and a potential blockbuster leukemia compound with biotech partner Pharmacyclics. It has a fantastic diabetes franchise and excellent immunological, antipsychotic and cardio drugs, as well as a promising potential Alzheimer's treatment. If spun off independently, I could see this business being valued at almost $55 a share when you stack up its products and its pipeline against its competitors.

Despite the lost children's product sales, the overall consumer business has been able to retain shelf space and is building back sales that were lost to others, notably store brands manufactured by Perrigo. If you give its sales a multiple relative to its peers, you could see a cash flow–spewing spin-off worth $15 that would be a natural to be acquired by Procter & Gamble or Unilever or Kimberly-Clark or even Church & Dwight.

Finally, its best-in-class medical device business, with its Cordis cardiovascular franchise and its Ethicon surgical products division, could easily trade for at least $40 a share when you compare it to its slower-growing and, yes, less prestigious competitors Becton Dickinson, Medtronic, Hospira and Boston Scientific. Collectively that gives you the possibility of more than $110 a share worth of value, unlocked simply by letting these three autonomous divisions stand by themselves, which many analysts would argue they already do.

Now, the great news about Johnson & Johnson is that, under Gorsky, the company has already gone far to repair its image with Wall Street, including, for the first time in ages, actually beating analysts' estimates for both the top and the bottom lines. Gorsky has said publicly that he will not tolerate any underperformance at any of the firm's vast divisions, and it would not surprise me if he does at least a partial spin-off of one of the less synergistic portions of the Johnson & Johnson empire. Either way, I think that JNJ has become a must-own in the health care space, with Gorsky once again returning the New Brunswick, New Jersey, company to its former glory—and the perennial fifty-two-week-high list as well.

3. Merck

I always laugh when people ask me how much it costs to start up a hedge fund, because it reminds me of how I was able to put enough money away to leave my job at Goldman Sachs and strike out on my own. The answer? Merck staked me all the money I needed. No, the giant pharmaceutical didn't give me money to manage. But in the 1980s, the Rahway, New Jersey, company did develop an anticholesterol drug, Mevacor, that my research showed Wall Street had badly underestimated. I helped manage the money of a bunch of smart doctors who had concluded that any diet or pill that could lower cholesterol could be integral in cutting down the incidence of heart attack in this country. Several mentioned to me that Mevacor could really catch on and become a potential billion-dollar blockbuster once Merck showed people how beneficial lowered cholesterol could be to a patient's heart. So I did what I always do when I want to speculate big on an idea: I bought call options on Merck as it slowly converted nonbelievers and set about creating one of the greatest blockbuster drug classes in history. When a pharmaceutical company produces a blockbuster drug, it's almost assured that its stock goes higher as the prescription data come out verifying the promise. But there's nothing better than a blockbuster drug that no one in the analyst community thought mattered, as almost all of them were using what, in retrospect, were ridiculously low estimates for the new drug. After a furious yearlong ramp as the strength of this anticholesterol franchise unfolded, Merck had made me more than enough money to quit my job at Goldman Sachs, take the plunge and go off on my own. I was extremely grateful, and I attended Merck's annual meeting the next year so I could personally thank then CEO Roy Vagelos for pressing the Mevacor case and making shareholders so much money. For years, Merck as well as Pfizer, with its own statin drug, Lipitor, the greatest blockbuster of all time before it recently went off-patent, rode this class of pharmaceuticals to levels that were unthinkable when first introduced. It was just a classic case of how wrong Wall Street can be and how powerful one drug can be for even a major pharmaceutical company.

But that was then, and this current iteration of Merck makes the old Merck from the Mevacor days look like a high-flying biotech stock. In fact, Merck, which used to sport the highest price-to-earnings multiple in the group because of its superior growth rate, now has the lowest because it has the slowest pace of innovation. That's why I have to suggest that the once unthinkable idea of breaking up Merck into little pieces is now not only plausible but is a must if this company wants to reward shareholders as it used to.

Heaven knows there's plenty to unlock. In 2009 Merck bought its rival and neighbor down the road, Schering-Plough, and while it has been effective in taking out costs, so far the acquisition has not produced the kind of return one would expect from a gigantic merger such as this one. There are a couple of reasons for that. First, Merck is getting hit all at once with some nasty patent expirations. Second, at the end of 2012 Merck had to stop U.S. development of a promising new successor to Mevacor after it had to pull the drug overseas, where it had been approved, because of some unforeseen side effects. Then in early 2013 Merck had to delay work on what was thought to be a promising new osteoporosis drug. It's just been a real tough run by any standards for the once best-of-breed pharmaceutical company.

But it isn't like Merck is sitting around doing nothing. In fact, Merck has one of the deepest drug pipelines of any major pharmaceutical out there, with thirty-five drugs in phase 2 or 3 development (close to approval), many of which could produce $250 million to $500 million in sales and one, a melanoma drug, with tremendous potential to be the next big Merck blockbuster.

It's not just all pipeline hope, however. Merck has a solid and growing diabetes franchise led by Januvia and Janumet, a pair of diabetes type 2 drugs that together generate $5.8 billion in sales. And the company has a vaccine division that's growing even faster, in part thanks to Gardasil, which has been shown to decrease the incidence of cervical cancer. The company also has a promising schizophrenia and bipolar disorder drug, Saphris, which causes less weight gain than other, similarly successful antipsychotics that currently generate multiple billions of dollars. I think this drug could be potential blockbuster material, as these kinds of drugs can take a while to catch on, and weight gain is a principal reason why patients stop taking these kinds of medications.

So there's plenty to get excited about. But the crux of Merck's dilemma is that Wall Street isn't the least bit excited about anything Merck seems to do. It's been such a snorer that most portfolio managers now view the stock as nothing more than a bond equivalent because of its bountiful dividend and its tremendous cash flow from existing medications that aren't threatened by patent expiration.

What can Merck do to revive its indolent stock? Pretty simple: it just needs to take a page from the incredibly successful recent Pfizer spin-off of its animal health division, Zoetis. When Merck bought Schering-Plough it got its own animal health division, a gem of a business that generates about $3.5 billion in revenue and a very handsome profit. That's almost the same size as Zoetis, but it grows much faster than that company, which currently has a market value of about $15 billion. It's easy to see how a spin-out of Merck's animal health division could produce at least a 10 percent bump to the current enterprise value. Then there's the consumer division, which gets $2 billion–plus in sales but no credit, because it's buried deep in the enterprise, despite housing such well-known brands as Coppertone, Dr. Scholl's, Tinactin, Lotrimin and Afrin. When I look at entities comparable to this division I can see it fetching $8 billion without too much of a stretch. Together that's almost $25 billion in assets that could be brought out instantly without damaging the core drug business. More important, remember how Wall Street works: it's addition by subtraction. Merck is obviously not satisfying anyone with this jumble of suntan lotions, foot supports and animal drugs alongside a fabulous pharmaceutical business. If Merck jettisons the consumer packaged goods and animal health businesses and takes the capital to either increase its dividend or buy back stock as Pfizer did, I could see the stock rallying 20 percent rather quickly. In the meantime you are paid to wait with a dividend that Merck is deeply committed to and has raised consistently for multiple years.

I know Merck won't return to those glory days of the 1980s, when it went from a decent drug franchise to one of the largest and fastest-growing enterprises in the world. That's now the province of the Celgenes and the Gileads and the Regenerons. Ironically, Dr. Vagelos is now chairman of Regeneron, which is developing what I think will be the next-generation blockbuster anticholesterol compound. But if Merck is as fed up with its stock price as the shareholders are, then it will most likely respond with a mimic of Pfizer's spin and give shareholders a very hefty return with almost no risk, giving you the careful path to getting rich that I so much want you to ride on.

4. PerkinElmer

PerkinElmer is another jumbled health care company I believe could unlock a tremendous amount of value by simply calling a banker and arranging a decisive divorce. This little $3.5 billion laboratory supply and life sciences play was formed by a merger in 1999, and since then the company has built itself up through a series of major acquisitions. Then, five years ago, management reorganized the company into two distinct units, a human health division and an environmental health business. On the human health side, which accounts for 56 percent of the company's sales, PerkinElmer makes diagnostics and tools that help detect diseases early in life, especially when it comes to prenatal screening, and it also develops tools that help research labs discover new drugs. The human health business is growing faster than its peers in the industry, and I think it would get a substantially higher valuation if it traded as an independent company. When you consider the 50 percent premium Thermo Fisher, the world's dominant life sciences tool provider, recently paid for Life Technologies, a company very similar to PerkinElmer's research business, you have to expect that PerkinElmer's best-of-breed research business would be worth much more standing alone. I wonder whether that new company would be able to stay independent very long, especially when you factor in that there were said to be several other bidders for Life Technologies left at the altar. Although even without a takeover, I think this breakup makes a huge amount of sense.

The other part of PerkinElmer, the environmental health division, is the premier maker of technology and instrumentation for detecting contaminants in everything from food and water to industrial end markets like chemicals, semiconductors and even construction. This is a slower-growth, lower-margin business that's also more cyclical than the human health side, meaning that the environmental business is more captive to the health of the overall economy, both here and around the world. It's kept the entire company's stock back with shortfalls that might be cured if a new, separate management gave the division its full attention as a stand-alone enterprise.

At the moment, PerkinElmer has faster organic growth than its peers in the life sciences space, but it gets a lower valuation; the stock is selling for less than twelve times next year's earnings estimates. In large part this is because management simply doesn't get full credit for its human health business, and it's pulled down by the momentarily sluggish environmental business, which happens to have substantial presences in depressed markets like Western Europe and Japan. Plus, even though the environmental side is ailing right now, this business is largely a play on increased consumer safety regulations, which are only going to be toughened, not lessened, over time. And it has a decent and growing exposure to China, where issues of water quality control are now paramount. If PerkinElmer management spun out the environmental business, the new entity could then focus more heavily on China and other emerging markets. Once the Chinese economy gets back on its feet, this part of the business could really roar. There isn't a company with technology as good as Perkin-

Elmer's, and I think an acquisitive company like Emerson Electric might want to buy the environmental health business, if only for a broader product portfolio for Emerson's burgeoning business in China. Everyone from DuPont to Honeywell to 3M has expressed an interest in adding to its safety portfolio. Maybe this company would whet their appetites.

Given the discount PerkinElmer trades versus its health care cohort, it's pretty simple to see that these disparate parts are worth much more than the whole. Let's do a quick sum of the parts analysis so you can see what I mean. First, there's the human health business, part diagnostics and part laboratory research tools. If you look at what Thermo Fisher paid for Life Technologies and give the same valuation to PerkinElmer's lab business, that equates to a $1.8 billion enterprise value. How about the diagnostics side? Well, that's similar to Gen-Probe, which was taken over by Hologic in August 2012 for six times sales. Give the same multiple to PerkinElmer and its diagnostics biz would be worth $3.3 billion. Add those two up and you get an enterprise value of $5.1 billion for the human health business. Right now the entirety of PerkinElmer has an enterprise value of only $4.4 billion. In other words, not only are you getting the environmental business for free here, but you're also getting the human health business at a discount. The environmental side has lower margins and more cyclicality, so if we say it's worth just two times sales, a rock-bottom valuation, that still gives it a $1.9 billion enterprise value, which means the total company is worth $7 billion. That's a 50 percent premium to PerkinElmer's recent enterprise value.

So if it breaks itself up, it's possible that these parts could ultimately be worth $4.8 billion, a price management won't be able to realize any time soon if it stays at a discounted whole. Will management see the light? I bet if it doesn't, an activist will soon come knocking and make the case for the breakup.

5. Manitowoc

Manitowoc, an oddly constructed industrial enterprise based in Manitowoc, Wisconsin, has two high-quality businesses, construction cranes and food service equipment, under one very constraining roof. Frankly, I don't think you could design two divisions to be more disparate if you tried. On the one hand, there's Manitowoc's old-school crane business, which is the number one supplier in the United States of lattice boom crawler cranes, as well as tower cranes, all-terrain cranes and boom trucks. The company is also huge overseas, getting 60 percent of its sales abroad. That's the part of Manitowoc that wears a hard hat and requires worldwide growth to produce strong earnings.

The other part of the company is one of the world's leading designers and manufacturers of commercial food service equipment, everything from refrigerators to ice makers, Frymasters, grills and beverage dispensers. This is the part of Manitowoc that supplies global companies such as McDonald's with machines to make fruit smoothies.

Manitowoc trades at a heavy discount to the average stock in the S&P 500 because it is viewed as a highly cyclical crane company, even though its fast-growing and less economically sensitive food service business accounts for 41 percent of its revenues and 66 percent of its operating profit. So Manitowoc will never get credit for its incredibly valuable food equipment business unless the company splits in two. Neither portfolio managers nor potential acquirers want to buy a consistent maker of food service equipment that's joined at the hip with a cyclical crane company whose results vacillate wildly depending on how well the economy is doing. And frankly, now that construction might be coming back in this country, why own a crane company that's joined at the hip with a maker of restaurant equipment that won't shoot through the roof whenever the economy gets going? Time for a hip replacement, for certain.

How much higher could the stock go if management were to decide to split things up?

Let's start with the crane side. This business is still well off its sales and earnings peak, even though construction trends are beginning to pick up worldwide. So if we value Manitowoc's crane biz using what people are paying for similar industrials like Terex, a decently run competitor, then based on the company's normalized earnings power—what it can make when business picks up—this could be a $2.5 billion business. And that's a fairly conservative number, not a super-bullish one.

How about Manitowoc's food service side? If we value this division based on what the market's paying for the average player in the space, then Manitowoc's food service business would also be worth $2.5 billion. Again, I think that could be a conservative number, because Manitowoc is anything but average. It's considered a best-in-class maker of food service equipment.

So let's add up these two potential valuations. Right now Manitowoc has an enterprise value—that's the market cap plus all the debt on the balance sheet; in other words, what an acquirer would have to pay for the company at the current price—of $4 billion. If the crane business is worth $2.5 billion as a stand-alone company, and the food service biz is worth $2.5 billion, then Manitowoc could be worth $5 billion if it simply decided to break itself up.

Manitowoc is a classic case of a company with the wrong packaging. A crane business and a food service equipment business simply don't belong under the same roof, which is why I think MTW could go so much higher if management would just announce that it was breaking the company up and forever freeing itself from the dreaded conglomerate discount.

6. DST Systems

You probably don't know DST, an information services and computer processing business chiefly for the financial services industry. It's a vast jumble of several businesses that could be highly valued on their own but are worth so much less being under the opaque umbrella that is DST. I see a number of signs suggesting that DST could be preparing itself for a sale, as management seems ready, at last, to face the inevitable fact that the parts are worth way more than the whole. In fact, it has already begun the dismantling process.

Right now DST Systems is kind of a cats-and-dogs company. For its chief business, DST provides information processing and software services, mainly to financial firms like mutual funds and brokers. Then there's a smaller division that does billing statement printing and mailing services for all sorts of businesses, especially telecom and health care companies. The financial side is a powerhouse, because many money managers outsource their mutual fund accounting services to DST, which is by far the largest player in this space, with 50 percent market share. The company provides transfer agency services to more than 101 million share-owner accounts. This financial outsourcer had been in decline for several years but has recently stabilized itself and generates a huge amount of cash. So does the ho-hum billing statement division.

But the real reason I like DST is because the company has a substantial portfolio of under-the-radar investments buried within the bowels of the company, so it gets no credit for them. For example, DST has a large stake in State Street, the fabulous custodial bank. It also has significant real estate holdings, major investments in private equity funds and some direct investments in private companies. When you add up all of these disparate assets on top of the core business, you get a sum-of-the-parts valuation for DST that far exceeds the current market value. Lately management seems to understand the discount. It has already started selling off some of its noncore assets, a potential prelude to a total breakup or perhaps a move toward going private.

The company could easily sell off noncore assets, including the hyper-competitive billing statement printing and mailing business, and it would be left with a pure-play financial services company that a private equity buyer or a financial services company might be intrigued to buy, given how little growth there is right now in that industry.

Not only that, but I think that DST could be a motivated seller, meaning that the people running this company seem like they'd be willing, even eager, to sell the whole enterprise. First of all, the longtime CEO, Tom McDonnell, a man who has worked at this company for more than forty years, stepped down in 2012 but has stayed on as chairman of the board and owns 1.7 percent. Another board member, George Argyros, who's in his mid-seventies, owns 22 percent of the company. Second, the new CEO, Steve Hooley, has a lot of experience in financial services and is precisely the kind of executive you'd bring in if you were planning to sell off DST's disparate assets in order to turn it into a pure play on the financial industry. All of these parts are easily monetized in a market eager for financial services companies without credit or interest rate risk.

Even if DST Systems doesn't catch a bid, this company has been gradually taking itself private for years, having bought back more than 60 percent of its outstanding shares over the past decade, 40 percent in the past seven years alone.

I would not recommend a stock on the basis of its takeover value, and the company has enough momentum that it could continue to generate above-average performance on its own. It's an archetypical divorce candidate that's still a winner even if it stays together.

7. Applied Materials

Sometimes even the best of companies get obscured because of actions taken to diversify away from a core business that had simply experienced a cyclical downturn. Manitowoc's management, for example, thought it could create more value marrying a less cyclical food service business to a massively cyclical crane concern. Similarly, Applied Materials, the best-of-breed semiconductor equipment manufacturer, set out on a diversification path not that long ago, and it's been holding back the enterprise value ever since. The core business of Applied Materials provides market-leading semiconductor-making machines and is the leader in half of its business lines. The company believes the semiconductor equipment business, which has suffered from a lack of orders, is now bottoming and should turn up over the next few quarters. In order to diversify away from the semiconductor manufacturers' episodic demand for equipment, the company has also built a display segment, which makes the equipment that's used to manufacture liquid crystal displays, or LCDs, and organic light-emitting diodes, OLEDs, for TV screens, personal computers, tablets and smartphones. This business has been in solid shape thanks to the strength in mobile devices and will get stronger as larger OLED devices are introduced in the next few years. The real problem for the stock, though, the real albatross, is the company's energy and environmental solutions division, which makes the equipment that's used to manufacture solar panels. The solar power market is rebounding hard right now, but there's still a ton of excess capacity, thanks to Chinese overproduction. Even though this is a minuscule part of the business compared to the semiconductor side, Applied Materials gets punished for the weak earnings from this af-

terthought division. It's a chief reason why AMAT has been a huge lag-
gard compared to the rest of the industry. Over the past two years, Applied
Materials has underperformed its peers, lagging the very similar KLA-
Tencor by 21 percent and falling behind the Philly Semiconductor Index
by 19 percent. Even though the stock rallied nicely in 2013, it is still way
behind the rest of its sector despite offering superior technology. I think it
still has a lot of room to run before it even catches up with the rest of the
industry, provided it takes action to unlock its value and free itself from
the discount brought on by the solar panel equipment division.

The best way for Applied Materials to outperform its peers is to break
itself up. In 2012 the company's solar division saw its revenues decline by
88 percent, resulting in a $184 million operating loss for the segment, ex-
cluding some big one-time charges that made the numbers look even
worse. Because of the weakness here, some analysts and investors feel that
Applied Materials should just shut down the whole segment. While that
would probably give the stock a short-term boost, I think it would be a
mistake, especially because the Chinese are beginning to show some ratio-
nality in their solar equipment production because of some very high-
profile bankruptcies in the past year.

Ideally, I think Applied Materials should spin off the solar business
together with the display business as a separate, more speculative company
that could appeal to those who favor investing in alternative-energy companies. The remaining semiconductor equipment business would instantly
be rewarded with a higher valuation as a pure play.

The fact is, even though this solar capital equipment industry is hated
right now, there's no denying the long-term worth of that renewable energy source business. The technology behind solar power is getting more
and more efficient, the payback period for buying a solar panel is shrinking, and the prices for solar panels are rising in Europe—the largest market for solar power in the world, as First Solar said recently at a very
well-attended analyst meeting.

You get this kind of breakup, and I think Applied Materials can go a
lot higher. If one assumes that the core semiconductor equipment business
can get the same valuation as KLA-Tencor, which trades at three times
sales, and I think that's a safe assumption, then you get a $22.2 billion

market cap for the core business alone—that's 25 percent higher than where the stock is right now. Then, conservatively, if the solar and display company trades at one times sales, you still get a business worth $800 million. The sum of the parts gets you $23 billion, or a $19-and-change stock well above where it has been trading.

Even if Applied Materials doesn't break up, Stephanie Link, co-portfolio manager of ActionAlertsPlus with me, who brought this discounted valuation to my attention, believes the company can earn $2 a share at the peak of the new semiconductor equipment cycle. At the last peak, the stock traded at eleven times forward earnings, so that means Applied Materials could go to $22 over the next two years or so on its own volition. That gives you a more than 50 percent gain from here, but you'll have to be patient to reap those rewards. With a breakup announcement, Applied Materials could take the stock to $19 in a much shorter period of time, then it can work its way higher based on that $2 number. So you have two ways to win: with the semiconductor equipment business coming back, the stock can go higher simply by virtue of stronger earnings over time; or management can take matters into its own hands, spin off the solar and display businesses as a separate company, and launch the stock higher overnight.

Just as I was finishing this chapter, it was announced that Applied Materials had agreed to merge with Tokyo Electron, a competitor with a similar profile, including both a semiconductor business and a solar division. The news about the merger focused on the semiconductor business, and I still think even a merged Applied Materials–Tokyo Electron can, and should, spin off the solar business and would get a much higher price if the regulators approve the merger.

8. Harris Corporation

One of the truly bizarre aspects of this market is that the defense contractors have been roaring higher, even though everybody's constantly talking about how the sequester has taken a big bite out of our government's defense budget. They've managed to run because these businesses were all well prepared for the cutbacks and because many hedge funds bet against them, expecting shortfalls. When the shortfalls didn't occur, they had to scramble to cover their shorts, helping to propel the stocks higher. However, there's one defense company that hasn't participated in this move, Harris Corporation, a stock that has underperformed the averages at a time when its peers Lockheed Martin, General Dynamics and Northrop Grumman have on average doubled the indices' advance. Why hasn't Harris moved in tandem with its cohort? I think it's because Harris doesn't have *enough* defense exposure.

Or, to be more on point, Harris gets a discount because it is not a pure-play defense contractor. In fact, it's not a pure play on anything. The company makes communications and information equipment, everything from wideband networking tactical radio systems for the military to secure telecom networks used by air traffic controllers, to voice, video and data connectivity equipment for ships at sea—they recently signed a five-year contract with Royal Caribbean—as well as comprehensive communications and information technology services to remote oil and gas drilling operations. Harris is the top supplier of tactical radios to the United States and NATO, and it has fifty antennae currently in orbit used to enable super-long-distance communications. It has a hospital services division that dramatically reduces the time to retrieve medical records. It's also helping to build out a national weather service data processing network.

In 2012 the company got 70 percent of its sales from the U.S. government, but that's down from 78 percent the year before and 82 percent in 2010 because Harris' commercial segment is growing so rapidly. These segments, however, don't belong under the same roof. The defense and commercial markets have very different purchase requirements and customer bases, and a stand-alone defense contractor, separate from these commercial operations, could be worth more than the entire enterprise.

Harris currently pays a decent dividend that yields roughly 3 percent, and the stock trades at ten times next year's earnings. Its defense business has slow growth, but it throws off a ton of cash. The commercial side is growing much more quickly, but the stock doesn't get credit for that growth because it's jumbled with the defense business. You split them up, you could have a defense stock with a higher yield and a faster-growing commercial communications stock with a higher price-to-earnings multiple.

Harris is a confusing conglomerate that would immediately create value if it would just split into several pure-play businesses. It would seem, given the immense outperformance of the defense contracting business, this split-up could be just a matter of time.

9. Occidental Petroleum

The oil patch has been home to some spectacular wealth creation via breakups, with Conoco and Marathon Petroleum simply dividing themselves into exploration and production and refining and marketing companies. It's time for Occidental Petroleum to do the same. Occidental, once the fastest-growing major oil company, has been unable to break out of the pack for the past few years, a victim of lassitude and a lack of creative thinking. The company has oil and gas assets all over the world, in Libya, in the Middle East, in South America, as well as some important assets here at home, especially in Texas's bountiful Permian Basin and California's Monterey shale, two areas formerly thought to be past their prime that have now been reinvigorated by nontraditional forms of drilling. OXY also has what's known as a midstream business, where it gathers, transports and stores oil, gas and carbon dioxide. Finally, it has one of the world's largest and finest commodity chemicals businesses. These assets, like the divisions that Conoco and Marathon comprise, are too disparate to work under the same roof, which is why the stock doesn't get nearly enough credit for what it owns.

But the good news is that Occidental's management, led by CEO Steve Chazen, recognizes the problem, and it may be only a matter of time before management does something about this disparity. Right now Occidental is considering a variety of plans to bring out value, and from what the company has been saying, I believe that by some point in 2014 this will be a very different-looking company with perhaps two or three separate entities no longer living under the same roof.

The first step would be for Occidental to either spin off or outright sell its assets in the Middle East and North Africa, which should bring in around $20 billion. While these properties aren't in the most stable places, they do represent just about the best assets that would be available on the market any time soon, certainly superior to the recent bid Apache Corporation received from the Chinese for just a portion of its volatile Egyptian assets. OXY could then use that cash to finance a gigantic buyback, one that would let the company shrink its share count by roughly 26 percent.

Occidental's remaining exploration and production assets in the Americas may be among the most undervalued in the entire oil patch. Management could easily split these into two separate companies, a more value-oriented pure play milking its deep assets in the Permian Basin that pays a hefty dividend and a growth-oriented operation centered around its gigantic unconventional holdings in North Dakota's Bakken shale and California's Monterey shale. The Bakken is a well-known field by now, rivaled only by Eagle Ford and Permian in Texas as the most prolific finds since Prudhoe Bay's discovery in the 1960s. But the Monterey shale could rival all of these, and Occidental is the number one player in the area by far.

How much would Occidental be worth if it actually follows through with this proposed three-way split—an international oil company, a domestic dividend play based out of the Permian Basin, and a domestic growth play built around its unconventional assets like the Bakken and Monterey shales?

Bank of America Merrill Lynch took a stab in 2013 at valuation of a split-up Occidental that seemed pretty cogent to me. The firm figured the international business could be worth $22 a share, while the American divisions together could be worth $126. If you add those together and subtract the roughly $7 a share in net debt on the balance sheet, you get a $141 stock. That's dramatically higher than where Occidental is right now, and those are just their base case numbers, not the more bullish analysis I've seen that puts the sum of the parts at $157 a share.

Of course, we don't know for sure what Occidental will actually decide to do. But that's where the opportunity comes in. Once we do find out the plan to unlock value, the stock is going to vault higher, perhaps to levels that exceed the wealth creation of Marathon and Conoco, because OXY offers superior assets. In the meantime, Occidental is paying you to wait for official word of the split with a not inconsiderable $2.56-per-year dividend. Good growth, good dividend, great locked-up potential; Occidental may be the most undervalued oil company on earth.

10. Johnson Controls

Some companies are just crying out to be broken up. One of those companies is Johnson Controls, an unwieldy auto-related conglomerate that has made no sense to me for years, even though, at various times, including now, my charitable trust would own it, thinking, *Ah hah! At last, they get it, they recognize that the considerable parts are worth more than the depressed whole.* But no, not yet at least.

Right now Johnson Controls has three main segments that each account for roughly a third of the company's profits. First, there's the company's building efficiency business, where it makes heating, ventilation and air-conditioning systems, along with building management and security systems. Second, Johnson Controls has a big auto supply business, where it builds interior systems for the car, things like instrument panels, information displays and seating. Third, the company makes batteries, both old-fashioned lead-acid car batteries, marketed under the name Interstate Batteries, and new-fangled lithium-ion batteries that are used in hybrids and electric cars.

For years, Johnson Controls has been trying to move into growth areas, away from its core auto parts business, because the auto supply game is a tough business with a lot of competition. That's why the company bought the venerable York International back in 2005 to get into the heating, ventilation and air-conditioning space. Meanwhile, within the auto business, Johnson Controls has been making acquisitions, buying specialty component manufacturers with strong franchises, particularly in seating, to get more vertically integrated. Yet while these moves have allowed the company to take share, the stock just doesn't seem to get any credit because it is an unwieldy conglomerate that Wall Street simply doesn't understand, so it trades at a big discount to its intrinsic worth. I can't blame the analysts, as there are no more synergies here than there were with American Standard, the archetypal breakup story.

So how much more would Johnson Controls be worth if it were broken up? If you value each of the components based on current estimates— the building efficiency business, the auto supply business, and the battery business—then it turns out that the sum of the parts only slightly exceeds the value of where the stock is trading right now. So why do I believe so strongly that this company should be broken up?

Because using current numbers is the wrong way to do the analysis. One of the key reasons why Johnson Controls should be split up has to do with the way each of the resulting companies would be valued. For example, the building efficiency division is what's known as a late-stage cycle business. Once a sluggish economy kicks into gear, a late-stage cycle business begins to show superior profitability compared to most enterprises and becomes much sought after by portfolio managers as a way to play the rotational shift in the world's economies. In other words, if you value Johnson Controls' HVAC business on the out years, what it could earn in 2015 or 2016, then it's worth a lot more than if you value it based on this year's numbers. If this HVAC unit were an independent company, the people who would be buying it would be much more likely to value the stock based on that longer time frame. The same thing goes for JCI's battery division. This is a high-growth business levered to the pent-up demand for autos, as the average age of America's auto fleet is about eleven years old. That means the earnings down the road should be a lot bigger than the earnings right now. And if the battery business were an independent company, it too would get a better valuation than it can right now, as it is buried within the disadvantaged conglomerate structure.

The auto parts business is highly cyclical, and with the weakness in Europe, where Johnson Controls sells a huge proportion of its wares, it's currently underperforming those auto parts companies with much more of a domestic orientation. If you believe, as a I do, that a worldwide recovery is in store by the middle of the decade, then I think this division would get more credit for its earnings on its own merits. But when you amalgamate these three businesses the way Johnson Controls is right now, nobody wants to value this company on 2015 or 2016 earnings because there are too many moving parts. It's just too risky and too hard to figure out.

If we use the out years—let's say 2015 because I don't want to be too aggressive—then JCI's building efficiency segment, the dressed-up name for its HVAC operation, could be worth $13 billion, its considerable battery business could be worth about $14 billion, and the auto operation could be worth $10 billion. Add it up, subtract the debt on the balance sheet and you get a company worth about $50 a share. That's a company worth holding on to, a perfect play on the worldwide recovery, with a breakup kicker.

Summary: Breaking Up

We've now seen how the prospect of breaking up can produce bountiful results from the first chatter of its possibilities through the execution of the deed itself. Let's recap the best candidates:

1. Baxter could be split into a slow-growing medical device company and a faster-growing biotech business to bring out instant value.
2. Johnson & Johnson could create value by dividing into a medical device business, a consumer products play and a pharmaceutical company.
3. Merck has a fabulous animal health division and a solid consumer products division that could be spun off from its intrinsic pharmaceutical business to create as much value as Pfizer did when it spun out Zoetis.
4. PerkinElmer is crying out to be split into an environmental services business and a life sciences company.
5. Manitowoc is a mismatched construction crane and food service machinery business that could easily be made into two separate entities.
6. DST is a company with three disparate parts—a financial services business, some real estate holdings and a stake in one of the best financial custodial houses in the country—that when separated are worth far more than the whole.
7. Applied Materials, a premier semiconductor equipment company, needs to divest its solar division as a separate, stand-alone speculative entry even if it does complete the merger with rival Tokyo Electron.
8. Harris Corporation is a defense contractor with so many different businesses under one roof that it's not getting the benefits of its high-growth defense business. A simple stroke of the pen means instant value here.

9. Occidental Petroleum should follow the path of Conoco and Marathon and split into an exploration and production company as well as a refining and marketing business.

10. Johnson Controls' three businesses—batteries, auto parts, and heating ventilation and equipment—would be better off on their own.

We can never count on management breaking up the businesses they created, but the path blazed by American Standard, Philip Morris and Tyco is so clear that you have to believe some of these companies will seek to bring out value in the ways detailed here. If not, given the current power of activist shareholders who take big positions and then agitate, often successfully, for their breakup plans, any one of these companies could easily be targeted for instant wealth creation. In the interim, fortunately, all ten companies have the earnings power and, often, dividend protection, to allow you to own them and wait for them to do the right thing by shareholders. In an era when the market itself simply isn't working right and the companies can't get their due no matter how hard management works to do so within the existing structures, these ten equities have lots of upside and a downside limited by both their breakup values and their undeservedly inexpensive price-to-earnings multiples versus their peers and the market itself.

CHAPTER 5

CEOs: The Bankable 21

Sometimes stock market analysts get it all wrong. Sometimes they are too constrained by the four walls of the spreadsheet and the desire to "model" or get right the next quarterly report. They don't understand what—or who—can really drive a stock over the long term. That can be helpful if you are working at a hedge fund trying to game the next upside surprise. But it's not all that valuable in an environment that's frightening for the average investor, who has been abused in the Flash Crash, betrayed by the Facebook debacle and stunned by a three-hour shutdown of the second largest stock market in the world, the NASDAQ, with no reason given for the "glitch" that makes any sense at all. Investors who have been put through that gauntlet need to redevelop faith in the stock market, or they will just hide in their wealth-destroying bond funds. They need touchstones. They need some faith in the equity process. Most of all, they need leaders they can believe in, people who can take the chaos of modern everyday business life and turn it into opportunities that their shareholders can profit from.

That's why, in *Get Rich Carefully*, I want to introduce you to a whole new way to pick good stocks. I want you to focus, going forward, on the jockey as much as the horse. Or if racing eludes you, I want you to bet on the head coach, because that's who plays the biggest role in determining the revenues and the earnings, while providing the priorities and the vision necessary to deliver superior performance for years and years to come. If we want to get wealthy over time, we have to identify who can help us get there and, in the parlance of wagering, lay money on them, or in the argot of Wall Street, buy shares in their companies.

I know many of you follow sports. Just for a moment, if you would, ask yourself if you would feel confident investing your hard-earned money on a legal bet this weekend on a team in the National Football League without researching or knowing the history of the coach of that team. Would you really favor the New England Patriots if they were run by someone other than Bill Belichick? Doesn't your confidence in the recent Super Bowl contenders, the Baltimore Ravens and the San Francisco 49ers, stem from the strengths and wisdom of their head coaches, John and Jim Harbaugh? When a team goes bad, do we blame the individual players on that team? No, we correctly blame the coach, because the coach must have a superior ability both to pick from the same talent pool as all other coaches and to outsmart those rival coaches through grit and innovation on the gridiron any given Sunday. When a club loses a couple of games in a row, it is the job of the coach to triumph over that adversity and get the team back on track. The coach has to manage the egos, keep the pay in synch with what the owners want and get the most out of his players. The coach makes the team, not the other way around.

Isn't that, I ask you, exactly what we expect of our CEOs? Don't we expect them to field a team of players who deliver every quarter and, if they falter, to get right back on track? Isn't the CEO responsible for the vision, the teamwork and the innovative spirit of an organization? As someone who has analyzed thousands of companies from the top down and participated in the hiring and firing of CEOs as a member of the board of directors of a public company, TheStreet, I can tell you that knowing the record and character of the CEO—what he's brought to the table before and what he can bring to the organization in the future—will determine, *more than any other factor*, whether you will be able to get rich investing with that leader. It is ironic that only in the business of picking stocks do we relegate leadership to the back of the investing bus and instead focus on the need to beat the estimates, as if, somehow, that's just

done no matter who is at the helm. I'm tired of it, and I want to change
the way companies are viewed to make the investing process easier, more
accessible and more successful. I intend to do that with this chapter, giving you the most investable twenty-one executives who have ever appeared
on *Mad Money*.

I want to salute these individuals for all they have done for their customers, their employees, and therefore their shareholders, as pleasing the
shareholders flows right out of the success in winning over the two other
constituencies. For my money, we don't do enough to celebrate the tri-
umphs of the successful CEOs. We revere sports figures with checkered
off-the-field standards. We fawn over actors and actresses who never make
us a dime. But when it comes to the business executives we bet on, we
think nothing of dismissing them all as greedy bastards who could care
less about us, unless it helps them to make even more money than they do
right now. We think they exist to line their pockets with money and pump
their egos with power. We focus on how much more they are paid than
their employees. We wonder why they don't relinquish more say to the
boards of directors. We think that he is surrounded by rubber-stampers
and yes-people who reward him with huge pay increases because they too
want the CEO's favor. After all, board members are often retired public
servants and academics, and the money they make from being directors is
so huge relative to their net worth that standing up to the CEO may be
risking the greatest job of their career.

Frankly, I don't care about any of that. Yes, I think almost all CEOs
are overpaid relative to their rank and file. The system allows that to be
the case, as compensation committees simply compare their CEO to what
other CEOs are making in the industry, regardless of their skill sets, and
agree to give them at least the same, if not more, compensation, no matter
how outrageous. But I don't let that lack of accountability—and the unfair reward system that comes with it—faze or blind me. I'm not here
to judge a CEO's compensation. I am here to judge the opportunity the
CEO is giving us to make money from his or her efforts. All I care about
is getting you to own the stocks of winning CEOs regardless of how much
they are paid. Salary morality is of no interest to me if the CEO is making
us fortunes with his stock. If they are overcompensated and it hurts the

stock price if they get that salary and bonus and stock package, then I am a willing seller and will find a better situation. My charitable trust did just that with Oracle after I learned that CEO Larry Ellison was paid the most of any CEO of any publicly traded company while earning nothing at all for his shareholders.

But if a CEO turns around an enterprise that would otherwise have gone bankrupt and gives you a gigantic return on a low-dollar stock, as CEO Alan Mulally did at Ford, I don't care what he gets paid. I got a terrific return betting on him. If a company is left behind the pack in its industry, I am going to assume it's the CEO that let the institution down, and I will recommend jettisoning that stock. However, if the company is being reinvented, the way Cheryl Bachelder reinvented Popeyes or Mark Papa changed EOG, then count me in as a buyer.

That's why I am going to reveal here the best of the best, the twenty-one people who have come on *Mad Money* and deserve your praise and your money. These are the twenty-one who will assuage your fear of owning stocks, or at least their stocks, and will let you profit alongside them as they practice their good works.

Getting to know management is almost impossible for the typical home gamer. It was difficult for me to do so as a professional money manager. We typically have to rely on scant interviews, brief three-minute question-and-answer sessions on television and the staged conference calls, with an occasional media profile thrown in to make our judgments about the effectiveness of the person in charge. With *Mad Money* I am trying to break that mold, giving chief executive officers some real time both on and off the set to explain their vision and tell us why we should own their stocks. This way I hope you can get more comfortable with the person leading the enterprise you might own shares in. I regard that comfort as the missing ingredient in trying to assess the bankability of a CEO.

I have always had mixed and often highly critical relationships with chief executive officers. I never hesitate to call out those who do poorly, particularly those who take boatloads of shareholder money while their stock stagnates or goes down. I have created my own *Mad Money* Wall of Shame to point out, in a constructive fashion, that some executives would do well to leave their enterprises to spend more time with their families, which could be a win-win for both constituencies. I've put CEO acquaintances on the wall—hey, I always start the show by saying it isn't about friends, it's about money. I've put people I thought should be in jail on the wall. And at all times I have said that the moment someone on the wall leaves or is fired, the stock of the company the executive labors at will go higher. I am proud to say that almost every single departure of a shamed exec has led to a higher price for shareholders.

All that said, I actually regard the vast bulk of the CEOs as competent, intelligent, and deserving of their accolades and their salaries and bonuses. In fact, when we look back at the period before, during and after the Great Recession, I think we will find more than a few hero CEOs, people who kept their heads and used the crisis to stretch the enterprise and take advantage of the crisis to build a more lasting institution, one capable of supporting a much higher stock price.

One thing is for certain: I can put together a list of visionary CEOs who weathered the Great Recession and allowed you to prosper along with them when things got better; it would be a lot harder for me to list politicians who brought anything positive to that most dire of moments.

Obviously, there are many CEOs who can be counted on to deliver for you, and I can't know them all. I never had the privilege of interviewing the greatest CEO of our time, Steve Jobs, although I feel fortunate that I got on the Apple bandwagon in the $50s by listening to my kids talk about Apple's products. If you bought the stock when Jobs started the company and sold it at its high, you gained more than 25,000 percent, a gain no one may ever top. I've had only the most cursory of interviews with Jeff Bezos, another CEO I admire tremendously, who has captained Amazon through a more than 17,000 percent appreciation from when he started the company. He is one of just a handful of surviving Internet wunderkinds.

Meanwhile, there are other CEOs who have been on the show who would most certainly be currently bankable had they not retired. There's Fred Hassan, who turned around Schering-Plough after it had fallen on hard times and then sold it to Merck for a huge price, his third giganti- cally successful pharmaceutical fix-up. There's Ivan Seidenberg, who took Verizon from an also-ran domestic telephone company to the best-in-class player in a global industry. There's Bob Simpson, one of the most successful oil and gas execs of our time, who built XTO into one of the largest natural gas companies in the world and then sold it to ExxonMobil near the absolute high in natural gas prices. Well done! And how about the redoubtable Peter McCausland, the founder and former CEO of Airgas, who prevailed upon shareholders to reject a bid from rival and archenemy Air Products, promising that if he were given the chance to continue to run the company he could do far better than the price Air Products offered. He did just that, giving you forty more points in the stock of Airgas than the suitor was willing to fork over.

There are so many others who are worthy of our twenty-one-gun salute, yet you might not know how important they are to the enterprise and to the stock value. The twenty-one winners I am about to give you are CEOs who have been battle-tested both in the real business world and in repeated trips to *Mad Money*, where I have had an opportunity to learn about them in a much more in-depth fashion than most analysts or shareholders will ever get to have.

These are the CEOs who I want you to consider betting on, jockeys who in this sport actually do control the horse, if not the race. When you see what they have done and how they have done it, I am sure you will agree with me and want to buy the shares of each of their operations as long as they are at the helm.

Bob Benmosche, AIG

So often people call into *Mad Money* and ask me whether I like the stock of a certain once great company. They will ask endlessly about Nokia or BlackBerry. Is this, at last, the moment to buy Xerox? Do you think the time has come when it is safe to pick up shares in AMD? I don't blame anyone for trying to call the bottom in these once great franchises. If the right executive comes in and the balance sheet isn't too shabby and the innovative spirit is still in the DNA, anything's possible.

That said, the successful, truly successful, turnarounds I can count on two hands. The vast majority of the time, these kinds of exercises devolve into "falling knife" contests, and and you don't want to end up being their butcher block. Leave that to the Crate and Barrels of the world.

Fortunately, some of the greatest turnarounds of our lives have happened in the past few years. Perhaps the mightiest is the effort led by Bob Benmosche to take American International Group out of government life support and turn it into what may be one of the great insurers out there.

I'm no stranger to Benmosche. A few days after the cataclysm of 9/11, I was with my erstwhile partner, Larry Kudlow, on *America Now*, the precursor to *Kudlow & Cramer*, and I wanted to interview a CEO in the insurance business who would come on the show and say that the checks literally were in the mail to the families of the deceased from that terrible tragedy. I made dozens of calls. No one would come on. No one except a guy I had never heard of, Bob Benmosche, then CEO of MetLife. I remember speaking to him on the phone as I booked him— hard to forget that booming voice. He told me he would come on that night because he had already told his organization to honor every claim immediately.

I guess I shouldn't have been surprised when he came to AIG on August 10, 2009, when the company was in tatters from the Great Recession. The man likes a challenge. The U.S. government had to bail out AIG to the tune of $182 billion in capital infusions because of a series of terrible insurance contracts the company wrote to insure abstruse instruments like synthetic collateralized debt obligations that were made up largely of poorly performing mortgages. Somehow AIG thought it would never have to pay off on them. Of course, as home values fell, the value of the underlying mortgages declined, and AIG had to reduce the value of the contracts on its books. AIG had been a very good underwriter of physical property, but in retrospect, it had no idea what it was doing when it was trying to assess the risk of financial instruments. The resulting financial catastrophe when these insured bonds blew up almost took down the entire financial world because AIG was so deeply embedded in the world banking firmament. In the end, AIG seemed to owe money to every large financial institution here and in Europe, and the U.S. Treasury was the only entity big enough to pay out on those obligations.

Enter Benmosche. While others were skeptical that the insurer would even survive, let alone pay back the $182 billion it owed the American taxpayers, the rough-and-tumble Benmosche saw immediately what had to be done. As was his way after 9/11, he was decisive in his plan and exacting in his execution, which, alas, included the execution of dozens of top-level personnel that he found totally wanting.

He quickly sold off AIG's asset management business, its life insurance operation in Japan. He then raised $36 billion by selling General American Life Insurance Company to MetLife and taking its Asian insurance arm, AIA, public. Those fast actions told investors that AIG, which they had thought to be in liquidation mode, could come back as a smaller, simpler, but thriving entity. That caught the eye of value investors, and they piled into it in droves as Benmosche delivered successful quarter after successful quarter while also bargaining to sell off pristine but extraneous assets like International Lease Finance, the aircraft financing arm. Oh, and the housecleaning was a thing of beauty if you like a Belichick type at the helm. It's Benmosche's way or the highway, and there were lots of sub-par AIG folks left crawling on to the Jersey Turnpike.

I too was skeptical when he began. I first brought him on the show a year into the turnaround, and he told me that he would be able to pay the government back by bringing out the entire book value of the enterprise, which was almost triple the value of the stock at the time. He would then retire the government's shares in the company through share buybacks and equity sales in the open market. Given how near death AIG was, the idea that this company could generate any free cash flow, let alone earnings, needed to buy back billions upon billions of dollars in stock seemed totally fanciful. "Who was that blowhard you put on, Cramer?" pretty much typified the reaction.

But he is truly a man of his word, and he got it done exactly as promised in a lot less time than he first thought he would need. When the government exited the last of its position, I brought Bob on to say thank you for all he had done. He told me that I was the first to do so and that no one from the government or from among his shareholders had bothered to say, "Good job. Thanks for your help."

That's ridiculous. Benmosche is a miracle man. When I chatted with him in the greenroom before the show, not long after he had beaten the cancer he had contracted early on in the turn, I speculated that he might be done with the job. Nonsense, he assured me, he was going to continue to take the stock to its book value in excess of $60 a share. But he also indicated that it could be worth much more than that.

You want to doubt the first man to say that he would pay all 9/11 claims in full immediately? You want to question the man who made the government whole on what could easily have been considered the most likely of the bailouts to be written off entirely?

I would rather own his stock. So should you.

Bob Iger, Disney

When I was growing up, I heard the silly adage that nice guys finish last. I had been brought up to believe that only the toughest—and perhaps the meanest—people could be successful. Now, it can easily be said that the most successful businessperson of our time, Steve Jobs, was indeed a miserable man, devoid of any personal skills and driven to humiliate just about everyone in his universe. I write "just about," though, because in any thorough reading of perhaps the greatest biography I have ever read, *Steve Jobs*, by Walter Isaacson, there's one executive whom Jobs revered: Bob Iger, chief executive officer of the Walt Disney Company. I think in some ways Jobs saw Iger as an alter ego, except one who was loved by all, not just loved by stockholders and tolerated by others.

If you ever get to meet Bob, you will know instantly why he's so amazing. He brings out the best in you, and he does so in a constructive yet competitive way. I first met him when he was chairman of the ABC Group, a half-dozen years before he became CEO. I had just finished my "hit" as a twice-weekly business correspondent on *Good Morning America*, and he was in the greenroom for a periodic check of how things were going. He took me aside when he saw me and immediately told me that he loved my stuff and what I was trying to accomplish, and then gave me a few helpful hints on how to do better. I came away glowing from the praise. Then, soon after, I realized that he had made many substantive suggestions that were actually critical of how I was doing my segments. He could have simply destroyed me had he just blurted out how he wanted the segment improved. But he took the time to present the changes in a remarkably breezy and supportive way, as if he had figured out, in advance, how to motivate me even though I was one of the smaller cogs, if not the smallest, in the entire on-air operation. He left me thinking he was my biggest backer, and I credit him with teaching me how to deliver a concept on television in a much more concise and pointed fashion.

While Disney had a long tradition of excellence, it had lost a lot of its edge by the time Iger came into the top job in September 2005. Since coming in he has revitalized product line after product line, taking on the broadcast network, the theme parks, the studio business, the merchandising and the cruise ships and hotels. In the meantime he has taken ESPN from a terrific sports property to perhaps the single most lucrative entertainment property in the world, responsible for 50 percent of the company's profits. And to think that it was just an afterthought when Disney bought it as part of a larger deal to take over Capital Cities ABC in 1996.

There are so many things to like about what Iger's done in his tenure. But what I like best is the multiyear vision he has outlined both in our off-air talks and in his on-air appearances on *Mad Money*. It is a vision of taking established fantasy franchises, refurbishing and revitalizing them and then blowing them out along all of the firm's multiple levels of distribution: movies, television, theme parks. He did it first with the buying of Pixar in 2006, then Marvel in 2009, and now Lucasfilm, the owner of the *Star Wars* property, in 2012.

Disney acts as a force multiplier of each of these amazing franchises by flooding all of its entertainment pipes with well-known characters and new ones from the lab. Through that remarkable amortization Iger turns what looks like a dilutive acquisition into an accretive one much more rapidly than expected. Plus, the worldwide love of the individual characters that comes with these purchases gives Disney a much more fabulous hit ratio in blockbuster movies than just about any other entertainment company out there.

Strangely, Wall Street was often slow to get Iger's vision of these acquisitions and sold the stock down each time he's done one, which was terrific for *Mad Money* viewers because we've been able to get in on each of the ridiculous and not long-lasting dips that come with these incredible buys.

By emphasizing the studio properties and their extensions into the lucrative theme parks, I don't want to minimize the immense profits that Disney books from the 80 percent of ESPN that it owns. As a sportswriter in an earlier life, I am in awe of the rigor of the operation and the way Iger has managed to funnel resources to take what may be the most valuable and least time-shifted entertainment property and make it worth more each year. No wonder we all pay more than $5 a month for the various ESPNs on our dial, whether we watch them or not. Everything else, other than news, we can watch later on Netflix or on demand.

As a fantasy football fanatic, first introduced to me by the legendary John Walsh, the executive editor of ESPN, back in the days when John ran *Inside Sports*, I can't believe how strong ESPN's hold is on those of us who live and breathe this oddly compelling and time-consuming game. There are tons of low-hanging fruit that could be harvested by Disney with their best-in-class website, including getting million-dollar sponsorships for the tens of millions of fantasy league players that they host. But frankly, as Iger would tell you—and he has certainly told me—as lucrative as that might be, Disney has so many irons in the fire of far greater magnitude that, while it will ultimately be monetized, there's too much money to be made for shareholders focusing elsewhere. Disney is a mine with so many veins of gold in it that you can't afford to spend time on the copper by-product that successful gold mining gleans.

Oh, and by the way, through all of this, Iger has never changed his nice and thoughtful demeanor. Most CEOs come out to Englewood Cliffs, New Jersey, where *Mad Money* is filmed, with a team of PR people, CFOs, security, you name it. Real posses. Iger? Alone. Just him. Sitting in the greenroom. Stretching his legs. Checking his cell phone and hoping you will swing by and visit before the show begins. And he's still the first guy every year to wish me happy birthday, no doubt because we share the same February birth date.

■ Marc Benioff, Salesforce.com

It's difficult not to be captivated by Marc Benioff, the larger-than-life founder of Salesforce.com, who cut his teeth learning about software from

Larry Ellison at Oracle while apprenticing with Steve Jobs, who was instrumental in Benioff's creating an ecosystem that now makes it the number one customer relations management company in the world.

Benioff is an inventor, an inspirer, a visionary and an uber-salesman all wrapped up into one life force who gave you an almost 2,000 percent return when his company came public in June 2004 versus a 65 percent return for the S&P. As someone who brought TheStreet public at the same time, I can only marvel that this company, which never lost the dotcom at the end of its name and uses the ticker CRM to emphasize its value as a customer relations management company, is one of only two companies from that whole Internet 1.0 era, the other being Amazon, that can truly be called winners when it comes to their shareholders. Benioff's vision is simple: He wants to be the undisputed king of customer relations software that can do everything from isolating potential sales targets to following up and converting them to keep them happy once they are in the fold. He also wants to wipe out the competition, whether it be SAP, Oracle or Microsoft, along the way to being the fastest public company in history to get to $5 billion in annual revenues. Who can doubt this man, given that his company was the fastest public company in history to get to $1 billion, $2 billion, and $3 billion in sales?

Remember, he traversed this trajectory in one of the darker times in American business history, and he did so without skipping a beat. Still, he has attracted more than his share of detractors, despite his company's stellar share performance, one of the top gainers of all stocks I have followed.

The skepticism involves Benioff's acquisitive nature. He has accumulated a huge number of properties to build out his customer relations management cloud-based software arsenal, and he's done so in record time. Along with his mentor Jobs, he pretty much invented the idea of the software-as-a-service model, where you download his product from the cloud. So perhaps he should be given the benefit of the doubt for his pursuits.

Benioff is in a hurry to win. He knows that if he doesn't move first to buy the companies that make Salesforce.com's tools superior to those of his competitors, they will catch up to the company's capabilities. So far he's done an amazing job of it, most recently nabbing an email marketing favorite of mine, ExactTarget, for $2.5 billion. I wonder if Benioff is trying to get a 10 in each category of my ten-point high-growth test. He's certainly earning top scores in each portion of the exam!

The detractors of Benioff and the stock don't understand two key elements of CRM. First, Benioff is the most transparent chief executive officer I have ever met. He regularly comes on after every quarter, and on several occasions I have demanded statistics and figures that others might be reluctant to give out for competitive reasons but I thought were necessary both to silence the skeptics and to make shareholders more confident and informed. He *always* adjusts to my questions and, in the next quarter's interview, provides all the data I want to see. He also puts those data points in an entertaining context so you can understand why Salesforce .com is doing better than everyone else in his sector. He wants you to understand every part of his company so you can be an informed shareholder who will buy more, not sell, when the stock goes down when the market takes a swoon. The second element the detractors don't understand? The customers love the product. I am always moved when I go to Salesforce .com's website and I watch the testimonials of so many Fortune 100 company executives about what Salesforce.com has done for their organizations. It's quite amazing to see the CEOs and chief marketing officers of companies as diverse as General Electric, Yelp, Burberry, Kimberly-Clark, Dunkin' Donuts, Home Depot and Wells Fargo sing the praises of Salesforce.com's sales, service and marketing clouds. I've used two different Salesforce.com products at two different companies and found them, like Apple products, revolutionary in their simplicity and in their usefulness in fostering productivity gains and more lucrative sales.

I am always looking for holes in a success story because I know that my viewers demand skepticism from me. As I always say at the beginning of the show, it's not about making friends; it's about making money. But every time I try to find holes in Salesforce.com, even when armed with the most critical of Wall Street research reports, I fail to find them. Not long ago I went to the Salesforce.com website and gave my name, address and phone number in order to sign up to view testimonials. Within an hour an incredibly smart and polite salesperson called to ask how he could best help me understand which products might be right for me. The persistence and alacrity amazed me.

As Benioff says of his enterprise, Salesforce "has always been a cata-lyst and evangelist for innovation in enterprise software. We've pioneered the shift from cloud to social to mobile." It's true. The defining test of tech success—dominance in social, cloud and mobile—is best found at Salesforce.com.

▪ Dave Cote, Honeywell

Not long ago, we on *Mad Money* decided to examine which companies had viable five-year plans that they had been successful in executing to figure out who's bankable over the long term. Well, they aren't easy to find. Most CEOs don't have enough confidence in their own or their enterprise's ability to navigate the world's choppy waters to even lay out five-year plans. Those who do? Let's just put it this way: only one of the executives managed to exceed his plan consistently and convincingly, Dave Cote, the CEO of Honeywell, a man I am proud to call my neighbor in Summit, New Jersey. (And, if you must know, he's not just being included in this list because he's never complained about the music blasting in the backyard during my daughters' festivities.)

Honeywell, which has advanced more than 250 percent since Cote came on board as CEO in February 2002, is a tremendous American manufacturer that makes everything from aerospace components, such as the cockpits on pretty much every aircraft regardless of the maker, including Boeing and Airbus, to automation and climate controls (think thermostats), security gear for fire and safety, specialty materials for plastics and refining and auto parts, including turbochargers that reduce gasoline use.

Honeywell benefits from strong current economic tailwinds, including builds of autos, trucks and aircraft after a serious downturn in the manufacture of all three. Nevertheless, Honeywell is not hostage to these tailwinds, as it also has tremendous exposure to secular-growth themes that work regardless of the health of the global economy, which is terrific news given the start-stop nature of the world's financial progress. Honeywell's biggest business, Automation and Control Systems, which accounts for about 40 percent of the company's sales, is all about energy efficiency, one of our favorite long-term themes on *Mad Money*. Honeywell is a leader in making energy-efficient heating, ventilation and air-conditioning systems, along with sensors and power management systems that help property owners lower their electric bills. Cote has told us several times in his multiple appearances on *Mad Money* that the United States could reduce its total energy consumption by 20 to 25 percent or more simply by replacing all of our existing equipment with Honeywell's more efficient products, a staggering statistic that, alone, should make you want to buy the stock.

The company thrives on "seed planting," as Cote calls innovation, and as he said on a recent analyst call, "When it comes to innovation, all of the things we've talked about, they don't happen unless you have the right new products. Whether you want to do a better job on margins, you want to grow share where you are, you want to grow into an adjacent market, you want to grow in a high-growth region, you have to have the products that people want at the price that gives them value." Case in point: Cote's team has developed chemicals for refineries that help enable the so-called dirty oils to become much cleaner. These chemicals allow for crude to be refined in much more efficient ways, stretching an oil company's ability to get more money out of whatever kind of crude gets pumped out of the ground.

Lots of CEOs give lip service to shareholders. Not Cote. He's been one of the most consistent dividend raisers, and he's committed to returning as much capital as he can to shareholders without hurting the growth of his myriad businesses.

We often speak of the need to unlock the value of disparate businesses under one roof. I just spent a whole chapter suggesting which companies should do just that. You may not think that heating and ventilation, safety, turbochargers, performance chemicals and cockpits deserve to be under one roof. But I am quite confident in saying that if you were to break this whole into the sum of its parts, those parts would be worth less than the whole, and the reason would be Dave Cote's steady hand on the tiller. My only fear is that Dave feels so passionately about the escalating U.S. government debt burden that he one day ups and quits and goes to work for the president, whoever that president might be. Right now, though, he's standing pat, and you should stand pat with him.

▪ Sandy Cutler, Eaton

During the old days at my hedge fund, every time the economy would falter I would be on the prowl for stocks to short, typically those that were known to underperform when things got tough. On my short list, always? Eaton. Here's a company that made key components for trucks, and in an economic downturn the last thing enterprises need are more trucks. So the stock would be hammered mercilessly.

All that changed when Sandy Cutler became Eaton's CEO in August 2000 and decided to reinvent the company as an electronics and power generation company with an emphasis on saving and cutting energy costs, something both the greens and the hard-headed businesspeople alike favor.

Over the past five years, Cutler has allocated 80 percent of Eaton's free cash flow to acquisitions, with an emphasis on strategic markets and regions, particularly Asia, with attractive opportunities for growth and profitability and proprietary content in products and services. The vast majority of these acquisitions were tuck-ins, augmenters of already strong franchises, until 2012, when Cutler made his boldest move yet, buying Cooper Industries for $11.8 billion, a transformative and value-adding acquisition I chronicled in a previous chapter. So often I read about how companies that make large acquisitions often find themselves overpromising and underdelivering. Not Cutler. Eaton and Cooper competed against each other for years in key electronic component jobs. Now they are united. Many of their product lines were compatible with each other, so the deal, which was wildly accretive from the get-go—meaning earnings estimates could be raised dramatically upon the completion of the merger—has brought in new business that one or the other couldn't get on its own. The Cooper deal makes Eaton either number one or number two in every kind of electronic market it plays in.

I believe that the merged entity will give Eaton at least two years of solid earnings surprises, even if the economy falters. No wonder Cutler's

Eaton receives the highest price-to-earnings multiple in the group. It deserves it. Even when it failed to meet expectations in the summer of 2013, the stock was able to maintain its lofty position, dropping just a few points on the news and then, miraculously, coming right back, as investors clamored to get in during the first real price break since the Cooper deal. It sure didn't last long, though.

While the stock is a big play on the domestic recovery, with about half of its revenue tied to the United States, Eaton's portfolio is fairly balanced across the entire economic cycle. It has so-called early cycle businesses, those that do well coming right out of a downturn, such as residential construction (think your fuse box) and vehicle production, both autos and heavy-duty trucks. It has mid-earnings cycle operations, which include hydraulics and midsize data centers, that are real energy hogs. And it has late cycle applications, namely commercial aerospace, utilities and nonresidential construction.

During the darkest days of the Great Recession I would ask Sandy to come on to talk about how Eaton was faring, knowing that the old Eaton would normally be thrown for a loop from that kind of economic activity. But its businesses had become so diversified among so many different verticals and geographies, with 30 percent of its revenues from Asia Pacific and Latin America and 20 percent in a now-turning Europe, that Cutler exuded the kind of confidence that allowed us to call a bottom in the stock, one of the best calls the show has ever had.

Sandy made it easy. He's all about raising the dividend on a consistent basis, which he can do no matter how difficult the environment is because his capital equipment company is probably the least hostage to the vicissitudes of the world's economies compared to any other cyclical I follow. His backing of the dividend was so powerful on the show that when the company's stock dropped to where the yield exceeded 5 percent—what I called the accidentally high yield that comes not from a company boosting its dividend beyond reason but from a company's stock falling beyond reason—I was able to tell people to back up the truck, now that Cutler's put his brilliant stamp on this amazing company.

▪ Chuck Bunch, PPG

In the 1990s, whenever auto sales or commercial construction numbers came out and they were disappointing, you could sit there and coin money by loading up on puts to bet against the stock of the old Pittsburgh Plate Glass. Few businesses are more susceptible to downturns than the commodity that is plate glass. Fewer cars getting sold? Fewer buildings being built? Less glass to be ordered from Pittsburgh Plate Glass. And down she goes.

But Chuck Bunch, the CEO of PPG, like Sandy Cutler of Eaton, recognized that no company has to accept its lot in life. You don't have to be a captain of a sinking cyclical when you can be the skipper of a long-term growth company. And that's just what Bunch did with PPG. He reinvented it as a proprietary chemical play, with materials that sold into markets that would grow no matter how the economies around the world were faring. I have had Bunch on the show for many years now, and over that time he has done a remarkable and continuing reshuffling of the deck to upgrade his hand, taking PPG from what some would say is a smaller, provincial American glassmaker that was Pittsburgh Plate Glass to a worldwide powerhouse proprietary chemical and coatings company that is the best in its class.

Bunch is always in motion to make a better company for you, whether it be making brilliant acquisitions, like stealing the coatings division from a hobbled Akzo Nobel to give it huge share in the fast-growing American paint market, or shedding the ultra-commodity polyvinyl chloride business that's classically used to make plastic piping in and around houses, sending it to Georgia Gulf in a very lucrative deal for shareholders. At the same time Bunch keeps increasing PPG's dividend at an amazing yet prudent pace, while also shrinking the float with a very aggressive share buyback plan.

What's the real impact of these moves? As you now know, portfolio managers don't like companies that swing in the breeze of the world's economies. That kind of economic sensitivity makes your stock hostage to too many factors beyond your control, giving it a much lower price-to-earnings multiple than it might otherwise receive. By shedding businesses like PVC that's used for pipe, Bunch's shareholders no longer have to fret about new housing starts or the scrapping or abandonment of big American infrastructure projects. Meanwhile the coatings business he's moved into has uses well beyond whether economies advance or contract. Plus, this isn't the same old glass or paint that PPG is famous for. PPG has developed lightweight plastic glass for cockpit and airplane windows—windows you can now actually see out of—as well as architectural coatings that can withstand the pollution and acid rain that have become lamented but accepted environmental evils.

And instead of selling commodity chemicals that are increasingly coming down in price because of bountiful new sources of energy feedstock, Bunch is a buyer of them, which allows him to routinely boost gross margins because of the low prices caused by the nation's natural gas glut, thereby beating the estimates in the process. Or he can just drill for them, because some of PPG's plants are right in the middle of the bountiful Marcellus shale, chock-full of the natural gas he needs to make many of his plastics. And when one of his own new business lines becomes too commodity-like, as was the case with the clear sunglasses his company created that darken when you step into the sunlight, he sells the division, usually for a hefty profit. He just won't rest until all of his products are best of breed, with the secular winds as their back.

Like so many of the terrific executives out there, Bunch isn't one to blow his own horn. He's a self-effacing, hardworking executive from the hardscrabble town of Pittsburgh. That said, like the new breed of heartland CEOs, he's as comfortable mixing it up in East Asia, Europe and Latin America as he is cheering for his beloved Pittsburgh Steelers. Like that terrific team, Bunch has given you winning seasons year after year after year. And I don't think next year will be any different.

Alan Mulally, Ford

Engineering one successful turnaround is tough enough. But how about two of them?

I first heard of Alan Mulally when he was an inspiration in turning around Boeing Commercial Aerospace after it had lost its lead to Airbus in the 1990s. He was known as the savior of Boeing for introducing a new line of successful jets just when people thought Boeing was down for the count. But when, somehow, he didn't get the top job in 2005, he moved over to run the Ford Motor Company, succeeding a young William Clay Ford Jr. With the possible exception of the creation of the Models T and A, Mulally may have been the best thing that ever happened to the Ford Motor Company, because, when things turned bad for the auto industry, he and he alone didn't have to ask the federal government for a bailout: he saw hard times coming and prepared Ford perfectly for them. He came in just in time to save the company from what might have been sure bankruptcy, given the sudden and shocking decline in auto sales during the Great Recession.

I have always had a fondness for Ford, ever since my first car, a silver Ford Fairmont with a fancy racing stripe, also became my first house during my brief homeless stint after being driven out of my Los Angeles apartment back in 1978.

But that isn't what got me to recommend the Ford preferred stock at $9 in December 2009, a move that gave you a gigantic gain in a short period of time as Mulally managed to steer Ford away from the shoals of insolvency. It's what Mulally chose to do the moment he got to Ford that won me over. I am a huge believer that when you want to fix a company, the first thing you fix isn't its product. It isn't customer service. It isn't morale. It's the balance sheet, stupid. All successful turnarounds start with getting the company to no longer hemorrhage money and then graduate to paying down debt. All failed turnarounds try to address issues like morale and new product, not recognizing that the good employees will run out the door and no new products will ever see fruition if you don't make payroll. In December 2006, shortly before the dawn of the Great Recession, Mulally recognized that his company was in no shape to handle a possible downturn, so he raised $23.45 billion in cash through some of the shrewdest bond issuance I have ever seen, pledging substantially all of the company's auto assets to raise that money.

No doubt, if he hadn't done that, Ford would have been in the same shape as Chrysler and GM, headed toward bankruptcy and receivership of the U.S. government. Instead Ford came out of the Great Recession hitting the ground running, and it's now gunning to be the number one car company in the country, with the highest profitability in the company's long history. Since the crisis, the company's balance sheet has seen a drastic improvement; it now has more than $10 billion in net cash, after having net debt of $12 billion just a few years ago. Ford debt had suffered from repeated downgrades, but now the company is rated investment grade, something that's incredibly important for a company that has to finance so much of the auto purchasing of its customers.

I spotted these changes early on, and when it was clear that Mulally simply wasn't going to let this grand brand go the way of his competitors, I pushed the preferred, not the common, and pushed it hard. I could tell that Mulally was bent on trying to save that balance sheet no matter what, and that meant he would pay off on the Ford preferred stock, a fixed-income piece of paper with a big dividend that sits above the common stock on the pecking order, before he could ever pay a dividend on the common stock. And that's exactly what he did, allowing many viewers to hit a five-bagger on a piece of paper that it seems nobody other than Mulally and I were focused on.

Alan is a huge fan of *Mad Money*, and when he saw a show I did where I said that because he saved Boeing, people were wrong to write him off at Ford, he gave me a call and said he wanted to come on the show. Soon after, he was on the set and laid out a vision of One Ford with Profitable Growth for All, or PGA, as he called it. That's profitable growth for the workers, the executives and the owners, the shareholders. He said he would rid the company of extraneous brands in order to simplify the product line and make it easier and cheaper to manufacture. He pledged that he would reduce the number of global platforms to nine from almost a hundred when he took over. At the time, many people I talked to thought that Mulally was a dreamer and that his company would soon join GM and Chrysler in the auto ICU, but he then proceeded to execute on every aspect of the plan, which, for the first time, has produced exceptionally good profit margins on every car and truck Ford makes.

Those changes have created a virtuous circle of more profits, better financial ratings, cheaper cost to finance and a further reduction in debt.

We saw it all in action when we took *Mad Money* to the fabled Ford

F-150 truck plant in Dearborn, Michigan, in 2011. You could see the effect of the positive changes on the faces of the workers on the assembly line. Ford's making about $10,000 per truck now, the most profitable vehicle it has ever produced. It should make a record number of vehicles next year and is set to pass General Motors in market share in the not too distant future.

Unfortunately, Alan and his team, like so many others, did not see the severe downturn in Europe coming. That's led to some disappointing numbers that have severely crimped overall profitability. Alan has pledged to me and to our *Mad Money* viewers that Ford will be able to scale back the losses quickly, but he will need Europe to return to profitability in 2015 if Ford is to make the $5 in earnings power that I believe it has if Europe could just break even.

That would lead to a huge move up in the common stock dividend— he has long since converted the preferred I liked so much into common stock—perhaps as high as the 5 percent yield I used to expect from Ford during the halcyon 1990s, before the company went on an ill-fated brand spree. That behavior almost surely would have caused the company to go under if Mulally hadn't stepped in with his One Ford view and shed all of those extraneous brands for much more than he would have been able to sell them even a few months later.

While General Motors too has gotten its act together, I prefer Ford because it has so much more runway, particularly in China, where it has only 2 percent share versus 14 percent for GM. Alan says he intends to increase the number of Chinese dealers by 50 percent in 2015 and spend $6 billion annually through mid-decade to boost Chinese sales. Some analysts on Wall Street think Ford has come too late to the party in China. I say that given his bankable ways in the United States, if Alan says he can take big share in China, I'm betting with him, not against him.

Many people have speculated that Alan will soon retire, but he has promised me he will stay on until the European operations are hitting their stride and the big earnings estimates that I am throwing out for 2016 and 2017 can be a reality. As long as Alan is running Ford, I think you have to make Letter F a core position in your portfolio, as I have for my charitable trust.

■ Ron Shaich, Panera Bread

Some guys just get it. They get the era and what people want, particularly the younger generation that will soon be the moms and dads and ultimately the big spenders who determine where families go, what they do and where they open their wallets.

Ron Shaich, the CEO of Panera Bread, gets it.

I found out about Panera, as I have found out about so many other good stocks, through my kids. My elder daughter played a great deal of field hockey and swam for her high school. Kids on both teams used to go to Panera after practice and games because they knew they would eat healthful food, so all of that working out wouldn't go to waste. It got to the point where my daughter, who was a vegetarian at the time, simply didn't want to eat anywhere else. She always had to have the signature salad, hold the chicken. Seeing that level of commitment, I pulled the books on the company, performing just the kind of analysis I outlined earlier when I contrasted Google with Amazon and Starbucks. When I compared Panera with other quick-serve restaurants, it came up as extraordinarily cheap, and I recommended it at $48. It's been a huge winner for viewers for years now. Of course, I wish I had gotten in at the beginning of this one, because Panera has made you about 3,500 percent after it was separated from its original owner, Au Bon Pain, which Shaich had started in 1981.

Shaich has managed to appeal to youth because he understands that the customer will pay up for what's regarded as more natural, more organic foods. He was among the first restaurateurs to display the calorie counts on the walls, and he's made Panera a bit of a treasure hunt, like Jim Sinegal did for Costco, with a menu that changes quite regularly. He's also been able to instill loyalty among his customers, as more than 15 million of them have joined the My Panera program in the time since he started the plan just a few years ago. It's not just a "Buy ten sandwiches, get the eleventh free," but an actual attempt to find out what individuals prefer and surprise them with offerings they might like. As with all successful affinity programs, Panera has been able to "take price," meaning raise prices to offset higher commodity costs, with nary a complaint nor a hitch in sales from its huge and, at times, worshipful customer base.

All of these moves have led to some super same-store sales numbers, even as other quick-serve restaurants, including some of the best out there, have stumbled during this period of inflated food prices and lower employment. Panera has strong unit growth, with fabulous and improving productivity per store. When I recently visited the first store in New York City with Ron, he showed me how, in just the past couple of years, he has figured out how to cut the time from order to serve rather dramatically, which has increased the amount of money that can be made during the busy lunch hour and brought tens of millions of dollars more to the bottom line. No wonder Panera has consistently delivered one of the highest operating income margins in the restaurant sector, 19.3 percent, which is substantially ahead of the industry average.

It's pretty amazing to me that Panera could have so many loyalists and still, for the most part, be a very small company, one-twentieth the size of McDonald's. Right now Panera has only about 1.5 percent of the limited-service market, and the average market share for a nationwide chain, excluding McDonald's, is double that. So it is conceivable that Panera could give you strong unit growth for many years before I would be concerned about cannibalization or the need to even consider moving overseas with the concept. Yes, despite the run, it's still really early in Panera's life, especially when you consider that to date Panera is still largely a suburban restaurant chain.

Not that long ago, Ron stepped up to chairman, and I feared that this man's intensity and vision might be lost too early. But he decided against moving out of day-to-day control and returned as chief executive officer, not unlike what Starbucks founder Howard Schultz did after a spell in a nonoperational role. I think he is integral to the spirit of the place and to its special bond with patrons, many of whom I encourage to be shareholders when Ron comes on *Mad Money*. As long as Ron stays at the helm, I am confident that the chain can double in size without much worry of overexpansion, and the stock will double right along with it.

▪ Howard Schultz, Starbucks

When I hear that our country isn't as successful as it used to be and doesn't have the edge that it used to, I wonder, *Have any of you doubters ever heard of Howard Schultz?* The man who founded Starbucks and is its chairman, chief executive officer and president, has in a quarter of a century created a chain of 19,000 coffeehouses in 62 countries with more than 160,000 employees and 70 million customers.

And I feel as if he somehow knows every one of them.

I've been an admirer of Schultz for more than two decades. Starbucks was one of the largest positions in my hedge fund after it came public in 1992 and was responsible for a healthy portion of my outperformance. But Schultz retired from day-to-day management in 2000, and while the stock continued to rally many years after he departed, the new management badly overexpanded and at the same time sacrificed both quality and cleanliness. The company totally lost its way. I had been extremely critical of the chain on air, concerned that the stock had become a terrible invest-ment. When he came back, Schultz promised me on the record that he would have things turned around after a couple of years' time. Sure enough, within the time frame that he promised, he managed to right the ship, and it's been a smooth sail ever since then.

It's funny, but as amazing as Schultz has been, he has rarely been given the benefit of the doubt when he tells you that things are on track. When Europe, which is an important market for Starbucks, turned weaker during the sudden downturn in the Continent's fortunes, Schultz ex-pressed some chagrin about the numbers, but just as he vowed to me that he would turn things around in a short time in the United States when he took back the reins, he made a similar on-air promise of a turn in Europe in one year's time. He was good as gold on the prediction, and we got a stabilization in the numbers one year later, even as Europe continued to falter.

Not long after that, though, when Yum!'s Kentucky Fried Chicken chain had a downturn in China, short-sellers attacked Starbucks as if it were going to have a similar shortfall. I heard Howard speak in New York at the end of 2012, when he said that China was actually going great guns and that his expansion plans were just beginning, with many major cities north of one million still not having a handful of Starbucks in each. Yet the analysts in attendance, almost universally, questioned whether Schultz had a handle on China. Some hinted that he was dissembling about how good things were, given how abysmal KFC's numbers were. When he shot the lights out the next quarter, and China was his biggest growth engine, it became pretty obvious the doubters were wrong again.

Currently Starbucks has 1,000 stores in China, and I fully expect that it can put up ten times as many stores before the chain runs out of room in the People's Republic. The profitability in China is magnificent, and the same-store sales numbers have been staggering, with consistent double-digit returns. I expect that within a few years China will surpass the United States as a source of profitability, and I believe China could ultimately have far more stores than the 13,000 found in the United States.

It's ironic that when Schultz left the company, it was a common perception that Starbucks had overexpanded and had too many stores in the United States. But when he returned, after an initial retrenchment, he took the United States back to growth mode, putting up far more stores and with no cannibalization to speak of. Starbucks has maintained higher comps in the United States than just about any other chain of retail stores, restaurants or coffeehouses.

Lately, as I detailed earlier when I ran Starbucks through my ten-part high-growth stock test, Schultz, in order to accelerate growth, has decided to step up two more initiatives: his consumer package goods business, which he took back from an ill-fated deal with Kraft, and his Teavana initiative, after he bought that boutique chain of tea stores in 2012. Starbucks has since launched Verismo, its single-cup platform, and joined forces with Green Mountain Coffee for an expanded relationship, both of which should add up to billions of dollars more in incremental sales in just a few years' time. But the real opportunity here may be the Teavana acquisition, which gives Schultz a separate platform for tea stores, which, he tells me, could be every bit as big as coffee someday, given that there are 40 million tea drinkers globally. That's something from the man who spotted the trend in coffee growth well before others did. Even though the Teavana chain was largely a retailer of teas and tea accessories, Schultz has the vision to use it as a platform for a whole new set of Starbucks-like teahouses. Once again I am hearing doubts that Schultz can pull this one off. Some people worry that he has bitten off too much; he already has the Tazo tea brand, so what's the point of Teavana? I hear that after its miraculous run from the lows reached at the end of 2012 the stock is tapped out and going nowhere, fast.

Me? Ever since Schultz promised me he would turn around a broken Starbucks within two years' time when he returned to the CEO job, I have learned to take him at his word. So I am presuming that Teavana will become a huge winner for a chain that has become the envy of the world for its hospitality, its product and a CEO who may be the best America has to offer.

Or, as I like to tell him, who else in the world could get me to pay five bucks for a triple venti cappuccino with skim, wet, when the guy down the block can't get away with charging me $3 for a cup of coffee twice the size?

Patrick Doyle, Domino's

When I first met Patrick Doyle in 2009, shortly before he accepted the chief executive officer title at Domino's Pizza, I didn't know what to make of him. After the obligatory "Irish guy running pizza chain" jokes—"Hey, Jim, I love pizza, that's what matters," he rejoined—I couldn't figure out what he could do to take Domino's to the next level. The company had been tremendously shareholder-friendly under previous CEO David Brandon, who had resigned to take his dream job as the athletic director of his alma mater, the University of Michigan. Brandon had made the extraordinary decision before stepping down to pay a $13.50 special dividend, a terrific gift to shareholders because dividends were taxed at such an advantage over ordinary income.

What could Doyle do to top that fantastic contribution to the loyalists who owned the stock of DPZ? He told me he had a whole new idea: he was going to make better pizza. There had been complaints that perhaps the pizza simply wasn't good enough. He didn't want to do financial engineering. He wanted to do pizza engineering.

Look, I am a numbers guy. I figured Domino's, with a terrific record of international expansion and franchise fees, didn't need to do anything to keep generating a decent return, let alone call everyone's attention to how second-rate the pizza really was. Sure, a couple of years before I met Doyle we slammed Domino's on *Mad Money*, saying Papa John's was both the better-tasting pizza and the better stock. Still, though, who cares? What's the price-to-earnings ratio of a better-tasting slice of pizza? I thought Doyle was wasting his time—and mine—when we discussed his mea culpa ad campaign.

Not long after that, we began to see a bizarre series of ads, real-life ads, where people commented on the taste of Domino's. Doyle had told me it would be far out there, but I wasn't ready for someone, on air, saying Domino's crust is like "cardboard" and "the sauce tastes like ketchup." Domino's spent $75 million to carpet bomb every major broadcast channel with the campaign, and, given its freshness and irreverence, it became the butt of many shows. Doyle, for instance, told me to tune in to Stephen Colbert when he was doing his take on the pizza, a hilarious send-up about how cardboard might have, indeed, been better-tasting than a Domino's pie.

I still didn't think anything of it. Neither did the potential investors; the stock languished at about $10 a share during the whole time the ad campaign ran.

A few months later, my kids wanted to watch some tube and order a pizza. We've been a Joe's family for years, the local pizza parlor, so I instinctively hit the place up on my preprogrammed cell phone. "Wait, wait," my daughter said. "Put the phone down, we're ordering Domino's."

I thought she was kidding. We'd been getting the same pizza for a decade. Domino's? I reminded her that they even ran a campaign saying their pizza was no better-tasting than cardboard.

She said to trust her. It was now the best-tasting pizza in the world. Okay, I said, I'll get the number. No need, she said, she'd do the ordering. Now my daughter, even at that age, was a shy kid. It isn't like her to offer to make a phone call. But she never reached for her phone. Instead, she went for her computer, and the next thing I knew I hear something that sounds like a baseball game, where an announcer tells you how far along the pizza is, from start to delivery. Darned thing had crowd noises and totally terrific graphics to go along with the order process, and we knew exactly when the delivery person was about to ring the doorbell, as well as the exact price we needed to pay.

Fifteen minutes later we were chowing down on one of the best pizzas I have ever had.

I spent the rest of the weekend doing the research, and I recommended the stock soon after. It's been one of the longest home runs since the show began, rallying tenfold since Doyle took over. Domino's has taken share from all of the local pizza parlors, like Joe's, around the nation.

Domino's has always been a global outfit. As Doyle has emphasized on the show many times, 95 percent of the population of the world is outside the United States, and everyone loves pizza. Half of Domino's sales are still domestic, but it now has over 10,000 stores in more than 70 countries and it's growing by leaps and bounds in places as disparate as India, Malaysia and Turkey. Turns out pizza is the ultimate American export. Doyle foresees Domino's equaling McDonald's and Yum! with about 20,000 international stores each and soon besting the over 7,500 stores that Dunkin' Brands has internationally.

Doyle has also revolutionized the technology behind pizza delivery, not stopping with just the cool app that my daughter plugged into our desktops and now our cell phones. He's used social media to expand the touch of the chain. He's gotten the system to accept credit cards. And he's added a "no cheese, you sure you want no cheese" two-button system that he jokes is for my vegetarian daughters but, ironically, has turned out to be a runaway hit in vegetarian India, which could soon turn out to be a top-five market for the company. Domino's was able to log more than a billion online orders in a very short period of time and a second billion in a period even shorter than that. It's a runaway stealth technology hit.

Domino's has a terrific franchise model; most of the franchises are owned by former staff and delivery people, making for a very loyal group of ambassadors. The franchise model allows most costs to be borne by the franchises, keeping gross margins very stable and reducing woes that would accrue to the company every time bread, cheese, tomato sauce or gasoline spikes.

Doyle's also keeping Brandon's tradition of the shareholder-friendly company. At the beginning of 2013, Domino's announced a resumption of dividends; there had been nine consecutive quarterly payments before the company ceased paying them when it gave the $13.50 special dividend to shareholders. Doyle can do that relatively easily, without stretching the balance sheet, because the franchise model throws off a huge amount of cash. The cash buildup also allowed him to pay a $3 special dividend in March 2012 on top of the regular dividend, which caused many of the analysts to presume that the run-up in the stock was now complete. But after bouncing around in the $20s, after Doyle had gotten you a double, the stock resumed its upward climb.

Doyle now comes on my show regularly, typically after still one more terrific quarter or a new product introduction, including a very successful gourmet pizza. He's not done innovating and always says he has a lot up his sleeve. I believe him. How can you not? He's the secret ingredient of the stock, just as he has secret ingredients in his now terrific-tasting pizza.

▪ Debra Cafaro, Ventas

On *Mad Money* I have highlighted the aging population as a bankable long-term theme. But with any theme you need a company that is uniquely qualified to profit from it and a CEO bold enough to see and capitalize off the opportunity. Debra Cafaro, the CEO of Ventas, is that person, and her company may be one of the chief beneficiaries of the trend.

Cafaro became CEO of this senior housing and skilled nursing facility company in 1999 and has given you a spectacular 1,800 percent return versus the S&P's 80 percent during the same period. She's the retiring baby boomer's hero.

Ventas, with more than 1,400 owned properties, is the largest private-pay senior housing company as well as the largest medical office building company in the country. Ventas has virtually no economic sensitivity, so it skated right through the Great Recession with flying colors. That's the kind of stock that defines Getting Rich Carefully.

How does Ventas do it? Cafaro is simply in a terrific business, as the demand for health care–oriented real estate is booming. With the number of people over the age of eighty-five growing three times faster than the general population, the supply of health care properties is constrained, especially given the inability of developers to obtain credit to build new facilities. Cafaro recognizes that she has a trillion-dollar market opportunity, and she has become the biggest force in senior housing, which is responsible for 60 percent of the firm's revenues. She has spent billions to buy properties nationwide, always being sure to keep the balance sheet strong by raising capital at opportune moments. Meanwhile she has consistently increased the dividend, doubling it over a seven-year period, giving it one of the highest yields—not from a declining price, like so many in the real estate investment trust business, but because of an ever rising payout. Initially Deb had been reluctant to come on *Mad Money* because of my skepticism regarding the long-term value of real estate investment trusts in a declining real estate price environment. But after realizing that the industry had far less economic sensitivity than I thought and admitting on air that I had gotten it wrong, while chowing down on a liberal amount of a salted mock crow, Cafaro accepted my apologies and came on to outline a story that I think can only get better and better by the year. That's why, when people now ask me how to play the aging-in-America theme, I don't hesitate: You invest in it with Deb Cafaro and with Ventas. This is by far the best-of-breed baby boomer story of all of the companies I follow.

▪ Manny Chirico, PVH Corp.

Sometimes a CEO has to take bold action, action that is often criticized instantly by those who aren't in the arena: the critics, the pundits who can only hope that one day they might run a gigantic enterprise. Such was the second-guessing when Manny Chirico, the best-dressed CEO ever to appear on *Mad Money*, purchased Tommy Hilfiger, the clothing company, for approximately $3 billion in 2010. What was the point of an already well-run company with 25 percent of the American department store shirt market and 50 percent of the ties, as well as a huge, successful, installed base of outlet stores, spending a fortune for a fashion line that may have peaked years ago? Perhaps they should have listened to Manny on *Mad Money* when he traced out a worldwide view of PVH, the old Phillips–Van Heusen, that enabled this largely Calvin Klein–based domestic sportswear company to become a worldwide powerhouse with 65 percent of its revenues outside of North America.

How wrong were the doubters? This acquisition, highlighted earlier in my major themes chapter, has managed to triple sales and give the company a fourfold increase in market cap, all during a period when Europe, a huge market of Tommy's, has been in a hideous downturn. Who knows how well it can do when Europe improves?

Chirico had big ambitions after he took the reins in 2006, wanting the company to be more fashion-forward and upscale, and he saw exactly that possibility when Tommy came on the block. Chirico married his sophisticated sourcing and superior materials at lower prices with Tommy to make PVH an international powerhouse.

Not done with his overseas expansion, Manny paid $3 billion for Warnaco in October 2012, a mishmash of a company that happened to have many of the most lucrative worldwide rights to Calvin Klein, the once flagship brand that had been eclipsed by Tommy. One of the more endearing characteristics of Manny's management style is his transparency. He had traced out certain goals for the Calvin acquisition that turned out to be too aggressive, particularly given the downturn in Europe. What did he do? Knowing that I am one of his biggest supporters, he came on the show to basically apologize for the stumble, which led to a 25 cent reduction in earnings guidance, the first that I could recall in all of the years that he has been at the helm. Of course, the fault wasn't with Manny. Calvin was just more of a mess than he thought when PVH bought it. But Manny blamed himself, not the people who were running Calvin Klein, for not seeing that ahead of time.

That said, there's no doubt in my mind that this acquisition was a must if, as Manny said, he wants to "reunite the house of Calvin Klein" under one roof. That's because Warnaco had the licenses to many of Calvin Klein's top lines, including underwear, jeans and sportswear, but it just wasn't generating the profits that the combined PVH will be able to.

I love the acquisition. It gives PVH the same leg up in East Asia, including China, that Hilfiger gave PVH in Europe. PVH can charge much higher prices for both Hilfiger and Calvin overseas, where the two brands have cachet, than in the United States, where investors have consistently underestimated their draw.

At the same time that he's made these two bold moves, Manny has resisted any attempt to jettison core "legacy" brands, though they have shown little to no growth, including Izod, Geoffrey Beene and the erstwhile namesake Phillips–Van Heusen shirts, although he recently disposed of his Bass shoe division, maker of the beloved penny loafer. That's a smart move; the stores generate a consistent cash flow and the outlet stores offer a nice stable base of profits through thick and thin. Ron Johnson, the former CEO of J. C. Penney, came close to bankrupting the company, but he did one thing right, at least for PVH: he gave the Izod brand prominent placement in his stores, allowing this legacy line to shine when the rest of apparel hit a rough patch in the summer of 2013.

I liked Manny from the moment I met him, when Cliff Mason, *Mad Money*'s head writer and my nephew, and I found ourselves sitting next to him at a lower-Manhattan restaurant. Like many terrific CEOs, he's a great salesperson for the enterprise. He's got me wearing PVH tapered shirts and skinnier ties on a regular basis. I know he's spotted the change, as he recently complimented me for getting out of the tent business, which is how he describes the shirts I wore before he gave me the sartorial insight I needed to go to the next level.

▪ Eric Wiseman, VF Corporation

When Eric Wiseman ascended to the CEO position of VF Corp. back in January 2008, some were concerned that without the steady hand of Mackey McDonald, his transformative predecessor of the old Vanity Fair Corporation, VF would founder on the shores of the incredibly difficult apparel industry. They were concerned that the soft-spoken Wiseman was more of a merchant, with a great eye for clothes, than he might be the CEO of the entire enterprise.

They were wrong. Dead wrong. Wiseman has taken this terrific domestic company that was once known for its Wrangler and Lee jean brands, before the acquisition of North Face in 2000, and turned it into a global brand powerhouse. While the stock of VF doubled from 2000 until 2008, when Wiseman came in, it's tripled in just five years' time as Wiseman has moved aggressively overseas and continued the long tradition of buying played-out brands and reigniting them in a fashion-forward direction. His most recent acquisition, Timberland, paid for itself in three years.

VF has a terrific coalition of brands. Besides North Face and Timberland, there's Vans, Nautica, 7 For All Mankind, JanSport, Lucy Active-wear, Eastpak, Kipling and now SmartWool, a product that Wiseman told me recently on *Mad Money* is taking the world by storm.

Wiseman understands that customers will pay a premium for top-notch brands, including customers in Central and Eastern Europe. Like PVH, VF Corp. has managed to continue the flawless execution all through Europe despite the downturn. Plus, now Wiseman is setting his sights on Asia, where North Face has shown remarkable sales growth in just a few short years. Meanwhile, Wiseman has continued his firm's generous dividend policy, giving shareholders a 40 percent payout ratio, despite being acquisitive and opportunistic, buying brands that need VF'ing to get them rolling.

Why, in this type of global market, where shocks can happen anywhere, is it important to get behind a Wiseman if you want to navigate the waters? Take the cost of cotton. Because of a poor cotton crop a few years back, the price of the material went through the roof. Short-sellers went gunning for Wiseman, thinking he would have to miss the quarter, and the stock was under heavy pressure for weeks on end. Then, when VF reported its numbers, the estimates were blown away, largely because Wiseman had figured out ways to cut costs, source the cheapest cotton around the globe and raise prices for his goods so that VF never skipped a beat. A lesser CEO might have had his head handed to him. These aren't ordinary times, when a domestic apparel company CEO worries about how his sales are doing at Macy's and Target. Now we have global enterprises where the sales in Germany, Russia and China can matter as much as the sales in the United States. That's the kind of market Wiseman thrives in.

That's why, every time VF dips on what's thought to be concerns about consumer demand in the United States or in Europe, I can recommend that you buy this stock with a level of confidence that I don't have for most other companies I follow.

▪ Sally Smith, Buffalo Wild Wings

You would think the name Sally Smith would be on everyone's lips given the 1,000 percent return she's given you since Buffalo Wild Wings has come public, versus about a 60 percent return for the S&P 500 during the same period. But Smith's not about promoting herself; she's about promoting a brand that has taken off in this country with a simple sports-bar menu of wings, beer and big-screen televisions.

I became enamored of Buffalo Wild Wings when I couldn't get a seat at one of its restaurants during the *Mad Money* college tour to the University of Michigan almost a decade ago. I pulled the file, liked the growth path—unimpeded for many years to come—and marveled at the crisp execution, and I have been pushing the stock ever since. After that time in Michigan, the *Mad Money* team has looked for the local BWLD whenever we decamp from our latest college venue, and when we can't find one, as was the case with Villanova in 2013, we bring Smith to the school instead. At 'Nova, Smith shone, announcing still one more quarter of excellent growth and higher profits, despite a big jump in raw costs.

Many restaurant chains develop a successful formula and then roll it out nationally with lightning speed to please Wall Street analysts who demand fast growth without regard to execution risk by untried management or cannibalization risk. I used to press Smith to do the same thing when she first came on *Mad Money* to tell the chain's story. I also wanted her to go overseas with a quintessentially American product that I think would be a home run virtually everywhere it opened. But Smith wants measured growth to be sure that she doesn't slip up, and that pace has been the secret behind these bountiful returns. Most of the stores are fill-ins around the country, often near universities, given the love affair young drinking-age adults have with the restaurant's formula. That conservative strategy makes her "hit" ratio, the successful-to-failed store metric, much greater than any other chain that I follow.

Still, despite the long-term growth path in this country, Smith has had to confront doubters all the way. The short-sellers, who have bet against her quarter to quarter, believe that at some point her concept will be defeated by rising wing costs, the chief variable for the stores, particularly because the company bears a lot of the costs, as almost half the stores are actually owned by the chain itself. That means the cost of the wings can't be laid off on the franchises, unlike AFC Enterprises' Popeyes or Domino's, two almost all-franchised chains where the owners of the stores bear the brunt of raw cost expenditures.

But Smith keeps surprising the skeptics, beating estimates even when the cost of this critical ingredient has spiked to levels that have crimped restaurant margins. Some of the costs have been recouped with beer, including store-made craft beer that's been a huge hit and allows for much higher gross margins than nationally branded beers. Smith has also been able to raise the price of her wing dishes as commodity costs climbed in 2012–13, and when they peaked and dropped quickly the gains flew right into the bottom line.

Smith has tied the chain's fortunes to sports, and the sales jump during the playoffs of pretty much every sport in every season, especially football and March Madness. The more national teams in the playoffs, the better Buffalo Wild comparable-store sales are. Smith's use of national advertising coupled with a huge commitment to social media have made Buffalo Wild Wings destinations for the games themselves.

Perhaps the most exciting development for BWLD is Smith's decision to commit to a second concept, PizzaRev, taking some of the company's bountiful excess cash to trial and then building out a pizza chain that allows you to craft your own pie. If this initiative takes off, I believe it is possible for Buffalo Wild Wings to continue to outpace the entire industry with its consistent growth. Besides her commitment to the quality of the product and the ambience of her stores, Smith is an excellent salesperson for the product. If I didn't have enough to do with my writings, the management of a trust and two television shows, she would have already sold me a franchise. There's plenty of room left for more, and I have just the right corner, about three miles from my house. But that will have to wait until another day.

▪ Richard Kinder, Kinder Morgan

It's tough to find a person who has created an industry as lucrative and shareholder-friendly as Kinder Morgan Energy Partners, the gold standard among oil and gas partnerships, one of the fastest-growing business areas in this suddenly energy-rich country. Rich Kinder and his master limited partnership namesake give you growth and yield, as this quintessential oil and gas man crisscrosses our nation with pipelines and rails to bring oil to the markets where it's most needed.

Kinder Morgan Partners was founded in February 1997, when Kinder acquired the general partner of a small, publicly traded pipeline limited partnership, the typical kind of tax-advantaged entity that develops these kinds of projects and then passes the profits right to shareholders. In that time he's grown his network to be one of the largest transporters of liquid and gas fuels in the country. When you hear about all of these oil and gas fields and you wonder how the product gets to where it can be refined, the answer is most likely a Kinder Morgan pipeline. Since its founding, Kinder Morgan Energy Partners has returned an astounding 2,653 percent versus 168 percent from the S&P 500 during the same time period, a phenomenal differential.

As I detailed earlier, when I described Kinder Morgan Energy Partners as a best-of-breed way to play the American energy renaissance, Rich has built up a network of 73,000 miles of pipelines and railroad tracks, which give you exposure to energy growth in the country without much of the price volatility of the commodity itself. I like that because it has afforded shareholders a much higher income stream even as the company acts more like a turnpike toll collector than an explorer and developer with finding and price risk. While Kinder is aggressive in his acquisition strategy, having bought El Paso Corp. for $38 billion in 2011 and then Copano Energy for slightly more than $3 billion in 2013, what unit holders of KMP care about is the "drop down" of pipelines owned by these new acquisitions into this master limited partnership, which allows for the continued increase of distributions over time. That's the key to the income growth and therefore the price appreciation. The more acquisitions, the more pipeline laid, the higher the distribution.

Kinder's a can't-beat-'em-join-'em kind of guy. He will not build a pipeline if he can't first find buyers that will fill pipes with oil or natural gas *ahead* of time. He never speculates with shareholder capital. He will also build rail lines only if they fit the need for faster time to market for oil and if they meet fewer environmental objections.

I love what Rich has accomplished in his time at the helm of this tremendous oil conglomerate. Like Mark Papa at the fast-growing EOG, Rich has become an advocate for energy self-sufficiency for this continent. He believes passionately that if we had an all-encompassing energy policy that included the use of natural gas as a surface fuel, perhaps to unseat diesel (which is made largely with imported fuel), the nation could be so much stronger than it currently is, with much cleaner skies and a lot more jobs to boot.

Every time I see or hear of a new shale field, I am always surprised to see that Rich already has the rights and the pipe or rail that allows it to be brought to the right market, where it can be most lucrative for his clients to sell. I shouldn't be shocked, though, as he is by far the best there's ever been in the master limited partnership pipeline field. If you met Rich, you would have no idea he was one of the wealthiest and most successful CEOs in the country. He's about the blocking and tackling of laying pipe and rail to get oil, gas, refined petroleum products and CO_2 from the source to the most profitable destination available. And he's a total gent.

▪ Jim McNerney, Boeing

Sometimes adversity defines the chief executive officer. Few have been up to the challenge more than Jim McNerney, the implacable CEO of The Boeing Company. Within a one-year period McNerney had to steer his company through the Scylla of a sequester meant to dramatically curtail defense spending and the Charybdis of the burning batteries in the problem-plagued 787 Dreamliner, the company's next-generation jumbo jet.

He came through the chasm with flying colors. Jim's the kind of guy who truly embodies the "head coach" concept of the corporation, a man you would bet on whether he was at General Electric, where he just missed being the CEO, losing out to Jeff Immelt, or at 3M or Boeing, where he took the helm on July 1, 2005. Boeing is probably one of the most difficult companies to manage, given its split between defense work and commercial airlines. On the one hand, Jim wants to sell aircraft to airlines in every country, but on the other hand, the government keeps him from selling his high-technology defense applications, including rotorcraft, missiles, satellites and advanced information systems, to countries where many of his potential clients are, including the Middle East and China. No matter, almost effortlessly his company has been able to sell commercial aircraft to the most well-off airlines in countries our government bans him from providing military products to, despite intense competition from Airbus, a company he describes as an unfriendly and fierce rival. Boeing is the nation's top exporter because of these efforts, providing products and support services to customers in 150 countries.

McNerney's biggest challenge came at the end of 2012, when authorities around the globe grounded the oft-delayed Dreamliner, key to his multiyear vision of the Chicago-based company, because the revolutionary electric battery system that powers much of the plane had several instances of onboard fires. Despite intensely negative media coverage, McNerney told me, he "never, never worried about it" because "it was a solvable problem." He showed his fortitude as a leader when he said, "The response with the people of our company was to roll up their sleeves and go to work and solve the problem," which they did far sooner than any of the myriad critics of this great company thought possible. Throughout this tribulation McNerney said his job "was to keep the distractions away from the people doing the real work in the company and satisfying investors and satisfying customers." He did both, which is why bookings for this plane never suffered and new customers can't get their hands on one until 2019 because of the immense number of back orders for the plane. No wonder this stock kept soaring through the ordeal and has become one of the best performers in the Dow Jones Average. It is a testament to Jim's remarkable stewardship of the 170,000 people who work for Boeing, 96 percent of whom are in the United States, that no customer canceled—not one—despite the horrendous round-the-clock publicity and an endless campaign from Airbus to steal customers by taking advantage of its temporary woes.

These days in the executive suite, "long term" may be a few years' time. But not for McNerney. He's so confident in the technology behind the 787 and the steady demand for the plane and its forthcoming iterations that he's issued a twenty-year plan for Boeing's growth. Talk about a coach you want to get behind for the long term. He's talking dynasty here. He traced out why he can be so confident of this long-term vision when he visited *Mad Money* as part of our "Invest in America" series. First, despite the Great Recession and similar downturns around the globe, the growth of air traffic never wavered and stayed consistent, growing at a 5 to 6 percent clip the whole time, much of the demand coming from East Asia, especially China. McNerney pointed out that "currently China is building ninety-three airports right now, and six of them are the size of O'Hare," the Chicago airport that is one of the largest in our country. Second, the planes McNerney is building use about 20 percent less fuel than those currently in service. Given that about 40 to 50 percent of an airline's cost is fuel—depending upon the latest spike in oil—it's a life-or-death matter for these airlines to replace their gas-guzzling planes with Boeing's latest iterations. I always re-recommend Boeing on *Mad Money* any time oil spikes; that's the spur for even greater plane orders from fence-sitting airlines. Finally, McNerney is confident that the creature comforts of the 787—more space, better seats, improved lighting and commercial-quality windows—will give his customers an edge in attracting passengers who may demand these extra amenities after experiencing them.

Many analysts and investors had been critical of the cost of building these new planes. But the tough-as-nails McNerney has developed a model program, Partnering for Success, that makes it very difficult for suppliers to say no to the behemoth that is Boeing without adjusting their costs in Boeing's favor. As McNerney has said, there's a "no-fly zone" for those suppliers who don't play ball, and that's going to lead to sharply higher gross margins for Boeing as work on the 787, the newly redesigned 777, and the workhorse 737 progresses over the next few years. So expect higher cash flow, increased dividends and bigger buybacks as time goes along.

McNerney's not happy about the sequester, but he had planned for it the year before, so he doesn't expect even a penny of additional hit to earnings. He expresses confidence that Boeing will fare among the best of all the defense contractors because of the uniqueness and dependability of its offerings.

The man has no regrets about the embarrassing Dreamliner gaffes. As he has said, "If your game is innovation you can tolerate a little more failure and learn from it." Consider his tutelage your gain. As long as McNerney's the head coach of Boeing, you want to be a buyer. If this company could come through the Dreamliner debacle with more orders than ever, and if the world's downturn produced barely a hiccup in Boeing's earnings, who knows how high Boeing can fly when the global economy begins to hum in unison once again.

▪ Indra Nooyi, PepsiCo

Sometimes you meet terrific CEOs in the oddest ways. A half-dozen years ago I had my daughter's swim team over to the house for an end-of-season bash, and I wanted to do it up right. I polled a bunch of the kids about what they wanted and was astounded at how down they were on snacks, including the snacks that I regarded as quintessential fare for these get-togethers, namely Fritos, Doritos and Lay's potato chips. Without even knowing it, I had run into a "body is my temple" set of kids who wanted to end the season strong and healthy.

That Monday I went on television with my friend and former CNBC colleague Erin Burnett during our old "Stop Trading" segment, and I described the weekend's swim party to her: how the young women all shunned fatty snacks like Fritos, something that could spell real trouble for PepsiCo's Frito-Lay division. The next thing you know, the company's investor relations people have sent me a box of all of the nonsalty, nonfatty snacks that Frito-Lay is developing, along with an invitation to their testing facility in Aberdeen, Maryland, to see what's in the pipeline. I spent a day there and came back convinced that PepsiCo will deliver on its promise of developing more healthful snacks precisely to deal with younger people who are in revolt against unhealthy food as well as public health officials who see these snacks as the proximate cause for the obesity epidemic in this country.

The commitment to change comes right from the top, with perhaps the most cerebral executive I have ever met, Indra Nooyi, who is determined to lessen PepsiCo's reliance on the historic namesake brand while building an international snack franchise of good and good-for-you products that are loved for their taste and, in many cases, healthful characteristics.

When I look at the PepsiCo that Nooyi inherited in 2006, I see a company that relied mostly on developed markets for profits, struggling against Coca-Cola in a worldwide slog. It had little in the pipe to change the impression that this soda and snack company could adapt to the needs of a developed world, where natural and organic foods are increasingly popular, while salty snacks are craved in emerging markets where PepsiCo had a meager presence.

In just a few short years Nooyi has upended that entire edifice, spending billions in acquisitions and marketing to become a leader in snacks in precisely the growing emerging markets that had been largely overlooked or ignored by her predecessors. From almost a standing start, PepsiCo has become the number one food and beverage player in Russia, India and the fast-growing Middle East. A partnership with Tingyi, a gigantic Chinese food and beverage company, has helped make PepsiCo a leading beverage brand in China, where stepped-up marketing could lead to big benefits in the next few years, benefits that are not currently in the analysts' estimates.

Plus, Nooyi has now set her sights on reenergizing the classic Quaker brand, which has been relatively fallow, lost in the shadows of the much larger Frito-Lay salty snacks division. Quaker is known worldwide as a delicious, nutritious and wholesome food provider, and Nooyi is refreshing and reinvigorating its product line, introducing yogurt bars and Quaker Real Medleys, fruit and nut bars that I sure wish had been around when I threw that swim party. She's done the same to Gatorade, extending its varieties and taking over valuable shelf space worldwide.

At the same time, she has moved aggressively in the "good for you" space with acquisitions, including Stacy's, Sabra, and Naked Juice, while repositioning Tropicana as a much more healthful drink, including offering an extremely successful reduced-calorie orange juice.

Nooyi, though, hasn't skimped on the billion-dollar brands that are more good than good for you; Lay's potato chips, Doritos, Cheetos and SunChips have continued their share-taking, while Mountain Dew, long a stepchild to Pepsi, has come on strong not just here, where it is now the number one convenience store carbonated soda, but in India, where it is has become the number one soft drink in the entire category. Yes, and I will admit that Diet Mountain Dew is the sole vice left in my daily routine.

Still, it's been a challenging time financially for PepsiCo. Nooyi had to buy in the bottling business that a previous management had spun out, in order to recapture profitability that had been left on the subsidiary's table. She's had to cut costs and fire thousands of people to streamline what had become a top-heavy organization. At the same time she has had to fend off an activist shareholder, Nelson Peltz, who wants her to split PepsiCo into a snack food and a beverage company or have her acquire Mondelēz, a spin-off of Kraft that Peltz has a position in. Peltz is a fabulous investor, filled with terrific ideas. I trust Nooyi to do the right thing by shareholders, and if that means breaking up the company, making a big acquisition, or standing pat, I am confident she will make the correct move. That's what great coaches do, and there's no need to second-guess them.

The recent restructuring at PepsiCo has produced palpable gains, including $1 billion in cost savings in the first year of its deployment. Nooyi's plan could save another $3 billion in the next several years. At the same time, she's accelerating the firm's organic growth rate to 5 percent, one of the best real growers in the consumer packaged goods segment. The restructuring, while wrenching, has allowed PepsiCo to post those terrific earnings that have given shareholders bountiful returns, well in excess of the S&P 500.

It's not easy, though, to put a money value on what Nooyi has done during her time at the top. She's worked hard to build up the good-for-you snacks and to make the plain old, reliably delicious snacks more healthful without sacrificing profitability or taste. She's become a tireless roving ambassador for PepsiCo, allowing the company to take meaningful share in countries that it hadn't even had a presence in before she took the job. And she's done it in a way that is in keeping with the high standards that PepsiCo has maintained throughout its long history of excellence.

Each year on *Mad Money* we look forward to "Green Week," when we highlight companies that do good things for the environment that are also good for the bottom line. I feel terrible about twisting Indra's arm each year to come on, but what can I say, she runs the only company that has consistently been able to shrink its footprint and become more profitable in doing so. She will tell you she doesn't do it just because it feels good, or even because it makes more money. She does it because it has given PepsiCo a competitive advantage in trying to get the best and brightest worldwide to work for the company.

Nooyi is every bit the embodiment of the new bankable U.S. CEO, someone at home around the world, taking tough action now to create far greater profitability later, and navigating the switch from developed world competition to emerging market dominance. Frankly, I don't know how she does it all, but I do know the results have been terrific, and shareholders have plenty to show for it.

▪ Mark Papa, EOG

We are accustomed to seeing oilmen in books and movies as wildcatting, swashbuckling, outsized characters. But real oilmen are busy exploiting and developing oil properties without a lot of publicity, visibility and fanfare. Real oilmen like Mark Papa, the true genius behind EOG, the old Enron Oil & Gas, which declared its independence from Enron long before the destruction of that once proud company. EOG has since gained more than 1,400 percent versus a little more than 35 percent for the S&P 500 during the same period. We think of tech and biotech as growth companies, but EOG, an oil company, is perhaps the greatest growth story of our era, and it is all because of the mild-mannered man at the top.

I first heard of Papa when I learned that EOG had become the most aggressive accumulator of properties in the two largest oil fields in this country since Prudhoe Bay, the gigantic Alaskan field that was discovered in the 1960s: the Bakken in North Dakota and the Eagle Ford in Texas. Papa came on *Mad Money* a few years into the show with bold claims—and at the time seemingly foolish ones—that the North American continent could become energy-independent by 2020 given the technology we had developed, including hydraulic fracking and horizontal drilling, and the vast underground pools of oil in this country that had hitherto been either uneconomical or unreachable.

Papa was also the first oil executive I had come in contact with to predict that these new technologies would allow for the discovery and production of so much natural gas that we would have a glut in this country. The surplus, he told me, would keep prices well below where companies could produce big profits drilling for the stuff. Unlike virtually every other oil executive, Papa fled from natural gas before the collapse in pricing from the surfeit he predicted, and went all in oil. The decision not only saved his company from oblivion but has now made it one of the largest oil companies in the world. In recent years we've seen a whole host of natural gas–focused firms try to become more "oily," as they say in the patch, including Chesapeake, Encana and Devon Energy, but only EOG has actually succeeded in a way that puts most of its peers to shame. The company now gets 86 percent of sales from oil and natural gas liquids and just 14 percent from plain old glutted natural gas.

Under Papa, EOG has been executing the game plan that the firm articulated years ago: it has captured world-class, low-risk oil positions, and it is driving the strongest organic liquids growth of any independent. It's doing so without loading up the balance sheet with debt or seeking to dispose of valuable assets to pay off high-cost debt lest they be seized by the creditors.

While many oil and gas companies claim to have made terrific discoveries in the Bakken and Eagle Ford, Papa's EOG is the biggest in *both*, with 600,000 acres of drilling space in each prospect. As terrific and as well publicized as the Bakken has been—including an on-location *Mad Money* show—it's the Eagle Ford that's been the real standout. Papa has told me the returns in that Texas field are equal to those that you get *only* in Saudi Arabia. He's pumping as much as 4,000 barrels a day from some of the newer wells, an amount well in excess of what other American companies have been able to produce in recent years. He says there's so much oil in EOG's Eagle Ford properties that you "can hit it with a straw."

Papa's not done with big finds. In a recent interview on *Mad Money* he indicated that he holds huge acreage in the Delaware Basin of the Permian oil belt, once thought to be tapped out, that might be as prolific as both the Bakken and the Eagle Ford. He's also finding more oil than he expected a few years ago in his stakes in two other fields worth watching: the Wolfcamp and the Niobrara shales in Colorado. He always points out how great it is that EOG has so many irons in the fire.

People often ask how I saw the big transformational changes coming in America's oil and gas revolution that I described in a previous chapter. I tell them I had Mark Papa from EOG on regularly. You pretty much had to learn about the renaissance unless you simply refused to listen to this quiet, thoughtful member of the new breed of wildcatters. He not only wants to make as much money as possible for his shareholders; he also cares passionately that continental energy independence isn't just a long-term dream but a short-term reality. And EOG is going to do everything it can to make it happen. I know Papa's stepping up to chairman status, but he has assured me that he will be with the company for many years. It's a wild trader, often going up or down three or four points with the oil futures, but as long as oil stays above $80 a barrel, this one's got the most upside of any play in the patch.

▪ Cheryl Bachelder, AFC Enterprises

When will Cheryl Bachelder get her due for what she's done for AFC Enterprises, the holding company that runs Popeyes, the number two chicken chain with more than 2,000 locations that is growing by leaps and bounds and has given you a twelvefold return in the past five years? For decades Popeyes had been the lowly stepsister to Yum!'s Kentucky Fried Chicken, known more for its down-and-dirty urban stores with a tired look and an even more tired menu. Don't I know it? I love Popeyes, have since my mom introduced it to me in the 1980s when a franchise opened near our house outside Philadelphia. But a half-dozen years ago I stopped going to Popeyes because many of the stores near me were so slovenly they didn't deserve my business. Then, in 2007, AFCE tapped Bachelder, who had been president and chief concept officer at Yum!, to come and reinvent Popeyes, bringing it up to the quick-serve standards of the finest in the industry.

Bachelder didn't just change the name Popeyes Chicken to Popeyes Louisiana Kitchen; she's turned the company into a go-to destination, with a host of new dishes to go with the traditional fried chicken, red beans and rice, dishes that are promoted nationally on television and with exceptional social media, giving her consistently strong same-store sales. There's no real mystery to what Bachelder has done. She started by cleaning up the stores with a nationwide remodeling effort, which is now about 60 percent completed. Newly redesigned stores have virtually doubled the performance of the older, drab Popeyes. Older, poorly performing units have been shut in an attempt to bring up the overall quality of the chain. She began to grow the company's bottom line in a consistent, steady fashion, which left money for further expansion and modest share buybacks. Then, beginning in 2013, Popeyes, which had been closing pretty much as many stores as it had been opening each year, started embarking on real growth with an accelerated opening of stores, choosing to enter new markets around the country, typically by buying up the failed franchises of competitors. Plus, the chain, which had always had a small presence overseas, notably in Turkey, has now set its sights on a global expansion with an emphasis on Asia, where Yum!'s KFC has had such success, but also Latin America, where the spicy fried chicken, red beans and rice are already staples in many countries.

I recently caught up with Bachelder at a remodeled Popeyes in Brooklyn that's been doing roughly $2 million a year, a phenomenal return for a stand-alone restaurant. Bachelder works closely with the franchisees, the majority of whom used to be cooks at other Popeyes, to monitor the guest experience and help build a pipeline of ideas for new dishes for its monthly promotions. At a time when many of the restaurant chains seem to run the same promotions year in and year out to no real impact, despite the national ad dollars spent, Bachelder's offerings, like its Zatarain's Butterfly Shrimp and its Garlic Pepper Wicked Chicken, have actually moved the needle on earnings per share. Hence the tremendous outperformance of the stock in the past few years.

I like Bachelder's poise and confidence. This restaurant chain could easily triple in size to 6,000 units before it runs out of runway, and given its billion-dollar market cap it wouldn't surprise me if it triples in reaction to that growth. Maybe, at that point, Bachelder will at last get her due as not only one of the best restaurant CEOs but one of the nation's best CEOs altogether.

▪ Terry Lundgren, Macy's

With the advent of Amazon, most people wrote off the long-term prospects of the typical department store as quintessential prey of the online retailing colossus. Terry Lundgren, the CEO of Macy's, was not one of them. Lundgren early on recognized that he could combat online encroachment and compete effectively against myriad discounters like Walmart and Target. He would offer superior service, localized, proprietary merchandise and lower prices on premium goods, which he would accomplish by holding the suppliers' feet to the fire through shrewd bargaining. After all, what apparel maker doesn't want to have his wares displayed in the nation's dominant chain of 800 department stores, including the country's largest establishment in New York's Herald Square.

Lundgren, who took over a tired and beaten Macy's chain in 2003, quickly realized it needed heft, and he went on a buying spree of many of the great local department store chains throughout the country. First, he amalgamated all of them under the Macy's name, giving him the buying clout he needed to get better bargains with the main providers of merchandise than any other chain could. Then he developed the concept of "My Macy's," localizing the buying in areas that were not conducive to a big-footing by out-of-town New York buyers. So if someone were to go to a Pittsburgh Macy's during football season, he would see yellow-and-black-colored clothes in honor of the Steelers. And someone shopping at the men's clothing department in the Macy's in Raleigh, North Carolina, is going to see a large assortment of bow ties and seersucker suits, which makes that store more competitive with the remaining local retailers.

Lundgren is a shrewd user of technology, rolling out what he calls the "omni-channel" of retail: if one store doesn't have a particular product, and the warehouse is also out of it, the product can be whisked to the customer from another store in the chain in no time flat. This is an important advantage over Amazon and shows that the brick-and-mortar retailer is fighting back with online innovation. As he recently told me on *Mad Money*, the Omni-channel controls the inventory better than ever before: "If it is not selling in Memphis, Tennessee, that's where I am going to pull it from, because I am going to avoid a potential markdown in the feature by pulling the slowest-selling store." Finally, he is retraining more than 100,000 associates to better relate to customers and to make a personal connection so these customers come back repeatedly.

Lundgren has figured out how to leverage his company's relationship with national apparel makers like Calvin Klein, VF Corp. and Ralph Lauren to make proprietary merchandise that can't be found at other stores. That gives Macy's a big edge when combating those discounters that also have a lot of buying power.

Many merchants are really very good at having the right merchandise but have not been adept at figuring out how to make the most money for their enterprises with those goods. They manage inventory poorly or they end up giving it away to TJX because they didn't sell it quickly enough. Others are just financial organizations without the pizzazz of a Macy's, whose signature event, the Macy's Thanksgiving Day Parade, is a national treasure. Lundgren's the unique figure who has mastered both, which has allowed him to deliver superior returns, an ever-growing dividend as well as a very substantial and real buyback that has reduced the float in a dramatic way since the downturn. Given the company's incredibly healthy balance sheet, even after it boosted its dividend and buyback to return capital aggressively to shareholders, I see much more to come.

So, not only has the department store not gone moribund, but it's flourishing, as one look inside the stores and one look at the ever-rising stock price would tell you. Lundgren has figured out the formula for mass and local, proprietary and cheap, and he's giving shareholders the real bargain.

• Alex Smith, Pier 1 Imports

Nothing like being the host of a big Thanksgiving Day dinner. And when we do it, we want to do it perfectly, right down to the napkin rings and centerpieces. But where do you go to get that stuff? I remember my mother going to a mall years and years ago up in Bucks County, Pennsylvania, not far from where I am from, where there was a Pier 1. Since then I had heard that the company had lost its way in the past decade, turning into a blah store filled with noxious-smelling candles, absurd Papasan chairs, and a lot of other ugly furniture and unattractive lamps. But I said to myself, *What the heck, there's one not far from my house in Summit, New Jersey, right on Route 10 in East Hanover, so why not check it out?*

The place was fabulous, with a terrific fall seasonal assortment, including the perfect turkey napkin rings and gorgeous as well as inexpensive wreaths of mock cranberries. We grabbed everything they had, and I grabbed the file on the chain. Turns out that there had been a remarkable turn in the stores thanks to Alex Smith, an actual merchant with a great eye for just such seasonal accoutrements, making the place a brightly colored adventure, a virtual treasure hunt of holiday gifts and housewares, a huge trove of decorative goodies for each occasion.

Soon after, courtesy of the Great Recession, an embattled Pier 1 stock—not the company, but the stock—traded at 10 cents a share, a ridiculous mispricing and a reminder that, unlike what many of the academics who don't actually know how stocks trade believe, many securities are woefully mispriced, causing incredible opportunities.

When it comes to turning around a business, few things are more difficult than bringing a failing retailer back to life, something the shareholders of J. C. Penney know all too well after the disaster that was the brief reign of Ron Johnson. Instead of boasting, like Johnson, to great fanfare that Penney's would be reinvented as a totally new store concept, with the end of couponing, the most valuable come-on to customers,

Smith took a different tack. He didn't make big, bold pronouncements about the distant future and then deliver subpar results. He didn't do it with sweeping changes that would alienate his old customer base. No, Smith turned Pier 1 around by focusing on brass tacks. He realized that if Pier 1 was going to survive, it needed better-looking stores and better, fresher merchandise, including all-new seasonal assortments, like Halloween and Thanksgiving and Christmas offerings. He tripled the number of buyers and planners in the organization to get the right look and feel for the stores and offer the best, most reasonably priced goods to sell. He dropped the emphasis on big-ticket furniture items and added smaller-ticket items. At the same time, Smith changed the way Pier 1's stores were laid out, adopting more open and pyramid-shaped fixtures that increased the visibility of the merchandise and made the retailer look and feel more approachable and friendly.

Smith also closed underperforming stores and put a stop to opening new ones. Pier 1 had 1,160 locations when he took over; he cut that back to 1,062 over a five-year period. He also revamped the labor force and the systems, allowing him to reduce full-time employees from 6,110 to 3,500 over several years, while taking low or negative same-store results to high single-digits or even low double-digits in rapid fashion. It wasn't done with discounting either, as Pier 1 sales tickets have increased from an average of $150 shortly after Smith took over to $225 several years later. He's now focusing on building out a terrific web experience, which he was unwilling to do until he was sure he got it right.

Smith heard me talk about the changes at Pier 1 and came on the show to trace out the future for multiple-year growth. He regularly checks in to see if I am still a happy customer, and with kids going to college, I can't think of a better place to help them decorate their rooms for each seasonal change. Smith is not done innovating, but he plays it close to the vest. So dropping by each season has become a must, as the unexpected appears regularly from season to season and holiday to holiday. Pier 1 had a rare quarterly report "miss" recently. Smith immediately came on *Mad Money* to blame himself for sloppy execution—even as many other retailers stumbled at the same time. Even the winningest managers slip up now and then, though, and that's precisely when you want to buy in them. Consider the stock decline an opportunity.

Summary: The Bankable 21

I know, after a period when so many CEOs seem to be lacking in character or given to outright chicanery, it is difficult to stand behind any executives, not knowing what could change, including their own personal mores and standards. But in the end, just as in the NFL, you get a feel for who is a winner and who is a loser, who is battle-tested and who can't handle the heat. We are in for some difficult times in the stock market. We've got uncertain growth, too much government intervention, a market that is fickle and machines that can wreck any stock. We have an SEC that's not tough enough and shareholders that are, for the most part, too apathetic to create change. We have directors of boards who chow down on big salaries and have a great reluctance to rock the boat lest they lose their hundreds of thousands of dollars in fees for their four-times-a-year gig. In that environment we should question why we should have any faith at all in these people. But the twenty-one I have just given you are not only worth saluting; they are worth banking with. If any of these people were to leave their companies, I would think twice about owning the "teams" they left behind and would willingly follow them to the next company that makes them CEO. Remember, I have looked these people in the eye on many occasions, gotten together with them in depth to learn who they are and what they have done, and they get my good housekeeping seal of approval for you to cheer for and to bet with as long as they are in the business of trying to make you money.

CHAPTER 6

Charting for Fundamentalists

Every Tuesday for many years now I have run a segment on *Mad Money* called "Off the Charts," where I discuss a particular kind of charting method as a predictive tool for the stock market, commodities and individual stocks. Given that I base almost all of my work on fundamental factors related to the companies I study, not the way their charts look, this segment is both heretical and antithetical to my traditional stock-picking methods. Yet I can tell you from my viewer mail and from Twitter @JimCramer that it's my most popular segment *by far* and has made me radically rethink my view about using charts as an aid to stock picking. Somehow, perhaps because so many old-style ways of viewing stocks have been tossed out the window by investors who simply don't trust the market to function honestly anymore, technical trading—examining the pictures of stock movements over different periods of time—has become a touchstone, a totem that more people rely on than ever before when they make buy and sell decisions.

Now, not for a minute have I become a chartist. I still make my buy and sell recommendations after studying as much publicly available information as possible about the companies themselves. Chartists could care less about doing this kind of homework. In fact, often they could care less about what the company even does. Some of the chartists disdain the notion that the fundamentals mean anything at all. They just want to look at a picture of what the stock has been doing over certain periods of time. They then make calculations and draw conclusions about the direction a stock is going to take based on the patterns they see on the chart and what has previously occurred after such patterns develop. They use these inferences to time when to buy and when to sell stocks.

They apply the same discipline when they examine charts of the entire stock market, usually as represented by the Standard & Poor's 500, sector ETFs, gold, or oil or any other commodity. Chartists are typically not interested in identifying long-term investments. They use their techniques to spot bottoms, tops and, best of all, breakouts and breakdowns, where stocks are on the verge of making major moves. Chartists are "timers"; they simply won't take action unless they can time it perfectly. I've become proficient at charting over the years, but I still rely on professional technicians to teach me the tricks of the trade, and I mention their work by name each Tuesday when I do the segment, as I will do in this chapter.

In my opinion, chartists can be a little too certain about themselves and their methods. Over the years I have found some of their techniques for divining big moves to be wanting, and I have systematically had to weed out some technicians from the *Mad Money* lineup who have not proven reliable with their interpretation of the data or their pictographs. They simply aren't correct enough. If you aren't a fundamentalist and you just buy a stock off a particular chart pattern, and the pattern doesn't hold up, you will find yourself up the creek without the proverbial paddle. Few things in investing are more reckless than buying a stock you know nothing about because you like the chart pattern. If the breakout fails to develop and a breakdown ensues, you will have no idea what to do, so, invariably, you will just kick the stock out and take a loss. That's just irresponsibly buying high and selling low, and I can't ever sign off on that kind of recklessness. Other chartists, though, can be tremendously helpful when their work is married with the fundamental work I do. For this chapter, I have isolated the most useful techniques and technical patterns that, in retrospect, have worked over and over again in the five years I have gone off the charts. I now believe that when you infuse your fundamental work with technical timing patterns, you increase the odds for successful investing. When you meld your research on a company with insights gleaned from the different technicians I highlight here, I think you can get a better entry or exit point when you make your moves. Plus, at a highly emotionally charged time in the stock market, when you are trying, as prudently as possible, to build your wealth, it pays to use every tool at your disposal. Why say no to something that can help you get rich more carefully, something that can't be rigged, jiggered or assaulted by a recommendation process that many no longer trust because of conflicts of interest and selfishness? Charts can't be conflicted, and they are definitely not selfish.

When I worked with Karen Cramer, or the Trading Goddess, as she was known back then, at my old hedge fund, Cramer and Company, she loved to integrate the charts with my fundamental work. She relied on them to generate lots of our best trading and investing ideas. She would start her chart work by examining the Standard & Poor's *Trendline Daily Action Stock Charts* booklet that would be hand-delivered to our house every Saturday morning, something I still have done to this day. The *Daily Action Stock Charts* catalogues the charts of hundreds of companies, and on a quiet Sunday night I like nothing more than to peruse each chart, looking to see which ones stand out as positive or negative based on the patterns I am about to share with you.

Karen would look at the unfolding pictures made when you connect the dots of the closing prices of stocks over various time periods: 20 days, 50 days, and her favorite, 200 days, because she thought those were the relevant periods that needed to be examined to establish or spot important trends. She would thumb through scores and scores of them, looking for potential breakouts (where a stock is about to jump up after treading water) and breakdowns (where a stock could be about to plummet) and then rip out the ones she thought were the most promising and actionable. She put the stocks we owned through a similar exercise and would say to me, "Something's wrong with this one, someone knows something," as she tossed me the picture with a breakdown circled in red ink. Or she would say, "We're about to get real lucky," when one of the stocks we owned had a positive pattern developing. Or she would study the charts of stocks in the same group to see if a sector rotation might be on the horizon. She was especially careful to spot "divergences," when one stock in a given sector was acting differently from others in that sector, and she would make a note to me that something's up, that something unusual might be happening at that company and I had to follow up with phone calls to analysts and with a perusal of publicly available documents, articles and research reports to find out what was behind that odd divergence.

Often she would give me a "nothing done," meaning that there was no action worth taking because the charts of most stocks were inscrutable or not compelling or we felt edgeless. On average, 200 charts might produce four or five good potential trading ideas once I had checked out the fundamentals and felt secure about them.

We would then put money to work in those new stocks if we were satisfied that we had a situation where the risk and reward based on the charts *and* my research made it worthwhile. Occasionally Karen might actually dump stocks in our portfolio that I liked simply because a pattern she regarded as horrendous was developing. She would then suggest that I start researching the stock all over again, because it was simply too risky to hold on to it while I did new homework. That's extreme, I know, but it worked more than I care to admit. Often this combination—insights gleaned from the technicals as a way to get started on the fundamental research—produced some of our most lucrative trades and let us avoid potential pitfalls, although I can tell you we did throw away some darned good stocks simply because Karen didn't like the way things looked on the pictograph she fretted the most about that day. "Charts never lie," she would say, though I often didn't know why charts told the truth. But she drilled it into my head that I had to care, or at least learn which patterns often flagged danger simply because there are enough chartists out there at big firms that they can make themselves right by taking the same action on the same patterns. That self-fulfilling behavior alone, she would say, is why the charts are so important. At a time like now, when hedge funds so dominate "the action" and so many money managers are technically inclined or use algorithms, or math inputs, that spit out buy and sell commands based on these identical patterns, you ignore chartists at your own risk. I can't tell you how many times I call around now when I see a stock dive to find out what triggered the decline, only to hear back "The chart's terrible" or "Its group is experiencing a technical breakdown" or "It just broke down below its fifty-day moving average." We're all chartists or, at least, closet chartists now.

It's not just the self-fulfilling behavior at work, though, that you are monitoring when you examine the charts. Karen liked to use charts because they can give clues to what large accounts might be up to but don't want you to know about. That's because chartists rely on volume spikes to detect what might be going on underneath the action. She said charts were like "polygraphs" that enabled you to figure out the truth about what the big trigger-pullers, like huge mutual or hedge funds, were doing with a stock. If you saw some sudden and aggressive buying, indicated by a quick change in the trajectory of a stock on large volume, Karen believed that someone might be "in the know" and have information that was worth piggybacking on. She would then have me check around to see if the company was speaking somewhere, or an earnings announcement might be due, or an analyst was getting cold feet about a recommendation or was warming up to the story. If we could get any insight about what might be happening and we liked the stock, she would pull the trigger herself, betting that the chart pattern would play out positively. Similarly, if a stock was "breaking down," she assumed someone knew that the quarter was awry or there would soon be something negative about to occur. She loved to short stocks that looked to be on the verge of breaking down and would do so if anything at all negative about that stock could be on the horizon.

Back then I was never as conspiratorial as Karen about these things. In retrospect, I was too innocent, though, because these past few years of financial failures and insider trading prosecutions have shown the wisdom of at least presuming that someone might be taking action on information few others have. These days, *not* paying attention to that kind of chart pattern seems a bit naïve, if not ludicrous, with whole wings of federal prisons filled with those who did know what was about to happen to the stock of a given company because they possessed material insider information that was illegally obtained and traded upon.

That's another important reason why it was so imperative to integrate the charts into *Mad Money*. Anything that can keep you from getting blindsided increases your chances of gaining great wealth through long-term investing. Your arsenal must be filled with every weapon possible, and if you can use charts responsibly, I am convinced you will do much better than other investors out there who rely solely on basic research.

In order to get you into the chart world, I want to start by examining what are known as the "internals," patterns about stocks in the aggregate that can give you clues to the direction of entire markets. Then I will show you how technicians use specific chart patterns to spot bottoms, to isolate larger moves and then, ultimately, to flag tops before they occur. I will wrap it up with some more sophisticated methods involving comparative techniques to flesh out big moves that might be on the horizon. Fortunately, almost all the charting techniques I am about to describe are available from software kits provided by almost every broker imaginable. Nothing in here will be beyond your ken. It's all available on the web; even the most abstruse techniques and patterns mentioned here can be Googled, as they are all listed and detailed if you are mystified and want to know more. And to think that we had to pay fortunes back at my old hedge fund for these very charting packages that are now available for free everywhere you look. Or we had to hand-draw the patterns when the software wasn't yet up to snuff. If you have just started out using charts, you have no idea how lucky you are.

I don't want to fill a whole book with technical tools. There are tons of those available already. I just want to give you the basics of what has worked and a few extra insights that most fundamentalists, whether hobbyists or professionals, need to know to be as informed as possible about how to use the charts and the technical data these software packages give you in responsible ways. I hope this chapter can separate the chart work that I think is worth your while from the methods that have failed to deliver consistent performance.

Confirmation of a Rally: Can It Be Trusted?

For years now, ever since the Great Recession showed the inherent weaknesses in our system, there has been tremendous skepticism about any advance. While I believe the systemic risks have been reduced, I know that each rally creates a worrisome set of risks. Callers and emailers often start their queries with "Am I coming in after a move has taken place?" or "Is it too late and we are about to get hammered again?" Good charting can be as simple as compiling enough indicators and data points to confirm that a solid rally is in place as well as determining its level of strength compared with previous rallies. Remember: charting, at is core, is simply a method of comparing what's happening this time, according to the charts and the technical data before you, to what's happened other times with similar inputs. So often we are fooled by big moves in the averages and what might be about to occur with them. The charts can help divine the possibilities that a move is for real. Portfolio managers running trillions of dollars are sifting through the same pictures and reaching the same conclusions you are, so the charts have a self-determinist quality to them.

Sometimes, to technicians, everything hinges on putting together the charts of individual companies and the charts of the bigger averages to create comparisons that elucidate conclusions about market strength. They are looking for "confirmation" of a move to detect its legitimacy. Here's a classic example: there is a historical adage that a new high on the Dow Jones Industrial Average will not be sustainable unless you have the Dow Jones Transportation Average, an index of trucking, rail, freight forwarding and airline stocks, also going to a new high, thereby "confirming" the rally. This particular pattern, known as "Dow theory" because it derives from the writings of Charles Dow, the founder and first editor of the *Wall Street Journal*, holds that a genuine bull market demands that both the Dow Jones Industrials and the Transportation averages should be rallying simultaneously to new highs. Dow was writing over a hundred years ago, and back then his logic made a lot of sense because the United States was a growing industrial power. Our factories made things and our railroads transported them—they were hand in hand—so any time you had a rally in one group but not the other, Dow theory considered it suspect. Chartists use a breakout in one average to confirm a breakout in the other. I like Dow theory and use it a lot to keep in check my enthusiasm for a rally. Transports are still a very powerful theme, and the index still carries tremendous sway over many investors. Often, on *Mad Money* and

Squawk on the Street, I will tell you that I don't like the way "the transports" are acting and that they aren't confirming the advance. That's my conclusion after overlaying a chart of the transports with the chart of the S&P 500 and finding the S&P's advance wanting. Dow theory keeps me skeptical, and that makes me a better investor. It does make me want to trim back stocks when I don't get a transport confirmation, because, historically, you don't buck the transports.

But, just like everything else these days, our economy has become a whole lot more diverse and complex over time; the transports and the industrials by themselves can no longer paint the whole picture. That's why I now look at the charts of many other sectors and compare them to the S&P 500 to buttress my thinking, including the technology stock cohort and the financial stock group, because they each represent nearly 20 percent of the Standard & Poor's 500. They are just too big and too important to ignore technically, so I monitor the SOX, which is the Philadelphia Semiconductor index, and I gauge the XLF, the financial ETF, and overlay them on the broader averages to try to confirm True North. I also examine the chart of the RTH, the retail ETF, because consumer spending is an important gauge of the health of the U.S. economy. We're a nation of spenders, not savers, although we have certainly become more frugal after the trials of the Great Recession.

As I look back over five years of "Off the Charts" I find that if you can get a rally where the transports, the financials, the techs and the retailers are all going higher in synch, then you need to put as many chips as you can on the table. That's been the precursor to every advance of any magnitude during the post–Great Recession period. It may seem almost too simple, but sometimes it's not worth rethinking, given how these patterns appeared again and again during the time examined.

The corollary is also true: you need to be skeptical of a narrow rally that's confined to certain groups of stocks that don't include the techs, the transports, the retailers and the financials. How important is this method of charting? During the entire advance leading up to the Great Recession, we had almost no "participation," the technical term for involvement, by the financials, retailers and the techs. That's right, these three critical groups, so important to our economy and therefore the stock market itself, sat out the rally, something you would never have known if you weren't charting them at the time leading up to the crash. Charting gave you the signal you needed to know that the market could not be trusted, as less important stocks were charging ahead, stocks involving the metals, mining, fertilizer, machinery and coal markets, while leaving banks, retailers and techs behind. In retrospect, the market had been hijacked by stocks that do well when China, not the United States, prospers, while "underneath," our economy, as represented by retail, banks and techs, was rolling over. When I go back over the chart work we did on the show leading up to that hideous decline, I think it may have been the technicians' finest hour. The move up could not be confirmed by the aggregate charts of important sectors, so you had to sell, not buy.

The Market's "Internals"

When you are a technician, you aren't looking at charts in a vacuum. You are also sifting through data as a whole that the charts generate. For example, you might be collecting information that gives clues about how the averages are really doing, not just how they look on the surface. When you create a chart of, say, the moving average of the S&P 500, all you are doing is taking the sum of the advances or declines in market capitalization of all of the stocks in the index and then adding that number to the end of a chart line that depicts the close of the previous day's, week's, month's or even year's worth of action. When that sum of the capitalizations of the stocks in the S&P 500 declines, that gives you a dip in the continuum; when the sum increases, it gives the line a lift. However, on a given day, if you measure the number of stocks advancing versus the number of stocks declining *within* the average, or what's known as the market's "breadth," it is often a better, more useful and more honest depiction of what could be occurring than the index as a whole might be showing. That's because some stocks might just be dominating the averages with big advances, masking weakness from many other stocks that you otherwise can't see without doing technical work examining the breadth of the stocks in aggregate.

CHARTING FOR FUNDAMENTALISTS

I always want to know the general sense of where the market might be going, so I like to eyeball aggregate charts that show the advances versus the declines to assess the real breadth of the market. You are always looking for broad participation to stay fully invested. If breadth "narrows," or fewer and fewer stocks are advancing each day, you have to trim, perhaps even aggressively, because the advance you are witnessing is long in the tooth.

I also find it useful to chart how many stocks are hitting new highs versus how many are hitting new lows. That comparison can give you a more rigorous look at what's really happening in the stock market than the broader index might otherwise provide.

We bandy about the new high list as if it is nothing special, par for the course even. But in reality it is extremely difficult for a stock to hit a new high. First, the company must be doing exceptionally well. Second, the sector has to be strong, as sectors matter so much to the overall action in a stock. Third, the larger forces—interest rates, the Federal Reserve, foreign markets—all those macro inputs, have to be aligned to not harm the stock and instead be giving it a boost. The gauntlet a stock has to traverse to hit a new high is challenging enough to make a definitive statement of that stock's strength. You don't get on the new high list simply because you're popular. And you never get on by mistake.

How does this work in practice, and how important is the charting of advances versus declines and new highs versus new lows? Go back to June 2011, the last time the market was in severe peril, yet so few people, except the chartists, using new-high, new-low and advance-decline measurements, knew the slaughter that awaited them. On the surface, the market looked to be "consolidating," another technical term meaning that stocks were pretty much marking time, hanging out, not doing anything. That's often a sign that while there's some profit taking going on by investors who have big gains, there's no particular selling pressure coming into the market. It's at equilibrium, usually a decent moment after a big run, certainly not one worth worrying about. I thought the market was acting fine, but the technicians were begging me to check the "internals," the data that assess how stocks as a whole are acting. Specifically, technicians were telling me that the number of stocks hitting new highs was diminishing each day even as it *seemed* we were just marking time. Concurrently, stocks making new lows were on the increase. Technicians were also showing me charts that compared how many stocks were advancing as a whole versus how many were in retreat, and the market's breadth was weakening by the day. Fundamentalists might be oblivious to these kinds of actions, but for technicians, high-low and advance-decline charting leaves telltale signs that the advance is in peril. Rather than consolidating in a safe way, the market has become quite dangerous. Consider the market as ice that you are skating on; it's getting thinner or melting, and you just don't know it unless you are using the technicians' new-high, new-low and breadth gauges. The middling action was masking a deteriorating market "underneath" and wasn't confirming the advance. Sure enough, with all these technical lights flashing red, even as the surface looked fine to stand on, the S&P took an 18 percent header, wiping out all of the gains for the year. If you followed the technicals, you could have avoided the worst sell-off since the Great Recession, because while stocks seemed to be stabilizing, it turned out that Europe had just begun its long slide down into a near depression and the federal government was headed to a showdown on the budget deficit that led to a ratings agency downgrade of the U.S. government's debt. Now remember, technicians don't care about what's going to "cause" the decline. No chartist was wise to Spanish and Italian bonds or to the machinations of the House of Representatives against the president. Chartists just know that certain patterns, like a decline in the number of new highs versus new lows, can signal that something terrible might occur. And in 2011 they were dead right.

Sometimes careful investing just means avoiding big losses. That's exactly what technical trading did for you in 2011. Ever since then I have kept a close eye on the new highs versus new lows indicator, as well as the market's advance versus decline breadth in general, to measure the real dangers lurking underneath the market's floor. Both those indicators were telling you far more than the broader averages about the true nature and health of the stock market. I consider them lifesavers; they are fabulous pictorial messages of the underlying pillars of the market. Right before that gigantic fall, they told you all that you needed to know, far more than the fundamentals did at the time.

Detecting Floors and Ceilings

When you pick individual stocks, you are betting that from the moment you buy them, they are going to go up. I know, that's pretty simple. But how often do you do solid fundamental work on how a company might be doing, and then just start buying it if you like what you see after doing the homework? Over time that technical ignorance might work out for you. But I am a huge believer that you want your basis, the price you pay for a stock, to be as advantageous as possible. You don't just want to say, "Okay, I've done all my work. Now it's time to buy." You want to say, "I know the stock, but I want to be sure the price is right before I pull the trigger." Charting can help you time that buy. It can increase the odds that you will start out from a stronger position and get a good basis. It's a terrific tool to help improve both your entrance and, ultimately, your exit, particularly in a rough, choppy market that tosses around all stocks, including the ones you might have your heart set on.

Let me demonstrate by going back a few years to show you how important it is to time your buy, especially when you are trying to pick a bottom in a stock that's falling in order to get the best entry point. Remember, I like to use weakness, not strength, to buy. That way I can get a better, cheaper basis, and I always like to get a bargain. I like to buy pullbacks. I like to buy discounts. That's because I view the stock market as if it were a merchandise mart, and I like to buy at wholesale, not retail. If I can get the same goods at an outlet mall much cheaper than I can at a full-price shopping center, then I am always going to head to the outlet. But I need to be sure that the discount is caused by a damaged or declining *stock*, not a damaged or declining *company*. Charting is an incredibly useful method of discerning between the two, allowing you to use the sale the market puts on to your best advantage.

It all seems so obvious, in retrospect, that the decline in 2008–9 was ultimately a fantastic buying opportunity. But who knew at the time? It sure didn't feel that way. Stocks just kept going lower and lower. In fact, each day just brought more fright and more losses as the sell-off thickened. The fundamentalists were often at a loss to explain the actions. They were fearful, emotional and, at times, extremely unhelpful in the process of finding a bottom.

At these big junctures it helps to call in the technicians, because they are unemotional and exacting in their terms of what bottoms look like, regardless of the fundamentals of the stocks themselves. Remember, to them every stock is just XYZ Corporation, as represented by a series of dots on a line. At times that line shows you a decent risk-reward level to do your buying, and that's what we are often looking for. But when things are as turbulent as they were back then—and I am sure we will hit similar dark skies again sometime—I like to call in not one technician or two or three but sometimes even four to be sure a dip is buyable before I take action. A bevy of agreeing technicians can be a wonderful thing to behold.

So let's go back in time to the summer of 2009, when stocks were still flailing on a daily basis and we were all trying not to drown in a sea of negativity. At that moment I was convinced that it was time to recommend something big and safe with a long-term history of performing well even in the toughest of times. In short, I thought it was time to buy AT&T, the phone company. The fundamentals, helped by a smashing roll-out of a new Apple iPhone, had turned positive for certain. There was no doubt that sales were increasing and profits would follow. The yield stood at an outstanding 6.2 percent, much better than just about any stock in the Dow Jones Average, and that dividend was backed up by the phone company's gigantic cash flow. But the stock itself, like so many others at the time, couldn't find any footing. It just seemed to be a dangerous time to own even the safest stock regardless of the fundamental strength of the enterprise.

Still, after determining my worldview as I showed you how to do earlier in this book, I decided the worst was over for the U.S. economy—and you need to buy when the worst is over. So I brought in four longtime technicians I trusted: Rick Bensignor, Helene Meisler, Dan Fitzpatrick and Alan Farley. I had followed all four for many years and had seen their work regularly either at my old hedge fund or at TheStreet, where there are a number of good technicians plying their trade. Even as fundamental analysts were wavering *because* AT&T's stock wouldn't stabilize, causing them to get cold feet on their buy recommendations, all four technicians said, simultaneously, that the charts were signaling BUY BUY BUY. And that's what led to one of my best calls ever, the "Off the Charts" segment back on September 22, 2009, when I said it was time to pull the trigger on AT&T.

What did they see? What made them all agree? They invoked concepts that are at the fundament of all individual stock charting: basing, floors, resistance and ceilings. Charting, if you analogize, is a lot like building a house. You need firm ground that won't give way to serve as the house's foundation. You accept that every house has a roof, a level that can't easily be gotten through. A good, buyable stock is one that has a sure foundation that allows it to turn up and head toward the ceiling. Eventually you want that stock to gather a head of steam and punch through that roof. Once that happens, the ceiling can, if the stock is strong enough, turn into a floor to launch it to a still higher level. So the chart pattern will ultimately show you the holy grail of technical trading: a series of floors that serve as launching pads to send stocks to and then through ceilings, all the way from new lows to new highs.

First, all four technicians agreed that AT&T had established what is known as a "climax" low at $21 back in 2008, with lots of sellers capitulating but buyers stepping up to create a base, or floor, in the stock at that level. They arrived at that judgment by looking at where the volume, the sum of all of the transactions during that period, had expanded to a level far in excess of that of a normal period's trading. That's a sign that the sellers have "exhausted" themselves. The volume levels, these technicians said, showed that most of the big portfolio managers who wanted out of AT&T had already left the stock. At the same time, buyers had stepped up to meet that supply with a concomitant level of demand. Think of it like this: Until you got the climax, there were so many more sellers than buyers at each level that they knocked the stock down with their own selling. As long as sellers overwhelm buyers with their dumping, no base can form. A climax is a sign that those sellers who have been holding out for some time are finally giving up en masse. Remember, technicians don't care why that might be the case; they are just monitoring prices and volumes. When they see that volume get much larger but the stock doesn't go down, that means you have finally found a floor, so it is safe to start buying. That's where the buyers are, at last, equal to the sellers, and a form of equilibrium is upon the stock.

NOW, JUST SPOTTING an absolute price low after a climax doesn't mean much to these analysts. A stock can stay at a low and do nothing. To get a tradable move from that low, they want to see a stock launch from that floor and then take out what is known as "resistance," a key term for understanding the world of charting.

To create an accurate chart of a stock, the technicians don't just look at the closing price and graph against the previous day's or week's close. That's not all that helpful because it can be herky-jerky and doesn't yield the smooth trajectory that they need to make accurate charts to further their judgments. So what they do is create what is known as a "moving average" chart to give a truer picture.

A moving average is formed by taking the closing prices of a stock over a period of time, adding those prices up and then dividing those prices by the days in that particular period. For example, you can measure a moving average over, say, a ten-day period, by adding up ten days' worth of closing prices and dividing the sum by 10, plotting the number on a graph. You then take the next day's close and add it on to the previous nine days of trading, dropping the first close of the previous ten-day period. Then you divide that number by the average of the new ten prices and plot that new point. Each subsequent day, you add in the new close and drop off the earliest closing price to get the sum of the new ten-day measuring period. Then you divide that number by 10 and arrive at a new point to plot. You arrive at a fifty-day moving average by adding up the closing prices of the previous fifty days and dividing the sum by 50, the number of days during that period. You then drop the previous fiftieth day and add in the current fiftieth day to arrive at the average you are plotting. Each technician I talk to seems to like different measuring sticks. Some are satisfied with just fourteen days' worth of depictions; others like longer periods. I personally like the 200-day moving average, again, taking 200 closing prices divided by successive 200 days to get each dot on the line. That length of time gives me a better sense of the longer-term strength or weakness of a stock and so, I believe, gives me a truer picture of how a stock has really been doing as a way to tell how it might do in the future. For me, it blocks out the noise that could be occurring in any briefer period and makes me feel more comfortable about the reliability of the trajectory I am examining. We all need to find our technical comfort levels; the 200-day moving average gives me the most confidence about how a stock has really been acting.

Those four technicians I checked in with on AT&T all used the 200-day moving average to come up with a view of the stock they trusted. They noticed that even though AT&T had most certainly found a floor at that $21 level that the stock repeatedly bounced off of, it kept failing to move up above the 200-day moving average they had plotted, creating what looks like a ceiling, or a point of resistance, at that level (see Figure 1). It capped the stock for ages and ages.

Then, at last, AT&T cracked through that ceiling of resistance visible in the 200-day moving average, and that was the signal to all of these technicians that it was game on at last for T and it was safe to buy.

Recall, the technicians tend to look at charts the way we look at houses. Once that 200-day roof was punctured, the chart changed coloration to them. The old roof became a new floor on a brand-new house. Every time the moving average went above the old roof, making a new floor, it would fall back and hold at that new floor. That just-established base emboldened buyers, as they recognized that the stock didn't sell back through that level. Instead, it held. And that's how a great chart was born.

Looking back at that beautiful pattern, it now seems so easy. Yet at that moment it was anything but easy, because at the same time these technical analysts were saying "Buy," the fundamental analysts were scared out of their wits that something that they didn't know about was wrong with the stock. They were totally unhelpful. Not one was as valuable to me with my AT&T pick as a technician discerning the stock's definitive breakout above the original 200-day moving average. That base, that floor, gave the stock a launching pad to head in an almost straight line into the $30s, one of the biggest gains a safe stock like AT&T could ever give you. It's the essence of what good charting is. You will see it again and again when you look at all the bottoms of that era and of many other moments when stocks stop their declines and an advance begins.

Lows that Hold

We know the proximate cause of the Great Recession was the bubble in housing. So many investors thought home prices could never retreat in value over any long period of time. It had happened only once in our nation's history, the Great Depression, and it seems that almost no one in the period that defined the bubble bursting back in 2007 saw it coming. I measure the health of housing by examining the chart of the ETF index of home builders, known as the HGX. After being in free fall since its top in February 2007 at $255, the HGX bottomed in March 2009, at the height of the Great Recession, at $55, which makes a lot of sense when you consider that the peak of the HGX came right at the beginning of the crash.

The HGX then took off from that $55 floor on a sustained run to $108 in January 2012, with only a dip to $76 in October of the previous year, a 41 percent move from that October low. It was a breathtaking advance, the strongest of all the indices off the 2009 lows. At that point many investors wondered if they had missed the big move and now it was over.

To see whether this fabulous move had run its course, I turned to Scott Redler of T3 Trading Group, who writes with me at RealMoney .com, the paid site of TheStreet.com. He examined the HGX daily chart for answers, and he came back convinced that there was much more to this move because the HGX had made more than five higher lows in a row (see Figure 2). Why do higher lows matter? Because they indicate that dip buyers, opportunistic pools of large money, had been coming in aggressively whenever there was a significant pullback, something we hadn't seen in that bedraggled sector in ages. Scott also liked the fact that the HGX had moved above all the short-, medium- and long-term moving average trajectories that technicians follow, showing that upward momentum was accelerating.

He then turned to a longer-term chart of the weekly performance of the index, dropping an old week and adding in a new week's worth of closes and dividing them by a large number of weeks to come up with a new point to plot. He noticed that HGX was bumping up against a very long-term ceiling of resistance created by a downward sloping line at $111 (see Figure 3). He predicted that a breakout above $111 would be the ultimate confirmation of the rally. Not long afterward, the index did just that. The result? A monster move to $189 without a breath, a move that you would have been able to grab had you analyzed the higher lows and the moving averages that took out long-term resistance. This is a pattern that constantly reoccurs after a sustained move has begun. It is the hallmark of a superb trader. Now, if you go back in time, you will see nothing positive written about the housing business when Redler made that bullish call. In fact, you will read a sea of negative articles, a veritable ocean of them. Those stories would have kept you on the sidelines. The chart put you right into the game, a game you could have won by obeying the principle of ever higher highs.

Overbought and Oversold

I have now introduced you to the different moving averages to show how a stock has been faring over a long period of time; you've learned about floors and resistances and what it takes to move beyond them. The next crucial theme for technicians? Whether a stock is overbought and therefore ripe for a pullback or oversold and ripe for a bounce. You determine whether a stock is overbought or oversold by charting the ratio of higher closes to lower closes, also known as a relative strength index. The relative strength index is a momentum oscillator that measures the direction a stock is going and the velocity of the move. The relative strength indicator compares a stock or an index to its price action historically. My favorite technical arbiters for relative strength measurement are Bob Lang and Tim Collins, both of whom have done remarkable work on the topic for *Mad Money* and RealMoney.com. Both like to use shorter periods of time, ten days or two weeks, to measure relative strength. They are looking for any pattern that reverses the action of the previous period, because that's the sign that a breakout or a breakdown of some magnitude might be upon us.

Typically when a stock gets overbought, it is ripe for a pullback because overbought stocks, ones with many buyers reaching to take in supply, tend to snap back after they've gotten too far away from their longer-term trend line. In other words, buyers have become too enthusiastic about a stock, and when their buying is done, unless something extreme happens to help the company underneath the stock, it retreats or reverts to the mean. Overbought stocks tend to be dangerous because they can pull back, sometimes quickly and violently, to a lower level of equilibrium. The inverse can be true too. A stock can fall so far, so fast that you should expect a snapback because it is technically "oversold." We see these patterns constantly; they are very reliable indicators that a change in direction is about to occur. I demonstrate the impact of stocks being overbought and oversold quite regularly as part of my "Off the Charts" segment of the show. They are terrific action points. If you are debating buying a stock after you have done all the research and find the stock is overbought, I usually tell you to wait for a pullback that almost always comes.

Periodically, though, some stocks break through all the ceilings of all the traditional significant measurement periods and then stay overbought for a week at a time, defying the historical trading patterns that have hitherto trapped them within bands of extremes. They defy the notion of the inevitable gravitational pull of the old equilibrium line and just can't be contained by any of the various ceilings that overbought conditions usually bump into and come crashing down from. When you spot these highly unusual moves, you may be able to strap yourself to a real moon shot. We saw exactly that occur to the casino stocks in July 2009, as Dan Fitzpatrick pointed out to me in an "Off the Charts" segment back then. That summer the stock of Las Vegas Sands, one of the largest casino companies, had been stalled repeatedly at the $10 level, failing every time it hit that barrier. Consider it an electric fence that repelled the bulls every single time (see Figure 4).

When the bulls finally broke out of the corral, there was no stopping them, and the stock gained relative strength after it pushed through, instead of regrouping to recover from its overbought status. That very rare pattern, when the buyers won't quit despite the stock being overbought, is a sign that the strongest positive move in the book might be taking place, which is exactly what happened with Las Vegas Sands. It proceeded to go from $10 to $48 pretty much in a straight line, with no substantive pullback to speak of. An overbought condition that can stay overbought is a golden opportunity for a huge move.

Remember, I like to marry the fundamentals with the charts so I am not too dependent on the pictorials. What was happening underneath that chart? That's when Las Vegas Sands went from being a Vegas casino with a small business in Macau, the only place in China where gambling is legal, to being primarily a Chinese casino company with an American affiliate because of a new Macau expansion and a simultaneous boom in Chinese gamblers, thanks to flush times in the People's Republic. The change transformed LVS from a so-so Nevada gaming company into an international powerhouse that might as well have been named Macau Sands. The chart told you about the transformation well ahead of the Wall Street analysts, who were still dazed that we had such a horrendous decline to begin with.

Discovering Bottoms

You don't always get the option to buy low and sell high. One of the most important insights you can learn from looking at the charts is that you can often make more money buying a stock that's already had a big run than you can by jumping off the stock to find something better. The problem for a fundamentalist is that after a big run, you can feel downright greedy if you don't sell and close. Watchers of *Mad Money* know that one of my adages is "Bulls make money, bears make money, but hogs get slaughtered." That's why, on the *Mad Money* sound board, I keep a button that sounds like a squealing hog and one that sounds like a guillotine in action as constant reminders of what happens when you are too greedy and are due for a fall.

Take Caterpillar, for example. Caterpillar had run up an astonishing 236 percent from its low in March 2009 and had hit a fifty-two-week high at $73 in the summer of 2010 when I asked a noted technician, Ken Shreve, to take a hard look at it to see if it was finished going higher. I liked the stock because even after its big run, it was selling for only about eight times earnings; historically, people were used to paying between ten and twelve times for its earnings. Plus, it was sporting a 2.3 percent yield, decent for a big industrial. But I thought I might be embarrassingly late to the party given its huge move.

Shreve reassured me. He first took a look at Caterpillar's chart versus the S&P 500's chart and noted that its relative strength was far more powerful than that key index in the face of severe market weakness (see Figure 5). Caterpillar had been trading sideways since April, but during the week of July 23, it closed above $68.35 and broke out from this consolidation area (point 1 on the chart). It then continued to power higher, after making a short pit stop in August, pulling back from $72.25, and went into another brief consolidation (point 2). Then it broke out once again.

Shreve also took a look at CAT from the longer-term monthly chart. He said at the time that it could be on the cusp of a nice run higher (see Figure 6). He pointed out a big U-shaped pattern that CAT had broken out of and noted that this kind of formation has often led to powerful rallies. CAT had drifted lower in May and June, which he said was a classic tell that the last remaining sellers had been shaken out of the stock, the ones who might have bought before the crash of 2008 and were just waiting for their investment to break even, behavior that often paves the way for a meaningful breakout. The weekly chart showed that CAT had at the same time vaulted over an important resistance line, the ceiling where the sellers had been overwhelming buyers, which in this case was at $72.83, where CAT had topped out back in April 2010.

Shreve also liked that the current rally was coming off a base that stretched all the way back to June 2008 and noted that anyone who had bought CAT at *any* time in the previous twenty-six months had made money as long as they held on to it. He told me that you get a stable launching pad from that kind of happy shareholder base.

When I queried, again, whether it was too late for me if everyone had already made money, he turned me on to another indicator technicians use: the percentage of mutual funds that own the stock. At the end of the second quarter of that year, Shreve said, only 381 mutual funds owned the stock, versus as many as 900 to 1,000 mutual funds in all of the other Dow components. He said that combination of *underownership* and a stable chart base indicated that there was still plenty of room to run.

The result? CAT gave Shreve a straight-shot gallop to $115. What we didn't know at the time—but perhaps the chart did—was that China had initiated an incredibly powerful stimulus plan with lots of shovel-ready projects that led to a huge wave in orders for Caterpillar's earthmoving machines. Those orders weren't "in the numbers," so to speak, meaning that the analysts didn't see the big increases in earnings that CAT had on the horizon. But the charts, as interpreted by Shreve, sure did.

Bankable Patterns

Some of the most important chart patterns look almost silly, as if they are mimicking body parts, letters or geometric shapes. Yet after perusing thousands of charts for this book, I have to admit that these patterns are indeed reliable precursors to real gains and losses and simply cannot be dismissed, no matter how wedded you might be to fundamental research. That's because they are often telegraphing what big money is doing, meaning what the smarter, often more informed players are trying to buy and sell. It makes sense to follow their footsteps as measured by the volume and price action in the stock, because they have access to information that the rest of us might not have. They may even have fancy information that shouldn't be legal to act on. That's okay. When we examine charts, we don't care about their information or their motivations; we just care about the footprints they leave and we follow them. Further, because there are so many chartists out there, once the pattern becomes self-evident, technicians pile on and the moves accumulate. Before I go into these, let me just add that many sound so silly or sophomoric that you might tend to bridle at my mere suggestion that you consider them before you buy or sell a stock. But I have tested these going back through five years of *Mad Money* and they have yet to be wrong or to have led folks astray.

HEAD-AND-SHOULDERS PATTERN

I learned not to ignore one of the most simple but by far the most reliable patterns out there, the dreaded head-and-shoulders pattern, when my charitable trust bought Alcoa in the low teens in 2010 and ultimately took a giant bath in red ink because of that ill-informed buy. We had become enamored of the work the terrific and erudite Klaus Kleinfeld had been doing at the helm of Alcoa—still are—and thought the stock, which had peaked in the $40s before the Great Recession, might be ready to return to its past glory.

Alcoa enjoyed a healthy run from the winter of 2010 right up until February 2011, rising from $13 to $17 as its earnings trajectory seemed to have finally turned around. Not long after the stock hit $17, it took a quick dive back to $15 for no reason that I could discern; then it quickly reversed and took out that $17 high, going to $18 on the eve of its quarterly earnings report (see Figure 7). I thought the quarter, when it was announced, was a fine one, beating Wall Street estimates on both the top line, or sales numbers, and the bottom line, the earnings. What worried me, though, was that after an initial positive reaction, the stock dropped to $16 and change on the news. A few days later it was back to $17 and I felt almost vindicated, thinking it could now be ready to take out that $18 level, and I went to buy more.

I could not have been more wrong. There was no vindication here. In fact, I didn't know it at the time, but I was about to be vanquished. That's because that $17 to $15 dive, represented on the chart as point A to point B, then followed the run to $18 (point C), then back to $16 (point D) and finally $17 (point E) had traced out a perfect head-and-shoulders pattern. Yes, just like a human's head and shoulders. That's the most frightening pattern in the technician's book.

I dismissed the pattern as something akin to Head & Shoulders shampoo. Hey, I was a pure fundamentalist; therefore, I thought I knew more than the charts. I knew Alcoa. I knew the company cold, how it had taken out costs, how it was busy fixing its balance sheet, how it was building the largest new smelting plant in the world in Saudi Arabia, where energy, the chief ingredient needed to smelt aluminum, was the cheapest possible. I pride myself on that kind of specific micro corporate knowledge. But I should have been keeping a sharp eye on the FXI, the ETF that tracks the Chinese stock market. That's because it was beginning to crack after a long run from its bottom, as the Chinese were struggling to keep their economy in high gear after their government's stimulus package had been completed and the economy had begun to falter. Unfortunately, the Chinese had been gearing up a huge amount of aluminum capacity to meet the new demand just when the demand was sputtering.

At the same time I was beginning to buy Alcoa, an aluminum glut of immense proportions was beginning to develop, courtesy of not just the looming slowdown in China but also a sharp contraction among Alcoa's biggest customers in Europe. The combination of a lack of production cutbacks and a huge burst of aluminum inventories worldwide caused the price of aluminum to suddenly plummet in breathtaking fashion, going to a level where Alcoa was losing money almost on every ingot produced. That basically stopped Alcoa's comeback from the depths of the Great Recession right in its tracks. Next thing you know, Alcoa's stock had been cut in half. Only after the big decline did we discover that Alcoa's earnings had hit a wall, and it's been pretty much downhill ever since.

This head-and-shoulders pattern allowed you to piggyback on someone who was more in the know than you. That was its true value. When that stock failed to make a new high on the better-than-expected earnings number, that was a "tell" that something was wrong, even though it was clearly not evident from the company's discussion of the quarter on its conference call nor from the results themselves. I didn't have the information to predict the decline. But the pattern, which occurs incredibly frequently, told you that someone else was taking action who might have known. That's the real strength of technical work. The best thing to have done, if I had paid more attention to the chart than to my company-based research, was to just take the trade and move on. It wasn't worth risking that the motivated sellers could be wrong.

Sometimes this business is humbling. I should have showed enough humility to recognize that someone, as represented by the sellers' fingerprints on the chart, knew better than I did about what the future held for Alcoa. To put it another way, I knew the micro, but the chart nailed the macro, and the macro trumped anything that Alcoa might have been able to do to arrest its decline in sales and earnings. I now make it a point to put all my stocks through a head-and-shoulders drill to be sure that never happens again.

Reverse Head and Shoulders

One of the things I admire about technicians is their intellectual consistency. If a head-and-shoulders pattern signals trouble ahead, an inverse head-and-shoulders pattern, also known as a reverse head-and-shoulders pattern, signals the opposite. That's right, when you spot what looks like an upside-down head-and-shoulders pattern—picture a human doing a headstand—you should run to it the way you would run away from a head-and-shoulders pattern. It's a terrific harbinger of things to come.

At the beginning of January 2013, lots of people thought the U.S. economy was building a head of steam. We had gotten through the fiscal cliff pretty much with flying colors, and there was a sense that perhaps it was time to start rotating cash from the staples, including food and drug companies, and putting that cash into heavy cyclicals, like Cummins, the truck engine maker, or Dow Chemical or Caterpillar, that thrive in a stronger economy. These are time-honored moves that fundamentalists always embrace when things are looking up, because that means the companies with the most economic dependency are about to have earnings surges. As I described earlier, money rotates toward whatever is growing fastest at that moment; if drugs, for example, are going to give you just some plodding year-over-year growth, money managers are eager to switch to something hotter, something with more earnings "leverage," meaning that they can make much more than they could previously selling that exact same product.

But Tim Collins spotted something else happening when many were anticipating the growing strength of the economy. He saw what was a developing inverse head-and-shoulders pattern for Pfizer, the world's largest pharmaceutical company. If you take a look at Figure 8, you can see that Pfizer traced out a left shoulder as it rallied through the month of October and then started declining aggressively. In November the stock bottomed to form the head, and then in December it caught a rally and then a pullback to create the right shoulder.

The key with this pattern is the neckline, the line that connects the high to the two shoulders. When a stock breaks out above that line it tells a technician that you are about to witness a big move higher. Pfizer's neckline was at $25.80, and Collins predicted that if it could take that neckline out, it could be in for a monster run. Given that money was pouring out of staples and drug stocks and headed for the industrials, this bullish reverse head-and-shoulders pattern from Pfizer, a classic slow-growth stock, was confounding me. I didn't trust it. Collins, a typical but excellent chartist, said he didn't care what the reason might be for Pfizer's stock to look like it was about to buck the prevailing rotation; you just had to close your eyes and buy as much as you could, because a reverse head-and-shoulders pattern shows that others know much more than you do.

He was right. The stock almost instantly jumped more than 10 percent after Collins told me to buy it with both hands.

What caused this move? Sure enough, soon after Collins flagged this Pfizer pattern, the huge drug company decided to spin off its animal health division into a new, publicly traded company, Zoetis, in a move that ultimately created $15 billion in value. Pfizer's stock told you something good was going to happen when it traced out the reverse head-and-shoulders pattern, and when the news hit, as surprising as it was, the people who had followed the pattern and had taken action made a ton of money. You would most likely *never* have known about this awesome wealth-creating move ahead of time if it weren't for the charts and Collins's interpretation of them.

Cups and Handles, Pennants and Wedges

Heads and shoulders and inverse heads and shoulders aren't the only chart pictures that can be relied on to tell us the truth when the fundamentals give us little insight into the direction of stocks. How about the cup-and-handle pattern? Don't laugh; this pattern has kept me from veering away from one of my most important recommendations, the stock of Domino's Pizza.

After an incredible run from $13 in March 2010, when Patrick Doyle took over as chief executive, to $37 in April 2012, Domino's finally looked like it was running out of gas. The stock began a huge drift down, trading at around $28 repeatedly and failing to rally from that level after multiple attempts. That's a sizable and worrisome retracement.

Now, I have been a huge supporter of Doyle from the day he came in, and I liked both the pizza and the earnings trajectory. However, as the stock languished and then trended lower, lots of analysts were concerned that the changes Doyle had made—the improvements in pizza, the technological advancements in ordering—had at last run their course. Could Domino's have lost its edge?

The analysts were iffy and split. The company wasn't talking. That's when technicians are most needed. So I went to Ed Ponsi, a technician at Barchetta Capital, to divine if Domino's moment had come and gone.

Nope, Ponsi said. Just the opposite. Right before we showed the Domino's chart on *Mad Money* the stock had begun to drift back up toward where it had been before the sell-off. But rather than being thrilled that it had managed to come back and then ringing the register, as I wanted to do, Ponsi said it was time to buy more, to double down even, because the moment was so special. Why? Because with that return back up toward $36 Domino's was tracing out a perfect cup and handle, one of the most reliable charts there is, a total launching pad for a much bigger move (see Figure 9). You caught the beginning of the cup at $36, then a gentle slope down to $28, where the base of the cup was being formed, then a return to $36, the right side of the cup, and then sidle to $37 and $38, which would be the beginning of a handle that almost always goes much higher. Sure enough, Ponsi nailed it, as Domino's then proceeded to double and then some from the base of the cup as earnings turned out to be accelerating precisely when it looked like they were breaking down. The iffy analysts, the trembling worrywarts only then, in the $60s, left their foxholes and told you to buy the stock. Hey, analysts, thanks for nothing.

Now, the cup can turn both ways, just like the head-and-shoulders pattern. You get an upside-down cup and look out, you could be in for a real bruising.

That was the case back in November 2011, when the FXE, which is the ETF that mimics the strength of the euro against the dollar, started showing some signs of weakness after a prolonged period of fairly solid action. That was the moment when the European crisis overtook all of the world's markets and threatened to bring down the single currency even as

European officials endlessly reassured us that the worst was over and there was absolutely nothing to worry about. Was the crisis peaking, or was it going to continue? The FXE would be the "tell," because if the euro was going to weaken, we knew that the worse was still to come.

So I went back to Collins and asked him what he saw. He noticed that there was a big arc starting at the FXE's lows of early October 2011, then cresting at the late October highs, and then ending near the November lows (see Figure 10). The FXE, according to Collins, was tracing out an upside-down cup and handle. He warned that if we saw any sort of continuation of the sideways action after what looked like the upside-down cup, we could see a sharp break to the downside. Sure enough, we got a breakdown that traced from $134 down to $126, the equivalent of getting smacked upside the head by a ladle. You paid attention to this one and you managed to avoid an 80-point decline from the 1,290 level on the S&P 500 as well as a plunge of 13 percent in Europe. That correction was one of the sharpest declines since the Great Recession, and it had to be avoided at all costs. Of course, you would never have sidestepped it if you had just listened to the oblivious head of the European Central Bank, who was tightening interest rates just as these European economies were beginning to roll over. Remember, nothing's keeping you from profiting from these bearish moves, as Collins suggested you do at the time, and a bet against both the FXE and the VGK, an ETF that tracks the stocks of some of the biggest European companies, was a very good trade to put on, one that gave you hefty profits at a very bad time for all markets.

We're not done with the shapes and sizes. When I went to figure out if Monster Beverage—at the time called Hansen—had run out of room near the end of 2011, I needed a chartist to give me the skinny. You see, I kept hearing that Red Bull competition was crimping Monster, one of the best performers of the era, and that there was also the very real possibility of regulatory intervention into the business. So I went back to Barchetta Capital's Ponsi, and he set me straight. He said that for months and months Monster had been bouncing off its 100-day moving average, his preferred viewing period, and that every time it looked like it might be down for the count, it rebounded right off that floor (see Figure 11). He said that Monster was making a series of triangles, also known as flag patterns or pennants, where you get a flat ceiling of resistance and an upward-sloping floor, and when the stock hits the new line of resistance it punches right through. He said that any time you get these pennant formations, which are just short-term consolidations that are preludes to what is known as a continuation pattern, you do not have to worry about a stock running on empty. If anything, it is just gathering strength. The stock, at $49 at the time of the "Off the Charts" segment, proceeded to jump right to $79, confounding the naysayers—including many short-sellers—who might have been less negative had they known they were fighting a pennant pattern. It was a remarkable gain, particularly when you consider that the other soft drink companies did nothing the entire time.

There are lots of variations of these different triangle and pennant formations. For instance, Collins identified that a big move up was about to occur in Citigroup back in June 2010, where the lows kept getting higher but the highs stayed the same (see Figure 12). That's what's known as a wedge pattern, and Collins finds it as reliable as the pennant and triangle patterns. They may appear to be just good-looking charts, but in the trenches it is these little consolidation and continuation patterns along with triangles and wedges that allow you to figure out when to buy, with the preferred moment being at the bottom of the wedge, the triangle, or the pennant.

Accumulation and Distribution

Volume is so important to chartists because volume shows when big money is making its moves. When there is a small move on light volume, the technicians ignore it. But when there is a small move on heavy volume, then the chartists drill down laser-like to see if it is a precursor to something much bigger and infinitely more tradable. Chartists are, at all times, looking either for "accumulation" on big volume, meaning that large money managers are beginning to accumulate stock in an aggressive way, or "distribution," the selling of a stock in a way that could telegraph a big decline. They measure these moves by something called an "accumulation-distribution line." While the calculation of the accumulation-distribution line is arcane, involving the charting of whether a stock closes higher on greater volume on any given day versus lower on lower volume—again any brokerage house will offer this kind of charting on its website—I care passionately about it because it can go against the grain.

Case in point: Monsanto in July 2012. I had been telling people that Monsanto had become a very rich stock, overvalued by most standards that I look at, including its historic price-to-earnings multiple, its PE multiple relative to the PE multiple of the S&P, and its growth rate versus the PE, also known as the PEG ratio. All three of these excellent relative benchmarks were trading at historic extremes. I wanted people to dump the stock at $80 before they really got hurt, and I put the stock in *Mad Money*'s "Sell Block" segment that I do on Thursdays. Chartist Collins heard me say these negative comments, and he said I could be stupendously wrong. The accumulation-distribution line showed that while the stock had down days, they were on light volume, but the up days were on heavy volume, a sure sign that more money was flowing into the stock than out of it.

Collins noted that such a consistent, persistent accumulation, or buying pattern, versus the distribution, or selling pattern, told him that large funds were building positions to own the stock long term, not to rent it for a quick move. There was something big afoot with Monsanto's stock, he said, and it wasn't being constrained by the traditional fundamental metrics I was using to value the stock.

Why does this matter so much? Because when the traditional metrics defy reason, when a stock stays expensive versus its growth rate for a longer period of time than you would expect, that usually means that some in-the-know people understand that something's changed at the company.

I still wasn't convinced. I needed more, a stronger sign to hang my hat on. So I asked Collins to chart a longer-term, multiyear moving average chart to see if something bigger and more lasting might be occurring at the company. I actually like to look at the longer-term charts because, while I used to be a trader at my old hedge fund, I have developed a more long-term view as part of my work with ActionAlertsPlus.com, my charitable trust, which doesn't allow me to trade because of restrictions related to my television show.

So we went back three years, one of my absolute favorite depictions, and traced things out over that continuum. Lo and behold, we found an inverse head-and-shoulders pattern developing, confirming that some large-scale transformation might be at work (see Figure 13). Now, charting is all about seeking clues. We had two clues: an accumulation-distribution line that showed a dramatic level of big-volume buying, the kind that could be done only by sophisticated, clued-in money managers, and we had a developing inverse head-and-shoulders pattern, one so powerful that, even though Monsanto was in the low $80s when we did this work, Collins thought it could punch through to $100 or even beyond if the right trigger occurred.

At this point, after you find a couple of extremely positive technical clues, it is time to merge the fundamentals, to bring them into the equation. What did we know about Monsanto? We knew that the CEO, Hugh Grant, had been saying that his company had become far more focused on genetically modified seeds and had developed revolutionary seeds to boost corn growth in drought-like conditions, exactly what prevailed at the time. He said the seed would be in high demand because farmers were switching from other crops to corn in order to receive the government subsidies for corn-based ethanol.

We then overlaid the chart of corn prices with the chart of Monsanto (see Figure 14). What did we find? Monsanto's stock price had become highly correlated to the price of corn, and because there was a developing drought at the same time that the ethanol industry had been taking an increasing amount of corn to refine into surface fuel, the price of corn was shooting through the roof. Monsanto was trading as a commodity, and the commodity it traded with was in super-bull-market mode. That's why its stock price was defying traditional metrics.

Sure enough, when Monsanto reported, we saw the impact of a huge surge in corn seed sales. Of course, by that time the easy money had been made, and you could have nailed it by doing this fundamental analysis overlaid on the accumulation-distribution line, which was confirmed by the inverse head-and-shoulders long-term chart. Few things are more satisfying than spotting a big move not from the fundamentals but from a correlation of seemingly disparate charts that explains what's really driving a stock higher.

And yes, within the next six months not only did Monsanto leave the $80s behind, but it rocketed through $100 as its transformation from a plain old chemical company to an agricultural biotech company had become obvious to all.

Volume as an indicator has served the "Off the Charts" segment well numerous times, but perhaps none better than with Google in 2011, especially because I am such a fan of the stock that I often let it blind me to the short-term swoons that it's prone to. As a fundamentalist, I could see back then that Google was really beginning to pull away from all of its competitors, not just in the lucrative search business but also in the wildly competitive cell phone market, courtesy of its Android software deal with Samsung.

More important, the October 2010 quarter was a standout, truly a remarkable number that showed customers were flocking to Google search in increasing numbers while abandoning both Yahoo! and Bing and some other, lesser search sites. The stock rallied, and rallied hard, instantly on the quarter. But as good as that quarter was, and as cheap as the stock was, selling at just fourteen times earnings with an 18 percent growth rate—and anything less than one times growth rate for a good company like Google is absurdly cheap—the stock ran into intense resistance at around the $630 level not that long after the stellar report (see Figure 15).

I went to Dan Fitzpatrick to figure out what the heck was going on. How, I asked him, could the $630 level be so difficult to punch through given these fabulous fundamentals? It was a genuine steel-and-cement ceiling on the stock. Every time it hit that level, it was thrown back to the $500s. Here's where Fitzpatrick's technical edge shines. He noticed that each increase toward $630 occurred on light volume, but each collapse occurred on much heavier volume. That, said Fitzpatrick, meant that Google had become "over-owned," meaning that the big institutions already had enough of the stock and didn't want to buy any more. He then looked up the institutional ownership and matched that against this volume supposition. It showed that institutions owned 80 percent of the stock already, an incredibly high proportion versus individual ownership. This was a red flag: you would like to see individuals, who tend to be long-term holders, owning at least 25 percent of the stock; a stock that's 80 percent institutionally owned is a stock that may have reached the upper limit, where everyone's in the pool (see Figure 16).

Plus, Fitzpatrick fretted that the last time the stock bounced off the $630 ceiling, it was beginning to swing erratically in much bigger moves each day, another red flag, because signs of increased volatility, as we will learn later, can presage big moves.

Fitzpatrick overlaid the volatility on top of the heavy distribution, or selling volume, on down days versus the light accumulation on up days and concluded that Google was headed for a big fall. Not long after that, Google endured a sickening slide of more than 100 points pretty much in the blink of an eye.

Now, here is where it gets interesting. There was *nothing wrong* with Google at the moment. Nothing. In fact, the next quarter was a magnificent one, and Google subsequently traded from $471, where it fell after Fitzpatrick's warning, to $671, right through the $630 ceiling. Anyone who had just bought Google and held on to it might not even have known the difference. I believe this sell-off was a quintessential example of the self-fulfilling nature of charting. This stock fell because the pattern stank, not the earnings.

However, I am a huge believer in having a good basis, or the price of ownership, and if you wanted to initiate a position in Google at a better price, you needed to pay heed to Fitzpatrick's warnings that a big sale was about to be thrown. You could have sidestepped the decline by selling some Google and then buying it back. Remember, we like buying wholesale, not retail, and we prefer picking up Google at the outlet mall, not at the pricey department store.

Either way, the distribution of stock coupled with the heavy institutional ownership and the lack of ability to punch through to new, meaningful highs after a terrific quarter all spelled trouble for the stock, *not* the company. And in many ways, for those who are trying to Get Rich Carefully, that's what will matter the most.

Just as heavy distribution helped Fitzpatrick dodge a bullet in Google, heavy accumulation coupled with a more sophisticated momentum indicator allowed Bob Lang to spot Boeing before it had one of the most counterintuitive runs I have ever seen in my career.

Beginning in the fall of 2012, a string of Job-like woes hit the Boeing Company one after another after another. First, the company was seen as a possible loser in the fiscal cliff talks, because it has a huge military business. Then Boeing's Dreamliner ran into humongous problems with burning batteries. On top of that, the sequester of federal funds that went into effect because of the usual dysfunction in Washington threatened Boeing's huge military business once again. So, many traders I know kept shorting Boeing on any lift, and big institutions seemed to be fleeing the stock at all costs. Many were saying Boeing was a goner.

Now, I am a huge believer in Boeing and its amazing CEO, James McNerney, and I simply didn't believe that this tremendous manufacturer would do poorly in an environment where airlines were flush with cash for the first time in ages and its competitor, Airbus, was having manufacturing problems of its own. I wanted to bet with Boeing, even though the numbers were coming down and prospects seemed to dim by the day.

Sometimes, when you believe in a company but it is surrounded by gloom, it's a good idea to go off the charts.

Just at the time of the original worries, Lang had been examining the accumulation-distribution line and noticed that even though the stock was either doing very little or going down—to be expected, given that plethora of woes—the meager rallies were made on heavy volume, and the much bigger declines were on light volume. In fact, Lang said the stock was simply marking time before a very big surge higher, because the light volume selling couldn't penetrate the $69 floor, which held repeatedly. Then Boeing had a session where there really wasn't much new news, and the stock vaulted $2 (see Figure 17). That increase was incredibly significant to Lang because it caused the stock to break through not just one moving average, the ten-day, which is important for the shortest-term trades, and not just two moving averages, crossing the fifty-day; it also broke above its long-term 200-day moving average. Those bullish crossovers in that one day's worth of trading led Lang to conclude that, contrary to what I was thinking and hearing, big institutions could not get enough of Boeing stock and it was most likely that the company could withstand any of the hits that were coming at it.

Lang didn't rely just on the accumulation-distribution line. He likes to rely on something called the MACD—pronounced "Mac D"—the moving average convergence-divergence tool, which is a momentum indicator that simply shows when the short-term moving averages are picking up the pace and accelerating faster than the long-term averages, helping to drive the price of the stock upward. The MACD can signal quick directional changes that you can profit from ahead of time. In this case, Lang plotted a twelve-day moving average over a twenty-six-day moving average as a way to take the temperature of the stock (see Figure 18). He was looking to see how the twelve- and twenty-six-day moving averages converged or diverged. The optimal situation is when the twelve-day moving average converges and crosses above the twenty-six-day moving average, signaling increasing momentum and more buying power. That's called a "bullish crossover," and it is a regular predicate for any big move in a stock. Any divergence that has the twelve-day crossing under the twenty-six-day is a "bearish crossover," signaling "Look out below!" The greatness of the MACD is that it gives you a head start, meaning it is predictive, not coincidental. (MACD software is available from every broker, along with a deeper explanation of the terms mentioned here if you need them to be able to take advantage of this tool.) At all times Lang is looking for that bullish crossover as a signal that a bullish setup, like the one with Boeing's stock breaking above the 10-, 50- and 200-day moving average, might be *about* to occur. While it may be fine and dandy to catch the move after Boeing establishes itself above the 10-, 50- and 200-day time frames, Lang likes to watch the MACD for signs of such a possibility beforehand, and his MACD analysis has been especially predictive for Boeing's stock.

The bullish crossover and the subsequent rallies above the 10-, 50- and 200-day moving averages were enough for me to decide to stick with Boeing. I told everyone that each time the stock got hit on the news, as long as it stayed above those averages, you could own it. I regarded the chart as a crutch, but a much-needed crutch, that gave me the support I needed not to get shaken out of the game. As it turns out, none of these woes had any real long-term impact on the stock; instead it began reaping

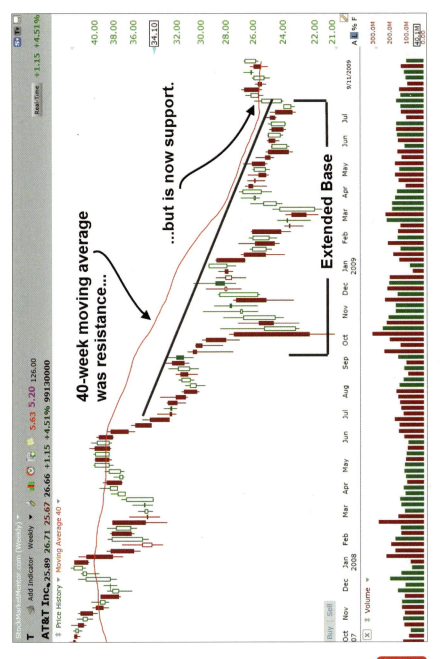

Figure 1

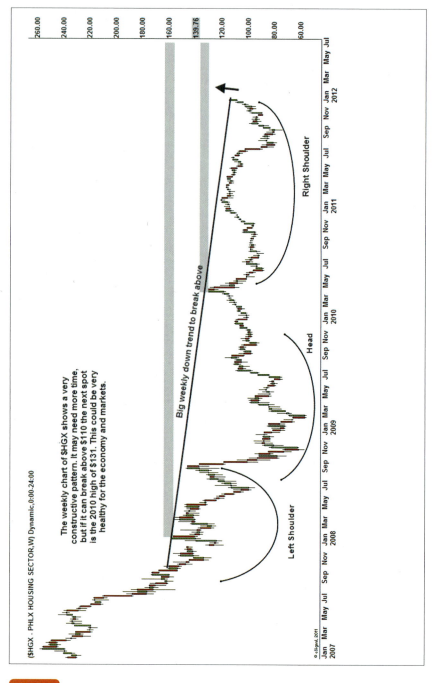

Figure 2

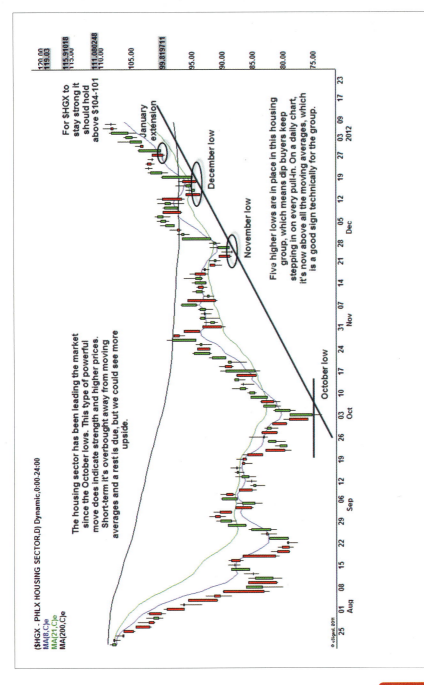

($HGX - PHLX HOUSING SECTOR,D) Dynamic,0:00-24:00
MA(8,C)e
MA(21,C)e
MA(200,C)e

The housing sector has been leading the market since the October lows. This type of powerful move does indicate strength and higher prices. Short-term it's overbought away from moving averages and a rest is due, but we could see more upside.

For $HGX to stay strong it should hold above $104-101

January extension

December low

November low

Five higher lows are in place in this housing group, which means dip buyers keep stepping in on every pull-in. On a daily chart, it's now above all the moving averages, which is a good sign technically for the group.

October low

© eSignal, 2011

120.00
119.03
115.91018
113.00
111.080248
110.00

105.00

99.819711

95.00

90.00

85.00

80.00

75.00

25 01 08 15 22 29 06 12 19 26 03 10 17 24 31 07 14 21 28 05 12 19 27 03 09 17 23
    Aug   Sep   Oct   Nov   Dec   2012

Figure 3

Figure 4

Figure 5

Figure 6

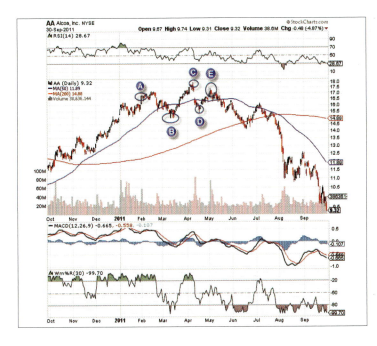

Figure 7

Figure 8

Figure 9

Figure 10

Figure 11

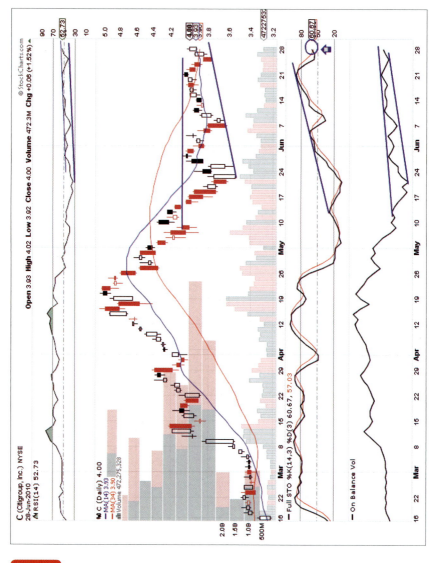

Figure 12

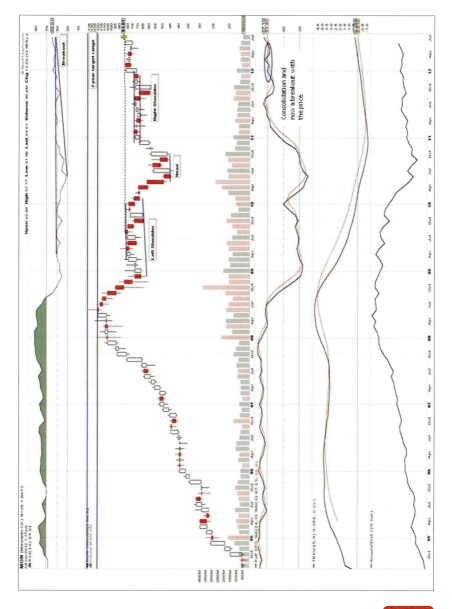

Figure 13

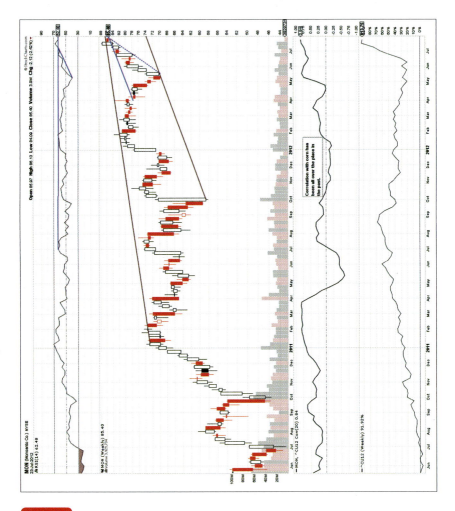

Figure 14

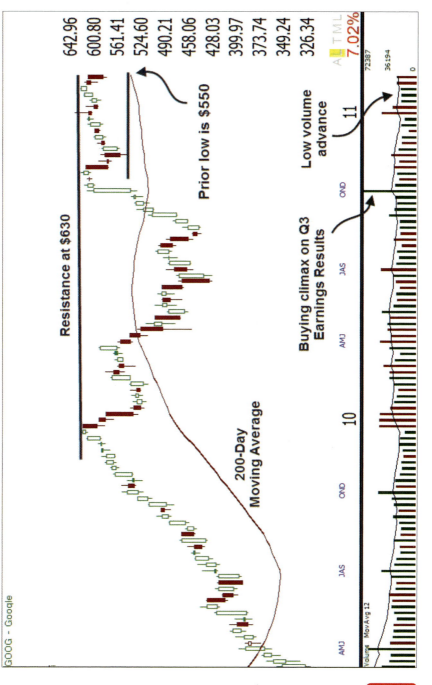

Figure 15

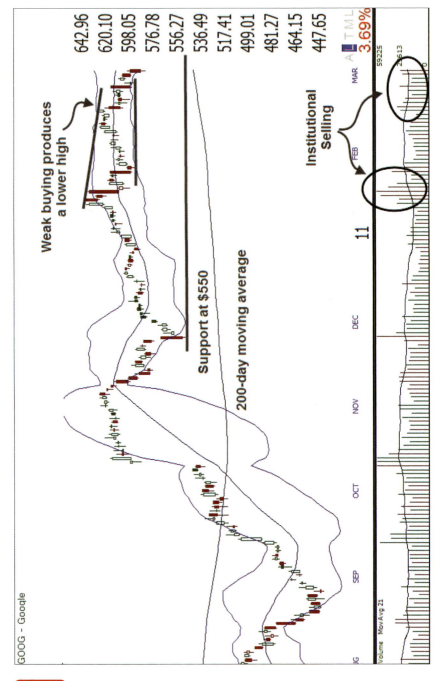

GOOG – Google

Weak buying produces a lower high

Support at $550

200-day moving average

Institutional Selling

642.96
620.10
598.05
576.78
556.27
536.49
517.41
499.01
481.27
464.15
447.65

A L T M L
3.69%

AG   SEP   OCT   NOV   DEC   11   FEB   MAR

Volume   MovAvg 21   59225   -613   0

Figure 16

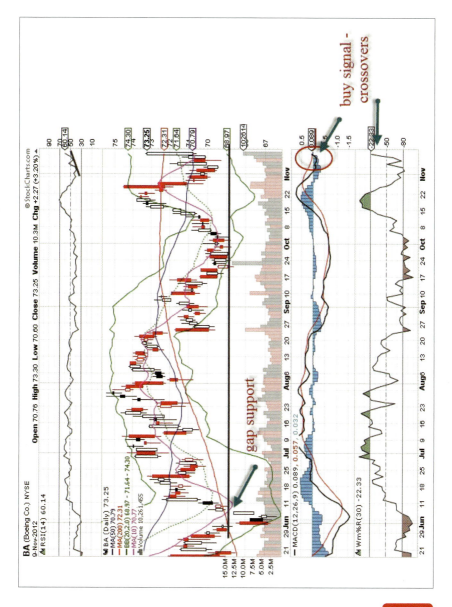

Figure 17

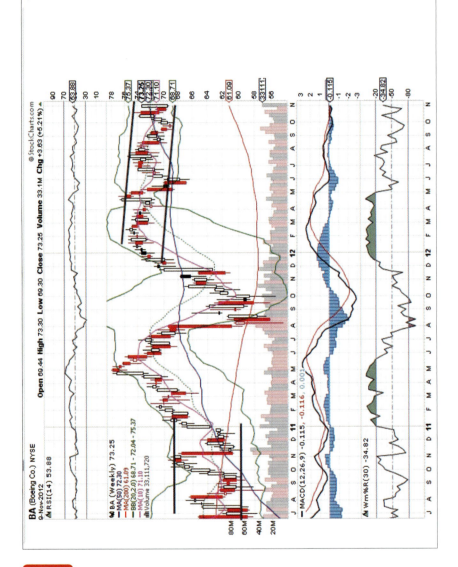

Figure 18

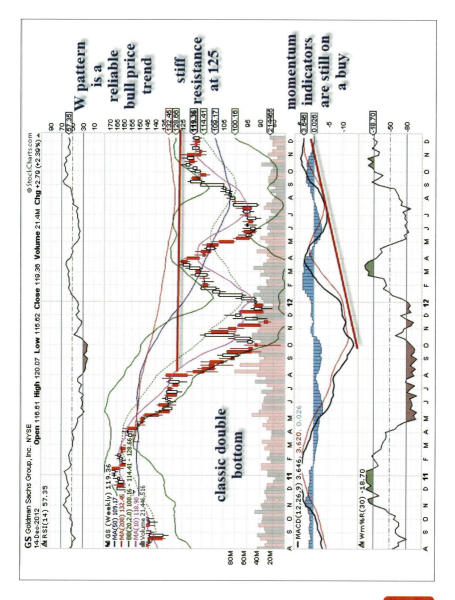

Figure 19

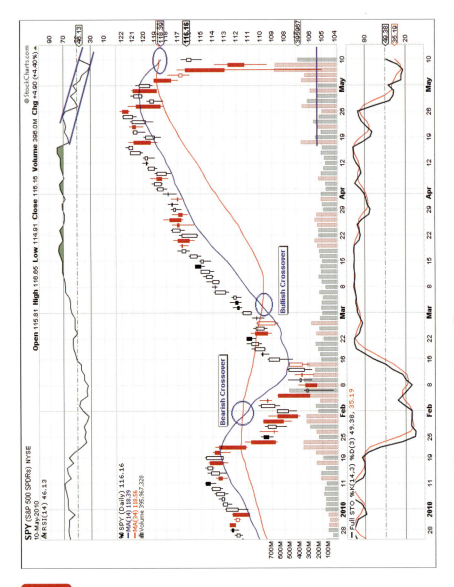

Figure 20

huge orders for its new planes, plus the old workhorse 737, that led to a remarkable and unlikely resurgence of the stock of this amazing American manufacturer, picking up an astounding forty-five points after Lang gave it the go-ahead.

Lang worked similar magic with the stock of Goldman Sachs back in December 2012. I had come to him to ask if the big move in the stock, from $90 to $120, made it too late to recommend the stock of the company I worked for in the 1980s. We were thinking of buying it for the charitable trust, but we hate being "late" with a move, meaning that the easy money had been made and we should just look for another stock, even as I thought that Goldman's prospects were improving in the new post–Dodd-Frank regulation world.

Again Lang liked what he saw (see Figure 19). The stock was trading above its 10-, 50- and 200-day moving averages, so it had strong support and was on a healthy trajectory. Goldman's MACD reading was similarly strong, with the short-term moving average in bullish crossover mode.

But what really got Lang thinking that the previous move could just be a springboard for a much bigger one was that Goldman's stock had traced out a very reliable "W" pattern, starting on November 6 with the stock at $126, then a trade down to $114 on November 14, back up to $120 on November 26, back to $116 (not below the first dip in the W), and then to $127 on December 18, which took out the start of the W back on November 6. This was not my first W. Over the years that I have been doing the "Off the Charts" segment I have seen W after W, and it worked every time as a precursor to a big move upward. This one, though, proved to be a real humdinger of a springboard, as Goldman's stock didn't stop going up from the right side of the W until $158 in mid-February 2013. I know it is a simple pattern, but it has been a regular winner on the show and can be a regular winner for you too, especially when combined with the rest of the technical positives.

Of course, these crossovers can cut both ways. After a remarkable run from what I call the generational lows of 2009, levels I don't expect to retreat to in our lifetime, the averages started to act funky in the spring of 2010. There was nothing in particular at work here, just a generalized feeling that we had come up too far, too fast. I never like to think that any market should get a speeding ticket like it's some high-speed car on I-95 about to be pulled over by a state trooper, but it did feel real heavy. So I went to Tim Collins for a quick check of the tape (see Figure 20). He didn't like what he saw: a bearish crossover using the time frames he measures, namely the fourteen-day overlaid on the thirty-four-day moving average. He said that once that momentum line had turned down, the conditions were ripe for a huge decline, perhaps as low as 1,180 for the S&P. The bulls should have been so lucky. This bearish crossover took the S&P down to 1,100, a horrendous decline, before it bottomed in December of that year. The bearish crossover foretold it all, even as the market took off at its conclusion and powered to much higher levels later on.

Summary: Watch the Patterns

Over the years, we have seen countless repetitions of all of these patterns, and they have become reliable staples of my thinking. I now rarely recommend a stock on *Mad Money* or buy a stock for ActionAlertsPlus.com without first checking the charts to see if I am running into one of the bearish formations outlined. Of course, I want to see bullish charts developing before I pull the trigger.

There are plenty of other proprietary methods to skin the technical cat. I have had tremendous success following the workings of Carolyn Boroden, the Fibonacci Queen, who is an adherent of Leonardo Fibonacci, the medieval Italian mathematician whose work I often talk about on *Mad Money*. Fibonacci discovered an important series of ratios that repeat themselves over and over again in nature: 23.6, 38.2, 50 and 61.8 percent. As it turns out, not only do they repeat in nature, but according to many technicians, including Boroden, they show up in the charts at key turning points in the price action of all sorts of securities. Twice during the incredible run the averages had from the bottom of 2012, Boroden has been able to use these ratios to call bottoms and tops that eluded so many others. But unlike the charts and technicals I have outlined here, I feel that without a skilled Fibonacci technician at your side, you will not be able to make much use of her material.

For the most part, however, by scanning the charts for some of the reliable patterns mentioned here, while monitoring the accumulation and distribution of stocks and staying focused on the momentum of the moving averages, you might be able to spot some terrific ideas and avoid some terrible ones. No matter what, though, don't use the technicals in isolation. Use them to help resolve conundrums like why Boeing doesn't go down or why Monsanto is trading at historic valuations or why Google can't seem to get past a certain level. Let the technical stuff help guide you through unforgiving markets that baffle so many and keep them from getting rich and taking advantage of the stock market's opportunities for magnificent gains. If you can take evasive action and dodge a decline because of the charts, you can make really big money, because it takes only one huge loss to wipe out even the biggest of gains. The combination of the charts and the fundies, as I like to call them, is so powerful that you need both in your arsenal. Unfortunately, the technicians often have tremendous contempt for the fundamentalists, and vice versa. I say abandon partisanship and use them both in conjunction, and you will be able to make some of the best, most informed decisions about how to invest your money wisely.

CHAPTER 7

Lessons Learned from My Charitable Trust

When I was at my hedge fund, I would spend a tremendous amount of time scrutinizing a box of trading tickets I kept in my closet, buy and sell tickets of different magnitudes, looking for mistakes or patterns of wrongdoing that needed correcting. It was perhaps the most rigorous and painful exercise that I could subject myself to. It was necessary, though, because you can learn much more from your mistakes than from your wins. What's to learn from a win? You were either lucky or you were doing it right, and if it ain't broke, don't fix that trading or investing style. But losses? You can spot patterns, identify tendencies and adjust accordingly.

At the end of 2000 I retired from my fund, fortunately with a record that was three times better than the S&P 500 in the fourteen years I ran the company, and I moved over to TheStreet, the online finance site I had created five years earlier. I decided I wanted to do something entirely different from running a hedge fund. I wanted to manage money publicly, to show how professional money management works, to show, in real time, how you make decisions about what stocks to buy and what stocks to sell. So I set up a charitable trust, put $3 million in it and started investing, agreeing that all profits at the end of the year would be given to charity. Before I made my buys or sells, I sent out an action alert telling

subscribers what I was going to do and why I was doing it. If they wanted to act first on the bulletin, that was fine with me. It's been a decade now, and tens of thousands of people have subscribed to ActionAlertsPlus.com to read how portfolio managers make decisions and to take advantage of the trades when they receive the bulletins, always ahead of when I execute my own trades. I've also acquired a terrific partner, Stephanie Link, who has moved over from running a research department at a big Wall Street firm and now co-manages the portfolio, as well as being TheStreet's chief investment officer and also a regular contributor to CNBC. She and I are a team; we make no decisions on the fund until we've huddled—and often clashed—over ideas to manage the portfolio as best we can. Which isn't easy, by the way, because if I mention a stock on television I am immediately frozen, meaning I can't touch that stock, for three days.

Why go over the past? Because I can give you all the ideas and themes I want to in *Get Rich Carefully*, but what about how and when to implement them? What about the execution? What about the "when do I pull the trigger on the theme, and when do I wait" guidance? With the reality of a tougher market, where the dangers are palpable, the cross-currents run amok over the fundamentals and flash crashes and flash freezes happen in a blink of an eye, any guide to investing must give you the new disciplines to cope with the vicissitudes of "the tape," that strange animal that runs at the bottom of the screen on your TV. Key dilemmas need to be resolved, such as how you can limit risk and yet still get a bountiful reward, and how you learn to cut your losses and let your gains run, even though the market's advance is so powerful that it seems like a sin to leave the table.

I know how I would have approached these gut-wrenching issues at my old fund. I would have gotten that box of trades out of the closet and tried to imagine what the heck I was thinking when I made that big mistaken buy at the top or sold out at the bottom. I would rack my brains to understand why I put money to work at that foolish level and why I did not see that headlight of an oncoming train when I wandered into that darned sector and that miserable stock.

With ActionAlertsPlus.com, though, I realized I had stumbled onto something even better than that corrugated box filled with trading slips

that couldn't talk or teach. I had stumbled onto the ability to look back at a real online diary, with real ideas traded in real time. Yep, I had created a contemporaneous compendium of what I was thinking when I bought or sold stocks for the trust. As I pored over the bulletins, I detected pattern after pattern of mistakes made because I had failed to assess the situation correctly or had been too eager or not skeptical enough or hadn't done the correct homework and had been too sure of myself. But I also saw what went right in difficult times and what disciplines did work even when confronted with a market that generates tremendous stress and confusion. Perhaps best of all, I saw and understood why standing pat was often the best decision, as counterintuitive as that seems to be at a time of tremendous turbulence, when your judgment is clouded by the fog of the stock battlefield.

As I read the old alerts and weekend roundups that we issue, I had an epiphany about why no other professional would ever agree to do what we are doing and why they like to keep their thinking and their buys and sells secret: it's too darned embarrassing! Hindsight and accountability are just brutal and punishing. But I play with an open hand and try to demystify the process to help you do it better yourself in this tougher environment. This review offers a much more rigorous look back than I would be able to give you if I simply scanned my best or worst trading tickets. That's all the better to illuminate your potential path to getting rich.

The five-year ActionAlertsPlus period I examined—covering the time since my previous book—represented the most tumultuous time in the stock market since the Great Crash in 1929. The averages flourished, were cut in half, and then got right back to even. Since then there's been a steady climb, punctuated by some pretty severe sell-offs, ones that have caused many people to buy high and sell low or to retreat from the market altogether. We can never banish fear or greed and the blindness they cause, but the insights gleaned from the contemporaneous alerts certainly will make you realize how vital it is to recognize that discipline and diversification are really your only friends in such unfriendly markets.

So, let me give you my as-it-happened, real-life lessons of how to manage your money carefully through these turbulent times when the bear is growling at the door, trillion-dollar trading glitches are all too common,

governments are all too intrusive and the gloom is so palpable that you can't believe the market will ever rally again. I've grouped these lessons into three separate chapters. In this chapter I discuss situations when you should take action to buy or sell and when you should just stand pat.

In the following chapter, I address what really matters if you are going to pick winning stocks and build a portfolio that lasts, and then, perhaps just as important, what doesn't matter, even as people keep telling you that it's key to your thinking. Then I detail some painful investing do's and don'ts that define prudence and recklessness.

In the chapter after that, I explain why you might need to sell a stock when the desire's not there or the gut can't take it. Consider this the equivalent of stocks as cards in a game of poker. You dealt yourself a hand, but there's a better hand out there if you throw back some cards and take new ones. The "buy and hold" orthodoxy insists that you keep that bad hand that can't help you and never trade it in for better cards that can augment your game. I will show you how foolish that thinking can be and how when I, mistakenly, follow the buy-and-hold dictum I almost always end up selling and folding at the worst time. I also explain what I call the "False Floors" of both stocks and markets, situations where it looks like stocks have bottomed but they really haven't, a key characteristic of a world in which AIG, Lehman and Washington Mutual can disappear in a heartbeat and new social media companies dive to levels 60, 70, 80 or even 90 percent below where they came public in record time.

If the post-Crash era is bewildering to this seasoned professional of more than thirty years, then I know it's one that's tough for you too. But here's the golden opportunity to learn from the mistakes I made so you can avoid them. You commit errors, you make mistakes and then you adjust. You misjudge and then you recalibrate. When the environment changes in a hard and fast way, you have to change with it. The company's fortunes take a turn, the CEO makes too many mistakes, the business is hit by an unseen nasty secular trend or disruption: you have to sell. When you are finished reading these confessional chapters I hope you will agree with me that this look back at my charitable trust is the perfect exercise to learn how to get rich in a prudent and careful fashion that has been the hallmark of ActionAlertsPlus.com.

When to Take Action, When to Stand Pat

Sometimes you just have to buy, even when your brain says, "Please, no, I can't tolerate that pain." Other times you should stand pat, do nothing, even as you itch to trade. In examining my bulletins, I discovered seven situations when buying might be warranted and seven when you need to take a pass, even if the logic behind making a move seems compelling.

1. Changing your mind about a changed company.

One of the biggest hits I ever had was when PPG, the old Pittsburgh Plate Glass, transformed itself from being a producer of commodity chemicals, including plain old glass and chloride for piping, into a specialty chemical commodity making polymers in use around the globe regardless of how strong or weak the economy is. When Chuck Bunch took over as PPG's CEO, as I detailed earlier in my "Bankable 21" chapter, he took a look around his portfolio of products and realized that any time the economies of the world, but particularly America's, got weak, his stock got hammered. So, systematically, one by one, he either closed or sold divisions that underperformed dramatically in a slowdown. He also built up or purchased units that sold product that was more in demand in emerging countries, particularly Asia. The result? When the U.S. economy slowed down, PPG maintained its earnings momentum and spectacular dividend record and the stock performed better than most industrials, and when the domestic economy improved, PPG was off to the races.

What Bunch understood is that the stock market rewards a company with proprietary technology and proprietary products, as opposed to commodity products that can typically be made in emerging growth countries like China and Korea for less than they can be made in the United States. Bunch turned his company from a low-value-added commodity cyclical company to a much higher-value-added secular-growth company producing coatings and plastics needed regardless of whether the global economy was weak or strong. These materials are specially made and can't be knocked off by countries with cheaper, less educated labor. The reward from this transformation means a higher price-to-earnings multiple. Portfolio managers like to be able to sleep at night, and they can do so with shares of PPG because the company is less likely to miss estimates now that it no longer needs worldwide growth to power the numbers. By making the switch, PPG gained control of its destiny from the economic fates, making it a totally different company than before Bunch arrived.

Contrast PPG's cyclical-to-secular change with Dow Chemical, one of the largest commodity chemical makers in the world. Despite multiyear attempts by CEO Andrew Liveris to make Dow the lowest-cost producer of a host of commodity chemicals, the company's fortunes are still heavily tied to the hopes of worldwide growth. And we know that old-fashioned consistent growth just doesn't exist in a world where Europe stagnates, China can slow down and the rest of the world struggles from too much debt and not enough demand. That's why Dow's stock has lagged that of so many others in its sector, especially PPG.

It's not an easy thing to change a company's cyclical stripes. Klaus Kleinfeld, CEO of Alcoa, has attempted to create as many value-added products with aluminum as he can and do so as fast as he can. But in the end, the company is hostage to the commodity that is its chief business line, the making and selling of aluminum, and there's way too much capacity for Alcoa to be able to complete the cyclical-to-growth transformation. Maybe one day enough of the company's business will be proprietary, like PPG's, and then the stock will soar. So stay tuned to it.

So, always be on the lookout for situations where companies are changing their stripes, becoming more proprietary, more specialized and therefore better able to handle a tough new world where a country's factories are always pumping out commodities. Those prices are the first to suffer in a downturn. Never let preconceived notions of a company's inability to change cloud your judgment. I had pretty much given up on PPG before Bunch, but the new man at the top changed the company, and when that happens, you have to change your view too.

2. Learn to like stock offerings.

We are all conditioned to believe that when a company issues stock, it's bad news for shareholders. I can't blame you. When a stock gets hit with a secondary, it does temporarily weigh on the equity. But these days, because interest rates are still historically low, companies can issue equity to pay back debt and de-risk their enterprises. These are deals worth running to, not running from. Real estate investment trusts have done a huge amount of these kinds of deals, and they have worked fabulously for those who participate in them. That's because, first, the money is used to help pay down expensive debt or refinance it with debt that carries a much lower interest rate. That new, cheaper rate falls right to the bottom line, allowing analysts to immediately raise estimates once the refinancing is completed. Second, the ratings agencies often upgrade when companies issue equity to expand their businesses, and that almost always produces a nice move up in a stock. Third, the new capital raised might allow the company to buy more properties, which will lead to greater earnings power and higher dividends in the future. The best place to look for these kinds of secondaries? All kinds of companies that were hit really hard by the housing crisis that are just now snapping back. The additional capital, for example, gave the private home mortgage insurers, who were down and thought to be out, the ability to write more policies on new homes. That is the essence of why the stock of Radian, a hitherto cash-strapped Philadelphia-based insurance company, was able to jump 50 percent almost immediately after its offering. When I suggested on *Mad Money* that people buy the stock on the offering or even ahead of the deal because the offering would be good, not bad, for the stock, I took a lot of heat on Twitter @JimCramer. Didn't the issuance of stock signal the top, people wondered? But there were so many sophisticated institutions out there chomping at the bit for this stock, ones that knew if Radian could get its hands on more capital it could flourish, that you had to take action the moment the deal was announced and buy it on any weakness that the announcement generated. Then you just had to hope to get more stock on the actual offering.

You must always be on the lookout for these kinds of deals and take immediate bold action. In hindsight, it doesn't look bold at all. But it sure was at that moment. I will do my best to point out which ones look good going forward.

Another kind of secondary I like? The kind that master limited partnerships offer, particularly the oil and gas pipeline companies are always issuing to finance their expansion plans to crisscross the country with pipelines to get oil and gas from Texas, Oklahoma, Colorado, North Dakota, West Virginia, Ohio and Pennsylvania to the rest of the country. Oil companies have made remarkable finds, but without pipelines to take the fuels to where they can be refined and processed, they can't profit from these discoveries. The cheapest and best way to get them there is through pipelines. But pipelines are expensive to build out, and the companies that build them need to raise cash pretty constantly in the stock market. Enterprise Products Partners, Kinder Morgan Energy Partners and MarkWest are best-of-breed pipeline players that have become serial issuers of equity to expand their networks. Do not fret over these deals; take advantage of them. They allow the pipeline companies to boost capacity to meet the demand from the explosion in oil and gas finds in the nation. More capacity means more dividend boosts down the road. So remember, when you buy the stock of a high-yielding master limited partnership on an equity offering, you should expect to be rewarded with a still higher distribution not long after the new financing.

Third, I like secondaries that are deliberately priced "deep in the hole," meaning they are being sold at dramatically lower prices than where the stocks were when the deals were announced. In September 2013, with LinkedIn at $246, the company announced it wanted to sell a billion dollars' worth of stock to raise money for corporate purposes. The brokers who handled the deal let it be known that the company was willing to sell it well below that price, and buyers queued up to get the discounted stock. Soon after the company was able to raise $1.2 billion, selling slightly more than 4 million shares at $223. It was a good deal for both sides of the trade: LinkedIn was able to raise $200 million more than it thought it could get, and buyers received a fabulous discount to where the stock had been trading. The stock immediately traded right back to where it was, and everyone who got stock made a huge amount of money. These kinds of "deep in the hole" discounts are available only from full-service brokers, as large corporate clients like doing these kinds of deals with their investment bankers. They are always worth trying to get in on. Many of the social media secondaries have been priced with terrific discounts similar to the gift LinkedIn gave investors.

Finally, we are in a period when many private equity firms are now issuing secondaries in companies they took private before the Great Recession that have come public since that dark time. In previous years I have shied away from these indebted companies for fear that the private equity firms "knew something" and the stocks were about to suffer a downturn. That's too cynical now, because these companies often have high debt left over from before the Federal Reserve cut rates drastically, and they have been able to refinance at lower rates with the new money. That means an immediate boost to earnings and subsequent lifts to the stocks. For example, we have seen terrific performances from the private equity deals in Dunkin' Donuts, HCA, Realogy and Dollar General. One to keep an eye on: any stock deals from Pinnacle Foods, a private equity that makes Birds Eye, Mrs. Paul's Fish Sticks, and Duncan Hines. I bet those will be fabulous opportunities too. I know the charitable trust is eager to get involved in the next offering of that newly minted consumer packaged goods company.

3. Buying an estimate cut.

Nothing could be more counterintuitive than wanting to buy a stock after analysts cut their earnings estimates for the company. But one of the best investments the trust ever made was back in March 2009, when Caterpillar, the big earthmoving equipment company, had been going down for weeks on end as analysts raced to slash estimates going into what looked to be a particularly hideous quarter. Analysts had all turned bearish at once after CAT's business globally took huge hits as customers struggled to get credit for new machines and orders seem to be canceled every day. When the company reported the quarter, it was even uglier than analysts had predicted, and some firms poleaxed estimates for the rest of the year, taking them down by as much as 50 percent. But the stock barely reacted, falling only slightly and then instantly stabilizing and returning to where it was when the hideous earnings announcement was issued. Bingo! That's how a bottom is formed. The stock was screaming, "Look at me. All the bad news is out. The worst is over." I know I am not smart enough to call a bottom myself. However, sometimes the market calls the bottom for you, and you must take advantage of it and buy. It makes sense: a careful investor waits until a stock is de-risked by bad news and then can build a position that could lead to tremendous profits down the road. CAT subsequently roared from that perch for months on end as business improved worldwide and earnings estimates had to steadily *increase* from those much too low levels. Yes, the big money was made on an estimate cut, not an estimate boost, because it turned out that Caterpillar's earnings had finally troughed, something you would have known only if you watched how the stock didn't take the hit that you expected when the slashing ended. The bad news was out; the good news awaited you.

Remember, if you want to find the single most important corollary to stocks bottoming, you simply need to find when the estimates are so low that they can, at last, be beaten. The market will tell you if they are low enough. It almost always does.

The best example of this rallying on estimate cuts was the bottom in JPMorgan that the trust was able to catch after the incident with "the Whale," that errant trader in the London office who caused the bank to lose $6 billion by hiding ever and ever greater losses. As the market kept trying to get a handle on the magnitude of the red ink stemming from the fraud, the stock just kept going down and down and down in synch with the estimate cuts. Then one day the *New York Times* reported that the losses might total as much as $9 billion from this one rogue trader, and several of the firms that follow JPMorgan took their estimates down to match that figure. However, the stock didn't take a hit on that last round of cuts. Instead it flatlined and inched up slightly as this final round of reductions was being made. The stock was telling you the estimate slashing was overdone. Sure enough, soon afterward we discovered that the bank's losses were contained at $6 billion, not the much larger $9 billion figure. That's why the stock failed to decline on that last round of cuts. Again, like CAT, the estimate reductions had gone too far, and the stock told you so. You had to pounce at that moment, as the stock rallied in an almost straight line from $31 to $50 and change and has never really looked back, despite the endless controversies and fines the whale incident and some faulty mortgage product issues engendered.

4. Buy when linked quarters bottom.

One of the most amazing processes is the journey a stock takes when estimates are repeatedly cut and a company reports a terrible number, then earnings estimates come down *again*, but this time the company reports a *similar* terrible number, not an even worse one. In other words, the quarter-to-quarter degradation has at last stopped, even though analysts expected it to continue. When this "no worse than the last quarter" pattern occurs, don't fool around, just start buying. The stock is almost always done going down. I call this the linked-quarter conundrum, because you would think that a company has to report better-than-expected earnings to rally, but that's far from the case if the numbers are continually cut but the business simply ceases to be worse. Sometimes all a company has to do is deliver a number that is no worse than the last time in order for its stock to start going higher. That's how General Electric bottomed in 2009. It didn't do anything spectacular; it just failed to continue to report a quarter lower than the previous quarter. That was a terrific opportunity to buy, and it led to a double not long after. Watch for earnings to stabilize from quarter to quarter after a horrific decline in numbers. My trust bulletins, in retrospect, show that's going to be a buyable bottom almost every time.

5. Know your metrics!

Most stocks bottom based on the earnings per share numbers. But some stocks in different sectors bottom on different metrics, and you need to be aware of when earnings are less important than a particular metric. You might be buying on something that just doesn't matter or passing up on a great opportunity to buy because there's a more important metric than just simple earnings per share (EPS) in the industry you are eyeing. I mentioned earlier that the two most salient metrics—the ones that trump earnings—are production growth for oils and average selling prices for technology. These supersede anything that involves estimate beating.

For example, Devon Energy repeatedly beat earnings during a period when we owned it for the trust. But its production growth disappointed each quarter. It just wasn't producing enough new oil. So even though it classically "beat" the Street's estimates, the stock went down because of the production shortfalls. The EPS number didn't matter. In fact, Devon could have reported a *lower* earnings number and higher production growth and it would have rallied! In contrast, the trust owned Chevron during the same period, and while Chevron didn't hit the EPS numbers that we were looking for, its stock advanced anyway because it showed superior production growth versus its peers, most notably Exxon-Mobil, which almost always hit the bottom line correctly but has had consistently disappointing production growth. It's no wonder that the stocks of ExxonMobil and Devon are two of the worst-performing equities in the entire oil patch, although I think Devon has the assets, it's just been undermanaged of late.

One opportunity that I missed for the trust because I didn't pay close enough attention to the key metric for its industry was the bottom in Micron. The stock of the memory chip maker has been a dog for more than a decade. When it recently reported still another terrible number I thought nothing of it. But the stock jumped higher. What did I miss? DRAMs, dynamic random access memory chips, the kind of semiconductors Micron makes, the most basic in the semiconductor food chain, had a bump up in their average selling prices during the quarter. That was extraordinary, something almost no one expected. It happened because the DRAM business had gotten so horrible for so long that many companies that made these kinds of chips had given up. So supply had become constrained, a real rarity in that commodity business. Be aware that as much as we would like to keep things simple and just focus on earnings per share, sometimes the *really* important metric can elude us. Micron subsequently went on to buy a failing Japanese DRAM competitor—and it's been off to the races ever since.

There's one other situation where you must be aware of a metric that doesn't seem important but may be all that matters: when a company is based in the United States but all we really care about is the metric in emerging markets, particularly China. One of the best buys the trust ever made was to pick up Yum!, the parent of KFC, off a sudden decline in Chinese sales because of a tainted KFC scandal. First, if you didn't know any better, you were flabbergasted that the stock could have gone down as much as it did on China alone. Yum! is a worldwide outfit, with KFCs, Taco Bells and Pizza Huts everywhere. But the *growth* for this American company isn't in the United States; it's in China. So when the Chinese KFC division had a shortfall, even though the rest of the company did well and Wall Street's estimates were still beaten, the stock got clocked anyway. Soon after, the company demonstrated that it had a plan to turn China around, one that involved heavy spending to promote KFC. The company let it be known that its earnings would be slashed as it boosted its Chinese advertising. No matter, even though EPS would be hurt, you had to buy the stock on that earnings shortfall. Not long after that, China began to turn, and Yum! headed right back up to its fifty-two-week-high. The Chinese KFC sales growth was more important to the stock than the actual reported earnings of the entire chain!

One more word on earnings per share. Ever since the stock market hit bottom in 2009, as I mentioned earlier, there have been endless criticisms about how the rally has advanced on bottom-line numbers only and not top-line numbers, as if somehow all that really matters is sales growth. That analysis is full of baloney. Those who waited for revenue growth missed the whole move. Never kid yourself: unless there is a key metric that is more important than earnings, like production growth for the oils or average selling prices for the semiconductors, don't be thrown off the scent by these people demanding to see big sales increases before they will turn positive on stocks. They don't understand that the new economy is about making do with less, and the companies that can fire as many people as possible and yet still have *some* revenue growth are now revered by the marketplace. These weak prognosticators think they are being careful when they tell you to wait for revenues to roar; instead they are being imprudent and have kept you out of some of the best stocks out there. Don't let them fool you; they don't know what they are talking about.

6. Don't touch that core holding!

When a football team wants to keep a player no matter what, they name him a franchise player. That means he can't be traded to another team. I can't tell you how many times I wish I had that designation for when we have owned a terrific stock for ActionAlertsPlus.com. What we do instead is deem a stock a core holding and write that we intend to keep it through thick and thin.

But so often we don't, and it's almost always a big mistake. Once a stock is dubbed a franchise player, stop giving it away. Hold out for better prices. And if it comes down below your basis, buy more. My Action AlertsPlus.com record is crystal clear on this issue. When I have a stock of a company that I think materially undervalues the enterprise, I have to do everything I can *not* to take the gain and eliminate it. I am willing to part with *some* of the stock, because bulls make money, bears make money and pigs get slaughtered, but it is vital to keep enough left in your portfolio so that it will still be meaningful if it continues to advance.

The temptation to take a gain is always so palpable that it can take every sinew to fight against. It's such a difficult task to keep a terrific stock riding in a portfolio, because you never want to turn a gain into a loss. But when I first penned that gain-to-loss rule I was speaking more of a trading win, not an investing gain. If you own a stock and you think that it could go up over the next few years because it is not expensive relative to where the stock is going, then by all means do your best to "franchise" it, or stick the "nontrade" label on it. You will not regret it, as long as the fundamentals stay positive. Of course, all bets are off if the business starts to deteriorate. You must immediately sell the stock if that is the case, or you will truly be to blame if you give up the win. But that's really the only case where you should rid yourself of a core holding, or I suspect you will leave a terrific amount of money on the table as it climbs without you.

What makes me so sure of this rule? Because we rate stocks 1–4 every week, and 1's are, by and large, meant to be core positions, hallowed ground where we want as many shares as we can get. But as I peruse the bulletins, it's unnerving to see how many 1's we have sold because of short-term market turbulence only for the stocks to continue roaring ahead without us. A core position is what it says it is: something that's basic to your portfolio, and it should not be so easily dislodged. I know that if we had been able to hold on to more core positions, we would have given to charity a heck of a lot more than $1.8 million since I started this project.

7. Make each buy matter.

Which brings me to my first major trading lesson from the trust: don't just stand there and pay the same price over and over again or you will have no room if the stock takes a hit. When you start a position, even if you intend only to buy, say, 150 shares, you need to leave room for that stock to come in so you can lower your basis with each buy. If you are starting to buy a stock that's $25, you probably do not want to buy any more than fifty shares at that price. After that you should not buy the stock again until it can lower your basis at least a full point. Anything more aggressive than that—and it is aggressive—is going to leave you little room for maneuvering if the stock gets hit big. You could arguably wait until the stock gets to $23 to buy another fifty, and then hold off until the stock gets to $21 to buy another fifty. That's pretty much the spacing I obey for the trust. You may think that you could be missing out on a quick run to $28 and have only fifty shares for that move. So be it. That's still a very nice gain. And you know what I say: no one ever got hurt taking a profit.

Portfolio management for the trust, though, is all about protecting yourself from the downside, and the best way to do that is to ask before you buy: Can it make a difference to my cost basis? If it doesn't, then you are being too eager and not cautious enough. You simply do not "create" a better price for yourself by buying too close to your last purchase. When Stephanie Link, my co-portfolio manager, and I duke it out every day, it is usually about this very issue, because we tend to like our top-ranked stocks so much that when the market is running we want to load the boat with them. But even in the best of bull markets, like the one from the bottom in March 2009, there are always price breaks caused by extraneous events—remember, the S&P 500 has a tremendous pull on all stocks— that give you a better opportunity. It does no good to just sit there and say, "Let's go buy more Abbott Labs, I really like it." That's what the undisciplined investor does. Far better to say, "Let's wait until that stock falls appreciably for no reason owing to itself, and then let's pounce when it helps us have a better cost."

Laying Down the Law on When Not to Buy

1. No worst-of-breed buying

There's a pub in Summit, New Jersey, that's my favorite place to grab a beer and watch a game. But I can't go there anymore. You know why? Because I told the bartender to buy Weatherford International, which my trust was buying at the time. You see, Weatherford was trading at what is known as a 30 percent price-to-earnings multiple discount to Schlumberger, its biggest competitor in the oil service field. They both do pretty much the same thing, but the market was valuing Weatherford's earnings far lower than Schlumberger's. I thought the discount was ridiculous because, while Weatherford was hardly best of breed, it simply wasn't so bad that it deserved to sell much more cheaply than Schlumberger. I could not have been more wrong. Soon after I bought the stock and recommended it to my favorite bartender, Weatherford reported a dramatic shortfall; worse, it owned up to some pretty shocking accounting weaknesses. It was the double whammy you most dread. Weatherford got cut in half. SLB inched higher at the same time. I didn't buy best of breed, and I got what I paid for. I miss that joint!

This scenario happens relatively constantly in this business. Worst-of-breed department stores that you try to take a flier on, like J. C. Penney, will almost never do as well as best-of-breeders Target and Costco. As much as Intel has been a dog, AMD, a worst-of-breeder from way back that competes with Intel, has been horrendous. And never forget the losses people incurred trying to buy Windstream, CenturyLink and, worst of all, Frontier Communications, hoping to pick up a little yield over best-of-breeders AT&T and Verizon in the telecommunications space. That yield chasing has had a devastating impact on many a portfolio. The yields were bigger because their common stocks were reflecting their poorer execution, reduced opportunities and their second-rate businesses, not because they were bargains that were mispriced. They were perfectly priced—for failure. Worse yet, CenturyLink and Frontier ultimately had to slash those dividends, the true sign of worst-of-breed behavior that leads to instant devastation, as many owned these stocks specifically for their higher yields. Reaching for yield from a worst-of-breed stock is a cardinal sin. Don't commit it.

2. Cash isn't always king.

What do Cisco, Microsoft, Oracle and Intel all have in common? People were lulled into buying their stocks at very high levels because they had so much cash on their books. You have probably heard that this stock or that stock had a gigantic percentage of its market capitalization in cash and therefore it has to be bought. As if cash per se is good news. Maybe in a high-interest-rate environment it might be good, because then companies get some extra interest income. Otherwise, though, it means very little. What matters is how they put it to work. Sure Intel, Cisco and Microsoft give you some nice-size dividends, but it hasn't meant much at all other than as a floor. They have also bought back a lot of stock. But they have bought it back badly, often too high, and they have not been opportunistic, using weakness to buy. They buy stock all over the place at any height and any time, oblivious to whether it's attractive or not at that moment. Contrast their behavior with that of one of the best-performing stocks in the S&P 500 off the bottom, Wyndham Worldwide, run by CEO Steve Holmes, who is one of the most shareholder-friendly executives running an S&P 500 company today. Holmes buys stock aggressively and when it makes a difference, particularly on those ravaging downturns when most other CEOs seem frozen and are unwilling to step in to take advantage of the pummelings, even though declines are market-driven and not specific to their company. Wyndham ratchets up its dividend far more than expected each time because Holmes thinks it is his duty to return the excess cash he has on the balance sheet to the shareholders if all of his needs for the business that year have been met. He doesn't sit with it and do nothing except watch it grow at an exceedingly low rate of return, if that can be considered growing at all. Holmes is part of a new breed of executives. He wants to fulfill his end of the social compact with shareholders. You stick with him, and you don't rent his stock, you own it. In return, he makes sure that you get your cut in the business, and he grows the business as fast as he can. He's the very model of what Intel, Microsoft and Cisco need at their helm: someone who understands that the stock price going up is very important and it is part of his job to figure out the best way to make it go higher.

3. Don't blame the customer.

I learned this one the hard way, when the trust decided to buy the stock of Juniper, a large networking and communications gear producer. The stock was in the low $40s back in 2011, when it had its first shortfalls. At that time it blamed some nameless Japanese customers for a lack of orders. That was totally plausible, as Japan's telco companies were huge users of Juniper's products, and the tsunami and subsequent Fukushima nuclear disaster hit the country hard. It was natural to think there would be a pause. Soon the stock dropped down to the $30s on more worries about missed customers' orders, this time from Europe and the United States. I stuck with Juniper because the company had a ton of cash, it was pretty clear that Europe had a lot of issues and we understood that the U.S. government had been a big customer of Juniper.

It wasn't until the stock got to the $20s that we realized that Juniper's blame-the-customer act was pretty darned lame. It turns out that Cisco was taking share the whole time and was simply kicking Juniper's butt with a better mousetrap. The Juniper customers weren't sitting on their hands. They were just buying elsewhere, which we didn't realize until we had delved deeply into Cisco's quarters, not Juniper's. The information was there to be had, but only from a competitor, not Juniper itself. There's a pretty easy moral here: When a company blames the customer, check to see whether the customer isn't still buying, except with a different vendor.

4. Don't tell us not to worry.

When you hear blithe assurances in the face of big stock declines, don't be calmed, be worried. In 2010 we decided to buy the stock of BP after a horrendous decline from the highs caused by the Macondo well disaster in the Gulf of Mexico. Right from the beginning, with the stock at $62, the company told you not to worry, it wasn't major, they had it all figured out. Their estimates showed that a very small percentage of oil was leaking out and that the decline from $62 to $52 made no sense at all. The decline just seemed ridiculous to BP. At the time, the market capitalization decline had exceeded the loss that Exxon experienced after the disastrous *Valdez* spill, which had to be the worst of all time, right? We decided to take the plunge, betting that BP had Macondo under control or it wouldn't be saying how minor the leak was. We figured the penalty for obfuscation was way too great, that there was no way they could be low-balling the losses here. When the stock dropped ten bucks, we figured this was one of the classic overreactions that happen. The company couldn't be this wrong.

Of course, we all know what happened. The company dissembled, and the losses were far worse than indicated. We ended up dropping $15 more on this one, one of the worst losses we have ever taken. Why? Because we committed the sin of believing. We trusted the endless denials. We weren't skeptical enough, something that careful investing now demands. I am not typically a gullible guy, but since the BP loss we have had to put in rules, including one that says stocks do not go down for no good reason after a company tells you not to worry. They go down because they deserve to go down. Sometimes you just have to trust the stock, not the company. It often knows a heck of a lot more. And don't forget, as I often say on *Mad Money*, there are so many noncontroversial stocks out there with terrific fundamentals that are undervalued, why play with fire? I wish I could have those BP points back. But they are basically the same points that you lose when you buy an "accounting irregularities" story, and we know that "accounting regularities" mean "Sell" until they are ameliorated, as I have explained many times on the show and spent a huge amount of time on in *Real Money, Sane Investing in an Insane World*.

5. There's more to life than cost cutting.

Companies that are good at cutting costs and only cutting costs, not growing revenues *at all*, may not be worth purchasing. Earlier, I praised the stocks of companies whose managers were able to cut costs but keep sales slowing improving. That's all I need to see for a possible buy recommendation. That's going to yield a higher stock almost every time, because that excess cash is going to be put to work either buying back stock or boosting the dividend if the chief executive officer knows how to help the market take his stock up. But companies that make their earnings by slashing without any real growth will truly disappoint you. That's what the two personal computer–making companies, Dell and Hewlett-Packard, did all the way down. They were totally adept at cutting costs but didn't know how to grow revenues. That's a sign that the businesses are in secular, not cyclical, decline, meaning, in this case, that the long-term trend is against their personal computer–heavy businesses. That's because the PC is losing share to other devices like smartphones and useful tablets. That's something to steer clear of, no matter what—*unless* the company does an acquisition that is *additive* to make the acquirer grow again or change its stripes. However, most of the CEOs in the position of the tailspinners have their hands full, and when they make acquisitions they typically make bad ones or ones that other companies don't want or have already passed on. I love cost cutters, but only if they have a plan to grow revenues. Otherwise, remember: Portfolio managers like growth, and you can't cut your way to growth even if you cut your way to profitability.

6. Stay true to your convictions.

Sometimes you work so hard, you do enough checks, you think you really know what you are doing—and then you lose your resolve at the worst possible moment. That's what happened to Stephanie Link and me in the fall of 2012 when we decided it was time to buy Bed Bath & Beyond. We didn't know it at the time, but we had just walked into the lobby of the House of Pain and were about to experience a nightmare I don't want you to have. Let me give you the object lesson—and the abject lesson—in blow-by-blow fashion, so you will know not to repeat our mistakes. Perhaps this tale will remind you in a giddy moment how tough and humbling this business can be and how sometimes even those who think they are playing with ice water in their veins freeze and can't handle the pressure. I need you to steel your resolve when you have done your homework and recognize a bargain for what it is, and not for what others tell you it isn't. Do not take counsel from your fears; stay clearheaded, and do not flinch, even when the temptation is so great that it's incredibly difficult to resist. For resist you must.

Bed Bath & Beyond is a chain I adore. I am two minutes from the first Bed Bath ever built. I love to go shopping there with my younger daughter before we go down to the shore, and, on the way home, we always stop across the street at the Harmon, a discount drugstore owned by Bed Bath & Beyond, to load up on all the bathroom stuff a teenager might need. Both stores have a scavenger-hunt feel that makes shopping with my daughter a huge amount of fun. Neither is expensive, and I always bring the coupon for Bed Bath to get the extra 20 percent off. Visiting these two places has been a ritual of mine since I moved to Summit, New Jersey, twenty years ago. That's historically what drew me to the stock. Any company that has a terrific regional concept that can go national—and Bed Bath had two of them: the flagship store and Harmon—is a company I always have my eye on, ever since reading Peter Lynch's *Beating the Street*, still my go-to investment book recommendation when people ask me @JimCramer on Twitter for a readable text for the stock hobbyist.

However, the stock itself was almost always too expensive for my taste. You've got your basic, consistent 9 percent grower with high-digit same-store sales that always seemed to sport a 20 multiple, meaning its price-to-earnings ratio was more than two times its growth rate. As much as I liked the company, that PE multiple was simply out of reach for me because I never pay more than twice a company's growth rate. Why the hard-and-fast rule, especially when some of the best growth companies sport those kinds of PEs? Simple. While I know I am going to leave some potential profits on the table, I also know that if the shares of a company that sports a high PE multiple stumbles, I could lose more than the whole rest of my portfolio might be able to make up in a couple of weeks' time. In other words, I would be so in the hole from one stock that the trust might be set back so mightily that I can't close the gap with the averages, let alone meet my stated goal of beating them.

Oh my, is it frustrating to watch the stocks you love trade through the stratosphere without you, knowing that if you just break your discipline those gains could be yours. However, it will always be that one time that you violate the rule that sends you into the abyss.

I continued to monitor Bed Bath, waiting for that opportunity when the PE multiple shrank to levels that lowered my risk profile. Sure enough, in the spring of 2012, right after my daughter and I took our annual pilgrimage there before going to the beach, the company reported a number that displeased Wall Street and the stock dropped precipitously, from $75 down to $59, as one analyst after another downgraded the stock and its acolytes ran to the hills. The analysts' refrain was pretty uniform: "What's the point of owning a consistent grower at a premium to the market when it is no longer consistent?"

The decline was stupefying. Like skydiving without a parachute. It was a living, breathing example of why I don't like to pay a premium multiple for any stock. That kind of pummeling can crush your confidence and really dent your performance.

Stephanie and I made our checks. We did enough research to know that the company's pledge that it would get right back on track seemed like a good one. And in reality, the quarter wasn't even that big a miss. The stock had simply been priced for perfection. We got our bulletin ready to tell people we were going to buy, but by the time we were ready to issue it, Bed Bath's stock reversed course and didn't look back as the market came to its senses about how good BBBY really was. We chalked it up as a lost opportunity, and we vowed to be quicker next time. We don't chase for ActionAlerts. We wait.

The stock proceeded to run back to $71, and we kicked ourselves all the way up. We swore up and down that if this company disappointed again, we would take advantage of it and just go buy some. After all, we would buy merchandise at Bed Bath that's 20 percent off. How could we resist buying the stock down almost the same amount?

We didn't have long to wait. After the breathtaking run back to $71, most of the investors who had bought the stock thought that whatever went wrong the last time was just a fluke and that this consistent company would right the ship.

Instead, we got another blah quarter, one that showed more disappointment in the comparable-store category. Business had not reaccelerated. The stock caught a couple more downgrades, mostly from people who had thought there was no way Bed Bath could miss again.

But there were several downgrades that suggested something far more insidious: perhaps Bed Bath & Beyond was being *Amazoned*. That's the single most dangerous verb in the Wall Street gibberish lexicon these days. It implies that people would rather browse for an item at Bed Bath and then go home and order it on Amazon. Bed Bath, like Best Buy, was becoming nothing more than an Amazon showroom. These were people who had decided that after a second miss there was no coming back for Bed Bath.

Frankly, at the time, this analysis made me laugh. I remember joking with Stephanie before she went on Scott Wapner's fabulous *Halftime Report* on CNBC, where she is a regular panelist, that I was sure none of these nay-saying analysts had ever even shopped at a Bed Bath. Did they have any idea how much fun it was? How cheap it was? Did they know Harmon at all? Who would check Harmon and then buy on Amazon? I thought the whole Amazon rap was fanciful. I figured we'd been given a second chance. The stock had gotten too cheap. Management would figure it out. Most important, the price-to-earnings multiple had now shrunk to a discount to the average stock as the remaining portfolio managers abandoned the equity.

We made our move and bought several thousand shares for the trust. Almost immediately the stock rallied from $61 to $63 and we felt vindicated. And then we heard the Amazon rumblings again. We didn't care. We knew this company was worth more than it was selling for and that management knew what had gone wrong and had made an acquisition to restore growth while changing up and freshening the merchandise.

The stock sank to $59, which had held the first time the stock broke down. We bought more. The stock then took out the low from the breakdown and quickly dropped two more points as the chartists, so powerful in a market like this, deserted the stock, as they always do when they spot a giant head-and-shoulders pattern. (See my technical analysis section if that term eludes you.) We nibbled again.

It still acted terrible and continued to drift lower as analyst after analyst now picked up the drumbeat that the company had become nothing more than an Amazon showroom. Several analysts said that Bed Bath had stepped up its couponing. I got the coupons, same as always. No changes at all. Others talked about how a recent acquisition wasn't working. It seemed like every day someone had something bad to say. We nibbled again, and, because of our "buy down" philosophy, it soon became one of our largest positions.

We would come to work early each day, look at each other, and know, almost telepathically, that we were both thinking about Bed Bath. Back and forth: "It's okay, don't worry. Things are fine." And every day the stock drifted lower, punctuated by an occasional 28 or 34 cent gain.

Next thing you know it was November, and we were having a terrific year for ActionAlerts. We were beating the market, and as I looked at Bed Bath, now trading at $55, well below our basis, I said to Steph, "This stock could kill our performance and *is* killing my good humor." The losses in Bed Bath were all we could think about, to the detriment of just about everything else in our work lives. I told her I couldn't take it anymore. We just had to get rid of it. She bucked me up and stiffened my resolve.

But the next week came and it still didn't stabilize. It just kept dropping. This time I had to buck up Stephanie. Then we got some lift for a couple of days, about halfway back to where we had first bought it, and both of us were so overjoyed that our losses had been cut to some degree that we decided, *Enough already! Just take the darned hit and be glad we got out alive.* I remember telling her that we were good managers and deserved back pats because we hadn't sold out at the low and had contained the losses to a level that didn't wipe out too many of our hard-earned gains.

It was like a huge weight, a grand piano, had been lifted from our shoulders. And you know what? The stock dropped back a couple of bucks after we sold it. We were giddy over how we had sidestepped the decline and were doing high-fives in the hallway at TheStreet.

We figured the quarter had to be horrible. Wasn't that what the stock was saying? So when Bed Bath reported and, once again, was nothing to write home about, we congratulated ourselves. They had only met expectations, not exceeded them. And those expectations had been shaded down several times already.

You know what, though? The stock didn't go down on the bad news. In fact, it went up, a classic example of a bottom that I traced out earlier. First it went back to the low it had bounced from the previous time, before our sale. Then it passed our sale price. Then it gained steam and went to where we first started buying it. Then it went up to the mid-$60s, the move we bought the stock for to begin with. Next thing you know the darned stock traded in the $70s as one analyst after another who had downgraded it changed his mind and slapped it on the buy list. They seemed to go out of their way to say that there was no Amazon threat after all! Finally Bed Bath hit an all-time high that was twenty points above where we sold it. With all of our averaging down, we could have had one of the best gains of the year. Maybe one of our best gains ever.

But no. We got impatient. We got scared. We let the fearmongers persuade us. We cut and ran at a terrible time. We didn't sell at the bottom, but, if you look at the chart, it was just about as close to the bottom as you can get.

Now, there's more than one lesson here. First, if you think a stock is cheap on the numbers, even if the numbers don't improve immediately, as ours did, why not hold on? At the bottom Bed Bath sold at the cheapest I had ever seen it. Yet I was more scared there than I was when it was higher, even though the company has a crystal-clear balance sheet, a hefty buyback and seasoned management. Second, when a stock is that cheap, it doesn't take much to send it higher. Stocks bottom when companies meet expectations after repeatedly missing them. It doesn't matter if the expectations are lowered. That's how it works. We abandoned Bed Bath right at the point when expectations were lowest, so low that it could finally "do" the number.

So, when expectations have come down, when the story still checks out—and believe me, I was checking plenty of their stores by that point—there's no reason to go other than you "can't take it anymore." That's never a reason to sell.

Finally, we should not have been afraid just to go right back in when the stock *failed to go down* on the okay quarter. We had done all of the work. We knew that the company was cheap, and we knew that stocks bottom when they meet the estimates. But we were both embarrassed to go back in and relieved that we wouldn't have to battle Bed Bath any more. Our bruised egos wouldn't let us do what we knew was right.

I want you to think about this example of two allegedly tough-as-nails pros who gave up on something they knew cold. I want you to remember this when you are certain you are right, provided that the balance sheet is intact, the company has a lot of cash and, if it is retail, the stores look as great as ever. We got worn down. We got beaten. Even when we were given a delicious second chance, we didn't bite.

Learn from this experience. If you ride something down, understand that as long as you keep checking, as long as the story isn't wildly off the rails, you can hold it for at least a better time to sell. If you have to, sell some of it, throw a maiden into the volcano, so to speak, if it helps to relieve the pain. But don't throw out the whole shooting match. If your conviction is strong and your discipline isn't violated, then ignore the sirens and wait for a better time to buy or a better time to sell. Sometimes just sitting there and *not* doing something, not giving in to your fear, is the best thing you can do for a stock that you may have lost patience with.

Oh, and of course, I have never gone back to Bed Bath. Can't bear it. Harmon? Nope, I now go to CVS.

7. Don't violate your cost basis.

Recall that in preparation for this part of the book I studied years upon years of trades. I was able to catalogue all of the good- and all of the bad-looking trades for patterns that produced the best possible returns. Of course, reality doesn't always follow a pattern. There are outliers, anomalies, luck even that can change the direction of a portfolio and of your performance. But my job here is to try to eliminate what was lucky and take out the positives or negatives that were one-off and most likely not going to be repeated. Just because you hit a double zero if you play roulette doesn't mean that you will regularly hit double zero. And while roulette may be the ultimate game of chance, the belief that a long shot is always going to pay off isn't something that makes a lot of investing sense.

That's why we have developed a very tough rule: Never buy any stock above your cost basis *unless* something absolutely transformative has occurred that you think has not been given its due by the marketplace. That's right, unless the company makes an acquisition or sheds a division or makes a big change at the top that you like or something else that is *material* to its expected earnings performance, don't buy above the price you just paid. This is a rule that most of you will hate. You might think, "This stock could be going higher, and we don't have enough of it. So let's just go buy some more, *even if* it is well above what we paid for it in the past." Stop it. You are simply chasing a stock, and unless the story has changed, you will most likely get hurt. You are just paying up because people like to pay up for winners. They just can't get enough of a stock that's going up, and they just hate stocks that are going down.

Chasing a stock because it is going up has cost me a great deal of money. I would have an established, good-size position; then the stock took off and I felt naked. I felt that I needed more stock even at higher prices because, what the heck, this one's going higher still. *Almost invariably*, though, that last bit of stock was purchased very near a short-term top. In fact, I will go a step further: that buy tended to be made precisely when I should have been trimming. That behavior has produced some of the worst results for the trust even as it seems satisfying when you first pull the trigger. It's why I am saying that buying above your basis without news must be considered a cardinal sin. That's what the empirical records say over a five-year period. Looking in a clinical, unemotional way at all of the mistakes I've made by averaging up, I can tell you it's just dead wrong. That's now my gospel. Sure, there will be times when you regret it, but the instances of regret *because* you bought above the basis will be far more numerous, so this hard-and-fast rule must be obeyed. Always wait and keep your bat on your shoulder, even if you believe in your heart of hearts that the stock is and must be going higher.

There's one exception that allows you to buy, and buy almost immediately unless the stock gets away from you: when something happens with the company that could lead to a further dramatic price appreciation but isn't being recognized for its possibilities. If you own the stock and know it well, believe me, you will be ready if something much better than expected happens, and you will understand it better than the marketplace. For example, if a company suddenly boosts the stock's dividend by more than anyone expected and the market yawns, you have permission to buy above your basis. If the company makes an accretive acquisition that doesn't move the stock even though you know it should, you are free to buy. And if there are multiple insider buys of real dollar consequence, again, I bless the buying. Because in the post–Great Recession world, I could find *no* instances in my thirty-stock portfolio where multiple insider buys—not sporadic small volume buys by a couple of directors, but a real capital commitment—were followed by stock declines of any magnitude.

In fact, I found that when I saw multiple insider buying, even at elevated levels, the stocks still, in aggregate, had terrific moves ahead of them.

I know this is an extremely difficult rule to obey, especially because there will be situations when a stock goes straight up after your first buy and you are kicking yourself that you didn't get more in because you followed my precepts and bought in stages, not all at once. But remember, we have learned from these tumultuous times, when stocks can go up or down swiftly for no reason intrinsic to the company itself, that *not* losing money must be our first priority if we are going to use stocks prudently to get wealthy. Buying and owning good stocks at good prices without chasing is how the biggest money gets made. I have seen it time and again with the trust. When I chase, though, and the bulletins are filled with self-justifications for those pay-ups, the next move is usually the beginning of a decline, sometimes of real severity, and the stock tends to plummet back to earth, often going below your first price. Don't be Icarus. Be inclined to trim after a big run higher, not buy more and ruin that fabulous basis that's so important after you have found that terrific investment.

Summary: Taking Action and Standing Pat

When to Buy

1. If a company you don't care for makes substantive changes that turn a bad situation into a good one, act on your instincts and pull the "buy" trigger.
2. Drop your negative preconception of secondary offerings. In this era they lead to higher, not lower, prices if it's the company that's selling the stock.
3. Not all earnings estimate cuts are harbingers of bad things to come. Some of them signal investable bottoms.
4. If a stock that has been under pressure from several bad quarterly reports, then reports a quarter that is in line with the last quarter, and not *worse* than that one, it is usually the sign of a bottom.
5. Sometimes you have to buy when a more important metric than earnings gets better than the previous quarter, *even if* the quarterly earn-

ings themselves don't look up to snuff. That's because you might be looking at the wrong metric to determine action.

6. Earmark stocks as core franchise holdings. Stick with them through thick and thin. Be inclined to buy more when the market turns down rather than kick the position out of the portfolio.

7. Buy only when it can be meaningful to your cost basis and helps bring down the average materially. No idle buying.

When Not to Buy

1. As tempting as it might be to buy a worst-of-breed stock because its price has come down so low, better to take no action. It will most likely lead to a loss.

2. Don't buy a stock simply because the company has a ton of cash. It's how that cash gets used that matters.

3. Pass on the stock of any company that blames the customers for its woes. The problem is most likely with the company, not with those it supplies or sells to.

4. Don't buy the stock of a company that tells you not to fret about the future. It's usually a concern for worry and might be a reason to sell.

5. Don't buy stocks simply because the managers are good at cutting costs. They also have to be able to grow revenues, or it just won't matter at all in the end. The stock won't go higher.

6. When you have done a lot of work on a stock and have tremendous conviction in its future, don't lose confidence and freak out just because all around you, especially the analysts, are panicking. You may very well be right.

7. Never buy above your cost basis unless something transformative occurs at the company. Otherwise you may just be buying momentum and ruining your discipline. That will cost you pretty much every time.

CHAPTER 8

What Matters? What Doesn't? What We Should Care About

We are inundated with facts and figures from government agencies, from companies and from news organizations that are supposed to make a difference. Every day I try to sift through them for my *Squawk on the Street* morning show. They come so fast and furiously that you don't have time to ask "Does this even matter?" You just presume it has import. Let's find out if that's the case. What should you care about?

1. Monthly Labor Report

But you know what? When I look back at my bulletins for five years, something stands out above everything else: The only data that actually have lasting impact on the market are the Labor Department's monthly non-farm unemployment reports, which get issued on the first Friday of every month. Now, understand that there are many different employment reports that come out in this market. Every Thursday we get unemployment claims. They are often considered to be important "tells" of what is going to happen. Forget about them. They are almost meaningless in the big scheme of things until there is a definitive trend in one direction, and even then they are fatal to trade off of as you get closer to the monthly compilation. Sometimes, by their own admission, they aren't even tallied right!

Also, the day before the big Labor Department nonfarm payroll report, we get a report from a company called Automatic Data Processing that handles payroll processing for many firms in the country. Ignore it. The number is meaningless; it has no reliability as a predictor of what the nonfarm payroll report will be, and that's the only number worth trying to predict.

However, you ignore the nonfarm payroll number at your own peril. As I looked back at each ActionAlerts bulletin that came out the Friday night after the monthly payroll release, I am astonished at the import this one number can have. Any disappointing number leaves a lasting impact on the market that can produce weeks of declines in its wake. If it is followed by another bad number, you will get a further decline, *even if* the market had fallen precipitously after the previous month's accounting. My bulletins show conclusively that until you get three months of stability— meaning no further declines, not necessarily advances—the market will most likely continue to drift or plunge lower.

The opposite is also true, though. Nothing can stoke a bull market or frustrate a bear more than a number that shows a job gain in excess of the previous month. Even better is when you get a job gain that's higher than expected. A big number that's better than expected coupled with an upward revision of the previous months' numbers is the ultimate triple whammy for the bears and can produce some spectacular results.

When these numbers come out, there are always pundits who want to see through them. They will pick apart some seasonal adjustment or try to asterisk the number to make it less significant. These people are charlatans. Strap yourself to the mast, hold your ears, ignore them and hope others don't so you can do some buying at lower levels than you deserve. These cynics are simply crafting things to say to justify their own existence or incorrect predictions. Or they have learned the lesson of the crash of 2008–9 too well and can't believe honest-to-Betsy good news when they hear it.

Further, as sexy as the actual percentage number of unemployed can sound, that piece of the puzzle is not as important as the sheer number of hires. That's what matters. If you are negative on stocks or underinvested after a second strong increase in a row of the number of hires—not the percentage of unemployment—a study of my bulletins tells you that you are going to miss a terrific opportunity to make money. I do not blame you if you want to wait to see a second good, higher number in a row, as that could be considered prudent. However, a really good report that's preceded by several flat reports can also be enough to get you to start some careful buying even if you have to pay up for positions. My study shows, though, that if you wait until 10:00 a.m. on the day of the report, you will get price opportunities that are an improvement over the opening because there is often a huge amount of short-covering in the first half-hour of trading as the hedge funds who bet wrong have to undo their trade. Once that buying is done, a vacuum exists and the market begins to decline. Wait for that moment to do your buying. Do not be "picked off" by a huge "up" opening on the day of even the best nonfarm payroll reports. If history be the judge, it most likely won't last. You will get better prices later that morning by waiting for those panicked short-coverers to finish closing out their wrong-headed positions. Do not be worried that you have missed a move, though, as there is still plenty of room for maneuver—and plenty of upside—once the job juggernaut gets rolling.

I just want you to get the best basis possible after a great monthly Labor Department report. Please, don't ever ignore these numbers. They are the most impactful ones that you will ever come across. So, when your eyes are glazing over from various inputs, take solace: the only number that really matters comes out at 8:30 a.m. on the first Friday of each month.

2. Breakups are initially undervalued by the market, so don't be thrown off the scent.

We all know that Apple, at its high, created more wealth than any other publicly traded stock in history. But you know what's a close second? The breakup of Philip Morris, the food, tobacco and beer conglomerate that I detailed earlier in these pages. About a half-dozen years ago the management of Philip Morris decided to split into two companies: Altria, a domestic tobacco company that would offer a high yield but slow growth, and Philip Morris International, the international tobacco business that had terrific growth prospects and a smaller yield. The funny thing about this breakup? When it was announced, no one cared. That's right, no one. Incredibly, the stock did nothing, even as the company itself had done extensive work showing how value would be created. And this company's managers are about as savvy as you will find when it comes to stock prices. I sat there and scratched my head. How in heck could this company be splitting into two and no one cared? Didn't that mean I shouldn't care? Maybe it wasn't as big a deal as I thought?

No, the market just didn't understand it. As I described in my chapter on breakups, these split-offs, of which Altria–Philip Morris was one of the great precursors of the era—may be the single greatest creators of wealth after takeovers, and in some cases, they can far exceed the wealth creation of a takeover if you just give them a chance to percolate. But the big moves didn't start until a couple of weeks in. Sometimes the market is simply too slow to recognize the bountiful nature of breakups; we have seen this lack of instant recognition on these momentous moves time and time again. My records show a lack of faith in several different breakup situations, including, most recently, Timken, a steel and ball bearing company that I thought we should sell because the market initially judged that the split wouldn't matter. Fortunately, co-portfolio manager Stephanie rather forcefully reminded me that we had done high-quality valuation work showing the breakup value far exceeded the current market price. Institutional investors are just perennially slow or initially indifferent to situations where the parts will inevitably be worth more than the whole. Patience mattered. By holding on in the face of ennui, we ended up making a great deal of money in Timken.

The moral here? Even if the market doesn't care, you must care when a company announces a breakup. Moreover, do not think that the move is over once it is announced or the split is effected. The best of the gains are often saved for last, when the smoke clears and you have two pieces that are both functioning in full glory. Impatience can be a killer in this game. Stay patient as the divisions multiply your wealth over time.

3. Not all insider buying is equal; some buys are more equal than others.

We all know that insiders sell for many reasons: estate planning, tax payments, divorce. Selling doesn't mean their company is falling apart. It only matters to me when they sell *all* of their stock.

But buying is different. Insiders buy only because they think their stock is cheap and undervalued. It's almost always a good sign. However, some signs are more effective reasons to buy than others.

The first is size. I don't care about any insider buying if it is fewer than 10,000 shares or less than $100,000. Chief executive officers and chief financial officers are the two most important executives at an enterprise, and I follow all of their trading. A CEO or CFO of a publicly traded company is almost always extremely well compensated. That means he or she has enough money to buy stock, and if the stock is as cheap as an executive says it is, then big buys should be expected. Small buys mean nothing.

The same thing can be said for boards of directors of publicly traded companies. They tend to be wealthy, particularly those who serve on the bigger corporations. Coincidentally, that's how I was able to spot and be patient with owning Philip Morris after it announced its breakup. While the stock did nothing on the announcement, soon afterward we read that four individual executives and board members had purchased sizable amounts of stock in the open market. Given that insiders have to own stock for at least six months after they purchase it before they can sell or they have to forfeit their gains, you couldn't get a more obvious endorsement for a stock than that.

One other consideration: Executives are often given options or registered stock units that vest over time. When the stock vests, you often see these execs sell some of it to pay taxes for the rest of the stock they take in. If you see a situation where an exec takes in the stock and *doesn't* sell some to pay taxes but instead shells out cold cash, then you probably have a winning stock on your hands.

What You Shouldn't Care About

We want to presume that everything released from the government—from the Commerce Department, the Labor Department and the Federal Reserve—is of great import, that somehow it will elucidate terrific trades or impact our investments. We listen or read, we wait for analysis from people who are supposed to know more than we do, and then we make decisions off these bits of data. We pick stocks from them. We buy and sell stocks off them.

We think we know what we are doing. But I can tell you from my study of all my public trades for ActionAlertsPlus that, other than the aforementioned Labor Department nonfarm monthly payroll report, we're just plain wrong to emphasize most of these data points. I know that probably seems inconceivable. The media spends so much time on each of these data points. Some of that is what I call the "day book" phenomenon: every editor has a list of the data that come out that day and, in advance of that release, has decided that a big story must be done around the information. Yes, there actually is a day book, although when I started in journalism it was a ledger and now it is a keystroke entry. But you will notice that every little gem or piece of fool's gold is held up as being "all-important." That hyperbole is, unfortunately, the grist of the business. Just remember where it comes from: the need for something to say, day in and day out, and not much more than that.

1. Read but do not act on the release of month-old minutes of the Federal Reserve.

Given that it's my job to tell you what really matters and what doesn't, we are going to start with an embarrassing revelation: the monthly release of month-old minutes of the Federal Reserve, considered the holy grail of investment decision making, means nothing at all. Worthless. The minutes are a total sideshow, and I, of all people, should know it, especially given that my most famous TV moment of all time—save my not-all-that-satisfying appearance on Jon Stewart, of course—came because I knew that the Fed knew nothing. Yet my contemporaneous notes from Action AlertsPlus.com embarrassingly show that I somehow acceded to their view that things weren't all that awry when it came to trying to make judgments about stocks.

First, let me explain the fixation with the Federal Reserve minutes. About one month after the Fed meets, this nonelected entity releases a summary of its thinking that took place at the previous meeting. It is awaited with bated breath by the media and traders alike. It is viewed as incredibly important, perhaps one of the single most actionable pieces of paper that hits investors' desks.

Forget that it is already a month old by the time we get it. Forget that many circumstances that appeared when they met might have changed: a spike in oil, a decline in employment, a cliff jump or two. The document is treated with reverence even though it should be viewed as irrelevant and often just plain inaccurate versus the current set of facts.

And don't I know it.

In the first week of August 2007, at the beginning of the horrific period that degenerated into the Great Recession, I was beginning to get hideous feedback from many of my sources within major investment firms that things had gone quite awry. Over my thirty-plus years on Wall Street I have managed to meet people early on who later graduated to senior positions at major financial institutions. These are people who trust me, and I trust them. I was getting an earful from these acquaintances that I wasn't doing enough to bring the real problems of the finance world to the attention of the public or the financial authorities.

Then one Friday, as I was listening to a conference call from a now vanished Bear Stearns about the current state of that firm, I was shocked at how defensive and fearful the executives seemed to be, point-blank laying out that they were having difficulties but that they were prepared for them. The only way for a brokerage firm to prepare for difficulties on Wall Street is to say nothing about them. That meant Bear wasn't prepared at all, as we ultimately saw in the collapse that followed not long after.

At the same time that Bear officials were yammering on about how they were holding things together, I was getting calls from several senior people in the mortgage business, including the now-extinct (and if it isn't extinct, it should be) subprime business. They were saying that if the Federal Reserve didn't start cutting rates—they were currently north of 5 percent after being raised repeatedly to stem growing housing inflation—there would be a huge amount of trouble ahead not just for the mortgage industry but for the U.S. economy.

At that time my good friend Erin Burnett anchored *Street Signs* at 2:00 p.m., and about halfway through the hour I would leave my office, walk the forty yards to the CNBC stage and join her for my regular 2:43 p.m. "Stop Trading" segment. My pattern was usually to tell her about a couple of stocks that I currently liked or disliked and what I thought would happen to them. We would banter a bit about the market, and I would disappear until *Mad Money* three hours and seventeen minutes later.

At that exact time the market was heading south in rapid fashion, in tune with the frightening Bear Stearns call, and on this Friday I just didn't feel like going out there to try to divine the next 40 cent increment that the stock of General Mills might advance or the next $4 fall for Google. In fact, I was steamed, steamed so badly that I violated my rule about being considered and not hot-headed, and I went ballistic on air. I started out slowly, talking about how things had gotten out of hand, and then began to rant, point-blank questioning the Fed's ability to do its job. As Erin gingerly tried to calm me down, interrupting me every fifteen seconds with a "Cramer" that I refused to acknowledge, I went on a tear about how the Fed was oblivious to the dire financial pain in the system. I said, "My people have been in the game for twenty-five years and they're losing their jobs and their firms are going to go out of business and it's nuts, they are nuts, they know nothing. This is a different kind of market and the Fed is asleep." The darned rant went viral on YouTube real fast and, aided by a *New York Post* piece saying that I was off my meds, it quickly racked up 2 million views.

We now know how everything turned out. The Fed did know nothing. The economy collapsed as the Fed held tight to its view that there was nothing really wrong at all, just a short-term, easily ignored hiccup. Their judgment may have been the worst economic policy error since the Hoover administration's insistence on balancing the federal budget going into the Great Depression. Here's what I didn't know, though: the Fed releases the full transcripts, not the minutes, but the actual full-blown transcripts, five years after the meetings. So I later learned that the Fed met soon after my "Stop Trading" appearance, and, as the five-year-old transcripts show, my rant actually came up in the conversation as a laugh line. Yep, the Fed thought things were totally in control and that I was comically out of control. They actually made a point of ridiculing my spot-on prognostication.

Well, it was a very dark comedy, as we learned. Those firms did go out of business, and those people I knew for twenty-five years were out on the street within a year, the proverbial apple cart sellers of the 1930s.

Not long after my rant the Fed released the minutes of the previous meeting—not the whole transcript, which we waited five years to see, but the curt monthly report—which revealed that all was well and that those who feared real stress in the system were just plain wrong. Things were better than we thought. The minutes emphasized that the Fed would cut rates if needed, but things were nowhere near that dire.

And you know what? When I read that, I actually believed that I—and my sources—might be too negative. Maybe I was too bearish and things were more in control than I thought. The minutes sounded so reassuring that I actually acted on the Fed's discrediting of those who tried to cry for help, including yours truly. How do I know this? Because I have the contemporaneous record from the ActionAlertsPlus.com bulletin. That's right, on August 17, 2007, after digesting some Fed comments, I took issue with my own statements, my own rants, and wrote, "At last I believe the worst is behind us," because the Fed had decided, however belatedly, to start cutting rates. I got fooled into thinking that was all that was needed. Even I misjudged the systemic risks of the crisis to come, and I had flagged it louder than anyone. I had put too much faith in the Fed and the minutes. I now know not to trust much at all that comes from these out-of-date notes.

Of course, the Fed turned out to be way late in doing so and took its time about it, so the damage occurred pretty much as I traced it out. Nonetheless, I failed to sell enough stock because I believed the Fed's statements were paramount. That's right, I actually violated the most important tenet of what's not important: month-old statements by the Fed instead of actual actions taken in real time by the secretive committee.

So, lesson number one about what doesn't matter: Ignore the minutes. Do not make any serious decisions when they are released once a month shortly after 2:00 p.m. I know, given the furious and volatile action that occurs once a month after their release, it seems almost impossible that these could be that irrelevant, but they are. These "most important" releases are dodges; they throw you off the scent and force you into making boneheaded decisions. If anything, now that you have this insight about them, take advantage of any price breaks they might cause—and they often do—to buy the stocks you've had on your shopping list and were simply waiting for the stock market to put them on sale. Go back to the themes and best-of-breed stocks for those themes that I traced out in an earlier chapter. What a tremendous opportunity to profit off an irrelevant release that everyone seems to think is one of the most important and impactful of documents. The minutes just don't matter—except to help get you better prices for stocks you have wanted to buy but thought were too high.

2. Don't act on the sells and buys of Big Time Investors.

Once a month we get reports from big investment firms, including hedge funds, about their dispositions, what they have decided to cut back or trim. We pore over what's known as 13-F forms that these managers file with the Securities and Exchange Commission, aggressively trying to figure out what a George Soros or a Carl Icahn or any other investing icon might be sick of or no longer likes. Then we think we are wrong if we own one of the stocks they sold and we should dump a stock we had done huge work on because the big boys must know better. Of course, the trail led by the greatest investor of our time, Warren Buffett, may be the most closely followed and acted on. I am telling you right now that this is a fool's game, one that you must ignore. How do I know this? Because, first, we have no idea why someone might be selling something. Maybe a portfolio manager left a major firm who specifically followed that stock. Maybe the stock is in a sector of the economy that has fallen out of favor with the money manager. Maybe a hotshot investor thought he had insight and bought stock and then turned around and sold it when the insight proved wrong. Or maybe, as in the case of Warren Buffett, there are specific reasons why he changed his mind that we will never know about. Or maybe he's just got a better investment up his sleeve.

I've got a painful example of the mistake of acting on a Buffett sell: my decision to get rid of Union Pacific in the $70s in part because Buffett's 13-F showed he had exited the position. What a regret! Not only did Union Pacific go on to double, but Buffett actually went and bought its competitor, the Burlington Northern, because he loved the rails so much. Of course, there was no need for him to keep holding stock in one railroad when he owned the other lock, stock and barrel. It was a valuable lesson and one that I managed to profit from soon after, when Buffett created a price break in the stock of Kraft by deciding to exit that company when he had a spat with the chief executive officer, Irene Rosenfeld. The result was a terrific bargain when, soon after, Kraft chose to break itself up in order to create more value, which it was quite successful in doing.

So take these releases, now widely talked about and acted on, with a grain of salt. Don't be shaken out of existing positions because of them. If anything, use the declines they precipitate to do some buying.

At the same time, I never want you to do any buying of a stock simply because someone you respect might surface in these reports as having taken a position. Remember, these reports are a month old by the time you see them and are just a snapshot of what an investment manager might own at that moment. He could have dumped or trimmed it since then, and you would have no idea that had happened.

Case in point: Right before the Great Recession a fund I admired tremendously, Atticus Partners, took a monster stake in Freeport-McMoRan Copper & Gold, the largest copper miner in the world. I knew that Atticus, run by the red-hot hedge fund manager Tim Barakett, did superb work and had an excellent record, and I decided to piggyback on their efforts and buy a stock that I had debated purchasing. When I read that Atticus had taken a stake, that was enough to push me into making the decision.

It was a disaster.

The stock was at $87 when the SEC release showed Atticus had taken a tremendous position. It shortly went to $8. Yep, $87 to $8. All the work they may or may not have done didn't matter. Not long after that, Barakett closed down Atticus, which had given investors horrendous performance.

I was able to escape the position before it did too much damage to my trust because I did my own work, which showed that the company's profits were decelerating quickly. Still, it was my decision to follow Barakett in the first place that got me in trouble. When I talk to individual investors about positions they may take, way too often I hear "So and so bought it, and I know that manager is terrific." Believe me, you have no idea why he did it, or if he will even be right. Managers make mistakes. If the idea goes awry, the manager won't be there to tell you what went wrong or whether things are about to get better. He doesn't care about you, and you shouldn't care about him.

Let the Atticus lesson be a sober reminder of how silly that kind of thinking can be. It's the opposite of careful investing, more likely to make you poor than rich.

In fact, in all the years that I have been running ActionAlertsPlus .com I have seen only one instance where an investor was worth following into a position. That's Nelson Peltz and his Trian Partners. Peltz is part of a particular group of managers called "activists" who, once in a stock, try to get management to make changes to bring out value. Peltz is a long-term investor. Bill Johnson, the CEO of H. J. Heinz, told me on *Mad Money* that after Peltz's Trian bought a large stake in Heinz, he met with Peltz multiple times. Bill found his ideas worthwhile and additive to the enterprise. Subsequently, Heinz received a takeover bid from Warren Buffett, and a great American brand name made you a fortune if you owned it. Peltz has also given you huge returns if you bought Wendy's, PepsiCo, DuPont and Mondelēz International, the Kraft spin-off, even after he's announced that he's taken his positions. This man does his homework, and his rationales are plain to see. He may be the best there is in the activism trade.

Now, there are many activist investors out there, and there will be more and more over time as hedge funds now increasingly like to make noise, particularly when a position goes against them. It's tempting to piggyback on them. However, our work has shown that by the time the filings become public, the bump from the news pretty much ruins any hope that you can profit from the stance. In fact, of all the activists we could find, Peltz was the *only* one with whom you could outperform the market if you bought on the news of his buys, even if you had to pay up when the release came out. Every other attempt to buy after the release of every activist we tracked produced returns that were less than you would have gotten if you were just stuck in the S&P 500. Careful investing requires you to do the homework, not trust the activist just because he has taken down a huge position and makes a lot of noise. Ask anyone who rode down J. C. Penney after Bill Ackman's long and loud stance was taken. One has to question whether Ackman did any homework at all or just didn't know how retailing works. We will never know.

3. Don't buy a one-trick pony, unless you know that pony can win.

Often on the "Lightning Round" segment someone will call in and ask if I like a stock because it has a brand-new product. Invariably the answer is no. That's because if the fundamentals aren't in tip-top shape, no new product will matter. And I can demonstrate how it can really hurt you. In the summer and fall of 2007, Corning, the glass company, introduced bendable fiber, which the company said would revolutionize the way cable companies build out cable infrastructure in apartment buildings. It seemed like a huge new innovation. At the same time Corning was developing Gorilla Glass, the acclaimed glass that Steve Jobs fell in love with, according to the biography of Jobs by Walter Isaacson.

I figured, how could you go wrong with Corning given these two innovations? Oops. It turned out you could go very wrong. Right in the midst of the rave review for these innovations, Corning reported a huge shortfall, courtesy of weak LCD television sales, which are the real drivers of their earnings. It was a major mistake to care about innovations that were way too small to offset the real—and flagging—business of the company.

Not long after that the trust purchased Trinity Industries because it had announced a major foray into wind towers, a renewable form of energy blessed by Congress with bountiful tax credits. It was a new line of business and almost immediately booked $400 million in revenues for Trinity, which was primarily a railcar builder. When the railroads suddenly cut back their railcar purchases, Trinity's stock was sliced in half. The wind business sure couldn't save them. We got crushed in Trinity, and wind simply didn't matter. It was way too small versus the railcar business. Still is.

The only exception to this rule? Drug companies that might be developing a potential blockbuster. Here one product can make a huge difference, as we saw in 2011 when Gilead, a major biotech company, paid $11 billion for Pharmasset, an 89 percent premium to the share price. No matter that Pharmasset had only eighty-two employees and only $900,000 in revenues and had lost a phenomenal $91 million in its previous fiscal year. No matter that it had already increased sixfold, in 2011, *before* it received Gilead's bid. What mattered is that it had a revolutionary compound to fight hepatitis C, thought to be one of the largest single opportunities left in the drug world, worth billions and billions of dollars. And even though the price tag was enormous, Gilead's stock soon tripled because of the success of the product.

On *Mad Money* we frequently recommend so-called orphan drug companies, even though they are one-product companies. These are companies that have one compound that conquers or eases an obscure disease that may afflict only several thousand people. Their drugs are protected by patent legislation, and the companies that produce them can often charge hundreds of thousands of dollars a year for the formulations. These companies vary in quality and need to be monitored closely. They are extremely speculative, too speculative to own for the trust, for certain. But these orphan drug stocks are the only ones I condone buying based on one innovation or new product.

By the same token, please do *not* write off a big drug company just because a particularly promising drug failed to perform. In fact, that is often a buying opportunity. At roughly the same time that Gilead purchased Pharmasset for its hep C formulation, Bristol-Myers paid $2.5 billion for rival Inhibitex, which also had a compound to combat hep C. Less than eight months later Bristol wrote off the entire purchase when the promising drug proved toxic in a handful of patients and caused a fatality. The stock of Bristol-Myers dropped 10 percent immediately. It was a fantastic time to buy, as others panicked, and the charitable trust scooped some up and was able to make a nice amount of money when the stock almost immediately bounced back well above where the bad news broke on a string of good new drug announcements. Bristol-Myers, like so many of its huge pharmaceutical brethren, has many multibillion-dollar products and can take a hit even the size of Inhibitex in stride.

Similarly, when Schering-Plough stumbled on a cholesterol drug, causing the stock to fall 20 percent, it was another terrific opportunity that the trust took advantage of. Not long afterward it started climbing again, and then the company was bought by Merck for a princely sum.

Big pharma can also handle repeated patent lawsuit defeats and bounce back rather quickly, as was the case with Abbott Labs. We got an amazing buying opportunity after it lost exclusivity for one of its drugs in a patent challenge. Abbott has a colossal pipeline of drugs to come, and this small loss didn't even figure into the earnings estimates that I tell you are the key fundamental to follow.

However, be aware that if a company has only one major drug and that drug goes off patent or gets caught up by a rival with a superior product, you *must* sell that stock immediately. We learned that the hard way, when we bought Teva Pharmaceuticals at $60 and watched it plummet to the mid-$40s when a competitor introduced a near copycat anti–multiple sclerosis drug, the only proprietary drug in Teva's entire franchise. Teva's stock never recovered from the challenge. One-product companies can, alas, be destroyed when that one product loses its raison d'être, outmoded by the competition.

4. Don't be fooled by contract wins.

Don't get caught up in giant contract wins involving engineering or construction projects. Several times in the past, I have been too jubilant and enthusiastic about companies that captured big multiyear contracts for seemingly big jobs that barely mattered and failed to move the earnings needle. Take Transocean, the world's largest offshore driller. All during its sickening slide from $140 to $40 during the Great Recession, it kept receiving giant contract win after contract win. The huge contracts didn't matter, though, because at the same time, the price of crude kept falling. When that price decline happens, you have to presume that projects will get canceled or price breaks will be given. Even with all of those wins, Transocean's stock ended up a big loser. Same with Fluor, the engineering and construction company that sank from $95 to $50 during the greatest streak of wins in the company's history. It turns out that not only did

Fluor have energy exposure, but it also had some huge losses from older contracts that went over budget, nullifying the new business that I thought was so important.

We also see the same in tech. You will see SAP AG get a huge win from Oracle, or Salesforce.com take a contract from Hewlett-Packard, and you might think when the stock does nothing you are being given a wonderful opportunity to buy. Nope, the stock's right. You are wrong.

Some companies report lots of good news that never seem to matter. It gets frustrating when these contract wins don't impact the stock. But that's because sometimes the only thing that does move the stock is the actual quarterly report itself. I learned this the hard way, when I got frustrated with the stock of John Deere, the agricultural equipment manufacturer. Deere had put out press release after press release enumerating good news, including lots of new big purchases of equipment. During this same period, we got crop report after crop report that showed Deere had to be having an amazing quarter. I couldn't believe the darned stock didn't move. Sure enough, when the company reported, it was terrific. But Deere is a famously cautious company, or I should say infamously cautious company, and it frequently throws cold water on anything positive. So even when things are good, on the conference call the company consistently refuses to acknowledge the positives and often simply stresses the negatives. Deere failed to turn all of that good news into the profits we expected, and it gave a downbeat outlook, saying that the good news might not even continue. It was that incident that caused me to tell *Squawk on the Street* viewers to dump the stock after it rallied in pre-market trading, as I detailed earlier in the text. Remember, in this new world, revenues matter, but profits are far more important in determining a stock's ultimate direction.

There's an important corollary here. You may have to sell the stock of a company that loses a big contract that's been on the books. We owned the stock of Chicago Bridge & Iron, a large engineering and construction company, when it announced that a huge oil and gas company had canceled a contract it had won to build a gigantic liquefied natural gas project in Australia. Analysts had presumed that the win would add a significant amount of money to the bottom line of Chicago Bridge & Iron for many years to come. When we saw the news, we hesitated and thought that perhaps the market would see that there were other gigantic projects on the books and CBI could make up the loss. But the stock got hammered because analysts felt compelled to lower their outlook as they had built the Australian project into their models and now their models had to change, negatively, to reflect that cancellation. If it's booked and it gets unbooked, then you may need to skedaddle, preferably ahead of others who are too sanguine after the loss.

5. No more crutches or alibis.

No chapter about what doesn't matter can be complete without mentioning some alibis that don't hold water and do not protect you from the downside. Often when you own a stock you try to justify that ownership stake by drawing ratios or making judgments that don't really hold up under close scrutiny.

For example, in 2008–9, when General Electric seemed to be taking it on the chin every day, we were trying to justify holding on to the stock. We came out with this rationale: the stock shouldn't be going down "because the industrial division was worth the price of the stock." The retort to that is simple: So what? If the company isn't breaking up, who cares what a particular division is worth? It's an abstraction. Moreover, the truth in General Electric's case was that while the industrial division was a gem, the financial division was much larger and it was doing awfully, wiping out anything good that was happening in the rest of the company. Careful investing requires clearheadedness and a jaundiced eye toward alibis that just don't hold up under close scrutiny.

6. Relative valuations don't justify a purchase.

The final all-important issue that doesn't matter? The relative rationalization. When we were frustrated with the underperformance of Cisco, the big networker, as it seemed to tick down a little almost every other day, we noted in the weekly bulletin that Cisco had a higher growth rate than the average stock in the S&P 500, but it sold at a lower price-to-earnings multiple to the average stock. This is the kind of complicated jargon that managers use all of the time, and while it seems to make ineluctable sense it doesn't always work.

Theoretically, yes, when you compare a stock to the S&P, you look at its growth rate, and if the stock is growing faster than the overall index, then you should pay more for those earnings than you would for the index. A company that grows 20 percent faster than the average of the 500 stocks in the S&P should not be trading at a 20 percent discount to the S&P 500's PE multiple, which was pretty much the case when we were buying a ton of Cisco.

However, there was one fatal flaw in the thinking: Cisco's growth rate was *slowing*. In other words, when you make a relational bet—meaning that one stock seems cheaper than another based on a particular function—you have to be sure that the reason for the "cheapness" isn't going away. That's exactly what happened in the case of Cisco. So the cheapness didn't matter at all after it reported a shortfall soon after, and the stock got hammered, leaving us holding the bag.

YES, SOMETIMES KNOWING what doesn't matter, what really isn't impactful, is extremely important, simply because you will make far fewer mistakes if you don't take counsel of irrelevant facts and figures. You often have to challenge the conventional wisdom, and that can be an expensive challenge. So, why not rely on someone who has already made it for you? Don't be fooled about Fed minutes, contracts or new products, and don't be frustrated by a lack of movement in a stock or a stock that doesn't comply with your wishes even though it seems it should. What you think matters may be illusory, as illusory as your profits will be if you believe the hype around the importance of something that, alas, isn't important at all.

Summary: What Matters and What Doesn't to Successfully Invest in a Topsy-Turvy World

What We Should Care About

1. The monthly labor reports are of tremendous significance and can color the investing firmament for months on end. You may have to

take evasive action if the reports show minimal growth or actual losses.

2. Don't be thrown off the scent of some important and positive actions by companies, such as breakups to bring out value. Sometimes the marketplace fails to understand the ramifications, and you have to step into the breach and buy.

3. Pull the file on a company, do some homework and get ready to buy a stock where there is concentrated insider buying. But when the buying is desultory, don't be confused. That's not a reason to buy.

What We Shouldn't Care About

1. You can pay attention to old Federal Reserve minutes like everyone else, but unlike everyone else, don't trade off them. They will lead you astray.

2. Don't act on the SEC filings of big-time investors. Piggybacking on their buys and sells will get you nowhere. Do your own work, because they certainly won't be there to help you when you need them.

3. Don't buy the stock of a company that brings out a "revolutionary" product unless you know that product can move the needle of the entire company. Most can't.

4. Contract wins are exciting to read about but rarely make an investable difference, so don't buy when you see contract news on the tape.

5. Don't dream up reasons to hold on to a stock when the fundamentals are declining. When you rationalize holding a stock that shouldn't be held or when the fundamentals have changed for the negative, just exit.

6. Relative valuations don't matter. When a stock goes down, don't express bewilderment and create ratios that show the stock is cheap and should be bought. Just because a stock looks cheaper than its cohort doesn't mean it deserves to trade higher. In fact, maybe it deserves to come down.

CHAPTER 9

When and How to Sell in the New, More Difficult World of Investing

When I penned *Real Money* more than a decade ago, I included a chapter about the art of selling. I just felt that the whole industry has a bias against selling stocks. It stems from the belief that once you researched a stock and decided it was right for you, that was it, you were done. You just owned it. At the time I said this kind of thinking is totally detrimental to your performance. The ensuing decade has proven that beyond a doubt.

But you know what? When I was explaining why you should be willing to sell stocks, my whole orientation was geared toward spotting tops. My chief concern was getting you out after a big run, when the getting was good. But when I reviewed all my trades for ActionAlertsPlus.com with an eye toward making myself a more careful investor in the future, I realized that there was so much more to selling than just spotting tops. There are multiple signals that tell you when to exit; if you are sitting around waiting for a top, you are going to end up losing a lot of money.

That's why I have compiled a list of ten warning signs that you must take heed of and act on when you see them. This is not an idle set of selling suggestions. I enacted these defensive and risk-management techniques after incurring significant losses that I don't want you to repeat, or you will never get rich, no matter how strong your other investments might be. I made these mistakes because I failed to take action when I knew things had changed or because I believed that the stock could withstand the newfound concern or because I simply refused to recognize the reality that the story had regressed and had become dangerous. Here's what you must do differently if you are not to repeat my errors.

1. When the thesis changes, cut your losses immediately.

Most people don't know where the exclamation "Booyah" comes from. I first heard it when I was doing my radio show, *Real Money*, which was the precursor to *Mad Money* on television. I had been extolling the virtues of the combination of Kmart and Sears that my friend Eddie Lampert had put together, and it had experienced a miracle run, from $24 to $170 in four years' time. A caller, who was listening to my New Orleans affiliate, simply wanted to thank me for putting him into Sears, a stock I had repeatedly stressed that I wanted everyone in the radio audience to buy. He had balked at first, but then decided to go all in and had made thousands of dollars on Sears. He said when something that bountiful occurs to you in New Orleans, you say "Booyah!"

These days, not a lot of people are saying "Booyah" about Sears. That's because Sears collapsed during the Great Recession, losing a huge part of its gains. My charitable trust was still able to get out, and get out with a profit, but I certainly should have gotten out earlier. I committed the cardinal sin of refusing to recognize that the reason I bought the stock had changed, and changed for the worse. When the trust got in during the early 2000s, the idea was that the hedge fund manager–turned-retailer would unlock the real estate value of the combined Sears-Kmart entity. In my bulletins to subscribers at the time, I highlighted that the nation seemed to be running short of available mall slots. Sears has anchor positions in many key malls all over the country. It had begun to shed under-performing properties in very good markets and in a total coup managed to sell eighteen stores to Home Depot for $271 million. Given that there are 4,000 Sears and Kmarts, you can imagine the visions that danced in our heads as the poorly performing stores were sold for their real estate value, allowing the excelling stores to shine.

Sears stock proceeded to double on the strength of that Home Depot sale and the possibilities of more and bigger asset sales. There were many rumors of imminent transactions right up until 2006, but they failed to materialize. Instead I began to hear rumblings from Home Depot about how it had been suckered into the deal by Sears and had dramatically overpaid for terrible real estate. Frankly, I blame Home Depot for not doing more homework. Still, the takeaway was clear from what I was hearing: now that Home Depot had been burned by Sears, there would be far fewer buyers kicking the tires of the properties Sears Holdings might have had for sale.

Next thing you know, the credit crunch ensued, and marginal retailers that might have been interested in Sears or Kmart properties fell by the wayside. Others were Amazoned, meaning they were not able to compete effectively with the online juggernaut. At the same time, highly leveraged mall owners had built out too many locations, leaving a stunning amount of vacancies. There simply was no need to buy up a Kmart or a Sears lease when there was so much empty lease space available pretty much wherever either had a store. In fact, there was vacant mall space pretty much everywhere in the country. Who needed those crummy Sears or Kmart leases or landholdings?

Did I sell it? Nope. I ginned up a new thesis. I no longer cared about the Sears real estate gambit. Now, I decided, it could be an earnings play. I held on to it, betting that Sears would find a way to reinvent itself and turn the stores around. If it wasn't going to sell them, then it would make a go of it.

What a fool I was. First, Sears and Kmart had been left behind by Walmart, Target, Home Depot and Costco, all better lower-cost operators with stronger balance sheets and greater physical store plants, much better locations and younger labor forces. Second, the Sears Holdings stores had a heavy housing aspect to them, with Sears being a huge supplier of home appliances. The result? Not only did it get outgunned by its competitors, not only was it felled by the housing crisis, but the main thesis, the breakup and monetization of the chain itself, the undervalued "real estate" theory was now over and it was time to move on. I was simply rationalizing my purchase, changing my thesis and abandoning what caused the big run-up to begin with. Management of Sears sadly had no idea what it was doing, and same-store sales began a long slide down that turned out to be irreversible. It became the fodder for every other store chain out there.

The trust was still able to evade a loss because I had followed my usual discipline of selling half of the position when it had doubled in value to play with the house's money. But I could have had an eight-bagger if I simply recognized that the reason I had bought Sears, the monetization of real estate, was gone. Now I was simply trying to come up with some alibi, perhaps an improvement in same-store sales, to justify the story. If you are in a stock for one reason—a real estate play, an earnings story, a breakup potential—and that story goes awry, do not dream up a new reason to own the stock. Just leave, even if it means taking a gain you don't want to take yet, because you will no doubt soon be taking a loss, which is always much more reprehensible than any gain of even the most marginal variety.

2. Don't risk it all for a small profit.

One of the most enduring concepts I have learned in my career is that nobody ever got hurt taking a profit. You've heard me say it many a time, and you've seen me write it in multiple venues. However, my review of all of my trades over this past half-decade of ActionAlertsPlus.com shows something else perhaps just as important: never regret taking a profit, even if it is a small one, when the worry exceeds the risk.

The time was August 2007. Some of us were growing worried about a potential housing bubble, but others, including many Fed members, said that the bubble was slowly losing fizz and therefore no one would get hurt.

At the time, people were piling into the stock of Fannie Mae, the mortgage packager and insurer that had an implicit guarantee from the federal government. While housing was overheated, Fannie Mae was known as a prudent lender that never took on a lot of investment risk and had been unfairly hammered as if it didn't know what it was doing. There was a tremendous demand at that moment for the kinds of mortgage bonds Fannie issued because they offered a yield in excess of treasury bonds but still had that implicit guarantee of the federal government. In fact, they were the mainstay of many an investment portfolio, particularly for banks looking to pick up a little extra yield.

I had been bothered by the idea that Fannie Mae wouldn't somehow *have* to be vulnerable if the housing market in the United States went bust. How much protection would the world's largest owner and seller of mortgages have if it got stuck with billions and billions of dollars in mortgages on its balance sheet without an ability to sell them because housing collapsed? But, then again, at no point in Fannie Mae's history had home values ever gone down more than two years in a row, and the declines were always of modest amounts. I was being overly cautious, I told myself.

The stock had been hanging around my $64 basis for several weeks as I mulled what to do. As I did more and more work on the mortgage industry, I became increasingly uncomfortable with all of Wall Street's reassurances, particularly because Fannie Mae was the biggest client for just about every major brokerage firm. I had become jaundiced enough to question whether these firms were so on the hook to Fannie Mae and its sister company, Freddie Mac, which had the same business model, that they had lost their ability to be objective.

Finally, I just said to myself that the risk seemed unfathomable if I was right about how housing could collapse, but the reward seemed minuscule. So, when the stock jumped a buck above my basis, to $65, I kicked it out, furious at myself for making only a dollar. Sure enough, the stock then rallied to $67, and I sent out a bulletin noting how angry I was with myself. If I had waited only one more day I would have done so much better. I wanted to buy it back because I had clearly made a mistake leaving it when I did; now the stock was going higher without me. How could I not have just been more patient? How could I have been so worried about the downside? How could I have been so darned cautious?

Sure enough, less than a year later, Fannie Mae was at $2. A year after that it virtually disappeared. Here I was stupidly second-guessing myself for missing a couple of points even though I had a real bead on the downside. Fannie Mae wasn't a "long"; it was a "short." My greed and insistence on trying to make some money even though I knew there were problems, compounded by my anger over missing two bucks, should be a reminder that once you have a problem position, one that you are truly worried about, don't worry about making a profit at all. Just get out. Sure, I would have liked to nail those last couple bucks, but considering that the $65 Fannie Mae stock was at $2 a year later, maybe the better way to look at things is that sometimes you shouldn't even care about the profit at all. If you want to exercise the prudence you need to Get Rich Carefully, after all of the chicanery and losses people have endured in this market, do yourself a favor and focus on the potential downside *more* than the upside. Holding out for a bigger win in an awful and deteriorating situation is just plain stupid. Cut your gains as well as your losses when the narrative changes for the negative, and don't kick yourself if the stock goes still higher after you dump it. Who knows? By next year it might be worthless.

3. If a stock goes down on great news, just sell it.

At the beginning of the market's turmoil in 2007, trading volume shot up huge. We were having some of the biggest trading days ever, more than double what they had been before things got nasty. To me that was a terrific opportunity to buy the stock of the New York Stock Exchange, which has since merged with the Intercontinental Exchange and no longer trades independently. I figured that, with volume up gigantically, the earnings estimates for the NYSE had to be way too low. Given that the most important propellant of a stock is how much the company beats the estimates by, this doubling of volume simply had to mean that Wall Street was being way too conservative in its estimates and the NYSE would crush the numbers when it reported.

But the stock just wouldn't go up. Day after day after day we would be blown away by the high-volume figures, and then we would see the stock act anemically or drip down a tad. Hmm, another buying opportunity? Had to be. I bought all the way down because my thesis seemed unassailable. Turns out that all of that good news didn't move the stock higher because the NYSE was *losing* market share to other exchanges. Much of the volume was trading away at new and often secret but SEC-sanctioned exchanges, and the venerable franchise was being diminished in stature and worth at the same time volume had taken off. They had nothing to do with each other; the exchange accrued no value at all from the exploding volume.

If you look back at the stock you can see the sickening slide beginning right when I thought it should have been going higher because of the volume gains. The stock quickly lost more than two-thirds of its value. The upshot? When a stock doesn't go higher on *repeated* good news, maybe there is news you don't know that's holding it back. Better to presume that you don't know something and others do, or that your thesis is bogus, and you should just sell the stock rather than waiting to find out what's really keeping the stock from doing what you would expect it to do.

I spotted a variant on this same issue not that long ago with Cisco, the Dow Jones stock and dominant Internet and telephone networking company. In July 2010, Cisco reported a fantastic quarter, one of a string of quarters that were exceptional, showing that growth was returning to the company after a long respite. The stock had already gone from $14 and change to almost $28 before the report, and it had pulled back to $23 before the company reported the ripping-good quarter. It rallied slightly that day on the better-than-expected quarter but couldn't hold its gains even as analysts spoke positively about the situation. I puzzled over it, wondering how the market could be so darned wrong about Cisco being back in growth mode. I thought that if I just gave it time, it would be like all of the other quarters of the past two years and begin to move the stock back to its highs.

It didn't, though. The stock just refused to budge on good days and went down on bad ones.

Sure enough, I rode Cisco down for what seemed like ages, traveling with it down to $18, not content to take a nice long-term profit for the trust. And the next quarter Cisco reported? It was a bust. The first in what was to be a long line of bad quarters.

The conclusion? When you get that muted reaction to a quarterly report that is better than expected after all of the other better-than-expected quarters have sent the stock skyward, you must take evasive action immediately. You *must* presume that you have just witnessed the last good quarter, that someone smarter or more informed than you is selling because he knows better, and you must ring the register.

These days you have to be hypersensitive to a stock's reaction to good news as well as bad. When a stock doesn't go down on bad news, you may have spotted a bottom. But when a stock doesn't go up on good news, sell first and ask questions later. Odds are that you just stumbled on the top.

When a company makes a bold strategic move that is additive, perhaps buying another company in what is known as an accretive acquisition, meaning that analysts can raise numbers immediately, you can hang on to the stock even if the market doesn't instantly award the acquirer a new valuation. You can stay with a stock after it announces a breakup and it doesn't react, because, as I have detailed, potential investors simply may not understand the magnitude of the acquisition and its impact on earnings or the wonders of a parts-worth-more-than-the-whole situation.

The market also often doesn't get the importance of unusually large hikes in dividends compared to previous increases or the bounty of rare special dividends from companies that usually don't give them. If stocks refuse to budge on those news streams, my work shows that you should just go buy some stock in the issuer. That's because management is demonstrating a level of confidence that is highly unusual and cannot be ignored.

These are all material positive changes that are reasons to buy, not sell. But if you are thinking that earnings estimates should be moving up because of something a company's doing, and the stock doesn't react either before the quarter, when you would expect everyone to see that the numbers are too low—the New York Stock Exchange example—or after, like the Cisco report that produced a dud of a move after the quarter was soundly beaten, then you have to sell and move on.

4. Upgrade clusters should be sold, not bought.

There's nothing like owning a security, waking up in the morning and finding that a major firm, a Goldman or a Credit Suisse or a Morgan Stanley, has upgraded your stock and slapped a strong buy on it, or a conviction buy, or whatever term they are using these days. You get the sense that you did well, that you worked and thought and researched the stock perfectly and you are being rewarded with an anointment. I know that's how I feel when a stock in my charitable trust gets recommended by a major investment house. I see the upgrade and think, *Hah! It's a good day, and I am in the right place.*

There's only one problem. As I discovered in the spring of 2011, with the stock of WellPoint, the large health maintenance organization, there actually *can* be too much of a good thing. The trust had bought WellPoint because it had been kicked to the curb by those who recognized that the Affordable Care Act might impinge on WellPoint's ability to raise prices on their contracts to companies, the chief reason why you own shares in one of these companies.

When Congress rammed the bill through and the president signed it into law, analysts uniformly downgraded the stock. But when the smoke cleared and Stephanie Link and I saw the details of the law and recognized that it wasn't as punitive as initially thought—in fact, it was the opposite— we bought some stock in this giant health care provider.

Of course, it didn't take long for the analysts to realize that they had gotten too negative on the stock. One by one they upgraded the darned thing, and it ran from $57 to $81. We sold some stock, just as I always tell you to do. Bulls make money, bears make money, but hogs get slaughtered. Nevertheless, we were giddy and flying high after each upgrade. How could you not be? You could tell by what we call the "gapped opening," an opening far in excess of where the stock closed the night before, that these upgrades were causing short-sellers who had stayed negative on WellPoint to panic and cover or buy back the stock to close out their positions. The shorts often don't care how high they cover, which is a big reason why you get these opening pops. They just want the pain to go away. So they reach and create the gap. I know it's sloppy, but I have been there and done that as a short-selling hedge fund manager, and I understand the undisciplined way you can be when you have been endlessly slapped upside your head by analyst upgrade after analyst upgrade.

We decided to hold on to a big slug of WellPoint, thinking that things could only get better, given all of these upgrades. They had to know something more, something even better than we thought, right?

Wrong. The stock had been levitating precisely *because* of each upgrade. At the top—and it was most definitely the top—there was no one left to recommend it. There was no one left to upgrade. The rocket fuel that had propelled the stock higher—the analysts who changed their minds coupled with the short-sellers who capitulated on each upgrade— was spent. The result? When the company subsequently reported a so-so quarter and gave tepid guidance, it got whacked beyond all reason and fell, you guessed it, right back to $57, where we got in originally. The fall was made all the more precipitous because of that dearth of short-sellers who can create some stability with their buying to close out positions. They had bought already. There was no one left to buy. We committed a cardinal sin: we gave up the gain.

In the end, the analysts were simply reacting over and over again to the same piece of news and the same reasoning: the Affordable Care Act didn't decimate WellPoint's earnings. But it certainly wasn't a win for it either, and at $81, the stock was reflecting a huge win.

So sure, be proud that you called the bottom or bought near the bottom. Feel terrific when you catch upgrade after upgrade as analysts recognize the error of their ways. But when the pool is real crowded and there are only a few stragglers left to dive in, don't overstay your welcome. Jump out, get dried off and ring the register on the whole darned thing.

5. Beware of multiple shortfalls.

When you run a hedge fund you are constantly making moves, daily moves, intraday moves, trades at the opening, trades at the bell. But most people are not hedge fund managers. And as I can tell from my Action AlertsPlus.com subscriber base, most are trying to buy stocks of good companies, stay in touch with these companies—my buy-and-homework dictum—and be ready to pull the trigger for more of a good stock if the overall market creates a sale, or sell the stock if something goes awry in the underlying business. That, in a nutshell, is what good, careful, prudent investing is about.

We've learned that stocks of individual companies have increasingly become dominated by sector pull, as described earlier, helped mightily in the past few years by the ETFs that serve to commoditize pretty much every industry. The good oil service stocks trade with the bad ones, except on the days surrounding earnings, where the differentiations are made. The terrible retailers get pulled up along with the savvy operators by the RTH, the ETF for retail. It's just a fact of life in modern-day investing, because so many have chosen ETFs as the way to go rather than bother to examine the underlying strengths and weaknesses of the enterprises that are all lumped together.

There is, however, another symbiosis, another relational pull that you must be on the lookout for, and that's the warnings of competitors. Many a time I have been needlessly blindsided, costing my charitable trust thousands of dollars, simply because I believed my chosen company was superior to other companies in the same industry and I didn't know that the whole industry was in decline.

Understand that spotting this competitor-takedown issue isn't always second nature. In fact, I have often used it to my advantage. When I look back at my buys and sells I am amazed, for example, at how many times I was able to pick up the stocks of good retailers simply because they had all been taken down by the report of a bad one. The classic case: how many times I was able to buy Walgreens or CVS, two very well-run drugstore chains, when the third national player, Rite Aid, blew up or reported extremely subpar earnings.

I used to put Rite Aid on *Mad Money*, before the stock fell so low that it no longer met our standard: no stock that falls under $2 is allowed on our show. Stocks that are under $2 tend not to be safe to invest in, and I don't want to traffic in them. Fortunately for Rite Aid shareholders, the stock has come back to life courtesy of a new marketing manager, but it used to provide a perpetual annuity for drugstore investors on a monthly basis. Rite Aid would announce that sales were weak either in the front of the store, where the consumables and over-the-counter drugs are sold, or in the pharmacy, also known as the back of the store. Each time the news broke, traders would dump their Walgreens or CVS, anticipating that they too would fall prey to whatever tripped up their fellow drugstore chain. Given that I owned Walgreens for the trust and would book Rite Aid for the show, it became evident to me that Rite Aid's problems were not only different and distinct from Walgreens', but they were zero-sum with Walgreens stores that were within short traveling distances from Rite Aid stores. WAG was taking share from the declining RAD stores. It was a terrific way to get a better basis, which ultimately led to a very nice gain for the trust.

The same thing occurred for years in the restaurant business, where Darden, the parent of Olive Garden and Red Lobster, suffered through multiple quarters of poor execution that continue to this day. Before Wall Street got wise to the faltering ways of a once great chain, every time Darden reported disappointing numbers, everything from Brinker, which owns Chili's, to Panera would get hammered. Another fabulous opportunity to buy a high-quality restaurant chain because of one errant player.

But the same thing did not occur in a different industry—the health insurance companies—even though I was in the best-of-breed player in the business at that time, United Health. Here my knowledge of the industry actually betrayed me. The health insurance industry is a very competitive one, with each company trying to get large-scale contracts from major companies, often trying to lure one company by offering a price advantage over the other guy. However, all of the companies try to portray themselves as independent of each other, offering superior, differentiated services beyond that of health insurance.

When WellPoint, one of its biggest competitors, reported a shortfall, the stock of United Health went down in sympathy, giving up a couple of points. I decided to buy more of the stock, betting that, as in the Rite Aid and Darden situations, United was getting dinged unnecessarily.

But soon after what I thought was that opportunistic buy, Aetna announced that it too, like WellPoint, had a weak quarter and gave a negative outlook about itself and the industry. United Health again dropped, although giving up nowhere near the points that WellPoint or Aetna surrendered. Almost all of the analysts who covered the industry reiterated their buys on United Health, no doubt after talking to the company, which had not signaled any weakness. Soon after, however, United lowered the boom on its own business and the stock got hammered, a vicious decline, no doubt exacerbated by the positive reiterations. I was devastated.

After that rude awakening I have instituted a new rule that has since saved me goodly amounts. When one player in an industry fails to deliver, you can logically hold on to a solid competitor. However, when a second entry blows up, you have to exit immediately, no matter where your stock is, even if you have to take a loss, because the vast majority of the time the competitor is either seeing the same thing that your company's seeing or is actually at war with your company and damaging the fundamentals. Since putting through this rule, we've passed up on some very nice opportunities that could have made the trust a little bit of trading money, but we have sidestepped major losses.

To sum up, it is fine to use a break in a competitor's fortunes to pick up some of your own favorites at a cheaper price—think Walgreens with

Rite Aid, or Panera with Darden. However, when a second company in the industry reports weakness, you have to exit your own stock too.

6. Sell stocks that don't participate in rallies.

Here's a new test for the careful investor: Examine your portfolio after a day when the S&P 500 registers more than a one percent gain. Take a look at the leaders and the laggards. As a hedge fund manager, I was always concerned if I dramatically outperformed the averages on an up day like that. It usually meant I was taking on way too much risk. At the same time, though, if I underperformed that day, I looked for the culprits. Invariably there would be some stinkers; there always are.

But when I perused old ActionAlerts bulletins, I discovered a disturbing trend. If you looked at the cohort of the stocks that didn't go up in a big rally, and you found that the vast majority of the stocks in that sector didn't go up either, then you needed to take action, and take action immediately. You needed to sell these nonparticipants from nonparticipating sectors, regardless of how you might have felt about them or their prospects.

Here's why. When I had stocks that disappointed on up days when the market rallied a percent or more, these same stocks tended to get absolutely clobbered on the inevitable down days. This pattern did not happen once. It didn't happen twice. It happened multiple times, and I incurred substantial losses that could easily have been averted had I just followed a simple rule: Sell the stocks of sectors that do not go up after several—not just one, but several—one-percent-plus days. You can revisit them later, lower, if you insist on doing so. Why not blow these out on the first day they underperform? There could have been a downgrade on that particular day that might have skewed the performance in a one-off way. Good stocks deserve more considered judgments than that.

Nevertheless, when I ignored several days' worth of underperformance, the losses were pretty eye-opening. For example, the stocks connected with personal computing technology, despite multiyear periods of excellent market performance, began to falter hard, even on big up days during the 2008–9 time frame. Steel, mineral and fertilizer businesses in the 2007–8 period failed to move higher when the broader market rallied.

There would be days on end when the market would go higher and these stocks would do nothing or go up far less than the market. Sure enough, it turns out that many of these stocks were not just in a cyclical funk; far more important, they were in a secular decline because they were being outmoded either by other technologies that they couldn't adjust to (in the case of the personal computer) or imports that they couldn't compete against (the steels and the fertilizers). In retrospect, these stocks, were screaming, "Sell me, please! Sell me before I hurt you!"

I know that you may be reluctant to part with these stocks, maybe because you have good gains or maybe because you want to get back to even with them, or their *past* earnings still seem strong to you. It doesn't matter. They should go. You can always buy them back. But as I learned back in the old hedge fund, once you have sold them, invariably you feel liberated and would rather *not* return to them. Remember, being in the best of breed in a sector that's in a long-term decline does not protect you from a fundamental sector sell-off.

When things are going well, even careful investors tend to get sloppy. In each case I didn't think it was all that imperative to take action because "they can't all go up at once." But the truth was, they weren't going up at all. They were doing nothing or going down. That's why this "sell 'em when they don't go up" lesson must not be ignored. There's too much opportunity cost, and there's too much money to be lost if you avoid this new rule.

7. Sector woes = sell.

You know why I want you to look at the sector of a stock that fails to go up on a one-percent-plus day? Because of an experience I had in 2007–8 when the trust bought the shares of my old alma mater, Goldman Sachs.

I knew the place was terrific, often thought to be head and shoulders above most firms. Indeed, looking back, almost every other firm I applied to or interviewed with has since disappeared. I had kept in touch with many acquaintances who had moved up to senior positions, and I was confident that they could steer the firm through any storm. Goldman had sidestepped many of the pitfalls of the era, including loading up the balance sheet with too much debt or moving big into the subprime mortgage business. It had always taken pride in being as transparent as possible when it came to using leverage, and I had tremendous confidence in both the chief executive officer, Lloyd Blankfein, and the chief financial officer at the time, David Viniar, to navigate the downturn.

That's why I told subscribers in a November 16, 2007, bulletin that Goldman Sachs, after a long slide, would most certainly have to stop going down soon because it was so much better than the other firms in its cohort. I wrote that with the stock at $233.

It would bottom a year later at $50.

Now, ironically, I was right about the fundamentals, just wrong about the stock. Goldman Sachs got through the period with no need for a government bailout. The closest it came to getting "in trouble" was when it decided to welcome the investment of Warren Buffett for additional cash in case things continued to go haywire.

It didn't matter, though. Goldman Sachs traded almost exactly like every other bank except the ones that ceased to exist. In the new world it didn't matter how "good" Goldman was. The banks were all tarred with the same brush and then feathered with the financial ETFs that bundled them together. Never ever presume that even the best can buck the homogenizing and pernicious ETF gravitational pull if that trend is headed down. The actual problems in the industry could be contagious to the stocks even if the company you are a shareholder in turns out to be immune, as Goldman was. Sure, a sophisticated trader might want to go short or bet against the ETF and go long or own the good one, such as Goldman, betting that the basket will go down more than your favorite. But if you think the stock you like is actually going to go up while the basket it belongs in goes down, I think you are wasting your time, and your money.

8. After the crash, no financial should be given the benefit of the doubt.

As someone who likes to pick stocks, not sectors, I recognize that I am an anachronism in this new age of stock commoditization. I actually like to do the homework. I like to listen to conference calls and make judgments about individual managements by watching investor presentations or, best of all, trying to get them on my show to hear what they have to say in person. I am what is known as a generalist, and I am agnostic about sectors. I will dig into every one of them. They all seem exciting and compelling to me. But I've learned a brutal lesson from the post–Bear Stearns/ Lehman/Washington Mutual era. The financial sector is different from all other sectors. When you buy the stock of a financial, any financial—a bank, an insurance company or a credit card company—you have to do far more work and have a much more keen understanding of what can go wrong than for any other kind of stock. You need much more faith to invest in banks than in any other group, faith that I often find is not backed up by the facts as they come tumbling out when things go bad.

This stance is quite a change for me. I have written in the past about the importance of owning bank stocks that can be taken over, in order for other, larger banks from out of the area to grow. I have always liked a business where you take in people's money and then pay them next to nothing for it while you do what you want with it. That's a recipe for a quick and easy profit. These companies can make money just by turning on the lights in the morning.

But even after all the investigations, all the laws and all the prosecutions—although there should have been many more of them— stocks in this group may simply be too hard for you to own, even though the fins, as we call them, make up the largest sector in the S&P 500. No matter how hard the government tries to get some transparency out of banks, or insists that the banks raise enough capital so they can't fail even with a degree of recklessness that might not be easy to spot, the banks can still confound you and can cost you more money than any other sector, including the volatile technology cohort. You simply can't make judgments about what you are buying or owning with the surety of, say, an industrial, a retailer or a drug company. They are black boxes, and I don't like black boxes.

I am not saying that I would shun all banks. Sometimes their prices go down so low that they can't be resisted. And when we get a yield curve with some inflection, meaning that banks can pay you little for your savings and checking accounts and minuscule amounts for certificates of deposit versus the huge amount they can make lending that money or investing it in higher-yielding but still risk-free assets, I am sure that it will be a more positive moment for them. But they have been a real bear to own, no pun intended, and most simply aren't worth buying if you can avoid them. As I perused bulletin after bulletin, I was astounded by how little in retrospect I really knew about the banks I had purchased. And, trust me, I knew everything that could be gleaned publicly about them during my ownership periods.

So I now feel it is important to have a dual standard distinguishing banks from every other type of security. Usually, when something goes awry for a company, I am willing to give it the benefit of the doubt if the issue can be explained away. Weather, for example, and calendar shifts can play havoc with retailers. An individual drug may not pan out for a pharmaceutical company. Tech product cycles can distort earnings, as a company won't do well in the last quarter hawking an old product when a new one is about to be rolled out. Oil companies regularly experience refining outages and can have declines in production because of storms and transportation problems. I can excuse all of them.

But my new rule is: When you get bad news from a bank, don't battle it, just exit it. In fact, the major lesson I take away from the incredible downturn in banks is that there is never just one issue or concern. Nothing is discrete or one-off with these companies. We find out they have screwed up in their lending practices? Sell. We find out that they poorly invested their deposits? Sell. We find out that they are being investigated by the Justice Department or the Federal Reserve for lying about their books? Sell. They miss the capital requirements set by Treasury or the Federal Reserve? Sell. It's the only way to protect yourself from a group that has destroyed almost as many portfolios as the dotcoms did at the turn of the century.

I know this is a very high standard, one that may cause you to rethink owning any of them. That's fine with me. My trust has a very small position, relatively, in this group, and while we have had big gains in JPMorgan, having bought it after the "whale" incident, I don't know if I will be so bold the next time. There's just too much risk in the group. In the old days, banks would be stopped from going too low by two unique elements: yield, because they almost always paid outsized dividends, and takeovers, because the lower a bank's stock went, the more likely it would be to catch a bid. These days the dividend policies are tightly regulated by the government, and the government is not thinking about how to reward bank shareholders with bountiful dividends. It's thinking about how to protect the rest of us from bank failures, so dividend boosts are heavily regulated and hard to come by. As far as takeovers are concerned, the Great Recession caused a level of consolidation that's become untenable to the politicians in Washington. It's more likely that they will break up the big banks than allow them to purchase any smaller ones. Plus, we are not seeing much regional takeover activity because banks are no longer trusting of other banks. They don't know what's on the other guy's balance sheet. If they don't know, believe me, we don't know either.

Unfortunately, there's a corollary to this rule of shoot financials first and don't even bother to ask questions later, and that's the unfortunate impossibility of mounting a real rally in the entire market without the help of the banks. The financials now make up about 17 percent of the Standard & Poor's 500, the largest group in the market, recently passing the information technology stocks in market capitalization title. But this group punches well above its weighting. Unlike every other sector I follow, it has the ability to push down or pull up the entire market with its bootstraps. And while a rally that's led by banks can be a terrific one, you can bet that a sell-off led by banks will *always* be a horrific one. Every single decline in the market in 2007, 2008, 2009, 2010 and 2011 started with a rout in the financials, either because of regulatory problems, like faulty bookkeeping or hidden, dubious investments, or because of shortfalls that couldn't be explained away. In other words, you could adopt my ultra-skeptical attitude toward the group, underweight it versus its representation in the S&P, and they could still take you down. Think about it, think about how much hurt the actions of the two best financials, Goldman Sachs and JPMorgan, have caused the market in the past half-decade. Then extrapolate that to those that aren't nearly as well run or take far greater risks.

Why is their power so inordinate? Several reasons. First, there is no such thing as a large, growing cash economy. Businesses need credit to finance everything from inventory to the additions they need to grow their companies. Banks supply the oil to the system's car. When they withhold it either out of an overabundance of caution or because the regulators demand it, then the economy can't grow as fast as it would otherwise, or it might not grow at all. Second, housing can be a major growth driver to the nation, and housing is uniquely dependent on credit. Only a small percentage of people in this country are wealthy enough to buy houses with cash. So if banks are stingy with mortgages, this job-creating industry stalls out, taking the economy down with it, as we saw from the origins of the Great Recession. Third, banks tend to be intertwined with other banks both domestically and internationally. The European contagion wasn't spread here by tech or utilities or food companies; it was spread by banks. The global financial system is built on credit. The etymology of the word "credit" is the Latin *credere*, which means "believe," and many investors have simply stopped believing in the solvency of the European banks. Although our banks have retreated aggressively from Europe, the linkage remains, at least psychologically, and the damage via the linkage has sparked every major sell-off since the 2009 generational bottom was reached. They are just too powerful for their own good.

Consequently, I have learned two lessons from my travails with the bank stocks: (1) don't own too many, and when you do, be sure to sell them at the first sign of trouble; (2) keep your eyes on the group even if you aren't involved, as it can help your portfolio if the group is inching up, but if the group is sliding down, it can take everything, from the oils to the minerals, health care and the industrials, down with it as surely as if there were something wrong with each of those groups themselves. Make no mistake about it, though, in the new world of careful investing, you never, ever have to own a bank again, and perhaps you never should and never will. We must all be risk managers now, and the risk to owning financials is just too great for most at-home investors to handle.

9. Retailing's tough: bad comparable-store numbers mean sell.

I don't believe in second chances for the banks. We have seen way too much hardship to allow any slippage of those rules, no matter how much "reform" has been visited upon the group. There's one other sector, though, that you must apply a higher standard to owning, although not as rigorous as banks, and that's retail. All kinds of retail: hard goods, soft goods, even food retailing, such as supermarkets and restaurants.

As someone who has cut his teeth on retail, I understand that these companies are almost always thinly capitalized and not built to withstand more than a short period of hardship. When I was growing up, I learned this lesson about not trusting the retailers the hard way. In junior high school I used to bring my lunch in a white kraft-paper bag every day, as most kids did. Then one day, my mom put my lunch in a black plastic bag with snap lock handles on it. Each side of the bag had a line drawing of a woman and the name Moana, with an address and phone number. The bag was pretty darned big, clearly not meant for the lunch function. But what the heck, I was a seventh grader, I didn't ask any questions and I threw the bag out after eating my usual fare: three navel oranges and a piece of Sara Lee pound cake.

The next day my mother put the lunch in another black plastic Moana bag. And then the next and the next. Finally, at the end of the week, I started wondering, *What's the deal with the Moana bags?* I asked my mother how much longer I was going to have to bring my lunch in these ridiculous contraptions.

"Forever," she told me. Mom explained that my father had sold 10,000 bags to the Moana chain of finer women's shops. But the Moana store didn't have a good Christmas and couldn't pay for the bags, or any of their other merchandise, and the chain had filed for bankruptcy. Pop was an unsecured creditor.

Obviously the Moana bags were of no use to any retailer but Moana, so my father brought them home. When I questioned whether we really had an endless supply of Moana lunch bags, my mother told me to go back into the laundry room behind the den to see for myself. Sure enough, every available inch of that little 12-foot-by-9-foot room was taken up with Moana bags. And for the next five years I carried my lunch to school in a Moana bag.

The Moana story is a cautionary tale about how retailers can live by the skin of their teeth and die virtually overnight. My father could not detect signs of Moana's folding. But public companies aren't able to hide from view. They release important numbers each quarter at a minimum, often each month, that tell you all you need to know.

That's why I want to stress the prism that must infuse all of your thinking: the retailer's comparable-store sales numbers, how the existing store count did versus the previous year's sales. These are the lifeblood numbers, the litmus test; they tell you how a store chain is really doing. Comparable-store sales allow you to analyze whether a store chain is executing right and selling out of merchandise at good prices or discounting merchandise at fire-sale prices. They give you a window into whether management is improving or going downhill. They allow you to ask whether you are getting more or fewer dollars out of your existing store base year over year.

To measure retailers, we must use comparable-store growth numbers, not overall growth, because, as I wrote earlier, overall growth can be easily skewed by a retailer simply putting up a lot of poorly performing stores that still can boost overall sales. You could add stores and mask the underlying deterioration of the total existing store base. I am not the least bit interested in overall sales when it comes to retail. Those mean nothing to me.

Many retail chains report same-store sales monthly, although several are trying to get away from such close scrutiny and wait for the quarterly report to break sales down. I don't blame the managers of the chains anxious not to reveal their monthly numbers. Retail's a tough game, and you don't want the Wall Street jackals breathing down your neck because you featured the wrong kind of sweater or too many shorts in the spring with weather that refuses to get warm. Still, I have now developed a hard-and-fast rule for careful investing: You are forbidden from owning a retailer that reports three straight months of negative comp sales. Mind you, I am not talking about numbers that are simply soft, meaning that a retailer might have recorded only a 3 percent comp gain after a 5 percent gain the previous month. I am talking actual negative numbers.

You see, the negative numbers tell you that the stores have too much inventory in them. The more negative, the more likely that they will have to discount that inventory. At a certain point the process becomes an actual tailspin that can't be easily arrested, and the retailer has to lay off salespeople and dump inventory at ridiculously low prices just to make payments to its creditors. That's why I insist that you do not stay beyond three negative monthly numbers, or one full quarter's numbers if the store does not release monthlies.

The only exception? If every major chain in the same segment of retail were to also report negative numbers, then forgiveness can be granted.

Some might think my three-and-you're-out rule is a harsh standard. I say I can count on one hand the retailers that were able to pull out of extended periods of negative comps. My rule would have gotten you out of every single teen apparel play before they began to lose big money. My rule would have forced you to exit J. C. Penney well before its calamitous drop when Ron Johnson's plan to resurrect the retailer's fortunes went badly awry. You simply can't afford to wait for a turn. You have to go before the hole is too big to climb out of.

It's not only negative numbers that you have to worry about with comp-store sales, though. Beware of the stocks of companies that have a sudden deceleration from a high comparable-store sales number to a low one. Again, one month can be explained away, but if the stock trades at a high multiple to earnings you can expect to take a bit of a hit. But three straight months of deceleration and you should be developing your exit strategy. Be especially wary of situations where you get numbers only once a quarter and you get a big drop-off in that quarter. Unless there is some sort of weather-related reason or a calendar holiday shift, you may have to jettison it if the stock sells at a premium price-to-earnings multiple to the other stocks in its cohort or the stock market in general. That's what kept me out of owning Chipotle for the brutal 87-point decline back in the summer of 2012. A few months before that decline the company had experienced a rather steep decline from low double-digit to high single-digit same-store sales. Given how expensive the stock was going into that quarter, you had no choice when you saw that deceleration. You simply had to sell CMG, regardless of how much you may have liked the stores, the Food with Integrity plan or the management, and I like all three. Sure enough, the next quarter showed a further degradation and you saw the 87-point plunge.

Yes, it seems harsh that you would have to leave a stock, a great stock of a fabulous company, after one sharp quarterly decline in same-store sales. And yes, you may miss the next move back up if it turns out that the previous quarter was an anomaly. But the downside is far greater in these high-multiple situations than the upside, so, again, the stringent rule applies: you must sell after what amounts to three months' worth of declining numbers.

Obviously, Chipotle is no Moana. Never will be. But it's my job to have you steer clear of situations of vulnerability that you may not see coming, and same-store sales remain the best defense against the retailing blindside. And with a losing stock, you don't even get any lunch bags to show for it.

10. De-diversification can be costly.

You know I am a fiend for diversification. We need it in order to be sure we don't fall prey to a sudden turn in a sector, and it isn't always obvious that you are overexposed to a particular group. The best example for this new era is the banking-insurance-housing complex, which barely existed before the Great Recession but should now be deeply ingrained in the prudent investor's psyche. In 2008 you might have owned Toll Brothers, Bank of America, and Metropolitan Life, thinking those stocks are from three different categories. You would be wrong, though. In order to buy a house from Toll Brothers, you need credit, a mortgage. If you can't get a mortgage, you typically can't afford a Toll Brothers house, most of which cost more than $400,000. You might go to Bank of America to get a mortgage. But if Bank of America is having a hard time with the regulators because of delinquent mortgages, it might not be willing to give you a mortgage loan. That will hurt Toll Brothers' sales as surely as if they were to raise the prices of their houses by hundreds of thousands of dollars. Metropolitan Life wouldn't help the cause. It is a huge holder of mortgages itself. Plus, it shares the sensitivity to interest rates that Toll Brothers and Bank of America have. These stocks sink or swim together. They are all portions of the same sector, even if you think they shouldn't be.

I found this out the hard way for my trust when I found myself backing into a portfolio that was way too heavily weighted to oil and gas. It didn't seem like that on the surface. The trust owned Quanta, a utility service company that builds and repairs large infrastructure projects, including electric lines. It owned Foster Wheeler, the engineering and construction company that's competent at building all sorts of giant projects in many industries. It had a position in National Oilwell Varco, the best-of-breed oil-drilling rig builder, and shares in Devon, Cabot Oil & Gas and XTO, three premier, independent oil and gas companies. Given that the trust typically contains thirty stocks and oil and gas represents about 10 percent of the S&P, it is reasonable to own three oil and gas plays, and perhaps as many as four if you want to "overweight" the area. So, Devon, XTO and Cabot Oil & Gas could serve as the oil-and-gas-weighted portion of the portfolio, with National Oilwell Varco being the overweighted component because you can't drill without rigs. And National Oilwell Varco is the go-to company in the industry for new rigs, with the finest technology to tap hard-to-reach shale oil and gas.

That's all well and good, but it turns out that at that moment a huge percentage of the book of business engineering and construction giant Foster Wheeler had involved building petrochemical plants and refineries. In other words, projects that would be canceled if oil prices fell. Quanta also had beefed up its oil and gas pipeline building division, so it too traded with the oil and gas companies' fortunes. To make matters worse, XTO, Cabot and Devon were all almost entirely natural gas plays, with very little oil.

When oil fell hard in 2008–9, natural gas fell even harder, especially when we realized that there was a developing glut in the product. The result? The trust fell victim to what I call creeping de-diversification: all of these stocks were trading off one commodity that was headed down. No company can buck that downward pull. This concentration contributed to the fund having the worst year it has ever had.

Oh, and to be sure, when you are doing commodity investing, picking the best-of-breed player means nothing. They are, after all, engaged in trying to profit in one form or another off that commodity. It goes down, they go down.

It's funny, but so many people complain on Twitter that I spend too much time discussing diversification and that perhaps it is time to suspend the "Am I diversified?" game that I have played pretty much every Wednesday of my life for the past dozen years. But when you consider how I was ensnared in a costly brush with antidiversification, you can't think about this issue enough if you are going to Get Rich Carefully.

If you find yourself leaning toward one particular group without realizing it, especially a group related to one commodity, something that can be found if some of your stocks are taking lockstep action for more than just a couple of days, start selling some of them immediately. Invariably lightning will strike your group, and the losses will be outsized. Know what you own, and know whether the stocks are trading together even if you think they shouldn't be. It doesn't matter what you think; it matters what the market thinks. The market, not you, is the ultimate arbiter. It's a simple rule, not easily followed, but it is gospel. So take your portfolio test today, and if there's too much concentration that you didn't know about, take action.

LET'S SUMMARIZE the selling lessons now, so you are ready to take action.

1. If the thesis changes, sell. If you bought a stock for a particular reason, say, a strategy to monetize real estate or a plan to break up, and the strategy doesn't pan out, just dump it. Move on immediately, and don't rationalize continuing ownership.

2. Never regret taking a profit, no matter how small, if you are worried about the risk. In the new world we can't kick ourselves if a stock goes still higher if we think it is riskier than we can handle. It's not worth the heartbreak if your fears are realized, because the devastation to your portfolio can be bleak. Don't be penny-wise; you could be pound bankrupt.

3. If a stock doesn't go up on good earnings news, presume that it's the last good quarter. When you get an earnings report that's solid after a huge run of good quarters and great stock performance, presume the run is over and take profits immediately.

4. Beware when multiple analysts issue upgrades at once. Don't congratulate yourself for being right; take action and ring the register. There's

probably no one, including short-sellers, left to do any meaningful buying after a slew of near simultaneous upgrades. The cushion to break the fall is gone, so exit the stock building.

5. When one stock in a sector warns, you can dismiss it, particularly if it isn't the best of breed. It just might be losing share to the companies that are executing better in its cohort. When two warn, get out immediately. The whole sector has probably gone bad.

6. If your stocks don't go up in a large stock market rally, presume that something's very wrong and take appropriate action. Don't create alibis for the stocks. Shoot first; you can always buy back later. But I bet you won't want to, because something's very much awry with a nonparticipant to a rising tide rally in the S&P that should lift all boats.

7. No stock is immune to its cohort's woes, no matter how good you think that stock might be, or perhaps even more important, even if the company itself doesn't fall prey to the sector's contagion. The stock will separate itself from the company and go down, rightly or wrongly, with its colleagues. Best of breed is no better than worst of breed in these situations.

8. In the new world of more careful investing, financials must no longer be given the benefit of the doubt. Too much money has been lost in this sector, and the assets they own are too opaque to make considered judgments for the vast majority of the stocks in the group.

9. Retailers are graded by how their same-stores compare year over year. If a company reports three straight months of negative comp store sales, don't take chances, just move on.

10. Beware of creeping diversification. Do too many stocks in your portfolio trade in lockstep with each other? You may be too undiversified without even knowing it. Watch the correlations. If stocks you think are not in the same industries are all advancing and declining with similar percentages on many given days, they are probably linked in ways you might not know, especially if they are related to the same commodity. You must trim the positions immediately. Presume that when bear lightning strikes, that's the group that will be hit.

False Floors

In a bull market, stocks have remarkable resiliency. It seems almost impossible to take them down. The moment you get a price break, buyers swoop in and snap up the stock. Some of my charitable trust's greatest gains have come from stocks that have been pummeled by short-term concerns—think Yum! with KFC's woes in China or McDonald's by a couple of weak sales or Bristol-Myers from a write-off of an expensive acquisition. Stocks seem to have an invisible floor beneath them that attracts money like a magnet. After you have determined that the downward catalyst isn't life-threatening—all bets are off if it is, of course—you simply need to figure out where the selling dries up and do some buying.

I don't mean to be glib about the assessment you need to make, especially after what we have just been through. For example, I never use price breaks that are the result of even a whiff of accounting irregularities, certainly not after what felled some of the biggest financial firms in the world. You must presume fraud now. Even though it is contrary to the American way, you must always presume guilt and sell rather than bet on innocence and hold. You can always get back in once the irregularity is cured. After the chicanery of insidious fraud throughout the financial system, I think you would be foolish to presume that any institutions in the crosshairs of the SEC might actually not have committed whatever is being charged. Remember, also, you cannot game fraud. You don't know what lurks beneath. You have to presume that everything you first find out is just the tip of the iceberg. If you think I am being too conservative, please, go over the Nortel fraud section of *Jim Cramer's Real Money*, where I kept believing that the company, and then the authorities, had gotten to the bottom of the fraud, only to discover, in the end, that the whole company was taken down by it. I also don't hang on after key executives resign without any reason given for the departure, or a reason that I think is plausible. I've been able to extricate people from some very hot stocks near the top simply by saying, "Nope, that doesn't smell right," only to be vindicated shortly thereafter.

But after what we've been through and the periodic bouts of selling related to fraud, fractured government and foreign woes, we have to tem-

per any enthusiasm we might have for a permabull environment and recognize that the moment we lose our skepticism is the moment we start
losing our money. In a tough market, different rules apply, as I found out
the hard way with my charitable trust during the big downturn that occurred in conjunction with the Great Recession. That hideous market
forced me to reexamine a lot of explanations for why I stick with a stock
and to change them, perhaps permanently, because the world is a different
place in light of the near total financial collapse we endured. Put simply, I
learned some valuable lessons, new rules to deal with the downside when
things go wrong with the market as a whole. I think the rules can apply to
any stock that you own that might be in the midst of a prolonged spiral,
regardless of the genus of the animal—bull or bear—that currently rules
the day. Specifically, what I find to be the most confounding part of the
new risk management I am urging is determining when a stock has finished going down. The possibility of a still more dramatic decline after a
sustained beating keeps us from acting in a rational way when great opportunity might be knocking. But the skepticism over whether a bottom
has been reached has also saved us. Of course, when we rush in too soon,
as so many did in the past few years, after what was thought to be a prolonged decline, we could end up crushed to smithereens.

Spotting a real bottom may be among the most confounding tasks
when managing your own money. As I reviewed all my ActionALertsPlus
.com bulletins, I found that I repeatedly moved too soon to buy and left
too late to sell. Far too often I thought a stock I was eyeing or owned had
bottomed after a prolonged spiral. So I catalogued all the instances where
I got it wrong—plunged too soon or had a misplaced sense of security
about the end of the sell-off—and grouped them into patterns I am label-
ing False Floors, situations where I made the same mistakes repeatedly.
There are a variety of phony bottoms, ones that can produce hefty losses
when you rely or just lean on them. After reading over these seven False
Floors, ask yourself whether you have used one of these self-justifications
to stay in stocks that you would otherwise be jettisoning. I know I had,
until I sat down and saw these same patterns where I could have cut losses
far earlier than I did.

The First False Floor? The BIG buyback.

A big stock buyback cannot put a floor on a stock in a severe market downturn or if the company isn't producing good numbers. Far too often, buybacks do nothing to prop up a stock and can be a huge waste of money for the companies that try to put their fingers in the selling dike. I saw this pattern creeping into my bulletins too often to count, and I was lulled into a false sense of safety in stocks as varied as Sears Holdings, which announced a $1.5 billion buyback when the stock was at $137; Cisco, which bought back billions of dollars of stock at incredibly high prices that did nothing to stem the decline; and Kohl's, which announced an accelerated buyback—another overrated term—when the stock was at $53 and then almost immediately got crushed after the press release heralded the repurchase.

Why don't buybacks give you any cushion? First, they are often just ways for companies to "make the numbers" by shrinking the denominator when it is divided into the earnings. Fewer shares divided into a slightly higher profit line can produce an earnings-per-share gain year over year that looks much more dramatic than it really is. I am not against shrinking the number of shares per se. It can produce greater profits for remaining shareholders. For several years after the stock market bottomed in 2009, for instance, the number one performing stock was Wyndham Worldwide, the hotelier, and much of that performance stemmed from a huge buyback that aggressively shrank the number of shares outstanding, allowing for much bigger earnings-per-share numbers than previous years and, at the same time, it put through ever larger dividend increases. That combination, not just the buyback, led to the tremendous outperformance that Wyndham generated.

But very often buybacks result in almost no net shrinkage of any kind because the company is busy doling out big option grants that offset the declines. Or the buybacks are done insanely stupidly, with no regard to price, just the same amount taken in each day. Many of the executives I talk to who are doing buybacks are clueless about the tactical importance of how a buyback should be done. The company should be aggressive when the stock is being hammered and walk away to keep the powder dry when the action is calm. So often we would have hugely volatile days, with tremendous selling pressure by the S&P 500 futures or ETFs that greatly impacted the stocks of companies doing incredibly well, and the managements were totally oblivious to the opportunity or didn't think it was even important to take advantage of. Any time you are buying stock, you must time it effectively or it can be a huge waste of firepower. The same is true for a company that buys stock. Lots of execs seem to check their brains at the door of the New York Stock Exchange or the NASDAQ when they go in to buy. They seem to revel in their own ignorance, as if someone taught them, "Look, price doesn't matter." Price *always* matters. They are lazy thinkers, and I think less of their companies when they intimate to me that they just do their buybacks by rote or take them out of the company's hands entirely and give them to brokers to fill. There's simply not enough incentive for that broker to do a good enough job when he's got a carte blanche order. He's certainly not going to stick his neck out and buy aggressively during a marketwide downturn caused by something, an event stemming from overseas, for example, that has nothing to do with the enterprise he's buying for. Yet that's precisely when the most help is needed for existing shareholders to fathom whether to buy more or cut and run. It is also the best opportunity to get in stock at prices below what you might normally expect to receive if the business is on track.

So please, don't be lulled into thinking that a big buyback must necessarily have an impact on a stock that might otherwise be falling, and falling hard. Most are simply poorly executed, and most certainly can't stem any decline. They are definitive False Floors because they either are not at work in the thick of a downturn or are not meant to be anything but automatic, the same amount per day at the same hour per day and nothing more.

False Floor 2: No stocks are too cheap to sell.

When I looked over the Friday-night bulletins that my charitable trust sends out, I was struck at how many times I justified owning bad stocks that were shedding points left and right by saying the stocks were "too cheap to sell." Sometimes I would purchase shares in one of these cascading knives because, I wrote, it was "too cheap not to buy." The alibi came up far too often, and it was often followed by further declines almost immediately after my buys were made.

Why is this idea so important? Because stocks that are too cheap have a tendency to get even cheaper and cheaper for a reason you don't know about at the time or for an overarching reason you are just not seeing but others are.

If you think a stock is getting "too cheap," I want you to think of that as your own personal red flag, a crutch that may not hold up under close scrutiny. If you find yourself using this logic, ask yourself whether you are looking at too small a picture. Is there something bigger happening in the industry? Is there something happening, say, in China that might be impacting your stock, as the United States may no longer be at the fulcrum of an American company's earnings? Is there something happening in Europe you haven't thought of that could be impacting the bottom line? How about some potential intervention by the federal government? Could someone have invented a better product? Is there a price war going on you don't know about? But please, do not contain your investigation just to the fundamentals of that company alone or the public research. There could be something looming away from the company, and that "too cheap" floor might be nothing but a sheet of dirty linoleum.

The "too cheap" rationale that you might be using comes in many colors, shapes, sizes and disguises, all of them just different varieties of fooling yourself. Several times our bulletins seized on the phrase "multiyear lows" as a reason to buy a stock, as if somehow the range of a stock contained the answer to where it could be stopped. Occasionally we diverged and wrote "multimonth lows" to give us a prop to take action.

Stocks tend to hit lows because they *should* hit lows. In a bull market, stocks often break out of long ranges. You would never think, Wow, I have to sell it because it has hit multiyear highs. You should be inclined perhaps to scale out of some stock to take out your cost of capital, but the range of the stock shouldn't really be part of the calculus. Maybe a stock hitting multimonth highs is trying to tell you something, namely that the company is operating at much better levels of sales, gross margins and profitability than anyone thinks. It stands to reason that a stock hitting multimonth lows might be saying the exact opposite.

Sometimes I justified mistaken buys with alerts that offered this gem: "It's cheap compared to what it could be worth." The problem here? Stocks tend to stay cheap versus their intrinsic value *unless* management chooses to bring out that value. If a company chooses to divide itself up and conquer, like so many of the oil companies that separated into refining and marketing and exploration and production companies, then your "cheap" thesis works. But just as often, a stock that's cheap tends to stay cheap, particularly one that can't be taken over. Unless you have unlimited patience and don't mind sitting out the upside that might be all around you, avoid the "too cheap" justification.

Another, slightly more rigorous-sounding floor is the "price-to-earnings multiple" alibi. I fell for this one hard during the Great Recession and its aftermath. For example, in August 2007, just when the economy was starting to roll over, we justified buying Caterpillar because it sold at only thirteen times earnings. Sure enough, not long after that it sold for only twelve times earnings. Then only ten times. Ultimately it sold at a single-digit multiple to earnings. There was one problem, though. My earnings estimates were way off because the company's sales fell apart as customers either couldn't get enough credit to buy big machines or they stopped ordering altogether because of a lack of demand for their own products. Turns out the stock wasn't selling at a cheap price-to-earnings multiple at all, because the earnings were cut, literally, in half. That meant the stock was selling at an extremely *high* price-to-earnings ratio exactly when I thought it was so cheap!

Here's another crutch that will invariably let you down: buying a stock because it seems "too cheap" on what is known as "normalized earnings power." All stocks have histories of what they have been able to earn over time. Most companies with long-term track records have a fairly well documented level of core profitability that can be easily estimated, which is referred to as normalized earnings power—the return it can be expected to give you in decent times. For example, banks that have deposits and make loans have had a fairly regular pattern of earnings based on the profits they make from your deposits and from lending. Sure, some loans will go bad, and some banks may not be able to make that much money on your deposits because interest rates are so low. Historically, though, there is a baseline of profitability, a normalized earnings power that you can value and figure out how much it is worth. When a stock trades below the average price-to-earnings multiple that's been paid over time for that normalized earnings stream, it is supposed to be a bargain.

That's exactly what I thought I was getting when the trust bought Bank of America at $16.78 in December 2009. I told readers that shares of Bank of America, which had plummeted from the $50s to the teens, "were discounting a lot of bad news" and were too cheap because the "shares trade at less than six times normalized earnings." In other words, I had calculated that Bank of America had a core level of $3 in earnings power just from feasting off of its deposits, and it seemed inconceivable to me that the stock could stay down at six times earnings given that core earnings power. It was just too cheap.

We know now that Bank of America at $16 turned out to be incredibly expensive because these weren't normal times, so there was no normalized earnings power to speak of. There were just losses as far as the eye could see. Sure, Bank of America might have seemed colossally inexpensive based on its long-term ability to earn $3, but it wasn't making much on those deposits because interest rates were so low and it was losing a huge amount of money on its mortgage business, as housing had broken its historic pattern of price appreciation. The losses on those loans overwhelmed all the traditional earnings streams and fees that banks get just by taking your deposits. The stock soon afterward traded down to $10, where it was then selling at three times that nonexistent normalized earnings stream. It finally bottomed at $5 because Warren Buffett took a stake in the company. The moral: don't buy stocks that look cheap on normalized earnings power because, when times are not normal, there may be no earnings at all.

It's not just hard times, though, that can destroy the crutch of normalized earnings power. In February 2010 I was drawn to the stock of Teva Pharmaceutical at $58 because it had historically sold at eighteen times earnings and, after several rough months, had fallen to a level where it traded at just twelve times earnings. When the trust bought the stock we told subscribers that this high-quality hybrid of proprietary medicines and generic drugs was trading well below its normal price-to-earnings multiple on its historic core earnings power and was, therefore, too cheap to ignore.

Sure enough, a few weeks later Teva fell to the low $50s and I was encouraged to buy more stock, as it now sold for just eleven times earnings. I reassured myself by checking that Teva's major drug, an anti–multiple sclerosis medicine called Copaxone, responsible for a huge amount of its proprietary drug earnings stream, was still selling well, and I knew that its generic business was going like gangbusters because it was copycatting so many blockbuster drugs that were coming off patent during that year.

Then the stock took another step down, shedding still one more multiple point. It was at that moment, with the stock trading in the mid-$40s, down gigantically from when I first starting buying it, that I learned that one of Teva's competitors had been able to come up with a generic challenge to Copaxone, something the company had repeatedly assured us could not happen. The challenge wouldn't arise immediately, so near-term earnings wouldn't be hurt. But when the generic launched, perhaps in 2015, or even earlier, the earnings from that drug would be cut to ribbons. Once a proprietary drug like Copaxone goes off patent or gets generic competition, it's pretty much finished as a source of growth and earnings. Sure, Teva seemed really cheap versus what it could earn in 2012, but in the out years, which I have told you repeatedly is far more important than the near term for most growth investors, Teva was extremely expensive because Copaxone's proprietary status would be challenged well ahead of when the company believed it to possible.

Teva's price-to-earnings multiple support on that core earnings power I was so excited about turned out to be chimerical, and the stock ultimately sold down to the mid-$30s. It never came back because the normalized earnings stream was disappearing before our eyes as the competition to Copaxone caused a dramatic and lasting long-term decline in the company's earnings ability. Oh, and believe me, the company never told you about this threat; I am not certain they even knew about it.

False Floor 3: The last man standing bottom.

One of the most foolish rationalizations available when all stocks in a given sector are in free fall is that a company you like and want to buy in this declining sector could be the "last man standing." I applied this analysis to various industries, including coal companies, banks and earthmovers, during the market's severe downturn. In each case I predicted that the company's shares I was buying had to bottom soon because times were so tough that many of its competitors were shutting down or moving on. It would be the proverbial last man standing.

It turned out that there were many competitors with more staying power than I thought. Plus, the pressure on the sector extended to even the best of breed, so my "last man standing" hypothesis didn't mean all that much when it came to what even the best company could earn in that environment. For example, my trust bought the stock of JPMorgan right before the last big bank downturn in March 2009. I said it was the only bank with a "fortress" balance sheet, so it would come out of the downturn with very little competition. It would be the last man standing among the big banks. In the meantime, though, its earnings were crushed by the downturn, causing the stock to take a real hit even as its business was holding up better than the others in its sector. Still, I had high hopes that many of the other competitors would be too hobbled to stay in business, and that's when JPMorgan would clean up. Things got so dire, though, that the government forced all banks to recapitalize, even the good ones like JPMorgan, and it bailed out most of the competition. That dilution from the equity that every bank had to raise to meet new standards set by the Treasury Department crushed JPMorgan, along with all of the other stocks in its sector. The competition never got a chance to be diminished, though, because the government simply wouldn't let it happen. Almost all banks, good and bad, were left standing in the end.

False Floor 4: Liquidation is no reason to buy.

I saw this happen during the period I analyzed on three different occasions, first with Freeport-McMoRan Copper, then with National Oilwell Varco, and finally with the gold stocks.

We were tempted by all three because we thought they had been knocked down unnaturally by hedge funds that had gone bust. We had read about how they had to be sold to meet hedge fund redemptions, and therefore the sellers were creating some terrific bargains for us in all three. In each case a large hedge fund was indeed liquidating, but in each case, despite the duress the funds were suffering, there were greater forces driving the selling, such as a worldwide slowdown, a decline in the price of oil or a slowdown in emerging market gold buying.

If you buy a stock because you thought that the liquidation selling had to let up eventually, you are going to be making a serious mistake. You see, there are liquidations going on behind the scenes all the time. The stocks that can't take it, the stocks that are being taken down by the selling, tend to be the stocks of companies where smart money knows not to buy because something's actually wrong with the companies. In other words, the stock of a healthy company can withstand liquidation pressure and you wouldn't even know the liquidation is going on. Stocks with weaker earnings or declining earnings break down quickly when a large holder is liquidating. That was the case in all three of the liquidation "bargains" I thought I was getting. These stocks weren't getting cheap on the way down because of liquidations. They were getting *expensive* on the way down because their earnings were about to be slashed.

False Floor 5: The bogus commodity bottom.

So often you will hear that the stock of a commodity producer should be bought because, although the stock is down, the commodity itself is still hanging on. The trust bought several oil and gas companies, big and small, because of this logic, and we lost badly by doing so. I discovered a pattern when looking back at these mistaken purchases. It turns out that the stocks peaked well ahead of when the commodities peaked. The commodities didn't predict the price; the stocks did. That meant that my fundamental tenet, that a stock's earnings would hold up because the commodity it produced wasn't going down in value, was fatally flawed.

In other words, if Chevron produces oil, and Chevron goes down but oil stays flat, do not presume that you have found a legitimate bargain-basement steal in Chevron. In fact, a decline in Chevron's stock, or any other oil and gas play, is far more often a precursor to the direction of the underlying commodity. So you end up getting hit with a double whammy: a stock falls in what turns out to be anticipation of a collapse in a commodity, and then when the commodity collapses analysts slash estimates for all of the companies that sell that commodity.

False Floor 6: The recognition that you owned something that you didn't think you owned.

Throughout the downturn I kept thinking that the stocks of makers of gigantic pieces of equipment like planes, earthmovers, tractors or farm equipment represented great value, and I could not understand for the life of me how they could keep going down despite their excellent *long-term* prospects. What I didn't realize was that companies that make these big-ticket items need to help the buyer finance the purchase. When things are going along fine, you never think that financing could be an issue. But when the economy slows dramatically, or the Federal Reserve tightens credit, the money needed to finance the product might not be there. At the bottom in the economy, Caterpillar, Deere, Joy Global and even General Electric traded more like banks than they did manufacturers, and I was blown out of the water by the subtle switch. So, ask yourself: Does it take financing for the company to do its business? If the answer is yes, be prepared to take evasive action if we get a sudden jolt to the economy. Of course, it's not just big manufacturers that have finance risk. Department store chains too need financing to stay in business; they can't afford the cash to buy all of the wares they sell. That's why I like to buy the stocks of the retailers with only the cleanest balance sheets. You can get crushed not knowing that the retailer you want to own might get its credit cut off before Christmas; almost no retailer can get through the holiday season without it. Think back to the fiasco that was J. C. Penney when it told us things were going well back in September of 2013 and then did a surprise 84-million share equity deal to be sure the most important constituency, the creditors, would give them the money needed to stock up for the holiday season. So make sure that balance sheet is a thing of beauty before you swoop in on a retailer that seems to be trading much lower than you think it should be. If it isn't, that solid floor you think you are standing on may be made of nothing that can withstand your portfolio's weight.

False Floor 7: The high dividend.

I spend a great deal of time on air and in my writings for TheStreet urging you to buy stocks of accidentally high yielders, meaning stocks that have fallen so fast that suddenly they have a very good yield relative to the return you can get from a comparable fixed-income security. But you have to be sure, beyond a shadow of a doubt, that the company itself can afford the dividend. If you think it can be cut, if you think that the dividend is at all not safe, this is a terrible place to try to bottom-fish. It might turn out that you are in the Mariana Trench of value fishing. I found out the hard way when I bet on Citigroup's yield as a potential floor. Same with General Electric, which had repeatedly assured you that its dividend would not be cut.

How can you avoid falling through the dividend floor? First, you can always just check to see what a company is earning, and if it is well short of the amount the company is paying out, just forget it, you have to sell it, unless the company has heavy depreciation and amortization costs that depress the reported profits. These measures can be difficult to calculate. But I have another way to flag it. You simply have to look at what other companies in the industry are offering. If the company's yield is well in excess of what the other companies in the cohort are paying, stay away.

We saw this happen with several telecommunications stocks with yields that were much larger than industry stalwarts Verizon and AT&T. That was a huge red flag. They had to be sold as soon as they were out of whack with the benchmarks, as shareholders of Frontier Communications and CenturyLink know all too well.

We saw the same phenomenon in 2012 when Excelon, the huge Chicago-based utility company, sported a yield well in excess of the rest of the industry. And we saw it in 2013 with Atlantic Power, whose yield was twice as high as the average power company's stock. Both eventually hacked their payouts, and the shareholders got hacked right along with them.

Let me make one thing perfectly clear: no outsized dividend from a financial is ever worth trusting again. As I wrote earlier, the financials demand a higher standard of scrutiny and are now simply too risky to own for most investors. Financials with exceedingly large dividends simply have to be passed up, no matter how juicy they may be or how intelligent the backers of the enterprise sound when they tell you the dividend is safe. Many operators, such as the execs who run mortgage real estate investment trusts, which borrow a lot of money to buy mortgage bonds, simply didn't understand what could go wrong if the housing market changed radically or the Fed backed away from its commitment to keep rates low. Most mortgage REIT companies ended up having to slash their payouts not long after they told you that all would be fine. I am not saying they would fail a lie detector test; I am simply saying that after what we saw happen to some esteemed, well-respected firms in the previous decade, it makes no sense to take our chances with these kinds of companies now. We will not get rich chasing these red-flagged yields. After what we have seen happen, they are the essence of what must be avoided. Don't worry, we will find a way to make money, just not with pumped-up dividends from companies that dwell in the world of finance.

Summary of False Floors: Don't Fall Through Them

What conclusions can we reach about floors after going through the seven that I crashed through? I think you have to ask yourself if you are simply making an alibi for the poor performance of one of your stocks. Are you just choosing to come up with some rationalization that verifies a mistake you made or a changed circumstance that you are not aware of? If so, be more critical. Stop pretending that your stock will cease going down because it has already struck terra firma. Face up to the idea that you might be standing on one of the seven False Floors I outlined and get the heck out of that floorless building!

1. A big buyback won't bail you out. It won't be there when you need it and is often for show or just to help execs make their numbers.
2. There is no such thing as a stock that is "too cheap to sell." Stocks go down for a reason. They may get even cheaper than "too cheap to sell" if you aren't careful and stop rationalizing about a bottom.

3. You might be tempted to buy more stock, thinking that the company you own will end up being the last man standing and you'll be the winner when it is. Often there are too many men left standing and the benefits from being the lone holdout never accrue.

4. Stocks can be brought down by sudden liquidations by strapped owners who turn sellers, but if there is nothing wrong with the company, the selling will quickly abate and the stock will go back to where it was. If the stock can't withstand the onslaught or if it doesn't bounce, the fundamentals have probably changed—and for the worse.

5. Don't buy or sell stocks because they are associated with a commodity that hasn't moved in lockstep with your stock. If oil, for example, stays flat, but your oil stock is going down, the stock is a lead indicator. So don't buy it thinking it's gotten cheap versus the commodity.

6. In times of duress, stocks of companies may reflect other concerns, ones that lurk under the surface. Companies that need financing to sell big equipment turn into banks in those situations, and the banks can and do run out of money.

7. Dividends can create floors, but dividends that are "too high" versus the rest of the cohort may not hold up and might end up being cut in the end.

CHAPTER 10

Check Your
Emotions at the Door

As someone who has invested in all kinds of markets in the past four decades, I can tell when something's different. In good times and bad times, we've always been confident that the world was not coming to an end and that the markets themselves could be trusted. A stock represented a business. There was honor to the process. We never questioned whether the market itself would work right. We never thought it could be run by machines so powerful that they could overrun their human masters. We never thought that a major stock market could just shut down for three hours for no real reason or that prestigious multibillion-dollar blue chips could lose half their value between 2:30 and 2:44 p.m. We always thought that Bear Stearns and Lehman would be in business, taking care of our money and offering us solid advice about what to do with it. The largest insurer, the largest car company, the largest savings and loan—these don't disappear. They thrive. The best initial public offering of the era, Facebook, doesn't pick the pockets of those hearty souls still attempting to make money in the stock market while they wait to see if they actually got any stock on the broken deal.

Yet all of that has happened in the past few years. We have seen an asset class itself—not just individual stocks, but an entire asset class—called into question. Every day people pull their money out of the stock market and hide it in inferior assets because it's become unfathomable, treacherous and, most important, unworthy of their trust. I have tried in this book to demonstrate that there are people and businesses and themes that can overcome the vicissitudes, reversals and turmoil that we have seen and experienced throughout this era. But I too fall prey at times to the emotions of the moment, emotions that will plague even the strongest and most thick-skinned.

If we are going to be the best investors we can be, we have to learn how to tame our worries yet stay skeptical enough to make considered judgments about when our investments have gone awry. A scared investor is a terrible investor. But the other bookend, euphoria, is just as toxic to our financial judgment. We are all human, but human nature can be the real enemy to investing with precision and prudence. You need to see, though, how much judgment clouded by fear and greed can really cost us. You need to see how a pro has learned to control those emotions by looking back and detecting patterns that weren't evident at the time mistaken decisions were made. You need to know we are all human, yet humans can still make a ton of money in the stock market.

I now want to show you how I have, at times, failed to check my emotions at the door of my trading and investing and the toll it placed on my money. I believe that if you see that I too made mistakes and yet still came out well ahead, you can recognize that mistakes don't need to derail you and send you back to certificates of deposit and bond funds that can't augment your paycheck in any real way.

I need you to know that you are not alone in committing errors, so you don't get discouraged when you try to Get Rich Carefully and make a mistake that causes you to lose money. I am cataloguing the situations where I failed yet managed to stay in the game, our ultimate goal, until things got better, so you do not say, "I can't do this, I am not equipped or qualified, and I am way too fearful or greedy to make money with my money." I am also showing you that we are all prone to these errors, something you wouldn't know if you simply watched the money managers who come on television and act as if they have never made mistakes. Some of them are so busy marketing 24/7 that they fear if they show that they goofed up or got too afraid or stayed in a stock too long or sold at the bottom, they will lose their assets under management and hurt their own bottom lines. It isn't worth it for them to be truly honest about their own weaknesses. The money goes elsewhere, to their flawless competitors, if they do tell the truth about their foibles.

I am not like these managers. I know my feet can be made of clay. I know that, at times, my head is too big to get in the door, and when that happens I am going to lose some big money. I am human. And I want to show you I am human, because I know you are too. Perfection can never be attained; if you claim you are winning all of the time you are lying to yourself as well as others. I have written about and have a video record of my mistakes; I can't get away from them even if I wanted to. That's because with both ActionAlerts and *Mad Money*, I play with an open hand, my rationales clearly stated in real time. That gives me a unique opportunity to show you when I get it right and, as always, when I fail. Typically when I go wrong it's because of unforeseen events. I was blindsided. Sometimes I make mistakes because my homework was faulty and I didn't follow through on my disciplines. But the biggest error I have ever made is listening to my emotions, the ones colored in fear or etched in greed, that made me lose money and confidence and stand squarely in the face of wealth-building. So sit back and enjoy, snicker even, as I flesh out my biggest boneheaded moves and reveal why they happened and how they better not happen to you. I've got twelve tales, the dirty dozen of emotions run amok, twelve stories that should have gone well for me but ended badly and were the essence of How Not to Get Rich, Recklessly.

Stop Falling in Love With Your Stocks!

I have liked Apple since the $50s. Every single book I have written has emphasized that Apple is the great American marvel. I have told the story about how I discovered Apple as a great investment when my younger daughter asked me to buy her an iPod for the holidays after I had already bought her one for her birthday in May. She was indignant. Of course she needed a second one. The first one was blue, and she needed a pink one, because they weren't mini–music boxes, they were fashion accessories.

From then on, whether it be the Mac, the Mac Air, the iPhone or the iPad, my family was all in Apple. Meanwhile, the sales at Apple kept getting stronger, the cash position larger, and the products more creative than any company I can ever recall—all because of the genius of one man, the founder, Steve Jobs. When Jobs died on October 5, 2011, I told people on *Mad Money* that Apple would never be the same, that it had now become just another stock—albeit one certainly better than average because of the deep product portfolio, the much-loved ecosystem as well as the fabulous cash-overflowing balance sheet—because the greatest inventor of our time was no longer with us.

Still, because of the love and respect people worldwide have for the company, the stock somehow, miraculously, managed to maintain its upward trajectory. I think it is fair to say that it didn't skip a beat pretty much all the way until April 5, 2012, when it hit $639. Even then, after falling to $527 on May 18, 2012, because of a broader market swoon, it proceeded to hit its peak of $702 on September 9, 2012.

My charitable trust owned Apple, and it was by far the biggest win we have ever had. So, like anyone else with a big win, I was reluctant to let it go. I did not show the usual discipline I exert, which would include selling some of the stock with the idea that bulls make money, bears make money and pigs get slaughtered, and I didn't want to be a pig. But in retrospect I sure was, because I had become a believer even as I professed skepticism when I declared the post-Jobs Apple just another stock. I wasn't analyzing; I was just plain in love and didn't want to let go. It was very clear that there was a lot more to Apple than Jobs, I told myself, and those of us who doubted that were already being shamed by the ever-rising stock price after Jobs had passed away.

Then, on October 24, 2012, I had the privilege of interviewing Walter Isaacson, Jobs's biographer, for the opening of a fund drive for a school I like very much, Bucknell University, because my friend and mentor from Goldman Sachs, William Gruver, teaches there and has shown me the wonders of a Bucknell education.

The interview was surreal. I have known Walter for many years and worked for him at *Time* magazine in the 1990s as a stock columnist. I believe his Jobs biography to be the best biography I have ever read. After a few questions about what Jobs was really like—not very nice, I must say—I asked Isaacson whether Jobs had placed some big things in the Apple pipeline before he died, some OMG products, I called them, not just line extensions, but breakthroughs. Isaacson had given Jobs his word that he would not talk about this issue for a full year after his death. Only then could he reveal what huge products Apple had been bequeathed. This would be the first time he spoke about them.

The answer? Basically none. I was astonished. None. NONE! Or at least nothing of any significance. I pressed: How about Apple TV? Isn't that going to be the next big thing? Isaacson said he didn't think so, because just as Apple needed the cooperation of the record companies to do iTunes, it would need the cooperation of the cable TV networks. And the cable companies are much better capitalized and can't be "rolled" like the music execs.

How about anything else, anything revolutionary, anything that would make us say "I love this company even more"? Nope, Isaacson said. What you saw is what you got and no more than that.

When I got back to New York, I huddled with Stephanie Link, my co–portfolio manager, and we let our subscribers to ActionAlertsPlus.com know that when we weren't restricted—tough call because I seem to talk about Apple every day—we would have to let some Apple go. No new OMG products meant the earnings momentum couldn't be maintained.

We eventually did sell half of our stock as soon as we could and got a price that was, in retrospect, pretty darned close to the top. But the trust held on to the rest because, like so many others, I believed. I had made so much money in the stock, I had ultimate faith in the company and, other than from Isaacson's revelation, I was getting no negative feedback about the future of Apple.

And then, on January 11, with the stock at $520, down almost 200 points from the high, I got the following text from my elder daughter, who, like her sister, had been so instrumental in steering me toward the products, the company and ultimately the stock. "Ugh can you please complain to someone that the new iTunes update is so confusing and doesn't make sense!!! Everyone hates it!!! Email Steve Jobs's replacement guy, it's horrible, ugh." She then proceeded to text me—we never seem to talk anymore, just text—about how much she hated having to carry two plugs because of the new products and how Google Maps was so much better than Apple Maps and that Steve Jobs would never have swapped out a good product by a competitor for a bad product by Apple.

I went on *Mad Money* that next week and said what I should have said 180 points before that: Apple's got real problems, and I, like so many others, was in denial. The rest, of course, seems pretty logical in retrospect: the hideous swoon down to almost half of its high, brought on by a combination of no OMG products for 2013, just line extensions and configurations, and fans who increasingly have turned on Apple in one way or another and gone to a competitive product, typically the wares of Korean giant Samsung.

I am not saying that the stock is a buy or it isn't. In fact, after the company instituted a nice-size dividend and a good buyback, I was confident that a bottom had been put in. And I felt even better about the stock after the new phones came out in September of 2013 and showed a ton of innovation that leapfrogged over the Samsung models now available. No, I am simply saying that with the stock at $700 near its all-time high, despite having superior information that cast legitimate doubts on Apple's future, I had suspended my judgment and didn't follow my discipline because I was smitten with the stock. I had gotten carried away, and I regret it as a serious error of judgment that should not be repeated by me or by you. It was a sobering public lesson in how falling in love with stocks blinds your judgment to doing the right thing. In the end, stocks are just pieces of paper, nothing more. I had insight from Isaacson, the acknowledged expert on Jobs and the company, and from the very person who first turned me on to Apple, my daughter, and I still hesitated to do the right thing.

It wasn't the first time I let my emotions get the better of me. I had gotten behind the stock of Chipotle, another company my vegetarian kids introduced me to, way back in the $40s, when I started *Mad Money* in the 2005. Here was a company that wasn't part of the fast-food chain complex as we knew it. It was about something different, about Food with Integrity, the company's mantra. It aspired to be organic with an emphasis on freshness and health, with no compromises on taste.

The culture at Chipotle is a lot like the culture at several other companies I admire, including Costco, Starbucks and Whole Foods—all the managements are friendly with each other, by the way—with an ethic that aspires to be more than just successful as measured by dollars and cents, although the profit motive is extremely important to each company. It's fair to say that if you asked the managements about the impetus for the success of all four companies, they would say it stems from a superior culture, which begins with nurturing and keeping the best employees, treating them with respect and listening to them. As I mentioned earlier, that's what the retired Costco CEO Jim Sinegal told me is the secret of Costco's success: a lack of turnover that makes Costco's training costs dramatically lower than the competition's, so he can keep merchandise costs dramatically lower than the competition's.

Only Chipotle pays as close attention to these important intangibles as Costco, and it's been integral to why I like the stock, beyond the Food with Integrity strategy. Chipotle is a classic growth stock, one where earnings "beats" (shorthand for better-than-expected earnings) had become a given. While the stock always looked expensive on current earnings, when you saw the future earnings estimates trounced in the out years, sometimes by as much as 20, 30 or 40 percent, you realized that it was quite cheap in retrospect. For example, in 2010 the stock was trading in the $90s, and the analysts who followed the company predicted collectively, via the consensus numbers, that the company was supposed to earn about $4, or a steep twenty times future earnings, when the average stock in the S&P 500 traded at just fourteen times earnings.

Turns out Chipotle ultimately earned $5.64, beating that estimate by $1.64, so what looked expensive in 2010 turned out to be darned cheap in 2011. That's what happens when you have such tremendous growth in earnings power, as Chipotle did because of its wildly popular fresh offerings and its aggressive expansion plans. It simply wasn't expensive retrospectively.

That's why I wanted to give the company all of the benefit of the doubt when it posted slower comparable-store sales numbers in 2012, the key metric, as I mentioned earlier, for any retailer, as you want to measure how a like-for-like store is doing. Yes, you can add tons of additional stores to bulk up on revenues, but if the older stores aren't doing well you might be cannibalizing them or not running them efficiently, and that could lead to real problems down the road.

When I first saw the 2012 slowdown materialize, I told people not to worry about the comparable-store sales slowing from 12.7 percent in the first quarter to 8 percent because it was just a blip. Chipotle had gotten out of trouble before, when it was a lot smaller and still intriguing and winning over the public. The numbers would bounce right back to the trend line. The reacceleration of growth was right around the corner. That's because, as with Apple, I "believed." I had tremendous faith in the company's ability to navigate any headwind and, in retrospect, was willing to suspend critical thinking.

Well, what I believed sure didn't matter, because when the same-store sales rebound I was looking for failed to materialize and instead accelerated farther downward, the stock plummeted from $403 to $316, an astounding and disheartening 22 percent decline *in a single day*. I had violated a cardinal sin, suspending discipline that simply can't be violated in this new world where stocks can get hit far harder than anyone believed possible.

But the tailspin was still not complete. The stock of Chipotle proceeded to give up another eighty points as comparable-store sales slowed the next quarter too. It wasn't just a one-time miss, or even a two-time miss. The slowing economy had overtaken even the great Chipotle.

Company representatives were somewhat chagrined when I questioned whether a pricier Chipotle was losing out to the other guy, a reinvigorated Taco Bell. Or perhaps people were just staying home or were ordering cheaper products on the menu, skipping the soda, trading down for a salad. Clearly there was a major degradation.

In retrospect, as in the case of Apple, I should have been advising people to take some profits, because even though Chipotle had been executing perfectly, the run had been so terrific and the gains so outsized that I should have been more forceful in trying to protect them for people. I let my emotions and my admiration for the management team get in the way of my discipline. The Chipotle folks were mortal after all.

The sudden deceleration didn't mean that Chipotle should be written off. The company is expanding overseas, it is nurturing a new noodle concept as well as a vegetarian theme, and the brand loyalty remains strong as well as the loyalty of the managers, in large part because the good ones are routinely promoted and given larger responsibilities. The corporate officers at the top are still best in show and the envy of the industry and because of that culture the stock did bounce all the way back. But I was blinded by the profit light and wasn't skeptical enough, because while management may be imbued with respect for the workforce and with the desire to improve the food chain and serve Food with Integrity, in the end they are just selling really good food at very good prices and are not immune to occasional glitches. In fact, had I been unemotional I would have simply sidestepped the decline and then come back in when the same-store sales eventually did get better, as I knew they would. In this tough time, though, you take evasive action when your discipline says you should, and then you can come back and make more money with much less risk. Again, I had fallen in love, and the love was, alas, in the $400s, no longer requited. Had I been cool and calculating and recognized that Chipotle could stumble if same-store sales had slowed, I would have been in the ideal position to come back to the story after the fluff was gone and the company was ready to fly high again.

Don't Be More Bullish Than the Company

Remember the theme of this chapter: Don't let your emotions get in the way of the cold hard facts, because if you are too joyous and too enthusiastic, you can distort those facts with your own mind-set. You won't hear people on television talk about this kind of flaw, because it is one that could easily come back to haunt them. They can be ridiculed. They can be embarrassed, as now, in the YouTube generation, mistakes can be played back endlessly. I know mine are played back, but because I am not trying to raise money and am just trying to teach and coach, I accept that, as in sports, you have to take the losses with the wins. That's vital for you because you too will make mistakes, and if you never hear any pros admit to mistakes you might surrender control of your money to them and go on autopilot, which I regard as a huge impediment to getting rich through the stock market. The "I never make a mistake" mind-set of very good money managers is, indeed, nonsense, as my trip to the iconic Ford F-150 plant on January 12, 2011, shows without a scintilla of doubt.

On *Mad Money* we are proud of American manufacturing might. Despite higher labor costs than some of our competitive trading partners, we are still the best manufacturers in the world of so many products, including the Ford 150 pickup, the best-selling truck of all time. So when Ford invited us to Dearborn, Michigan, to do our show from the factory floor as part of our "Invest in America" series, we jumped at the chance. Who wouldn't? Unlike the other members of the Big Three, Chrysler and General Motors, Ford didn't need a bailout. Its CEO, Alan Mulally, one of my Bankable 21 worth backing wherever he goes, is the rare combination of someone who knows cars and how to build them as well as a man who knows the finance side of the world. Amazingly, you could say the exact same thing about him when he managed commercial aircraft during his days at Boeing.

When it became clear to a very prescient Mulally that the United States could be in for a downturn like no other in our lifetime, he went to the bond markets and raised billions in relatively cheap capital so his company was fortified for the losses that all of the automobile manufacturers experienced in the Great Recession. I consider Mulally a miracle worker, and our trip to the factory was as much a celebration of his stewardship as of Ford Motor Company itself.

Oh, I had a grand time. While filming in Alan's office, I met Bill Ford, chairman of the namesake company, and joshed with him about how he was having a tough year. Bill was momentarily taken aback and sprang to Ford's defense, until I set him straight that I was actually talking about the horrendous season the Detroit Lions, the team Ford owns, had just concluded. Good chuckles all around.

Mulally gave me a tour of the plant; we test-drove some early versions of what would end up being Ford's best-selling car, the Fusion; and I sat in the trading room where Ford hedges its raw products that go into every car.

So I was pumped to the max when we got to throngs of workers who took time off from the line to hear the show. How could I not be? Go back and take a look at the chart of Ford on the day of the show, January 12, 2011. Ford traded at $18 that day. A new high for the era. Even better, *don't* take a look at the chart, because it mocks my judgment. Ford's pictograph looks like the peak of Everest, with the right side encompassing the cliff that starts forming literally the week after our visit to the factory. In other words, the stock topped right when I had come to praise it and cheer it on.

After I congratulated Alan for delivering the company through this rough patch that felled the others, I started the questioning by asking whether he thought Ford had the capability of earning $5 in 2015, about two and a half times what Ford had racked up in profits the previous year. Alan demurred. I egged him on, prodding whether, given the fact that Ford was firing on the equivalent of eight cylinders, that big number wasn't a given. He resisted again, assuring me that nothing in the auto business is a given but that he had created a fortress balance sheet and would soon restore Ford's dividend to its old fat glory if all went well.

I told him that while he might be shy and cautious, I saw $5 in the cards and a stock that could go considerably higher given what I was seeing in the turnaround for the Dearborn giant. Mulally simply refused to take the bait, and after another round of questions I circled back and made my prediction that this would be the beginning of a multiyear run for Ford Motor given its tremendous new earnings power.

I could not have been more wrong. Eighteen months later, the stock had lost more than half of its value, falling from $18 to $8. The culprit? While the United States continued to gain steam and gain share, Ford has a huge business in Europe, and Europe had just begun its long slide back into recession, destroying Ford's longtime profitability and generating hideous losses that literally wiped out any earnings Ford North America could report. Because of Europe, Ford's earnings hit a retaining wall and actually *fell* more than 20 percent soon after I visited Dearborn. My $5 earnings estimate for 2015 was just an emotional pipe dream.

But here's what's important: that was *my* pipe dream, not Alan Mulally's. I had become intoxicated with Ford's success. I had become too proud of what Ford *had* accomplished and projected it to a very uncertain future. It was my enthusiasm that had led me astray, not Mulally's.

Now, of course, you could easily say, "Wait a second, Jim. Ford let you down." Alan didn't see the severity of the European downturn coming and didn't trim operations fast enough. However, neither did anyone else. Tough to blame Mulally for not being able to see around the corner when no other executive I know did either. Nope, it was all on me. I had failed to check my enthusiasm at the door of the F-150 plant, and the subsequent sickening decline in the face of my hubris is a reminder of just how difficult this business can be and how humbling the results are when you think you know more than the man who's making the trucks rolling off the assembly line right in front of you.

Even the Best CEOs are Not Miracle Workers

When I speak about my bankable CEOs, I am saying that these twenty-one people can transcend the toxic environment we find ourselves in and inspire their companies to thrive, no matter what. But what happens when a company is stuck in an industry so horrid that even the best and the brightest can't pull it off? That's the story with Alcoa and how I became intoxicated with the possibilities of the company after meeting Klaus Kleinfeld, its truly brilliant chief executive officer.

Many companies had been whacked and whacked hard by the Great Recession, but few had been poleaxed as badly as the nation's number one aluminum maker. The stock had traveled from the mid-$40s before the bruising downturn, where it had been a leader in the Dow Jones Average, to the mid-teens as earnings collapsed for this commodity metal that is incredibly sensitive to the economy.

Most international companies that are headquartered here in the United States, after years of attracting some very parochial chief executive officers, including Alcoa, began hiring far more cosmopolitan people as their businesses expanded well beyond our nation's borders. They had to, because this country has little real growth, and growth, as I always tell you, is the most important ingredient to a higher stock price. You can't be based here and sell raw materials here and expect to prosper. You have to sell into all markets, especially the emerging ones that can maintain growth for years to come. Earlier in the decade Alcoa, long a parochial company, chose a total anomaly for even the most forward of American companies, the erudite Klaus Kleinfeld, a sophisticated German who is a man of the world.

But don't mistake his refined manner for someone who wouldn't take on the high costs of refining aluminum. Kleinfeld's both a cost-cutter and a builder, quick to shut down unprofitable mills, particularly ones that aren't being utilized enough, like Alcoa's European plants, and instead expand in low-cost areas where energy costs are cheapest, including Saudi Arabia, or where demand is most needed, such as his plant in Tennessee, close to some of the biggest truck-making operations in the country.

There are some executives who can really teach you about how their business, alien to the generalist, actually works. You sit there rapt, knowing that they know so much more about their business than you ever will. But a jack-of-all-trades such as myself has to know a little bit of everything to be able to write and talk about stocks as much as I do, and each time I sit down with Kleinfeld, as I try to do after every quarter, I glean more eye-opening wisdom that makes me a better student of the ways of the business world.

That's why I figured that such a smart man would be able to turn Alcoa from a company with very big losses during the Great Recession to hefty profits in better times. His ruthless lack of toleration of losses pretty much assured those of us who follow Alcoa that his ardor for his job would be rewarded with a higher stock price. That's what I told viewers when the stock traded in the mid-teens, as the company seemed well on its way to its $40 perch, where it stood before the hideous collapse of its earnings.

But I hadn't counted on several issues. First, the Chinese, who are high-cost producers of aluminum—and egregious creators of pollution in doing so—simply didn't cut back at all as the downturn progressed. If anything, they kept adding capacity. Second, while demand held up for some of the critical operations that need aluminum, namely airlines and autos, one of the biggest users of aluminum, commercial construction, was put on hold around the world. Third, at the same time, financial interests, namely hedge funds, leaned heavily against the commodity as a way to play the downturn, and they have never let up. They have exerted tremendous pressure on the metal and have slammed it down every time it picks up its head. That's all part of the new, treacherous world, where stocks and commodities are playthings for these giant pools of capital.

Sadly for Alcoa and its shareholders, the demand for aluminum softened at precisely the time when supply boomed. There was simply no place to put all of the aluminum that the world's smelters were producing. The result? Despite one of the most amazing cost takeouts I have ever seen, Alcoa simply couldn't generate anywhere near the earnings that would have been expected at that point in the comeback cycle. And just when it looked like demand was stabilizing, Europe, a continent with 700 million people, hit a wall, and demand dropped precipitously. At the same time, China's property market had gotten overheated, and that led to a huge decline in the only country that had a growing commercial construction business, the type of construction that creates the biggest demand for the distinctly nonprecious metal.

The result was a glut of insane proportions that, despite Kleinfeld's best efforts—and they were herculean—it just didn't matter. Alcoa's stock price collapsed right along with the price of the raw metal. I had learned, brutally, that despite the near miracles Kleinfeld had performed, there was just too much capacity putting out too much aluminum for too few users. No one man can change an industry this complex, particularly when one of the main participants in the industry, China, simply won't cooperate with what's economically or medically rational. People have to be put to work in that country even if their chances of respiratory illness are far greater than for just about any profession in the world. Ultimately the stock fell to the mid–single digits from my mid-teens recommendation and then suffered the indignity of being booted from the Dow Jones Industrial Average after forty years of inclusion.

The lesson: never become so enamored of an executive, even one as talented at Kleinfeld, when his company faces monumental commodity headwinds. Ultimately, I am confident that Alcoa will rise again because of changes put through by Kleinfeld. But I misjudged the dangers of commodity investing even with a fabulous CEO at the helm.

Sometimes You Can Be Too Skeptical

Sometimes you let your emotions get to you the other way: you grow too skeptical, too negative or too fearful simply because you don't believe an executive is capable of navigating the waters of an increasingly difficult world economy.

Such was the case with me and Greg Wasson, the chief executive officer of the nation's largest and oldest drugstore chain, Walgreens. I had been recommending Walgreens as a terrific value play in the mid-$30, but I didn't truly see the potential for Wasson's work until he purchased the Duane Reade chain in New York and turned the dowdy and often dirty chain into a dominant powerhouse.

I was smitten when Wasson opened a palatial Duane Reade down the block from me in the newly residential downtown Wall Street area, replacing the dungeon I use to drag myself down the steps of when I had to get my prescriptions filled. The store, which encompassed the former residence of J. P. Morgan, had gleaming aisle after gleaming aisle, a beauty parlor, a doctor's office and a twenty-four-hour food store offering darned good sushi. In fact, the store was so gorgeous that I asked Wasson if he would fly east to allow us to film an interview there. He graciously and immediately accepted.

We had a grand time as he strolled down the aisles, demonstrating how he had leapfrogged all of the other drug store chains with this one-stop charming experience. The stock, at the time flirting with the $40s, was a must-own, I said, simply because no one could compete against these glamorous emporiums.

Not long after, however, Wasson picked a fight with Express Scripts, an important pharmacy benefits manager who steered a lot of business to his store. After the tiff, customers of companies that had hired Express Scripts to rein in drug costs were then steered to rival CVS to pick up their prescriptions. The fight clobbered the stock to the low $30s.

Then, in June 2012, Wasson did the unthinkable: he shelled out $6.7 billion in cash and precious stock to buy a controlling stake in Alliance Boots, a European health and beauty retailer. Walgreens' stock immediately dropped almost 6 percent on the news of the deal. At the same time, the company opened a brand-new Duane Reade 150 yards from my own store, albeit on a different street, one that had heavy tourist traffic.

That was the last straw for me. As the stock was pummeled into the high $20s, I said that Wasson was too aggressive, had overexpanded—how else to explain a store so close to another one—and had bitten off way more than he could chew. I said that the costly Alliance deal was too great a gamble for shareholders to bear.

Wasson called me right after my comments and walked me through all of the benefits of the Alliance deal and the need to stick to his guns with Express Scripts. He even defended the virtue of opening a new store so close to the one we did the show from. He assured me there was no cannibalization; they had a different clientele and were both immensely profitable ventures.

As much as I admired Wasson, I was unmoved. No way could he pull all of this off. And at $29, I said so on air. I had lost faith in the company, and it was now too risky to hold. You had to dump one of my favorite recommendations.

It was the exact bottom. Soon after that he settled the war with Express Scripts on terms wildly favorable to Walgreens. He announced a groundbreaking partnership with AmerisourceBergen, another prescription drug provider, that gave Walgreens a huge boost in terms of its own profitability and the lowered prescription costs to customers. Plus, the integration of the Alliance deal has been spectacular, with lots of Alliance products now supplanting some of the big cosmetics players in the stores because of the higher quality the brand offers. The stock never looked back and has outperformed all other drug store chains with a remarkable twenty-five-point run from the bottom, in an almost straight line.

Wasson was a hero for these bold moves, moves that I was too skeptical to believe in. I just couldn't take the jarring nature of all of the changes. Wasson was right; I was wrong. I knew he was a visionary, but when he put his vision into action, I was too blind and small-minded to see the opportunities. I just didn't have the imagination Wasson did, and I paid the price. So did my viewers.

Lots of people believe you can't be critical enough of executives these days. They believe that doubt, if not a guilty-until-proven-innocent attitude even toward the best of companies, is vital in order to make money and not be fooled by the CEOs who make bold claims about what they can do for shareholders. Greg Wasson deserved better. He deserved the benefit of the doubt for his years of profit-making decisions, and I didn't give it to him. I didn't check my emotions at the door.

I THOUGHT I had got taken in big-time when I took my show to Tulane University in the fall of 2010 and interviewed Jim Bernhard, the founder and CEO of the Shaw Group, a huge construction company famous for building all kinds of power plants and the admitted best construction company when it comes to nuclear power. I told him I was worried about the nuclear book of business because the plants had become so expensive to build. He assured me that demand would be there and that President Obama's energy secretary was going to do his best to expedite the building of more plants because they emitted zero carbons. He was adamant that he had the nuclear and nonnuclear orders to have a bang-up 2011. Even if some orders got canceled, shareholders would do just fine if they stuck by the company. His bold predictions took me aback, but he had been a man of his word before my Tulane interview and had given us no reason to doubt him.

But then along came the Fukushima tragedy, the horrendous tsunami and subsequent destruction of a series of nuclear power plants in the worst accident since Chernobyl. Even as Bernhard insisted to me that shareholders should have faith in Shaw, I thought only a true Pollyanna would stick with this recommendation. So I backed away, thinking that no matter how special Bernhard might be, this one pretty much put the nail into Shaw's coffin.

I pulled my recommendation of Shaw and watched it sink about 10 percent soon after. I felt better immediately. But the really stalwart CEOs out there aren't going to let even incidents like Fukushima keep them from not bringing out value for their shareholders. In the beginning of 2013, Bernhard sold Shaw to the Chicago Bridge & Iron Company for $3 billion, which was a 72 percent premium to where the stock was before he made the deal, and well above where I told you to drop the equity. Seventy-two percent! Not only was Bernhard not delusional about his firm's prospects, but he single-handedly created value through this amazing combination. I had underestimated his resolve and his knowledge about what could happen to his own company. I was playing the informed skeptic, the know-it-all who knew more about nuclear power construction and power plant engineering in general. I had become too emotional after Fukushima and showed too little faith in Bernhard. I was not only wrong, I was dead wrong.

VARIATIONS OF THE MISTAKES I made judging the vision of Wasson and the determination of Bernhard can be instructive to you home gamers.

For example, when Frits Van Paasschen, CEO of Starwood, the 1,000-plus hotel chain that includes W, St. Regis, Westin and Sheraton, came on *Mad Money* and talked about his aggressive expansion plans into China, I was initially ecstatic. Starwood was putting up 100 new hotels all at once in the biggest growth market for travel in the world. Frits knew what he was doing and had even moved there for a time to oversee the work. In a world starved for China plays, this one had to be among the most exciting.

But the moment we caught a whiff of China's slowdown, I told people to be careful about Starwood and that the China thrust could lead to an earnings decline. I was simply reading the suddenly negative Wall Street research and marrying it to the headlines about the China regression. Even though Frits came on the show to tell me the fears were overblown, who was I to take the side of a wide-eyed executive when the steely, highly paid Wall Street analysts were telling me to back away? My trust dumped the stock soon after.

What I didn't realize, and Frits did, was that the Chinese, even in a downturn, are inveterate travelers, and there's a definitive hotel shortage in the dozens of Chinese cities that have one to two million inhabitants. Even in the downturn Starwood couldn't meet the demand for hotel rooms just when I had turned most negative. Next thing I know, the company delivers some huge numbers, well above those that had been shaded down by the "community" of analysts, as well as myself, and the stock roars from the $50s, where I had exited it, to almost $70, above where it had started its China-related decline. My skepticism had gotten the better of me, and I had let Frits down, not vice versa.

Sometimes it is difficult to believe how high a stock can go, and you can let your own caution get in the way of a big idea that you yourself believe in. Such was the case when International Paper paid $3.7 billion to buy out one of its competitors, Temple-Inland, in a grab for greater share in the huge worldwide corrugated box market. When International Paper was in the low $30s, its CEO, John Faraci, came on *Mad Money* and laid out the advantages of this merger. There had always been too much capacity in the container board business, he explained, something I knew because my father used to sell container board at International Packaging Products, his gift wrap and box jobbing company. The Temple-Inland deal would lead to some needed capacity closing, he explained. It was clear to me after the *Mad Money* discussion that Faraci had negotiated a fabulous deal for his shareholders, and I urged people to buy the combined company. Once International Paper closed the Temple-Inland deal, Faraci took the slack out of the corrugated market and prices began a sustained climb for the first time in recent memory.

But when International Paper soared from the low $30s to $38, I thought the move was over. Sure, Faraci remained bullish, but wasn't it my job to be the cynic, to question all assumptions, particularly because of the dramatic advancement in price? So I fell back on one of the time-honored phrases on Wall Street that often mean not a thing. I said, "Stop buying, do some trimming, and then wait for a pullback to make a new commitment to the stock." But International Paper's stock didn't blink, and it quickly put on ten more points without skipping a beat.

I had been a doubting Thomas and chose to ignore Faraci's estimate of the far-reaching consequences of this amazing deal to buy its competitor and then take out capacity. I didn't respect the power of what amounted to a new oligopoly in corrugated, which allowed for price increases even in the face of both a European and a Chinese downturn. I had learned a valuable lesson. Sometimes your enthusiasm is entirely justified, and when it comes to a landscape forever changed by the end of cutthroat competition, you have to be less critical than you would otherwise be. I learned this International Paper lesson well and managed to get behind both the bountiful airlines' and the rental car companies' stocks when the Justice Department blessed a series of wildly anticompetitive mergers in both industries. Faraci wasn't some cockeyed dreamer; he was a cold realist who had changed the playing field, tilting the pricing toward the box makers and away from the customers. His steely approach took advantage of a moment when the Antitrust Division didn't see the power of the combination—any more than it saw the power of the airline and rental car mergers and the early airline takeovers—to at last create an environment of rational pricing. These kinds of moves don't just give you a quick trade; they give you colossal long-term gains. I've never forgotten that, at times, you can remain enthusiastic and keep championing a situation much longer than you would otherwise, provided there's been a real secular change to the industry in which it toils.

Some Things Can Change for the Better

Sometimes being set in your ways, not willing to believe that anything or anyone can change, can lead to some real bonehead decisions. Sometimes thinking in broad generalizations can do the same. Judging a stock by its cover and presuming that just because a pattern has often been right means it always will be right are two emotionally wayward decisions I make far too often.

The best example of my inability to get beyond my own prejudices was my multiyear abhorrence of the refinery stocks—Valero, Tesoro, Marathon Petroleum and HollyFrontier—despite some structural changes in the market that brought some gigantic gains to those who opened their eyes and saw them coming.

I had looked at refiners over a twenty-year period and had developed a terrible bias against them. They seemed always to be engaged in price wars and were never able to earn more than a teeny bit per gallon above what they paid for their crude oil feedstock. There seemed to be no way they could change their stripes. All of the refiners were being squeezed by having to import expensive crude oil and then having to refine and market it in an endlessly cutthroat environment. In short, they were ripping their lungs out competing with each other. There was no way, I thought, they could change their ways and boost their profit margins.

But in September 2012, with the major refiners Marathon Petroleum up 43 percent, Tesoro up 70 percent, Valero up 41 percent and Western Refining having advanced 68 percent, I decided I had to take a look at these stocks to see how I could be so wrong. Frankly, I was flabbergasted and pained about how I could have missed such a move. So was Mike Jennings, the president and CEO of HollyFrontier, a huge U.S. refiner that's a combination of Holly and Frontier, two famous old-line refiners that got together after the brutal, multiyear price wars had decimated the industry.

Mike had called me up and asked to be on *Mad Money*, in part because he was tired of my not understanding the changing dynamics of what had been, at least for me, an uninvestable cohort for the past twenty-five years. What Mike knew, and I didn't, was that the revolution in oil shale drilling in this country, which had produced millions of barrels a day more than we thought available just a few years ago, hadn't just changed our import-export ratio of oil and gas. It had also changed the equation for the profit margins of some of the biggest American refiners. What I hadn't bothered to realize was that refiners were buying a lot of this newfound American crude, sometimes at prices $15, even $25 less than they would have to pay for imported crude, turning it into high-grade refined gasoline and then charging consumers for that refined product at the same prices they got with imported oil. That's right, they were, at last, able to charge far more than their cost of raw feedstock because of that American glut. They could buy the oil well below the benchmark Brent crude price because of all of the newfound reserves: the Bakken shale in North Dakota, and the Eagle Ford and Permian Basin shales in Texas, as well as other prospects that were just beginning to ramp up in Colorado and Ohio. The refiners were able to maintain those outrageous prices for their finished product, relative to their own domestic feedstock, because not only was demand strong in the United States, but they could export refined product overseas. Plus, it didn't hurt that the many lean years of U.S. refining had produced a dramatic consolidation that had, at last, led to a much lower degree of competition than most of us realized. The dogfight had ended precisely at the moment that domestic crude had become bountiful and cheap.

That lack of competition, plus the higher price the refiners could charge, had led to fabulous profit margins. Mike explained that this meant refiners could afford big dividends for shareholders—including special dividends that HollyFrontier paid—courtesy of the newly discovered crude in this country. Such bounty was unheard of in the industry.

My emotional bias against this group, rooted in years of dislike because of multiple shortfalls and guide-downs, had blinded me to the changes afoot in an entire industry. Your takeaway is simple: beware of preconceived notions in the face of radically positive moves that are based on reality, not fantasy.

SOMETIMES PRECONCEPTIONS of the chief executive officer can cost you dearly. I have always been a fan of Procter & Gamble, the fabulous consumer packaged goods company that has one of the best brand names worldwide and has been a serial raiser of its already bountiful dividend. But with the appointment of Bob McDonald as CEO in 2009, the stock of this great company had begun to fall behind its cohort. The lack of upward movement wasn't lost on the analysts. For several quarters in 2012 it seemed like there was open revolt against McDonald on the conference call, as the normally docile analysts repeatedly asked him if he actually had a handle on his company. The tough talk by the analysts and the pronounced underperformance of the stock led me to slap McDonald on the Wall of Shame, a place of dishonor I have created on *Mad Money*, reserved for those who I believe would allow the stock of a company to rise simply if they were to announce their resignation. I said the same would happen to P&G if McDonald were to leave the company.

But in the ensuing months McDonald made it clear that he recognized that he hadn't taken bold enough action in the three years he had been running the enterprise. He had let underperformers in the organization hold on to their job. He hadn't cut the considerable fat at the firm that he had inherited. A renewed McDonald made it clear to those of us who followed the company that, beginning with the last quarter of 2012, they would be quite surprised with the actions he would take.

After years of doing *Mad Money*, I was loath to give McDonald the benefit of the doubt. My mind had been made up: he couldn't change. But after spending some time with him, I took him down from the Wall of

Shame, betting that any generalization that left no room for the possibility that a person could change would end up backfiring in my face.

Sure enough, McDonald announced a much better than expected quarter soon after I took him down from the Wall, and he laid out a plan to cut expenses even more dramatically than anyone thought possible while accelerating the company's organic growth rate. McDonald had changed his stripes. He had proven the doubters wrong, and the stock had its biggest move up in years.

The resurrection of McDonald is a reminder that staying negative because a CEO hasn't delivered is not necessarily the smartest move. I am not suggesting that you change your mind and start liking and believing in some no-account chief executives. I am saying that when someone the caliber of Bob McDonald admits, out loud, that he hasn't done a good job—a big thing for any chief executive officer to say—and vows that he will do things differently, perhaps you should keep an open mind about the man. Had I kept McDonald on the Wall of Shame after he confessed to not doing as good a job as he could, I would have prejudged the man in a way that was undeserving and, ultimately, costly to your pocketbook.

Amazingly, after McDonald got the company back on track, he then reported a weaker quarter than expected, and P&G ushered him out and brought back its old CEO, A. G. Lafley. I think Procter made a mistake; McDonald had put the company back on course, and while the stock initially jumped on the move, not long afterward it fell back to where McDonald was shown the door before it began advancing again. Corporate America can be tough and unforgiving, even to those who changed their ways and started doing everything right, as McDonald had done after several years in the Cincinnati wilderness.

TALK ABOUT PRECONCEPTIONS. Early in 2012 I sat on a panel with some of my television colleagues, and we were astonished to see a big move in Kimco Realty, the largest neighborhood and community shopping center real estate investment trust. One of my on-air friends expressed awe and skepticism about how Kimco, which has almost 900 shopping centers with 131 million square feet of space, could be doing this well. After all, wasn't Amazon supposed to destroy the brick-and-mortar retailers?

David Henry, the CEO of Kimco, was watching the show. He wasted no time coming on *Mad Money* to straighten us out. He explained, patiently, that not only was Amazon not damaging his business, but his business was thriving, with seven straight quarters of positive same-store net operating growth and the beginning of a sustained period of rent increases when tenants moved out. In fact, those stores that had indeed been Amazoned had made way for higher rents for stores that sold items like pets, perishable food or hair care that could never be duplicated by the Internet colossus. He said the business wasn't just surviving in an Internet world; it was thriving because of the lack of financing for new shopping centers. The inability of developers to get loans from banks to develop commercial real estate had kept a lid on the competition, allowing the prices to rise.

Not long after Henry's appearance, Kimco rallied 30 percent; not bad, and much better than the S&P 500, especially when you consider the bountiful and rising dividend this real estate investment trust pays. Again, a knee-jerk analysis can keep you from cashing in on some of the best gains.

Stocks with Accounting Problems Almost Never Go Higher Until They Are Resolved

Sometimes the emotionalism that blinds your judgment doesn't happen the first go-round. I had no reason to question the bona fides of a little $6.40 speculative play, Magnum Hunter Resources, when *Mad Money* decided to book Gary Evans, the CEO of the company, back in February 2012. We had spent a huge amount of time on the show exploring the possibilities of three big oil and gas shale plays in the country: Eagle Ford in Texas, Bakken in North Dakota and Utica in Ohio. So how could we say no to a company that has a stake in all three? Magnum Hunter seemed like just the kind of speculative stock that people were looking for to play the American renaissance in oil and gas. Undercovered by Wall Street, unknown by many, it seemed like the kind of long shot where the odds were just wrong. What the heck was it doing at $6? Sure, its balance sheet was stretched, but every oil and gas company I have interviewed during the past few years, except for Devon Energy, has had stretched balance sheets, because the opportunity to drill and discover oil and gas was too great not to exploit it headlong. It's no coincidence that Devon, by the way, had been among the worst performers of the oil and gas stocks, precisely because it has chosen a conservative approach instead of the aggressive stance that has made so many of these oil companies, like Anadarko, EOG, and Cabot Oil & Gas, such success stories.

When Evans came on I immediately liked him and everything he had to say. Here was a man with properties that could be worth two, maybe even three times the price of its stock. I made that clear in the interview and when I blessed the company.

It traded a few cents higher after the interview and then was cut in half over a matter of months as various logistical problems—all seeming pretty reasonable—got in the way of the oil and gas delivery from the wellhead. The company had also done a massive secondary offering in May 2012 to raise capital and augment their balance sheet, and the market didn't handle it well, especially when the company reported a gigantic shortfall in November 2012. Finally, the company had recently discovered an accounting error and had dismissed its chief accounting officer.

So Magnum Hunter had a lot of explaining to do when CEO Evans expressed a willingness to come back on *Mad Money* tell his story. Evans once again told a compelling tale, this time that he was going to sell assets, including his terrific Eagle Ford properties, to bring out the true nature of his undervalued company. I figured it was a can't-miss opportunity, especially given that the company was due to report the following week and the stock had fallen so hard already. I knew Evans couldn't answer any specific questions about the quarter, as he was in what is known as the quiet period right before earnings, when company representatives are not supposed to talk about results until after they are published. But there was certainly plenty else to talk about, given these colossal miscues that had crushed the stock, especially given the endless lightning-round questions I had received about the company since my first recommendation.

Eight days after the appearance, Magnum Hunter decided to delay issuing its quarterly report. Oh, boy: $4.16 at the time of the appearance goes to $3.75. Eighteen days after that, Magnum Hunter told the SEC that it may have discovered a material weakness in its accounting.

A month later, on April 3, 2013, Evans said he wanted to come on again. He had terrific news: he had sold his Eagle Ford assets for $400 million, which would relieve the pressure on the balance sheet and take some of the sting out of the losses. Reluctantly, I agreed to book him, given that this transaction sounded like a huge positive. Evans came on and said that things were going back to normal now that the sale had been made and he could concentrate on his vast oil holdings in Ohio's Utica and North Dakota's Bakken.

At last I felt better. Until April 17, two weeks later, when Magnum Hunter fired Pricewaterhouse as its accountant and the stock went to $2.50. That was it. Finally, I had had enough of Magnum Hunter.

What happened here? It's pretty simple: I was so enamored of the speculation because of the buzz—the Utica, Eagle Ford, Bakken buzz—that I overlooked one of my most important rules of investing: when there are accounting issues, you should sell, no matter what. In truth, I should have just cut my losses the moment I learned of the accounting discrepancy. I would have left much higher than where the stock was in its last two appearances. I was blinded by the chance, and no stock, whether it be speculative or blue chip or just a plain solid growth situation, should ever be recommended if there's an accounting problem. Of course, there will be stocks that can go higher and there will be accounting issues that are resolved positively that will cause you to miss a chance to recoup money lost. But the lesson of Magnum Hunter was simple: accounting irregularities must trump all emotional attachment, and that must *never* be violated. Let me add one last corollary and a positive coda to the story: Once the accounting issues were cleared up and Magnum Hunter was given a clean bill of health, the stock doubled. Still, if I had simply said "Sell" when the problems surfaced and "Buy" when they were resolved, viewers could have dodged a bullet and made a ton of money.

Summary: Check Your Emotions at the Door

All twelve of these tales demonstrate the hazards of violating your discipline and letting your emotions control you. Being blind to opportunity, being frozen in the face of danger, not being tough enough mentally and being too stubborn when you thought you were just being skeptical—these are all actions born not of rational thought but of emotional weakness.

In sports we would call these unforced errors. All were avoidable had I sat back and said, "What the heck am I doing? Why am I closing my eyes to something that might be so obvious to someone else more distant?" Let the dirty dozen remind you that we are all fallible, but we must not be fallible over and over again in the same situations. Let's recap so you will not make the same errors I made when you are confronted with the same kinds of situations.

1. Apple and Chipotle: Stop falling in love with stories. The love may be unrequited through no fault of their own.
2. Ford: When the CEO hints that you are too bullish, listen to him.
3. Alcoa: Some headwinds are so pervasive and threatening that even the best of CEOs can't beat them.
4. Walgreens, Shaw, Starwood Hotels & Resorts, and International Paper: Don't let your skepticism turn into nihilism. You may pass up some darned good opportunities.
5. Refineries, Procter & Gamble, and Kimco: Don't let your biases against certain industries and companies blind you from their journeys from ugly ducklings to swans.
6. Magnum Hunter: When accounting irregularities surface, sell even if you love the store. You will be getting in at a lower level once the issues are resolved.

Conclusion

So much about the stock market has changed in the past five years. We've seen the destruction of a huge amount of capital, followed by a miraculous resurrection. Sadly, the comeback has left millions sidelined, perhaps rightfully so, because the market itself has done nothing to restore our faith in it. People should have thronged back to stocks, given the success of the averages. However, the losses were so extreme, the trust so despoiled and the risks so outrageously imbalanced against the rewards that I blame no one for fleeing these pieces of paper purported to be linked with companies and executives whom no one seems to believe in anyway.

Never for a moment in *Get Rich Carefully* have I tried to paint a positive picture about how the stock market works anymore. I accept that the old days, when you invested in tremendous American companies and were presumed to come out ahead, are long since gone. We know the machines now run amok, unchecked by a government that still hasn't figured out the damage they can do and how they've driven away the nation's core investor class.

We understand that stocks have become unhinged by financial engineering that's been blessed by an industry that has long since forgotten that you exist or matter to the process of national wealth creation. It's obvious that many firms in the financial services business can't make enough money off the 99 percent of you who want help. So they leave you to your own devices or throw you to the jackals of dumb indexing or bond funds that were sold as being risk-free but are actually risky as all get-out and *reward*-free now that interest rates are done going down.

Our eyes have now been opened to the wealth-destroying flash crashes, flash freezes and Facebook fiascos, which seem to be with us each day. We still don't know, after all of these preposterous events, what exactly went wrong. Our only certainty? That these machinations will continue and no one will do a thing about them. The incentives just aren't there to clean up the mess or regulate those who have created it.

The litany of corrosive questions depresses and frightens us. Can we really be protected from the machine guns of the high-frequency trading bandits? Is it worth it to go against crooked hedge funds and brokers that bet against you to make their profits? Hasn't all the easy money been made, and now it will just be given back, as has been the case since the new millennium began?

Now that you have gotten to this conclusion, I hope you recognize that stocks are indeed worth the trouble and the investment, but only if you have the right tools to navigate the shark-infested corporate seascape. You now understand the new ways and disciplines to guard yourself from the financial-engineering scoundrels who want to separate you from your money. By combining the prudent methods you've learned here with the fresh ideas and themes you need for long-term wealth creation, you should feel confident enough to go forward on your own to profit from the chaos that so many others have given up on. If you work closely with a professional to build your wealth, you should now be a more informed client. As someone who has been helping people make money for more than three decades, let me assure you that the more wizened and informed you are as a customer, the better and more lucrative the relationship is for all involved, not just the broker. I think you now have a fighting chance in a market that's making money for those who dare to challenge it with discipline and creativity.

Let's go over what you've learned. You should know that stocks routinely become divorced from the "fundamentals" in ways so predictable that you can profit from these dislocations. You are ready to harness the seemingly capricious rallies and sell-offs to your best advantage, getting terrific bargains while others, terrified by the volatility, flee from these opportunities. You are all set to capitalize on the daily stock market chaos with the confidence that eludes so many who are traumatized by the new battlefield realities. You now presume that declines will occur at the drop of a hat, sometimes for no good reason, and you are ready and waiting with your buy list of best-of-breed names to exploit long-term themes that aren't hostage to the whims of the domestic or international economies. You can now regard these mini-crashes and rapid-fire retreats as gifts that give you a better entry point to accumulate stocks that others toss out by rote or ignorance.

Consider how far you've come. You've had multiple stock market anatomy lessons. You know, mechanically, how a stock goes up or down a point. You've learned how and why stocks fall in and out of favor, and you are ready for either contingency. You now know who and what to listen to in order to form an outlook and pick the best investments to exploit it. You don't have to waste your time sorting through irrelevancies because they've already been sorted for you. Nor are you going to just take what the indices give you, because you've learned a new kind of security analysis that lets you identify the proper metrics and the important inputs that determine which stocks will thrive and which ones will dive.

We've come to accept the primacy of slow worldwide growth, but we don't moan about it. We find chief executive officers who refuse to be stultified and, instead, seek to create value no matter where it can be found, even if it means tearing their institutions asunder. They know how to generate huge returns in any environment and can be trusted to not let you and your portfolio down. If the economy falters, we don't have to falter with it, because we are confident that they will figure out ways to exploit the economic hazards to our advantage.

This market challenges us every day with its inscrutable moves. So we must use everything at our disposal, including charts that, when married with the fundamentals, can give us better entry and exit points than we've ever had. We know how to spot bases and floors that can hold our weight. We know, technically and fundamentally, what to look for, what can punch through ceilings and take us to new highs.

You will still make mistakes. Some will be very costly. Hopefully, though, the lessons learned from the scrutiny of my own foibles openly on display through my charitable trust should reduce the number of errors and limit the losses that could otherwise overwhelm you. We know we have to stop rationalizing bad investing behavior. We must try to augment whatever stock hand we've been dealt with tactics that work in this more treacherous environment. The disciplines and do's and don'ts I have traced out here should make sense to you because I have shown you how expensive they were to my trust when I didn't obey them. Hopefully, now that I've described my most foolish moves to you, they will generate more than a laugh or two, and perhaps even some hefty profits.

We know that no matter how hard we try, our emotions can and will attempt to get the better of us. I have shown you how necessary it is to conquer them if you are going to get rich by prudently buying and selling stocks. If it takes my own mortification to modify your behavior so you won't repeat my sins, then so be it.

Finally, know that you are not alone. Know that hubris and foolishness and recklessness and greed dog all of us. We just need to know when we're committing or exhibiting those sins so we can correct course quickly, before too much financial damage occurs. We understand that shortcuts lead to dead ends. We can now avoid them and stay on the proper, prudent paths that will eventually get us to prosperity.

We've got a journey ahead of us, and we're ready for what comes. That sell-off lurking around the corner? Come and get it. That confusing rally? We'll use it to sell our losers and improve our portfolios. Those confounding pieces of data? We're mast-strapped and oblivious to the sirens that want to throw us off our profitable course.

Remember my words: we've learned our valuable lessons. We are now ready to triumph over the daily trauma of markets that we no longer fear. We have each other's backs. But we know that there is no such thing as overnight wealth. That's for fools who will never obtain it. We're busy taking our time, avoiding the pitfalls, trying to see around the curves and tiptoe past the endless land mines as we attempt, carefully, to get very rich and not give it back when we get there.

Acknowledgments

You are now at my favorite part of every book I write, where I get to thank all of the people who make my work life and my daily life possible so I could write *Get Rich Carefully*. First, my whole work existence, whether it be the shows I do, the books I write, the columns I blog or the charitable trust I run, depends on you. If you didn't think you could learn from me and trust me I, would have vanished from the financial scene ages ago. If you didn't call in or stop me on the street or tweet me asking for help, I would, no doubt, have given up to return to the hedge fund world so I could figure out the direction of Apple or 3M or Boeing on a minute-to-minute basis, as I did before I started my television and Internet career.

So I thank you for sticking with me through the bountiful times and the lean times, allowing me into your homes to help you manage and grow your money. It's funny, most people are so uncomfortable talking about money, now more than ever after the Great Recession, that it seems pretty outlandish when I say that I want you to get rich. But that's been the goal of the public portion of my career, and that goal has suffused this entire text.

I am acutely conscious that no one actually wants to Get Rich Carefully. You just want to get rich. But I also have no doubt that if you aren't careful, you just aren't going to succeed. We've seen so many people try to make big money in a hurry. It's no different from chasing that rainbow to get to an elusive pot of gold. It just isn't there. Wealth creation is about preparation. You do the homework, you don't break discipline, you keep mistakes to a minimum, and I am confident that you will make more money with your investments than you ever thought possible. However, the corollary is true too: If you don't do the homework and you don't follow the rules, I am equally confident that you will lose much more than you would have made by doing it right. That's a statement about how tough it has become to protect yourself from the downside of a damaged asset class, not about your own financial foibles.

When you actually sit down to write a book, you recognize that the task can be monumental. So you need help. For this book I got an extraordinary degree of help from Nicole Urken, the research director for *Mad Money*, who dealt with my emails, days, nights and weekends, as we labored to create a lasting text that can address so many of your concerns and questions. We started with the premise that people are more bewildered than ever about the way wealth can be created using stocks, despite the sharp rise in the averages. We brainstormed repeatedly about how to get you to where you have a fighting chance to grab your piece of the capital gains pie. She was instrumental to what we have tried to accomplish, and—highest compliment—I would not have done the book without her.

Of course, there would be no book at all if David Rosenthal, publisher of Blue Rider Press, hadn't kept after me to write one to explain the new realities of a financial world that's become a virtual Garden of Eden but with far more than its fair share of poisonous apples. David is a fearsome advocate for his writers, as we are for him. He's demanding, and he should be, because he wants only the best from you and nothing less. You pray he likes it; you dread that he might not. Isn't that the essence of what a fabulous editor is about? Thanks, David, for convincing me I had a new book in me. A nod, of course, to David's excellent team, starting with Aileen Boyle, who never ceases to amaze me with her support and her sponsorship. I also want to thank Linda Rosenberg, Meredith Dros, Phoebe Pickering, and Tanya Maiboroda. Also, just another shout-out to all the brilliant chart mavens I mentioned and thanked in chapter 7.

Much of what I can accomplish in life can be laid squarely upon my colleagues' shoulders, not just mine. Which is why Stephanie Link is such a fabulous partner. Stephanie runs ActionAlertsPlus.com, my charitable trust, with me, and she has the best research mind of anyone I have ever worked with on Wall Street. She amazes me with her knowledge and her insight and her writing ability every day. Together we are a battle-tested, rigorous team that invests openly to help you learn how to manage your own money. I can never figure out when she sleeps because there has never been an email after 4:00 a.m. that she didn't respond to a minute after receipt. I wish you could be a fly on the wall when we go at it about the stocks we buy or sell, but then again, you'd probably get smashed when we pick a stock that sets the trust back. Losses always sting, but when you play for charity, any setback seems as though you are taking money from the needy and giving it to a furnace to burn. Stephanie has done fabulous work not just with the trust but on CNBC, where she's become one of the most popular faces on the network. She's indispensable and indefatigable, and one day I will let her get all of her work done and stop regaling her with stories of the brutal old days.

These past few years at CNBC have been a whirlwind, as television now bookends my daily life. I start my morning with the *Squawk on the Street* gang, David Faber and Carl Quintanilla, over at *Post Nine* on the floor of the New York Stock Exchange. Each morning we rip through the headlines and try to put the business news in a context that makes sense but is also fun. Why not? Why shouldn't that be an imperative? In a world where people have a million things to watch any time they want, it's guerrilla warfare to get viewers to tune in, so you better make it compelling. You know what makes that show work? We like one another, and we hang out with one another; our only real friction is the sports teams we root for. After years and years of knowing Faber, I have figured out that the teams he follows lose because he's rooting for them. May he never root for the Philadelphia Eagles. Special thanks to many of the other terrific people we see on air in the morning, including Simon Hobbs, Kelly Evans, Bertha Coombs, Bob Pisani, Steve Liesman and Rick Santelli.

Squawk on the Street has so many people who make you look good each day that it's almost impossible to mention them all. But I want to especially thank our executive producer, Todd Bonin, as well as Chip

Aiken, Gillian Austin, Ben Berna, Deb Findling, Brad Rubin, Sally Shin, Lisa Villalobos, Brian Swartzfeger and Pat Smith. They all help make *SOTS* the fastest hour of business television going.

After I leave the Exchange I go right across the street to TheStreet, where I get to work with Elisabeth DeMarse, the chairman and CEO of the company I founded almost twenty years ago. I never hide that The-Street has been troubled for some time, so I also cannot hide that it's now about the best it's ever been run, and I am thankful to Elisabeth for straightening out the joint. She's tireless in her enthusiasm for reviving the company, and it's working. May she never stop doing what she's doing, because she understands that there's so much more to TheStreet than just, well, me.

TheStreet is where I see Stephanie and Nicole each morning, as well as Ted Graham, another fabulous *Mad Money* researcher, who has done a terrific job, especially with the complicated health care stories that so many regard as signature *Mad Money* pieces.

Some of the heavier lifting at TheStreet these days gets done by Erwin Eichmann, who has breathed new life into the company's subscription business, including *Real Money* and ActionAlertsPlus.com. I never stopped believing in the subscription model, which includes the more than 35,000 stories I have written for TheStreet over the years, and he's proving me right. So many people helped me with this book at TheStreet, most of all the amazing technical support folks Jeff Kessler and Yossi Benchetrit— one day I promise I won't screw the files up! Adam Leverone is my @Jim-Cramer doppelganger on Twitter. Can't start your morning without reading Doug Kass and the gang on RealMoneyPro.

After a couple of hours doing TheStreet business, including a slew of videos orchestrated by Ruben Ramirez with Debra Borchardt, Brittany Umar and the dynamic duo of Nicole and her brother, Ross Kenneth Urken, who runs the wildly successful MainStreet.com, it's off to Engle-wood Cliffs with the incredibly loyal long-time driver Kayhan "Kyle" Si-lahtaroglu, to get all fired up for *Mad Money*. You need to be stoked if you are going to do a one-man stand-up entertainment show about business every single night, and given that I have now done 2,000 episodes, that's a heck of a lot of stoking. So many fabulous people go into making a television show, and you rarely get to see any of them. I try to thank them daily, but it's never enough, so let me give it a whirl here. In the control room we've got Bryan Russo, our director; George Manessis, our senior line producer; as well as Tim Dewald, Robert Aouad, Brandon Teitel, Linda Dimyan, Heather Gaines, Kate Kohlbrenner, Kathy Spencer, Vildana Hajric and Maryann Lateano. The people out on the floor for the show, Steadicam operator Keith Greenwood and his sidekick, Dave Frendak, as well Justin Johansky and Kareem Bynes and Dale Knoth, provide the oxygen, and stage manager Kyle Remaly provides the match. Kyle has had to pick me up off the floor more often than I would like to admit. He knows the show must go on.

When people ask me what's the secret to the longevity of the show, though, I know better than to say that it's my enthusiasm or my love of investing. The success stems from the work of two amazing people. The first is Cliff Mason, our head writer and the son of my sister, Nan, and her husband Todd. Cliff has been with the show the whole time, and it can't be done without him. What you hear every night is often the distillation of a huge amount of research put into a readable 1,400-word segment that Cliff bangs out three times a day. I don't know if anyone else on earth could be that productive or that flawless. We're all intimidated by him, justifiably, because he's a genius. Everyone who has ever met him knows this, so why not just shout it? Oh, and may I just add that when so many thought that Europe was about to be blown to smithereens, Cliff persuaded me to go all in for Europe—perhaps the best call the show has ever made.

The second person behind the show's success? You see her now and then when I ask cameraman Keith to pirouette toward her, but you must know that what you see each night is the creation of our executive producer, Regina Gilgan, and she can never get enough credit for what she's accomplished with *Mad Money*. Regina has a vision of what must be done and a love for our viewers that suffuses that vision on a nightly basis. Her strength of character and her leadership need to be bottled and passed around from newsroom to newsroom so all can learn from her skills and her demeanor. People walk through brick walls to please her. I'd walk through tungsten.

You don't get to stay on air as long as we have without the backing of management who believes in you. We are blessed with two fabulous executives, Nik Deogun, CNBC's senior vice president and editor in chief, and Mark Hoffman, chief executive officer and president of CNBC.

When you ask newspaper people who the best editor in business news is, they don't, at first, want to admit it because they are so used to print superiority. But after a little prodding they own up and say it is Nik. His judgment, skill, nurturing and love for business and business news makes him a one-of-a-kind journalist. How blessed we are to have this amazing editor in chief. Nik makes everyone better at his job, and I can't thank him enough for what he's done for me as a journalist and as a friend.

I wouldn't have a show to begin with if it weren't for Mark Hoffman. Most people in business news have worked at only one or two places. At one time or another I have worked for ABC, CBS, Fox, the *Wall Street Journal* and the *New York Times*, and all I can say is that our network practices the best, most rewarding journalism of all of those esteemed networks and publications. Notice I didn't write "business" journalism. I am talking all of journalism. When I analyze any business, I know that its culture, its ethos and, yes, its numbers come from the person leading the company, and Mark's the reason CNBC is the dominant business news outlet on earth. I am so grateful that he encouraged me to "go for the nine," to take on the cohosting of *Squawk on the Street*, because it's allowed me to do live journalism with the best people in the game. Thank you, Mark, for all you have done.

I've got special thanks to offer Brian Steel, Jen Dauble, Tom Clendenin and Steve Smith, who have worked so hard to promote our efforts and have done so much to ensure the strength of the *Mad Money* franchise. Our show's longevity depends on their efforts, and they perform them magnificently. Special thanks to Steve Fastook for making both the *Mad Money* and the *Squawk on the Street* sets so incredible. People need to stop and watch you before you can generate any success. All of these terrific people make that happen.

We are surrounded by amazing on-air talent at CNBC. Each morning I get to joust for a time with the incredible team on *Squawk Box*, the show that will always define the morning for me, as it has for the past twenty years. Thank you so much, Joe Kernen, Becky Quick and Andrew Ross

Sorkin, as well as my longtime friend and executive producer Matt Quayle, for letting me play in the closing moments of your fabulous show. Colleagues Scott "Judge" Wapner, Sue Herrera, Tyler Mathison, Brian Sullivan and Mandy Drury always make me feel at home on their terrific hours, where they are total joys and I thank Melissa Lee for her gracious lead-in to *Mad Money* I will miss my back-and-forth with my great friend Herb Greenberg, which was an almost daily feature on *Street Signs*, but I don't know whether the crew on that show will. Those visits to the set to duke it out with Herb were all unscripted, and they sometimes had to bail me out, unmiked. Fortunately, Herb still appears on CNBC and he writes with me daily at TheStreet, so we have an additional venue in which to beat each other's heads in about stocks that I love and he likes to red-flag. He's always been instrumental in my thinking about risk and his new *Reality Check* newsletter from TheStreet keeps me on the straight and narrow about some of my favorite high growth stocks.

Everyone tells me I lead a complicated life, so I guess it must be true. The only reason I hesitate to admit it is because there are people in my life who make my life happen, who actually allow me to go forward without falling off the rails. When I started in this media business I was, how do you say, rough around the edges? It seemed like hardly a week went by when I wasn't detonating, just an unstable vial of TNT dressed as a man. But my fabulous agents, Henry Reisch and Suzanne Gluck from WME, have helped me change all of that. Suzanne, along with David Rosenthal, encouraged me all along the way with *Get Rich* and is the best friend a writer could ever have. I couldn't make a move in television without Henry, so I don't. They don't make advisers more trusted than he is.

How did I get so lucky as to have the best lawyer in the world, Bruce Birenboim from Paul, Weiss? Because he's one of my closest and dearest friends and an actual miracle worker, that's how. It is true that my agents have kept me on the straight and narrow, but when I fall off, I land in Bruce's arms. He and his wife, Ellen, are always there to catch me. Bruce's partner, Chuck Googe, has helped me through tons of successful negotiations, too.

Thanks to my good friend William R. Gruver, a chaired professor at Bucknell who served as a director of TheStreet for a tumultuous decade

ACKNOWLEDGMENTS

and lived to tell about it. Bill has been teaching me about business and about life from the day I first met him at Goldman Sachs more than thirty years ago. I am always thrilled that he uses my books to teach his terrific students.

Two fabulous women keep my head from exploding on a daily basis: Deb Slater and Noreen Shevlin. Deb's been steering me to where I have to go for fifteen years now. Believe me when I say I would have no idea where I was or where I am supposed to be without her. She's the assistant who's also your mother and your close friend. Noreen is my life's chief executive officer, and I don't know where I would be without her. She's why I can do two shows, write books, run a charitable trust and tweet and blog around the clock.

A special thank-you to Matt Horween, who is my closest associate on so many fronts, including economics, politics, charts, the numbers and, most important of all, ethics. I don't make many moves without running them before Matt first, and I am blessed that he's been so helpful on so many fronts. Matt's my most faithful and fearless critic, just as it should be.

Now let me turn to the true inner circle that allows me to do my work and also have a life. First, to my best friend, Michael Haley, who, along with his wife, Ellen, critiques everything I do, including this book, as well as the rest of my life. To my sister, Nan, and to Pop, who never waivers even when I do: I sure do wish I were more of a picnic, but if I haven't figured it out by this time, I guess I am not going to, so I apologize for my daily demeanor. Never too late to start trying, though. Thank you, guys, for putting up with me for fifty-nine years.

Finally, I want to thank the love of my life, the person I dedicated this book to, Lisa Detwiler. She's the one who had to deal with the 3:45 a.m. alarms I need to write a few pages a day. She's the one who has had to deal with my endless griping and my tiresome tirades about how I will never get this book done. Thank you, Lisa. I promise I won't write another book after this one . . . until, of course, I do.

Index